A Survey of the New Testament

Edited by
H. D. Harrison

Randall House Publications
114 Bush Road, P.O. Box 17306
Nashville, Tennessee 37217
1983

A SURVEY OF THE NEW TESTAMENT

Randall House Publications
Nashville, Tennessee

Printed in the United States of America
ISBN 0-89265-090-7

CONTENTS

PREFACE

The materials contained in this survey were first prepared in manuscript form for audio cassette production. They have enjoyed a wide circulation in that medium. The nature and quality of the work are such that an even wider circulation, in a more permanent form, was felt necessary.

The authors of the survey of the New Testament are Dr. Stanley Outlaw, Dr. Charles A. Thigpen, the Reverend F. Leroy Forlines, Dr. Robert Picirilli, and the Reverend Milton Worthington.

Dr. Stanley Outlaw wrote the survey of the books of Matthew, Mark, Hebrews, and James. Dr. Charles A. Thigpen authored the survey of the books of Luke, John, and Acts. The Reverend F. Leroy Forlines penned the survey of the books of Romans and Galatians. Dr. Robert Picirilli wrote the survey of the books of First and Second Corinthians, Ephesians, Philippians, Colossians, First and Second Thessalonians, First and Second Timothy, Titus, Philemon, Jude, and Revelation. The Reverend Milton Worthington authored the survey of the books of First and Second Peter; and First, Second, and Third John.

Dr. Stanley Outlaw received his B.A. From Free Will Baptist Bible College; his M.A. and his Ph.D. from Bob Jones University. He has, since 1966, been teaching New Testament Greek and Bible at Free Will Baptist Bible College in Nashville, Tennessee.

Dr. Charles A. Thigpen holds a B.A. degree from Bob Jones University, Greenville, South Carolina; a M.A. from Winona Lake School of Theology, Winona Lake, Illinois, the M.Ed. and the D.A from Middle Tennessee State University, Murfreesboro, Tennessee.

Dr. Thigpen has been an able pastor, and has served as Dean of Free Will Baptist Bible College in Nashville, Tennessee from 1948-53 and from 1957 until June 1, 1979 at which time he was named as President of the college and continues to serve in that capacity.

The Reverend F. Leroy Forlines is a graduate of Free Will Baptist Bible College, Nashville, Tennessee; holds the M.A. from Winona Lake School of Theology; and was graduated from Northern Baptist Theological Seminary with the B.D. His most recent degree, the Th.M., was awarded by Chicago Graduate School of Theology. Professor Forlines has been teaching at his alma mater since 1953. For many of these years, he has been both professor of Systematic Theology and Dean of Men.

Dr. Robert Picirilli earned his B.A. at Free Will Baptist Bible College, Nashville, Tennessee; his M.A. and the Ph.D. at Bob Jones University. He was awarded an honorary D.D. by Bob Jones University in 1967. Dr. Picirilli is a notable author, lecturer, professor of New Testament Greek and is presently serving as Dean of Free Will Baptist Bible College where he has served since 1955.

The Reverend Milton Worthington received his B.B.E. degree in 1959 from Columbia Bible College in Columbia, South Carolina. He has pastored churches in Florida, North Carolina, Mississippi, Tennessee, and Michigan. He is presently pastor of Central Free Will Baptist Church in Royal Oak, Michigan. He is also chairman of the Sunday School and Church Training Board.

It is the desire of the editor and publisher that these materials bring knowledge and blessing to those who read and study them.

Harrold D. Harrison
Editor

A SURVEY OF THE GOSPEL OF

Matthew

by Stanley Outlaw

The following outline of the Gospel of Matthew will be used as we survey the general contents of the book:

I. THE BIRTH OF CHRIST (1—2)
II. PREPARATION FOR THE MINISTRY OF CHRIST (3:1—4:11)
  A. Ministry of John the Baptist and Baptism of Jesus (3:1-17)
  B. Temptation of Jesus (4:1-11)
III. THE MINISTRY OF CHRIST (4:12—25:46)
  A. The Public Ministry of Christ (4:12—16:12)
  B. His Private Ministry (16:13—20:34)
  C. Climax of His Ministry (21—25)
IV. THE TRIAL, CRUCIFIXION, AND BURIAL (26—27)
V. THE RESURRECTION AND COMMISSION (28)

I. THE BIRTH OF CHRIST (1—2)

Matthew introduces the birth of Christ by giving a genealogy which traces Christ back through Abraham and David. These two important figures are mentioned in 1:1 because David was the king of Israel whose throne Jesus Christ would occupy forever, and Abraham was the father of Israel through whose seed God had promised to bless all the world (Genesis 12:3). One unusual thing here is that the names of four women are mentioned, a thing which was quite uncustomary in Jewish genealogies. Furthermore, there is something strange about each of the women mentioned. Tamar in 1:3 was the daughter-in-law of Judah by whom twins were born to him; Rahab, the harlot (1:5), was delivered from Jericho; Ruth was a Gentile, a Moabitess, a descendant of Lot (1:5); and Bathsheba (1:6) was the woman with whom David committed adultery. It must have been that Matthew wished to show us God's grace in including these women in the genealogy of Christ that he chose to specifically mention them. Note also that the customary form of the genealogy is "Abraham begat Isaac; and Isaac begat Jacob," etc., but when we come to 1:16 concerning the birth of Christ, Matthew very carefully avoids the word "begat" in reference to Joseph because of his knowledge of the virgin birth of Christ. The three divisions of the genealogy which are mentioned in 1:17 exactly match the three main divisions of the history of Israel: Abraham to David, which represents the theocratic form of government; David to Babylonian Exile, which represents the monarchy or period of kings; and Babylonian Exile to Christ, which represents the Hierarchy, or rule of the priests over Israel.

In 1:21 the name "Jesus" is introduced by the angel. The Greek word "Jesus" is the exact equivalent of the Hebrew word "Joshua," and the meaning of both words is "Jehovah is Savior." Twice in the King James Version this name is translated "Jesus" when it should be "Joshua," in reference to the Old Testament figure (Acts 7:45, Hebrews 4:8). In Matthew 1:23 the writer points out the prophecy of the virgin birth of Christ which is found in Isaiah 7:14. It is interesting to note in these early chapters of Matthew how many different aspects of the birth of Christ had been prophesied in the Old Testament.

In the second chapter the visit of the wise men (the Greek word is "magi") reveals the part which Gentiles played in the birth of Christ. These men were probably from Persia or some of the other eastern countries which were especially known for their observation of the heavenly bodies. They apparently knew of the birth of Christ by a direct revelation from God. It seems that Mary and Joseph had remained in Bethlehem after the birth of Christ since they were now in a house when the wise men visited them. Judging from the age of the children whom Herod killed, it seems that it had been more than a year since the birth of Christ when the visit of the wise men took place. The Herod mentioned in chapter two is the infamous Herod the Great who had been honored by the Roman Emperor with the title "King of the Jews." The bloody history of Herod the Great, who killed his favorite wife and two of his sons when he became suspicious that they were plotting to take the throne, reveals that the merciless slaughter of the innocent children of Bethlehem was not at all unusual for him.

The providence of God in protecting his Son is seen in the flight of Joseph to Egypt. Jesus Christ came to die, but His death must be at the right time and in the right place, and God would see to that. Note that this mention of Egypt seems to be consistent with the usual Biblical picture of Egypt representing the world and worldliness for the believer. This is seen in that Matthew quotes the fulfillment of the prophecy of Hosea 11:1 which says, "Out of Egypt have I called my son." The emphasis is placed on separation from Egypt, and for the Christian separation from worldliness. When Joseph returned with the baby Jesus to Nazareth, Matthew remarks that this fulfilled the prophecy, "He shall be called a Nazarene." The problem here is that there is no specific Old Testament passage which says this. But note that Matthew says that this was "spoken by the prophets," not one, but several. Since the little village of Nazareth had a lowly reputation, this apparently refers to the many prophecies which said that the Messiah would be a humble and lowly person. The word "Nazarene" refers to the place where Jesus grew up and has absolutely nothing to do with the Old Testament vow of a Nazarite.

II. PREPARATION FOR THE MINISTRY OF CHRIST (3:1—4:11)

A. Ministry of John The Baptist and Baptism of Jesus (3:1-17). In Matthew 3 and 4 the baptism and temptation of Christ are seen as the two significant events that especially prepared Him for and instituted His ministry. John the Baptist was actually slightly related to Jesus and was about six months older. He was from the hill country of Judea, and his father and mother were Zacharias and Elisabeth (see Luke 1). Everyone was excited about John the Baptist because he was the first prophet in Israel since Malachi some four hundred years before. Although related, he apparently did not know Jesus personally but was given a sign by which he would recognize Him (John 1:33). John's message, "Repent: for the kingdom of heaven is at hand," was the same message which was preached by Christ (Matthew 4:17), and later by His disciples (Matthew 10:7). John used the rite of baptism, which had been used by the Jews to initiate Gentile proselytes, to mark the occasion of the repentance of his converts. Jesus apparently submitted to John's baptism for two basic reasons, to mark the inauguration of his official ministry and to identify himself with sinners. The ministry of John the Baptist fulfilled the prophecy of Isaiah 40:3 which gives the picture of an oriental king visiting one of his subject nations and sending before him a representative to see that the way is clear and that everything is prepared for the king. God's audible approval from Heaven at the baptism of Christ (Matthew 3:17) is one of the three occasions when this occurred during Jesus' ministry, the other two at the transfiguration (Matthew 17:5) and just before the crucifixion (John 12:28).

B. Temptation of Jesus (4:1-11). The temptation of Jesus is very important in the ministry of Jesus Christ as Savior and Redeemer. His temptation served the two-fold purpose of proving His sinlessness, thus making it possible for Him to become the sacrifice for the sins of others rather than His own, and qualifying Him to be our intercessor because He can be "touched with the feeling of our infirmities" since He was "in all points tempted like as we are, yet without sin" (see Hebrews 2:18 and 4:15). It seems that the three temptations which the devil hurled at our Lord represent the three basic desires of the human heart. The challenge to turn the stones to bread represents temptations connected with the necessities of life; the challenge for Christ to cast Himself off the pinnacle of the Temple, which would have resulted in His being heralded as a great prophet, represents the desire for fame and recognition; the invitation for Christ to worship Satan in exchange for his usurped possession of the kingdoms of the world, thus causing Jesus to bypass the Cross, represents man's desire for wealth and possession. Indeed, these three basic desires are also seen in the devil's first temptation to Eve in Genesis 3:6 when he caused her to see that the tree was "good for food . . . , pleasant to the eyes, and a tree to be desired to make one wise" as well as in the Apostle John's description of "all that is in the world, the lust of the flesh, and the lust of the eyes, and the pride of life" (1 John 2:16). The devil's temptations are basically the same today as they always have been.

III. THE MINISTRY OF CHRIST (4:12—25:46)

A. The Public Ministry of Christ (4:12—16:12). From the latter part of chapter four through the twelfth verse of chapter sixteen, Matthew records the ministry of Christ as it was directed primarily toward the multitudes. In the last verses of Matthew four Jesus calls His first disciples, two sets of brothers, Peter and Andrew, James and John, all of whom were fishermen. In 4:23 we see the three means through which Jesus presented His message: teaching, preaching, and healing. The first two seem to have been equal in importance, only emphasizing a difference in technique and quite often combined for the utmost in effectiveness, while the latter, healing, was always secondary and complementary to the first two. From the areas mentioned in 4:25, Galilee, Decapolis, Jerusalem, Judea, and beyond Jordan, we see from a Bible map that Jesus' influence very soon covered all of Palestine.

In chapters five through seven Matthew records perhaps Jesus' most famous discourse, the Sermon on the Mount. In 5:1-12 Jesus gives a series of eight blessings or beatitudes which describe the desired characteristics of disciples of Christ. The word translated "blessed" here may also mean "happy," and it is interesting to substitute the word "happy" in each beatitude and note Jesus' description of true happiness. Happiness is realized in the life of a Christian to the extent that he seeks to pattern his life after the characteristics of his Lord, and these characteristics are those of the beatitudes. Then Jesus mentions that His disciples perform two services in relation to the world; like salt, they preserve the world from total corruption and the outpouring of the wrath of God, and like light, they serve as a beacon and source of illumination to the world. In Matthew 5:17, 18, Jesus introduces the very important subject of His relationship to the Old Testament Law. The Jewish leaders accused Him of breaking and disregarding the Law of Moses, but Jesus insisted that He did not come "to destroy, but to fulfil" the law and the prophets, and that not the smallest part, not "one jot or one tittle shall in no wise pass from the law, till all be fulfilled." Jesus freed us from the law, not by violating it, but by completely obeying it and becoming Himself "the Lamb of God, which taketh away the sin of the world" (John 1:29). In the remainder of Matthew five Jesus explains the true interpretation of many parts of the law. He especially explains that the two commandments, killing and adultery, may be broken not only by the very act itself, but also by hating and lusting. In other words, Jesus stressed that sin can be committed by the thought as well as the deed. Jesus closes this discussion of the law by pointing out the goal for the disciple, to be "perfect, even as your Father which is in heaven is perfect" (5:48). In this context the word "perfect" must be taken in its absolute sense; however, Jesus is not here saying that any Christian will be perfect, but rather that this should be every disciples' aim and desire.

In Matthew 6:1-18 Jesus deals with three religious practices which had been improperly observed by the Jews: giving, praying, and fasting. Contrary to the practice of the Pharisees, Jesus said that His disciples were to do each one of these "in secret," that is, not for the eyes or ears of men, but as a true act of honor and worship toward God. In connection with His discussion on prayer, Jesus introduces what is popularly called the Lord's Prayer, but which is more accurately "the Disciple's Prayer." Note that in this prayer Jesus introduces a new title for God which no Old Testament character ever had the privilege of using, the term "Father." This term in itself speaks of the great possibilities which lie open to the Christian in his prayer life. In the rest of chapter six, verses 19-34, Jesus emphasizes the great need for putting service and love for God ahead of any desire for material gain. He illustrates God's concern for our daily needs by pointing to objects of nature, the fowls of the air, and the lilies of the field. In 6:33 Jesus sums it up when He says, "Seek ye first the kingdom of God, and his righteousness; and all these things [these material needs] shall be added unto you."

Matthew 7:1, "Judge not, that ye be not judged," has been taken by some as an admonition never to be critical of anyone or of any doctrine. But if this were true, this passage would be contradicting other passages of Scripture which admonish us to "try the spirits whether they are of God" (1 John 4:1). Matthew 7:1-5 is not an exhortation for Christians to be gullible and naive, but rather a warning for us to severely judge ourselves before we make any attempt to judge others, and to be willing to be judged on the same basis by which we judge others. Matthew 7:7, 8 is one of the great prayer promises of the Bible, "Ask, and it shall be given you; seek, and ye shall find; knock, and it shall be opened unto you." Jesus follows this invitation to pray with a reminder of the greater care of our Heavenly Father over our earthly fathers, who even themselves often granted our requests. Matthew 7:12 gives us what is usually called "the golden rule," and 7:13, 14 emphasize the difficulty and definiteness of the way to Heaven compared with the ease and laxity of the way to Hell. Matthew 7:15-29 warn against the clever deceitfulness of false prophets, wolves in sheep's clothing, who cannot be discerned by their words but rather by their works. The basic difference between the true and the false concerns the type of foundation upon which each is built. The false builds upon the sand (salvation by works, by human effort and ingenuity) while the true builds upon the rock (salvation by God's grace, through the blood of Christ).

Chapters 8 and 9 record a series of ten miracles in the ministry of Christ which Matthew seems to group together topically rather than chronologically. In these miracles he demonstrates the complete sovereignty of Christ over all realms: over disease, in the miracles of healing; over nature, as He calms the sea; over the devil, as He casts out demons; over sin, as He forgives a man's sin; and over death, as He raises Jairus' daughter. But, since Jesus has returned to the Father, this dominion can be maintained today only through His followers on the basis of His finished work; therefore, he admonishes us to pray "the Lord of the harvest, that he will send forth labourers into his harvest" (Matthew 9:38).

In chapter 10 Jesus officially commissions and sends out His twelve disciples to warn Israel of the presence of the kingdom. It is interesting to compare the list of the twelve here with that given in Mark 6, Luke 9, and Acts 1. Each list has some variety in order, but in each one the same four apostles are always mentioned together and in each foursome the same apostle is always listed first, Simon Peter in the first group, Philip in the second group, and James, the son of Alphaeus, in the third group. This seems to indicate that the apostles were officially divided into three groups of four with an appointed leader of each group. On the subject of rewards and fruitbearing, Matthew 10:42 indicates that such a small thing as giving a cup of water to a disciple simply because he is a disciple is considered as fruit for the Master and will not go unnoticed by Him.

In 11:1-19 Jesus answers the doubts of John the Baptist by quoting from a Messianic passage in Isaiah 35 and showing John that He was accurately fulfilling what had been prophesied about Messiah. John the Baptist was apparently subject to the traditional Jewish misconception that Messiah would immediately restore Israel to her former glory and set up a political kingdom here on earth. In spite of John's human misconception, Jesus commends and exalts him to the highest place in the Old Testament dispensation but emphasizes the fact that the least in the new dispensation of the kingdom of Heaven, the present day church age, is greater in position and knowledge than John the Baptist. In 11:20-27 Jesus condemns the cities of Chorazin, Bethsaida, and Capernaum who had been eyewitnesses to His personal ministry and yet had not received Him. In this passage Jesus seems to teach degrees in eternal punishment on the basis of the opportunities which an individual or nation has had. But He closes the chapter in verses 28-30 with one of the most compassionate invitations in Scripture, "Come unto me, all ye that labour and are heavy laden, and I will give you rest."

In chapter 12 Matthew emphasizes the rising hostility of the Jewish leaders, especially in relation to his performance of that which was needful and good on the Sabbath day. They went so far as to accuse Jesus of casting out demons by the power of "Beelzebub the prince of the devils" (verse 24). Jesus pointed out the fallacy of their charge and warned them of the seriousness of their sin, a sin which was at least bordering on the "sin against the Holy Spirit," this is, the sin of willfully ascribing that which you know to be the work of God to the devil. In this chapter Jesus also points out His superiority to the Jewish ceremonial institutions in that as priest He is "greater than the temple" (verse 6), as prophet He is "greater than Jonas [Jonah]" (verse 41), and as king He is "greater than Solomon" (verse 42).

Chapter 13 gives the seven great parables on the kingdom of Heaven: the parable of the sower, the wheat and the tares, the mustard seed, the leaven, the hidden treasure, the pearl of great price, and the net full of fish. In this chapter Jesus gives us the interpretation for the first two; and thus, they become for us the key to interpreting all of the parables. Remember always that a parable is trying to get over one main thought; therefore, do not press every detail of a parable into a doctrinal teaching, for in doing so many false and contradictory doctrines will be developed. In chapter 14 Matthew records the tragic circumstances of the death of John the Baptist, followed by the feeding of the five thousand, and Jesus' walking on the water. The love of Christ is especially seen as He tries to find a place to be alone following the death of John but is plagued by the multitudes who follow Him. Instead of being angry with them for disturbing His privacy, He "was moved with compassion toward them, and he healed their sick" (verse 14). The feeding of the five thousand is the only miracle of Christ which is recorded in every Gospel.

Matthew 15 begins with the complaint of the scribes and Pharisees concerning Jesus' disciples neglecting to observe the ceremonial washings of the Jews when eating. The Pharisees were the strictest Jewish religious sect, while the Sadducees were the most liberal. In addition to stressing the letter of the law, the Pharisees also added many of their own ceremonies to the Law of Moses. The scribes were the official copiers of the law, and many of them were also Pharisees. Jesus answered their complaint here by charging them with the much greater sin of disregarding the law of God by allowing men to escape their obligation toward aged parents by simply pronouncing the hypocritical oath, "Corban," meaning "it is a gift," thus pledging all their earthly possessions as dedicated to God while keeping them for their own selfish use. Here Jesus points out that the heart of a man and that which comes from his heart indicate much more clearly what a man really is than do his outward religious acts and ceremonies. Matthew 15:21-28 reveal a unique conversation which Jesus had with a Gentile woman while He was visiting outside Palestine in Syria or Phoenicia. The woman recognizes Jesus as the prophesied Messiah, the "Son of David," but Jesus seems peculiarly cold. However, it becomes evident that He only wishes to emphasize His present ministry toward Israel and to prove the woman's faith. And what faith this Gentile manifests as she willingly submits to being "the master's dog." Note that Jesus always commends faith when it appears where it is least expected (see also Matthew 8:10) and condemns unbelief when it appears in those who should believe (see Matthew 16:8; 8:26). Chapter 15 closes with the feeding of the four thousand, similar in many respects to the more familiar feeding of the five thousand, but taking place on the Palestinian side of the Sea of Galilee.

Jesus closes His public ministry in the first part of chapter 16 with the Pharisees' demand for some special sign and a warning to His disciples against their doctrine. The sign of the prophet Jonah in verse 4 is, of course, the resurrection, for Jonah was a picture prophecy of the resurrection as he stayed three days and three nights in the belly of the fish. Indeed the resurrection is the focal point of Christianity, for upon its truth Christianity stands or falls (and so agrees Paul in 1 Corinthians 15).

B. His Private Ministry (16:13—20:34). After Jesus' rebuke of the Pharisees for seeking a sign, He takes His disciples out of Jewish territory to Caesarea Philippi. It is certainly appropriate that Jesus introduces the doctrine of the church in Gentile territory, for indeed the Church of Jesus Christ today is mainly a Gentile church. Matthew 16:13-20 has become quite a controversial passage, perhaps mainly because of the use made of the passage by the Roman Catholic Church in claiming Peter as their first pope. After Peter's marvelous confession in verse 16 Jesus replies, "Thou art Peter, and upon this rock I will build my church." The three principal views on this passage say that the "rock" here refers to Christ Himself, or to Peter's preceding confession in Christ, or to Peter himself. In the final analysis, perhaps there is a truth in all three, for even if we concede that Jesus here refers to Peter, it is to Peter as the spokesman and representative of all the apostles, and in this connection even Paul taught that the Church is "built upon the foundation of the apostles and prophets, Jesus Christ himself being the chief corner stone" (Ephesians 2:20). Immediately following Jesus' commendation of Peter's confession, our Lord begins to reveal to His disciples the approaching Cross, but because of their warped views of Old Testament prophecy, they were not able to imagine a cross in the plan of the Messiah. Note that Jesus clearly prophesies His death four times, here in 16:21, then in 17:22, 23; 20:17-19; and 26:1, 2. Contrary to the claims of some, Jesus did not become a martyr for His cause, or the victim of circumstances; He rather laid down His life of Himself because He had "power to lay it down" and "power to take it again" (John 10:18). Jesus closes this first mention of the Cross by inviting His disciples to take up their own cross and follow Him. To take one's cross primarily stresses identification with Christ in all respects.

The two main subjects in chapter 17 are the transfiguration and the tribute money. The record of the transfiguration in 17:1-13 at least partially explains the strange statement in 16:28, "Verily I say unto you, There be some standing here, which shall not taste of death, till they see the Son of man coming in his kingdom." In other words, the three privileged disciples, Peter, James, and John, are here given a glimpse of what the kingdom of Heaven will really be like. Many feel that Moses and Elijah are here seen talking with Christ as representatives of those two groups which will be involved in the resurrection, that is those who are dead in Christ and those who will be alive at His second coming. It is important to notice that the tribute money mentioned in 17:24-27 was a Temple tax received for the support of the Temple in Jerusalem and not a Roman tax.

In Matthew 18:1-10 Jesus uses a little child as an example of the attitude one must have in order to undergo conversion. We must remember that Jesus does not say here that Christians should be like children in every respect, but rather only in the example of a child-like faith. Unfortunately, sometimes Christians become very childish in their conduct which is certainly not well-pleasing to God. This passage, along with 2 Samuel 12:23, offers circumstantial evidence for the teaching that children under the age of accountability are safe under the protection of God's mercy. Matthew 18:15-20 relate important instructions concerning personal offenses among Christians. Many weak Christians could be saved for the church if we would follow carefully these instructions. The church today is in great need of giving attention to this matter of discipline. Verse 20 gives us the basic definition for the New Testament Church, that is simply a group of people, it matters not how small, who are meeting in the name of Christ. Matthew 18:21-35 relate Peter's question concerning forgiveness and Jesus' answer in the form of a parable. In this parable Jesus makes an attitude of forgiveness toward others necessary for us if we would obtain the forgiveness of our own sins. Chapter 19, verses 1-12 give us Jesus' teaching on the subject of divorce. In answer to the question of the Pharisees, Jesus goes beyond the Law of Moses to creation itself in order to find the basis for marriage as He quotes from Genesis 2:23, 24. In verse 9 Jesus clearly teaches that there is only one ground for divorce and remarriage, that is adultery on the part of the offending party. Some question as to whether the idea of remarriage is involved here, but it must be for at least two reasons. First, the Jewish idea of divorce always involved the possibility of remarriage, and second, the passage itself says, "Whosoever shall put away his wife, except it be for fornication, and shall marry another, committeth adultery." In other words, if remarriage does not take place, the sin of adultery is not at all involved. We should stress, however, that even in the case of unscriptural marriages forgiveness may still be obtained if the person comes to God with a genuine attitude of repentance. Remember that there is only one unforgivable sin, and that is the sin of blasphemy against the Holy Spirit. Note that in verses 10-12 Jesus' disciples come to the conclusion that if marriage is so binding, perhaps a person ought not to marry. Jesus' reply indicates that the question of marriage lies completely within the individual's choice and accompanying circumstances. Marriage is blessed of God; if a person wishes to remain unmarried in order to devote himself more to the work of God as Paul recommends in 1 Corinthians 7, that then is certainly commendable.

In 19:16-26 Matthew records the account of the rich young ruler. It is interesting to notice that the commandments which Jesus quotes to the young man are the last six of the ten commandments which involve man's duty toward other men. The young man claimed a measure of excellence in relation to these commandments. However, he fell far short on the first four commandments, the first of which requires complete devotion to God. His God was his money, and he was unwilling to give it up, even for eternal life. Jesus closes this passage with a statement concerning the difficulty of rich men in being saved. The question is not whether God is willing to save rich men, but whether a rich man is willing to put his trust in God rather than in the power of his riches. In verse 24 the "eye of a needle" is to be taken in its literal sense as referring to the eye of a small sewing needle, for Jesus' whole point is the impossibility of such a thing with men. Verses 27-30 seem to indicate that the apostles of Christ will have some special place in His future kingdom. The emphasis of verse 29 is that Christ rewards everyone who serves Him faithfully, both in this life and in the life to come.

The parable in 20:1-16 is an illustration of the teaching of Matthew 19:30, "Many that are first shall be last; and the last shall be first." Some have taken this parable as evidence that there will be absolutely no difference in rewards in Heaven, no special recognition of any kind whatsoever. But they miss the point of the parable as well as the clear teaching of other passages of Scripture, such as Matthew 19:28, 1 Corinthians 3:8, and 3:12-15, Matthew 10:42, Luke 19:17. This parable, rather, teaches that the basis of rewards lies in the sovereignty of God and the opportunities of men. God will reward men according to His good pleasure and according to the advantage which they have taken of their opportunities, not according to some special privilege or position. In 20:17-19 Jesus again prophesies His fast approaching death. In 20:20-28 Salome, the wife of Zebedee, comes with her sons, James and John, to request for them privileged positions in the coming kingdom. Notice that Jesus does not condemn Salome's request or say that such positions do not exist, He rather reminds her that special privileges of this nature will be given according to the good pleasure of the Father. Someone has remarked that the resulting indignation of the other apostles, after finding out about the request of James and John, probably came as a result of their not having thought of it first rather than because of some special piety on their part. The healing of the two blind men in Matthew 20:29-34 is probably the same incident as the healing of blind Bartimaeus in Mark 10:46-52. Matthew tells us that there were actually two blind men, while Mark, who likes to focus on special details and personalities, chooses to emphasize the more colorful of the two men, blind Bartimaeus.

C. Climax of His Ministry (21—25). Matthew 21:1-11 record the triumphal entry of Christ the King into the city of Jerusalem, an event which had been prophesied in Zechariah 9:9. By doing this Jesus was announcing that His kingdom was drawing very near. The death, resurrection, and ascension of Christ would institute a new dispensation in God's dealing with men. It is important to notice that the New Testament seems to stress both a present and a future aspect to the kingdom of God. Verses 12-17 of this same chapter record the cleansing of the Temple which Jesus carried out before His death. Jesus cleansed the Temple twice during His ministry, the first time in John 2:13-16 in the early part of His ministry, and the second time in the close of His ministry as recorded in this passage. Jesus uses the barren fig tree in 21:18-22 to teach a lesson about the need for fruitfulness as well as a lesson about the power of faith.

The remainder of chapter 21, as well as the first fourteen verses of chapter 22, concerns the Jewish leaders' questioning of Jesus' authority and Jesus' answer to them. Jesus first embarrasses them by asking them a question concerning the authority of John's baptism which they were unable to answer because of their hypocritical position. Then Jesus follows with three parables, the parable of the two sons, the parable of the householder and his vineyard, and the parable of the marriage feast, all of which emphasize the rejection of Jesus as the true Messiah by the Jewish leaders. The parable of the two sons points out that God judges men by what they do rather than what they say. The parable of the householder and the vineyard, apparently based on Isaiah 5:1-7, pictures the unfruitfulness of Israel in the face of all of God's blessings as well as her rejection of God's messengers, including his own son. The parable of the marriage feast in the first fourteen verses of chapter twenty-two shows Israel's rejection of God's gracious invitation, which results in God's turning from Israel to the Gentiles. The man without the wedding garment apparently represents those who try to enter God's kingdom on their own terms rather than coming by the terms which God lays down. Salvation must come only through God's method, not through human schemes or devices.

The remainder of Matthew 22, verses 15-46, concerns four different questions, three of which were asked by the enemies of Christ, and one by Christ Himself. Jesus was asked the first question by the disciples of the Pharisees and by the Herodians. The question was, "Is it lawful to give tribute unto Caesar, or not?" The tricksters thought they had Jesus in a corner because, if He said, "Yes," they would accuse Him of being a traitor, and if He said "No," they would go straight to Pontius Pilate and charge Him with instigating a conspiracy. Jesus turned their question upon them by stating a principle which is very applicable today, "Render therefore unto Caesar the things which are Caesar's; and unto God the things that are God's." It is perfectly right for a Christian to demonstrate loyalty toward his government as laong as that loyalty does not interfere with his service to God. Verses 23-33 record one of the few appearances of the Sadducees in the gospels. They were far less popular with the common people than were the Pharisees. They claimed only the five books of Moses as Scripture and rejected all the traditions of the Pharisees. They also dismissed almost everything that was supernatural, including the resurrection, about which they asked their question. Their aim was clearly to present a human case which to them made a resurrection impossible, a woman in Heaven who had been married to seven different men. Jesus' answer dealt with their amazing two-fold ignorance, first concerning the Scripture and its teaching, and second, concerning the power of God. The third question was asked by a lawyer from among the Pharisees; it required Jesus to give the greates commandment of the law. It is interesting that Jesus' answer in essence summed up the two parts of the ten commandments, the first four commandments dealing with man's duty toward God and the second six dealing with man's duty toward his fellow man. Jesus Himself asked the final question concerning whose son Christ was to be. Jesus' purpose in quoting David from Psalm 110:1 seems to be to show the Pharisees that the Messiah was both the son of David and the Son of God.

Chapter 23 of Matthew reveals a side of Jesus which is often overlooked by modern day commentators and preachers. We certainly see in Jesus an enormous love and compassion, but we also see in Him great anger in His denunciation of hypocrisy. The religion of the Pharisees was solely a religion of demonstration; when there were no eyes to view their religious activity, they had none. Jesus sums it up in verse 5 when He says, "All their works they do for to be seen of men." Jesus follows His description of their character and actions by a series of eight "woes" or denunciations of their hypocrisy. He declares in verse 35 that they and their generation will soon be the victims of the judgment of God on a careless and hard-hearted people. It is interesting to notice that this chapter, which contains some of Jesus' strongest words, also closes with one of Jesus' most compassionate expressions, "O Jerusalem, Jerusalem, thou that killest the prophets, and stonest them which are sent unto thee, how often would I have gathered thy children together, even as a hen gathereth her chickens under her wings, and ye would not!" (verse 37).

Matthew 24 and 25 contain Jesus' popular discourse on His second coming often called "the Olivet Discourse." In attempting to interpret this passage of Scripture, it is of the utmost importance that we notice the questions which the disciples asked Jesus in verse 3. In the minds of the disciples, it is likely that all of these things were viewed in connection with one event, but in the answer which Jesus gives it seems that there are two or three separate events. It seems that verses 1-26 and verses 32-34 refer primarily to the destruction of Jerusalem in A.D. 70 by the Roman General, Titus. Verses 27-31 form a parenthetical contrast between the destruction of Jerusalem and the second coming of Christ. Verse 34 clearly states that everything which has been mentioned in the preceding verses, with the exception of the parenthetical statement in 27-31, will take place within that very generation. Verse 36 is a very important verse because it forms the transition from the subject of the destruction of Jerusalem in A.D. 70 to the subject of the second coming of Christ. Everything in the remainder of the Olivet Discourse from verse 36 forward concerns the second coming. Note that this method of interpreting the Olivet Discourse does away with the teaching that certain specific signs must precede the second coming of Christ, and this is certainly more consistent with the doctrine of the imminent return of Christ, that is the thought that Christ may come at any moment. To illustrate His teaching, Jesus gives us three parables, the first one concerning the faithful and evil servants in 24:44-51, the second concerning the ten virgins in 25:1-13, and the third concerning the talents in 24:14-30. Together these parables emphasize the importance of ever being watchful for the Lord's return and of ever taking advantage of our opportunities and abilities to their fullest since Jesus could come back at any time.

IV. THE TRIAL , CRUCIFIXION, AND BURIAL (26—27)

Matthew 26:1-46 record the last events before the death of

Christ. Verses 6-13 relate the anointing of Jesus by Mary of Bethany, the sister of Martha and Lazarus. Verse 12 seems to indicate that Mary was the only one who actually realized that Jesus was about to die. Verses 17-30 give us an account of the institution of the Lord's Supper which Jesus commanded to be continued in the church as a symbolical reminder of the importance of His death. Verses 36-46 record Jesus' final hours of agony in the Garden of Gethsemane as He shrank from the knowledge that He was about to have all the sins of all the world placed upon Him on the Cross. The rest of chapter 26, verses 47-75, concern the betrayal, the mock trial before the Jewish high priest, Caiaphas, and Peter's denial. Contrast the action of Peter in 26:75 with that of Judas in 27:5 and you will have a good example of the difference between true and false repentance. Because the Jews desired the death sentence for Jesus, they were forced to bring Him before Pontius Pilate, the Roman governor, since they did not have the authority to carry out capital punishment without the permission of Rome. Pilate certainly asked one of the most important questions of the ages in 27:22 when he inquired, "What shall I do then with Jesus which is called Christ?" Pilate rejected Christ, not by open opposition to Him, for he declared that Jesus was a "just person," but by simply refusing to stand for what he knew to be the truth.

A contradiction is sometimes supposed in the report by the Gospel writers concerning the sign over Jesus' Cross. However, by comparing the words of the sign in all four gospels, we come to the conclusion that each of the Gospel writers probably reported only a part of the sign, and that the sign in its entirety actually read, "This is Jesus of Nazareth, the King of the Jews." There is absolutely no contradiction. In reading the account of the crucifixion in the four gospels we find that Jesus made a total of seven statements or "sayings" from the Cross, only one of which is reported by the Gospel of Matthew. This is found in verse 46 where Jesus said in His native Aramaic tongue, "Eli, Eli, lama sabachthani?" which means, "My God, My God, why hast thou forsaken me? " a cry of agony which was actually a Biblical quotation from Psalm 22:1. This cry reveals the mortal agony which Jesus suffered on the Cross as He experienced the totally unique feeling of having God the Father turn His face from Him as He bore the guilt of our sins on the Cross. The "veil of the temple" in verse 51 was the veil which separated the Holy Place from the Holy of Holies where God's presence dwelt, and the rending of this veil symbolized the fact that the way to God's throne of grace was thrown open to every man through Jesus' death on the Cross (see Hebrews 4:16). Many feel that the rising of the saints in verses 52 and 53 indicates that believers who died before the cross were, at the time of Christ's resurrection, taken from their temporary Old Testament abode to be with Jesus in Paradise. The account of the burial of Christ in verses 57-61, along with the parallel account in John 19:38-42, reveals that at least two important Jewish leaders, who were members of the ruling body of the Jews called the Sanhedrin, had become disciples of Christ. These were Joseph of Arimathaea and Nicodemus. The sealing of the tomb which the Pharisees requested in verses 62-66 serves as a very forceful argument for the truth of the resurrection of Christ.

V. THE RESURRECTION AND COMMISSION (28)

Chapter 28, the final chapter of Matthew, records the resurrection of Christ and His great commission as it was given to His disciples in Galilee. Note that each one of the gospels, as well as the Book of Acts, gives the great commission of Christ to His disciples. Here in Matthew it is found in 28:18-20, in Mark 16:15, in Luke 24:47, in John 20:21, and in Acts 1:8. The truth of the resurrection is perhaps the cardinal doctrine of Christianity, for as Paul said, "If Christ be not raised, your faith is vain; ye are yet in your sins. Then they also which are fallen asleep in Christ are perished" (1 Corinthains 15:17, 18). The great commission here in verses 18-20 is composed of a basis followed by three different commands. The basis of the commission is the universal authority which has been given to Christ according to verse 18. The first command is found in the words, "Teach all nations," which literally means, "Make disciples of all nations." The second command involves baptizing these disciples in the name of the Trinity, and the third command involves "teaching them to observe all things" which Christ commanded. Each part of the great commission is important, and no part should be neglected or played down. First, people must be saved through faith in Christ, then they should be taught the doctrine of Christ in order that they might "grow in grace, and in the knowledge of our Lord and Saviour Jesus Christ" (2 Peter 3:18). Note that in verse 20 Christ promises to be with us as we faithfully carry out this great commission.

A SURVEY OF THE GOSPEL OF

Mark

by Stanley Outlaw

I. THE SERVANT'S PREPARATION—BAPTISM AND TEMPTATION (1:1-13)

Mark starts his account of the ministry of Christ by telling us about the work of John the Baptist and the baptism of Christ. He calls this, "The beginning of the gospel of Jesus Christ." Indeed it was with Jesus' baptism that His official ministry began, and not before. The word "gospel" itself simply means "good news," and the beginning of Jesus' ministry at His baptism was certainly good news for all the world, for this was the "Lamb of God, which taketh away the sin of the world" (John 1:29).

In introducing the ministry of John the Baptist, Mark, in verses 2, 3 quotes a two-fold Old Testament prophecy. It foretold John's work; first, from Malachi 3:1, and then from Isaiah 40:3. Both of these prophecies picture John's ministry as that of a "forerunner" who goes ahead of an oriental king to prepare for his approaching visit by announcing it publicly and seeing that the subjects are made ready for the presence of royalty. Mark identifies John's baptism as "the baptism of repentance for the remission of sins," that is, a baptism which marked the fact that they were now turning from the old way of life to a new way which would prepare them to be servants of the king. Of course, we must insist that there was nothing miraculous in the baptism itself which would take away a person's sins. The baptism only marked the profession of an attitude on the part of the candidates, just as Christian baptism marks the profession of repentance and faith in the finished work of Christ.

Those who would exalt baptism to the position of a regenerating act remove it from its proper position in the Scripture and come dangerously close to making salvation dependent upon an act of man rather than upon the finished work of Christ. Those who submitted to John's baptism were saved just as any Old Testament saint was saved who came with faith in God's promise and a truly repentant heart. The difference between that baptism of John and Christian baptism is the difference between the Old Testament and the New Testament dispensations, the difference between the absence and presence of the abiding ministry of the Holy Spirit. Those who submitted to John's baptism prepared themselves to participate in the work of the king. Those who, with a true heart, submit themselves to Christian baptism receive the commission of the king to administer the rites of his kingdom while he is away. This they do as His official ambassador through the abiding power of His Holy Spirit. This difference is plainly illustrated in the incident where Paul rebaptized those twelve men at Ephesus who had only received the baptism of John (Acts 19:1-7).

In verses 9-11 we see Jesus Himself submitting to John's baptism. The question immediately arises, "For what reasons would the sinless Christ submit Himself to such a baptism?" The answer is at least three-fold: (1) To serve as an official initiation for the beginning of His ministry, for indeed up until this time Jesus' Messianic activity had been very limited. (2) To identify Himself with sinful man for whom He came to die. (3) Some would go so far as to suggest a vicarious element in His baptism. The idea is that here Jesus made full repentance for those who would be saved through His death on the Cross, but who, because of an imperfect heart, would be unable to make a satisfactory repentance for a holy God without this help of His Son. Since Scripture is not clear on this aspect of His baptism, certainly too much emphasis should not be placed upon it; but we must admit the truth that our salvation comes through the entire ministry of Christ, from beginning to end, and not by just one part of it.

In verses 12, 13 Mark gives an abbreviated account of Jesus' temptation, omitting the details of the three major temptations, but adding the facts of the dangerous presence of the wild beasts and the comforting ministry of the angels. The purpose of Jesus' temptation is clearly explained by Hebrews 2:18 and 4:15, which tell us that this, and the other trials throughout His ministry, fully qualified Him to "help them that are tempted," and to compassionately "sympathize with our human weaknesses."

II. THE SERVANT'S WORK (1:14—13:37)

In Galilee (1:14—7:23). If you will check a Bible map, you will find that there were three Roman provinces in Palestine in Jesus' day. The northernmost province was Galilee, in which He spent most of His ministry; the middle one was Samaria, occupied by the despised Jewish-Gentile mongrels; and the southernmost province was Judea. In Judea was located the capital city, Jerusalem, and the sacred Temple which Jews came to from all over the world, and where Jesus visited at different times during His ministry. Mark uses nearly half of his Gospel, from 1:14—7:23, to tell about Jesus' work in His home province of Galilee. In verses 14, 15 of chapter 1, Mark introduces us to the ministry of Christ in Galilee and tells us that his message was one of proclaiming the arrival of the kingdom. In verses 16-20 we are told of the call of the two sets of brothers who were to help make up the chosen twelve disciples. It is interesting to notice that Jesus called men to be His disciples who were busy at work already, not those who were sitting idle. Lazy men never make good followers of Christ. Jesus invited Simon and Andrew to follow Him in words which related to their occupation, "Come ye after me, and I will make you to become fishers of men." Often the talents which a man has acquired in a secular life can be applied for beneficial results in his life as a disciple of Christ. Just as these men had used every legitimate means to catch fish for a living, Jesus would now teach them to put that same zeal and some of those same methods to work in catching the souls of men for eternity. In verses 21-27 Jesus makes His first appearance in the synagogue in the city of Capernaum, an important trade city where Peter and Andrew had made their home after moving from their hometown of Bethsaida, just across the Jordan River (see John 1:44). Almost every major city, both inside and outside Palestine, had a synagogue where Jewish people gathered to study the law. There was only one Temple location, and it was in Jerusalem, but there were many synagogues scattered throughout the world. In this synagogue at Capernaum, Jesus gave some of His greatest discourses.

The people were most impressed with the "authority" with which Jesus spoke; He spoke in such a way that the people were persuaded that He knew what He was talking about. Certainly we too, as preachers and teachers of His Word, ought to be so convinced of our message that we could speak with "authority" and with His convincing power. During this first appearance of Jesus in this synagogue, we see Him manifesting His power over the realm of Satan as He casts out the unclean spirit. Demon possession is very prominent in the gospels, and we should remember that demon possession and demonic influence is still a very important factor today in explaining the actions of some men and women. No doubt America in the past has been largely spared of this phenomenon because of the thorough permeation of the gospel, but as this nation turns her back on God, we may be sure that we will see more and more of the reality of demonic influence. Almost any of our missionaries who work in those benighted areas which long ago turned their backs toward God can already tell us of many incidents which aptly illustrate this bold manifestation of Satan's work.

The remainder of chapter 1, verses 28-45, tells us how quickly the good news of Jesus' work spread over the province of Galilee, and how Jesus sought to cover as much ground as He possibly could in the short time which He knew that His ministry would cover. Verses 29-31 show us Jesus' compassion in the healing of Peter's mother-in-law, and of her appropriate response of immediately arising to serve Him and His followers. How appropriately she illustrates the true slogan, "Saved to serve."

Verses 32-34 point up the fact that Jesus performed multitudes of miracles of healing which are not recorded in detail in any of the gospels. Note that in both verses 25 and 34 Jesus forbids the devils to speak of Him, although they knew who He was. The Son of God did not wish to be associated with Satan and his helpers, even when they testified of the truth of His deity. True it is that we too ought to be careful that we do not become associates with the enemies of God and of His Son. In verses 35-39 we get a glimpse of the fervent prayer life of the Son of God and His complete reliance upon the strength of His Heavenly Father as He continued His heated pace to get the message "throughout all Galilee." Verses 40-45 record the account of the faith of a leper manifested in request to Christ's, "If thou wilt, thou canst make me clean." He does not question Christ's ability to heal him, but only wonders about his willingness to thus show his love toward Him, and how pleased he must have been at Jesus' ready reply, "I will; be thou clean."

In 2:1-12 Jesus returns to Capernaum and is immediately surrounded by the crowds as He ministers to them in a local home, probably Simon Peter's. But among all the throng, there stands out the incident of the four courageous men who are so intent on getting their palsied friend to Jesus that, when stopped by the crowds at the door, they immediately go upon the rooftop and dig through the flat roof to lower their friend to the great physician. Note in verse 5 that Jesus saw "their faith," not just that of the sick man, but that of his friends as well. But on this occasion Jesus made a strange statement which aroused accusations of blasphemy from the critical Jewish leaders. The statement to the palsied man was, "Son, thy sins be forgiven thee." The fact that the man was healed showed the connection between sickness and the curse of sin, while at the same time it displayed Jesus' authority to forgive sin. The answer which He gave to His critics in verses 9, 10 is very interesting. The very fact that Jesus had direct power over a man's body proved His deity as well as the fact that He had power over a man's soul, for no mere man possesses either of these.

In 2:13-20 Mark records the call of Levi, or Matthew, who immediately shows a favorable response by inviting his friends and associates to a banquet so that he might introduce them to Jesus Christ. Again the Jewish leaders are critical of Jesus for His associations with "publicans and sinners." Some professed Christians have used this passage of Scripture as a defense for worldliness and compromise, but we must recognize the difference between becoming the genuine and compassionate friend of sinners, as Jesus did, and the tendency to find our companionship among sinners to the extent of deceiving the unsaved man and the false religionist into thinking that he is all right. Certainly, if we follow the pattern of Jesus both in His compassion for sinners and in His separation from sin, we cannot go wrong. Many seem to misunderstand the thrust of Jesus' meaning in verse 17 when He refers to "they that are whole" and to "the righteous." Jesus here seems to be using a note of sarcasm in reference to the Jewish leaders who claimed to be "whole" as well as "righteous." Until these leaders came to the place where they realized that they were very sick and that they were themselves great sinners, Jesus could do absolutely nothing for them. The first step in the salvation of any man is the realization of his awful sinfulness in the eyes of a holy God.

Mark records the answer of Jesus to His critics' question about fasting in 2:18-22. By the illustrations of the bridegroom, the new cloth, and the new wine, Jesus teaches a lesson about the purpose and time for fasting. The hypocritical Pharisees regularly observed a ceremonial fast twice each week, on Mondays and Thursdays. Jesus here seems to indicate that fasting should be a natural outgrowth of a burdened heart, rather than a ceremonial rite set aside for regular observance. Certainly there ought to be more fasting among Christians today, but it ought to be over sorrow for sin and prayer for sinners rather than a determined effort of the flesh to give a pious appearance.

The closing verses of chapter 2, verses 23-28, reveal Jesus' correction of the Jewish misuse of another Old Testament institution, the Sabbath. To the Old Testament Law, which was burdensome enough in itself, the Jewish rabbis had added a long list of requirements which dealt with every aspect of a man's life. By referring to the incident of David and his men, when they were fleeing from Saul, eating the sacred showbread which was reserved for the priests alone, Jesus wished to teach that commandments which God gave for the benefit of man from the beginning could become flexible if a greater necessity presented itself. God did not mean for man to be a slave to the day, but for the day to serve to the benefit of man. From Christ's additional statement in verse 28, perhaps He was also hinting at the liberty He would bring from the bondage of the law through His death on the Cross.

Mark records another Sabbath incident in 3:1-5 in Jesus' healing of the man with the withered hand. Here Jesus uses another argument against the Jewish misinterpretation of the Sabbath day, that is, that it is right to perform an act of goodness or of saving a life, even on the Sabbath day. Note that in verse 5 we see in Christ a mixture of emotions. He experiences the emotion of anger at the rebellion of the Jews, but at the same time, sorrow because of the hardened condition of their hearts. Jesus would teach us that it is right to be angry with those who oppose God and rebel at His commandments, while at the same time we must guard ourselves with a balance of compassion lest we allow that anger to cause us to act irrationally.

Verses 6-12 inform us of the extent of Jesus' reputation by this time, as well as the fact that again He had performed numerous miracles of healing which are not recorded in detail. Jesus' choosing of His twelve disciples is given in 3:13-21. From a comparison of the four lists of disciples recorded here, and in Matthew 10:1-4; Luke 6:12-16; and Acts 1:13, we find that, in spite of the differences in order, there are at least three important similarities between the lists: (1) Simon Peter is always first, and Judas Iscariot is always last: (2) Although the order within each group differs, each of the three groups of four disciples always contains the same four names: (3) Each of the three groups is always headed by the same man, Simon Peter in group one, Philip in group two, and James, the son of Alphaeus, in group three. This seems to imply that Jesus divided the disciples into three official groups of four disciples with an appointed leader at the head of each group.

Verse 21 indicates the extent to which Jesus was misunderstood when even those who proposed to act as His "friends" sought to seize Him because they thought that He was insane. Mark 3:22-30 is a very solemn passage containing Jesus' warning to the Jewish leaders of their danger in committing the unforgivable sin of blasphemy against the Holy Spirit. Many deep sermons have been preached on this Scripture in an attempt to define this sin, but it is quite clear what the sin is in this context. It is the sin of willfully and rebelliously, and in the face of unshakable evidence, ascribing the clear work of the Holy Spirit to the power of Satan. The next question often asked is, "Can this sin be committed today?" Again the answer is simple. If men today can ascribe the clear work of God's Spirit to the devil, then they can commit this sin. Certainly in this dispensation, the very age of the Holy Spirit Himself, this sin can be and is committed. However, though the sin can certainly be committed, I doubt that it is the job of the Christian to try to determine who has or has not done so; for indeed if a man has, God will not forgive him in spite of your efforts, and if the man has not, but thinks he has, and you succeed in getting him saved, then you have certainly done right, and God will bless you for it. This passage serves as a warning to an age of mockery, when almost nothing is regarded as sacred by some, that God will not fail to deal harshly with those who treat His precious Holy Spirit with such insult and disregard.

Verses 31-35 close out chapter 3 by revealing an incident which Jesus used to teach a very important lesson. As His mother and brothers sought His attention from the outskirts of the crowd to which He was speaking, He pointed out that blood relation or any other external factor is not that which determines a real connection with Him. It is rather the earnest determination of the individual to do God's will which pleases God and His Son. There seems to be some hint in this incident of the doubts which we know Jesus' brothers entertained about His ministry until after the resurrection, and perhaps His mother had some of the same misunderstandings.

Four of the five parables in the Book of Mark are found here in chapter 4. In verses 1-20 we are given what is no doubt the best known parable of Jesus, the parable of the sower. Jesus gives the interpretation to this parable, as well as the parable of the wheat and tares in Matthew 13, as a key to the interpretation of all His parables. He stresses the importance of the parable of the sower in 4:13 where He says, "Know ye not this parable? and how then will ye know all parables?" In this parable the "sower" is the preacher or teacher of the Word of God; the "seed" is the life-giving Word itself; while the "soil" represents the different responses in the hearts of men who hear the Word along with the accompanying circumstances. It is important to notice that there is a progressive element in the first three responses to the sowing of the Word. The first type of soil is "by the way side," that is on the well trodden paths where men walked and packed the earth so that no seed could possibly sprout. This represents the hearer who demonstrates no response to the gospel call though he hears the best of preachers. His attention and concern are elsewhere, and his untended heart is left open so that Satan steals away the precious seed.

The second type of soil is "stony ground." The actual picture is not that of a soil full of small stones, but rather of a large flat rock covered by a thin layer of top soil. Seed sown upon that rock will quickly sprout, spurred on by the heat of the sun reflected from the rock. But when the tiny roots of the plant try to reach down into the soil for food and moisture, they are stopped by the rock, and the plant quickly withers. Thus many make a dramatic, and often emotional, response to the gospel, but then just as quickly and dramatically withdraw when some slight persecution or hardship arises in connection with the Word and the new life.

The third type of soil is that "among thorns." The response of this soil seems to involve the production of at least some superficial fruit, for we are told that "it yielded no fruit." It manifests some earnestness in its response, but "worldly cares" and the desire for riches keep it so busy that it just simply has no time to tend the growth of the seed of the Word of God, and these cares eventually choke out all semblance of fruitfulness.

But, for the encouragement of the sower, thank God for the fourth response of the seed sown upon "good ground." It, of course, is richly productive, but even in this instance not all good soil is of the same fertility. In the same sense, genuine Christians possess different potentials in regard to ability and opportunity, and thus Christians will vary in the amount of fruit which they bear, "some thirty, and some sixty, and some an hundred." But note carefully that all genuine Christians do bear fruit. There is absolutely no such thing as a fruitless Christian. Remember, however, that Jesus' definition of fruit is somewhat broader than is sometimes imagined, for He stated in Matthew 10:42, "Whosoever shall give to drink unto one of these little ones a cup of cold water only in the name of a disciple, verily I say unto you, he shall in no wise lose his reward."

In the parable of the sower, the Word was represented as seed, but in the next parable in 4:21-25, the Word is "a candle," first making those who receive the Word an illumination and guide to those who see the Word in their lives, and second, as a light to reveal the secrets of the heart that a man may see himself as he really is. Those who energetically respond to the Word will receive more understanding and ability; those who refuse the Word will gradually lose what interest they had.

In Mark 4:26-34 we are given two parables about "the kingdom of God," the parable of the unconscious growth and the parable of the mustard seed. The first of these parables is found only in Mark. The parable of the unconscious growth emphasizes the small part which man really plays in the production of fruit from the Word. Man sows the Word through preaching and teaching it, but he must then wait for the harvest. God Himself produces the fruit through the power within the Word itself and through the Holy Spirit's use of the Word. Paul points this up in 1 Corinthians 3:6 when he says, "I have planted, Apollos watered; but God gave the increase." The emphasis of the parable of the mustard seed is that of the growth of the kingdom of God from very small beginnings, as was the case with the original disciples and the early church, to a greatly enlarged position in history so that Christianity has changed the fate of nations and of the world itself. Some see in the mention of the "fowls of the air" a reference to the evil and compromise which would creep into the church, but it seems likely that it is merely a part of the overall picture showing the strength of the kingdom (see also Daniel 4:20-22). Jesus' power over nature is illustrated in the miracle of the stilling of the storm in 4:35-41. Just as the sovereign Savior calmly stilled the sea with a simple rebuke, so He is able to still the turbulent human heart with those beautiful words, "Peace, be still." The prophet Isaiah gives authority to this comparison with his declaration, "The wicked are like the troubled sea, when it cannot rest, whose waters cast up mire and dirt. There is no peace, saith my God, to the wicked" (Isaiah 57:20, 21).

In chapter 5 we are given the accounts of the demoniac of Gadara, Jairus' daughter, and the woman with the issue of blood. Mark's interest in small details can be seen throughout the incident of the demoniac of Gadara in verses 1-20: in the detailed description of the man's condition; in the giving of his name, Legion; in the number of swine; in the statement of his condition after the demons were cast out; and in his request to accompany Jesus (you can see this better by comparing the parallel account in Matthew 8:24-34 and Luke 8:26-37). The account closes with two contrasting requests, the requests of the people of that region that Jesus would leave lest they lose more of their precious swine, and the request of the liberated demoniac who owed his new life to Jesus and could thus do no less than follow Him. But Jesus had something more useful for this man; He would send him as an ambassador into an area where Jesus Himself was not wanted with the simple but specific order, "Go home to thy friends, and tell them how great things the Lord hath done for thee, and hath had compassion on thee."

In this miracle we saw demonstrated Jesus' power over Satan. In the next two miracles we see Jesus' power over death, in the raising of Jairus' daughter; and His power over disease, in the healing of the woman with the issue of blood. These last two miracles are intertwined in verses 21-43 of chapter 5. Jairus, one of the synagogue rulers, shows his faith in Christ's power by begging Him to go touch his daughter that she might not die; and the loving Master, who never turned anyone away, quickly follows him toward his home. But even while Jesus is on this urgent journey, being pushed this way and that by the hurrying, curious throngs of people, He feels a peculiar touch of faith from a miserable woman plagued by a dreadful blood issue for the last twelve years. Jesus' inquiry as to who was responsible for this peculiar touch brings out the woman's confession and His commendation of her faith. The curious throngs often accompany Jesus today in the midst of some excitement, but it is usually only the few who, with a feeling of great need, reach out to Him with a touch of faith and have their needs met. But as Jesus is ministering to the needs of the woman, messengers come with word that they are too late to save Jairus' young daughter; but Jesus quickly stops Jairus' discouragement with the words, "Be not afraid, only believe."

As He proceeds, Jesus allows only "the inner-circle" of disciples to accompany Him, Peter, James, and John, who are seen alone with Jesus also at His transfiguration and in Gethsemane. In verse 39, when Jesus says that the little girl is only asleep, He does not mean that she was not physically dead, but that everything was in His control, and He would now wake her as if she were only asleep. The New Testament constantly refers to the death of believers, who have the hope of the resurrection unto eternal life, as merely sleep (see John 11:11-14; Acts 7:60; 1 Corinthians 15:51; 1 Thessalonians 4:15). The devouring viper of death has been robbed of his power by the resurrection of Christ, and we can thus proclaim victoriously with Paul, "O death, where is thy sting? O grave, where is thy victory?" (1 Corinthians 15:55). By a simple beckon from the voice which calls forth life, Jesus presents to the anxiously waiting parents their precious little twelve-year-old daughter.

Mark records a visit of Jesus to His hometown of Nazareth in 6:1-6. Jesus spoke with great power, as usual, but the people of Nazareth felt that He was just one of them, and thus no better than they were. Jesus' power to perform miracles was greatly hindered here because of the refusal of the people to accept Him and His message. From verse 3 we find that Jesus had brothers and sisters who were born after Him, and in verse 4 Jesus gives a principle which is still very true, the fact that a preacher usually has honor and authority in every location above that which he has among his own relatives and home people. In 6:7-13 Jesus sends out the twelve in pairs, for protection and mutual encouragement, with specific instructions.

Mark 6:14-29 relate the account of the death of John the Baptist. It is sometimes hard to understand why God would allow such a great hero of the faith to meet such a dismal end at the hands of a wicked man like Herod, but we must remember that the reward of the righteous is often not realized in this life, but rather in eternity, even as Paul declared when he said, "There is laid up for me a crown of righteousness, which the Lord, the righteous judge, shall give me at that day: and not to me only, but unto all them also that love his appearing" (2 Timothy 4:8). In verses 30, 31 the weary but jubilant apostles (the word means "the ones sent") report the success of their campaign to the Lord and receive His invitation to take a well-earned rest from their labors. But they are unable to find any privacy, and the compassionate Savior looks upon the pursuing multitudes as "sheep not having a shepherd." In 6:32-44 He stops to teach them and then commands His disciples, perhaps in preparation for their future spiritual responsibilities, "Give ye them to eat." Of course, the disciples are unable to feed such a multitude, either physically or spiritually; therefore, Jesus takes their five loaves and two fishes and feeds the 5,000 men with their women and children, and thus demonstrates to His disciples that through His power they too will be able to feed the multitudes which will later look to them for spiritual food. In 6:45-52 we find the miracle of Jesus' walking upon the sea, which once again demonstrated to His disciples His sovereign control over the laws and elements of nature which He had created. Mark closes chapter 6 with verses 53-56 by telling us of Jesus' visit to the land of Gennesaret and gives a brief summary of His work there, thus again reminding us that Jesus performed multitudes of miracles, the details of which are not recorded in the Scriptures.

In 7:1-22 we read the story of the Pharisees' accusation against Jesus and His disciples for failing to observe all the details of their Jewish tradition in the ceremonial washing of the hands before a meal. Jesus answers their accusation by quoting a verse from Isaiah

29:13 which aptly described their attitude, "This people honoureth me with their lips, but their heart is far from me." The religion of the Pharisees, like the religion of many today, was a religion of the hands and the head, but not of the heart; a religion of externals rather than internals; a religion which said, "Do and live," rather than, "Live and do." Jesus continued to answer their accusation by pointing out one instance of their hypocrisy in their excusing the violation of the fifth commandment relating to honoring parents by merely allowing people to pronounce an oath, "It is Corban," which deceitfully dedicated their possession to the Temple and freed them from supporting their aged parents. In closing His answer, Jesus declared, by way of contrast, that carnal externals are not really that important, for even in relation to health God has made the body so that it will take care of many of the germs, but the determining factor as to the real character of a man is the condition of his heart.

In Gentile Territory And Return To Galilee (7:24—9:50). After the above incident, Jesus symbolically departs from Jewish territory and visits the Gentile area of Tyre and Sidon, where, in 7:24-30, a Greek woman from Syro-Phenicia approaches Jesus in behalf of her demon possessed daughter. Contrary to fashion, our Lord at first seems to rudely turn her away, appealing to the privileged position of the chosen "children" of Israel in relation to the gospel, but it appears evident that Jesus was merely testing the woman's faith, and what faith she does manifest in her appropriate answer, "Yes, Lord: yet the dogs under the table eat of the children's crumbs." Jesus always responds to faith, though it be only as a mustard seed, and with this strong manifestation of faith, He grants to the woman her full request. Chapter 7 closes with Jesus' visit to the Gentile area of Decapolis (an area of ten Greek cities) and His healing of the deaf man with an impediment of speech in verses 31-37. The strange thing about this miracle is that, instead of just commanding the healing, He uses a process and first puts His fingers in the man's ears and touches his tongue with His own spittle, and then gives the command, "Be opened." It seems that Jesus does this to demonstrate His sovereign Lordship as creator, for He touches the man's ears and tongue in a communication of His own powers of hearing and speech, just as in the beginning God took the clay which He had shaped and "breathed into his nostrils the breath of life; and man became a living soul" (Genesis 2:7). In verse 36, Jesus' reason for commanding this man not to spread abroad the news of the miracle was obviously to prevent further hindrance of His ministry by the jealous Jewish leaders; and in verse 37, the words of the people fitly describe the ministry of Christ in the simple declaration, "He hath done all things well."

In 8:1-9 the miracle of the feeding of the 4,000 is found, similar in its teaching to the feeding of the 5,000, first, as it shows Jesus' concern for the physical needs of men as well as their spiritual needs, and second as it teaches His disciples their need to prepare themselves to feed the longing multitutdes the spiritual food of the bread of life. From 8:10-21, Jesus again comes to the western side of the Sea of Galilee to the area of Dalmanutha where the Pharisees immediately demand from Him a special sign from Heaven to prove His claims. What mighty miracles Jesus had already performed in their very presence, yet they still demanded some other sign to satisfy their doubts. Those who are always demanding of God a special sign would not believe regardless of how much evidence He gave to them. In answer to the request of the rich man in Hell for Lazarus to come back from the dead to appear to his lost brothers on earth, Abraham said, "If they hear not Moses and the prophets, neither will they be persuaded, though one rose from the dead" (Luke 16:31).

As Jesus and the disciples entered their boat and left the Pharisees, He warned them of the "leaven of the Pharisees, and of the leaven of Herod" (verse 15). Although Jesus spoke of the doctrine or teaching of these two groups, His disciples, with their minds so trained to think of material things, feared that He was rebuking them for failing to bring along enough bread. Jesus was disappointed that they were so concerned about material things and had so soon forgotten the feeding of the 5,000 and of the 4,000. The doctrine of the Pharisees, which He warned them against, was that of religious externalism, while that of the Herodians was a grasping desire for worldly power.

In 8:22-26 Christ arrives at Bethsaida at the northern end of the Sea of Galilee, on the eastern side of Jordan. When a blind man is brought to Him for healing, He leads him outside the city, for He would allow Bethsaida, which had already rejected Him, to witness no more of His miracles (see Matthew 11:21). Again, the unusual thing about this miracle is that He heals the man by a process: first, to teach us that He was bound to no particular method, for in our own day He can heal directly or through the use of modern medical knowledge; and second, to increase the man's faith in the process of His healing. Then, after the man is healed he is commanded not to give the witness to the rebellious city of Bethsaida.

In 8:27-33 Jesus proceeds north, outside the border of Palestine, to the Gentile area of Caesarea Philippi. Here Jesus drew from His disciples the confession upon which His Church was to be built, a Church made up largely of Gentiles (see Matthew 16:18). In answer to Jesus' request for their opinion, Peter, speaking for all the disciples, said, "Thou art the Christ." "Christ" is the Greek word for the Hebrew "Messiah," which means "the anointed one." Upon the basis of this confession, Jesus immediately made His first direct prophecy of His coming death but was strongly rebuked by the same disciples who had just made such a bold confession in Him. Peter, like most Jews of his day, and even John the Baptist (see Matthew 11:3), had misunderstood the mission of Messiah and thus was serving as a tool of Satan to turn Jesus away from His necessary death on the Cross (see verse 33). Chapter 8 closes with verses 34-38 which give the qualifications (verse 34), the value (verses 35-37), and the responsibility (verse 38) of discipleship.

Mark 9:1-13 record the account of the transfiguration, which gave Jesus' three closest disciples, Peter, James, and John, a glimpse into the glory of the future kingdom, as well as a witness of those who will be included in that kingdom; the dead in Christ, represented by Moses; and those who will be alive at Christ's coming, represented by Elijah who had the privilege of going to Heaven without dying (see 1 Thessalonians 4:16, 17). As they were descending the Mount of Transfiguration, Jesus replied to the question of His disciples about the coming of Elijah, as prophesied in Malachi 4:5, 6, by telling them that Elijah had indeed come as prophesied, but that the nation as a whole had also rejected Him. We learn from Luke 1:17 and Matthew 17:13 that John the Baptist fulfilled this prophecy. The incident involving the powerless disciples in 9:14-29, immediately following the transfiguration, taught the disciples the tremendous power and hold which Satan may have on a human being, while at the same time it showed them that there is absolutely nothing that cannot be accomplished through the persistence of faith and the power of prayer. Jesus makes His second direct prophecy of His death in 9:30-32, and in 9:33-37, after the disciples had been boastfully debating their individual greatness.

Jesus taught them the necessity of a genuine spirit of humility, a low opinion of self, and a corresponding exalting of others, if they would be accepted by Him. In 9:38-42 Jesus teaches His disciples that doctrine, not affiliation, is the true factor in determining who is a true servant, for no man can have power through the name of Christ without being on His side. Verse 42 declares the seriousness of the offense of one who in any way becomes a stumbling block to a young believer. It is our job to encourage those who are just starting their life for Christ, and not to discourage them in any way.

Verses 43-50 close chapter 9 with a series of warnings concerning the drastic measures one should be willing to take to avoid eternal punishment. The cutting off of the hand and foot and the plucking out of the eye are to be taken literally in the sense that it would truly be better to take such drastic measures, if by doing so it would stop the sin that is about to send you to Hell. In other words, no effort is too great if it will keep a soul out of Hell. Note Jesus' description of Hell, which He repeats three times in verses 44, 46, and 48, "Where their worm dieth not, and the fire is not quenched." The first part of this description clearly teaches, not immediate annihilation, but the continuous, eternal existence of the soul in Hell, while the last part describes the continuous, eternal punishment which will be suffered by those who here neglect their souls and thus face in eternity the wrath of an angry God.

On The Way To Jerusalem (10:1-52). Chapter 10 records incidents which occurred during Jesus' final trip to Jerusalem. In verses 1-12 the Pharisees ask Jesus' opinion about Moses' teaching on divorce in an effort to show Him in conflict with the Law of Moses; and in answer to their deceitful question, Jesus gives us His teaching on divorce. Jesus pointed out that God in His wisdom and mercy allowed Moses to permit divorce because of the hardened condition of the nation of Israel; but He goes back before the Law of Moses to the creation of man and woman and declares that God ordained marriage as a permanent bond, and those who take the vows of marriage so lightly and divorce and remarry are guilty of adultery. However, in the parallel passage in Matthew 19:9, Jesus does seem to indicate that remarriage would be permissible for the innocent party in a case where the marriage partner had been guilty of adultery. Verses 13-16 demonstrate Jesus' compassion toward children, and His statement in verse 14, "For of such is the kingdom of God," seems to teach both the necessity of conversion, of the new birth, of taking the humble attitude of a child for salvation, and the fact that children under the age of accountability are somehow taken care of by the grace of God and are not held accountable for their sins if they die within this period. In verses 17-22, in reply to the claim of the rich young man that he had obeyed all the commandments regarding his relationship with men, Jesus demanded of him the one thing which he was unwilling to do, that was to give us his riches that he might follow Him. This He did in order to show the young man that in spite of all his good intentions, he had not obeyed the first and greatest commandment, "Thou shalt have no other gods before me."

In verses 23-30 Jesus compares the difficulty of a rich man being saved to that of a large camel going through the eye of a small sewing needle. His disciples, who according to Jewish tradition thought of riches as a sure sign of the blessing and favor of God, were astounded and asked the question, "Who then can be saved?" But Jesus declared that even this humanly impossible feat is possible with God, so indeed a few rich men will be truly saved and will be in Heaven. Noticing Jesus' demand upon the rich young man, Peter, with some pride, points to the sacrifices which he and the other disciples had made to follow Jesus. Rather than rebuking this rather evident display of self-righteousness, Jesus lovingly declares that all those who make such sacrifices will be richly and abundantly rewarded, not just in eternity, but in this life as well.

In verses 32-34 Jesus makes His third direct prophecy of His approaching death and resurrection in Jerusalem. Verses 35-45 relate the eager request of James and John for the honored positions at Jesus' right and left side in His coming kingdom. Note that Jesus does not deny that there are such positions, but rather declares, "It shall be given to them for whom it is prepared." With equal jealousy the other ten disciples demonstrate their anger toward James and John, no doubt regretting that they had not first made the request themselves, but Jesus puts a stop to their pulling for positions by declaring that the guiding principle of the Christian ministry will be one of humility and service to others, not a striving for higher positions. Chapter 10 closes in verses 46-52 with the colorful account of blind Bartimaeus and Jesus' manifestation of Divine power in restoring his sight. His faith in Jesus as the promised Messiah was manifested by his loud and repeated cries, "Thou son of David, have mercy on me."

In Jerusalem (11:1—13:37). In Mark 11:1-11, as Jesus enters Jerusalem for His final visit, He deliberately fulfills every detail of the Messianic prophecy of Zechariah 9:9 in His triumphal entry, and thus declares to the city and the Jewish leaders that He is the Messiah, the King of the Jews, to which all Old Testament prophecy pointed. As Jesus and His disciples leave the city of Jerusalem at the close of this day to return to Bethany, no doubt to the home of Mary, Martha, and Lazarus, He pronounces a curse upon a fig tree which He finds bearing "nothing but leaves," and by so doing emphasizes to the disciples the necessity of fruitfulness, both in the individual and the nation. Returning to Jerusalem the following day, Jesus, in verses 15-19, demonstrates His Divine authority by driving out from the Temple those who had misused it by making it a place of commerce and crooked business. In verses 20-26, as they came toward the city the next day, Peter noticed that the fig tree which Jesus cursed was already dried up and dead, and he expressed his amazement at the Lord's power. Jesus uses this opportunity to teach a second lesson from this fig tree, the lesson of the power of faith in prayer to the extent that He promises, "What things soever ye desire, when ye pray, believe that ye receive them, and ye shall have them" (verse 24). However, in verses 25, 26 He reminds them that an unwillingness to forgive on their part will also keep God from forgiving their sins.

Chapter 11 closes with verses 27-33, which relate the demand of the Jewish leaders to know by what authority Jesus did His work, especially the purging of the Temple. Knowing their deceitfulness and dishonesty, and that they were unwilling to accept the truth, Jesus avoids their question by asking them a question concerning the authority of John's baptism, which because of their hypocritical position and their desire to please the people, they are unwilling to answer.

In 12:1-12 we find the parable of the householder and the vineyard which Jesus apparently adapts from Isaiah 5:1-7. Obviously the parable gives a picture of God's continuous efforts to bring Israel to repentance and to fruitfulness throughout the years to the extent that He finally sends His own Son to bear witness to them. Jesus' account of the manner in which they treat the Son serves as another prophecy of His soon coming death. This parable, which so clearly pictures the attitude of the Jewish leaders toward Christ, intensifies their opposition to Him through a series of questions designed to trap Him. The Pharisees and Herodians ask the first question in verses 13-17 concerning paying tribute to the Roman emperor, Caesar. Jesus avoids the trap of either a "yes" or "no" answer by replying, "Render to Caesar the things that are Caesar's, and to God the things that are God's." Proper duties to man and proper duties to God do not conflict. The Sadducees next make a rare appearance in verses 18-27 with their question about the woman married to seven different brothers, a question designed to make the resurrection, which they rejected, seem impossible. Jesus subjects them to great embarrassment by accusing them of two counts of gross ignorance: first, concerning the teachings of the Old Testament Scriptures, which they claimed to believe; and second, concerning God's almighty power to work out humanly insoluble problems.

In verses 28-34, one of the scribes, with some apparent honesty, next asks Jesus to give the greatest of all the commandments. Jesus' reply is actually a summary of the two parts of the Decalogue, the Ten Commandments, in which the first four deal with man's duties toward God, and the next six reveal man's duties toward his fellowman. Jesus thus declares that the first obligation of man is a right relationship with God, while the second obligation, which automatically develops from the first, is a right relationship with other men. Jesus Himself closes out the questions in verses 35-40 with His own question. By requiring the Jewish leaders to explain how the Messiah is both the Son of David as well as the Lord of David, He faces them with the prophetic fact that He, as Messiah, was, humanly speaking, heir to the throne of David, and Divinely speaking, He was also David's Lord.

In chapter 13 we find the Olivet Discourse, Jesus' last major teaching to His disciples before the crucifixion. This discourse is also found in Matthew 24, 25, and Luke 21. Astounded at Jesus' prophecy of the destruction of the Temple, four of His disciples in private ask Him when this is to take place, and by what sign they may know that it is about to be fulfilled (verse 4). It is apparent from the wording of their question in Matthew 24:3 that they thought of His coming and the end of the world as accompanying the destruction of the Temple. It is this misconception that Jesus attempts to clear up in the Olivet Discourse. In verses 5-9 he points out certain events which will be repeated again and again before A.D. 70, and in verses 10-13 He declares that the gospel will be "published among all nations" during this brief period, involving a great deal of persecution for His disciples. We see this being fulfilled throughout the Book of Acts from the day of Pentecost, when Jews were present from all over the world, and through Paul's missionary journeys which covered most of the civilized world at that time. Note also

Paul's declarations in Romans 1:5, 8 and Colossians 1:6. In verse 14 Jesus gives the important sign of "the abomination of desolation," which Luke identifies with the sight of "Jerusalem compassed with armies"; at this sign the Christians are to flee Judea, knowing that she has been abandoned to the wrath of God administered by the Roman armies. Verses 15-23 warn the disciples of the difficulty of those days and of the deceitful claims of deliverance by false messiahs. Verses 24-27 point out, in contrast, that the coming of the Son of man will be visible to all in the clouds of Heaven. In verses 28-31 Jesus again refers to His prophesied destruction of Jerusalem and, with a reference to the parable of the fig tree, He declares that the signs will soon be fulfilled and that the entire prophecy will take place in that very generation.

In the closing verses of the chapter, verses 32-37, He presents in bold contrast the conditions of His second coming; absolutely no one would know when it will take place, not even the Son Himself at that time, and there would be no specific signs to warn those who are unprepared. He rather gives one word of advice which will ensure our constant preparation, and that word is, "Watch!"

III. THE SERVANT'S DEATH AND RESURRECTION (14:1—16:20)

In chapter 14 we are told about the plot of the Jewish leaders (verses 1, 2); the anointing of Jesus by Mary, the sister of Lazarus (3-9), apparently showing that she was the only one who actually understood His prophesies of His coming death; Judas' plan to betray his Master (10, 11); the institution of the Lord's Supper, which was to be observed as a continuous reminder of the price which Jesus paid on the cross (12-26); His final prophecy of His death and resurrection, as well as the denial of Peter, in spite of Peter's self-confident protests (27-31); His final hour of agony in Gethsemane, accompanied by the sleepy inner-circle of disciples, Peter, James, and John, in which He pleads with the Father, not because of fear of death, but in dread of the awful thought of bearing the sins of the whole world in His sinless body on the cross (32-42), and then the betrayer's kiss and the arrest (43-52).

In 14:53-65 Mark begins the account of the mock trials of Jesus, first, before the Jewish High Priest and the Sanhedrin, the governing body of the Jews, who are unable to find witnesses who will agree together in their condemnation of Jesus. However, when Christ honestly confesses that He is the Messiah and that they will see Him coming in judgment upon them, they quickly find this as grounds for condemnation and cast their vote, "guilty of death" (verse 64). Verses 66-72 close the chapter with the sad account of Peter's denial under pressure, contrary to his boastful declarations.

The main difference between Judas and Peter was that Judas indeed felt remorse for his sin and the way things turned out but made no real repentance, while Peter, realizing the full consequence of what he had done, wept bitterly and made full repentance of his cowardly denial (verse 72).

Mark 15:1-20 record the trial of Jesus before Pilate, the Roman procurator of Judea, whose headquarters was actually at Caesarea, but who usually came up to Jerusalem for the Passover to help prevent additional trouble. It was necessary that Jesus appear innocent before both a Jewish and a Gentile court. Pilate knew Jesus' innocence, and made several attempts to effect His release, such as offering the Jews a choice between His freedom as opposed to the freedom of one of the worst criminals then imprisoned, one Barabbas. But when the people, with the encouragement of the Jewish leaders, cried for the release of Barabbas and for the death of Jesus, Pilate made a cowardly surrender and ordered that Jesus be subjected to their desires. In 15:16-20, the Roman soldiers mock Jesus' royalty with a purple robe, a reed for a scepter, a sharp crown of thorns, and pretended worship. Verses 21-41 record the crucifixion of Jesus, undoubtedly the most agonizing form of capital punishment ever used, as well as the continued mockery of the Jews as He hung on the cross. Jesus was crucified at 9:00 o'clock in the morning; darkness came over the land at 12:00 o'clock noon and continued until Jesus died at 3:00 o'clock in the afternoon (15:24, 33, 34).

Mark records only one of the seven statements which Jesus made from the cross, "My God, my God, why hast thou forsaken me?" a statement expressing the mortal agony felt by our Lord as His Father deliberately turned His face and His favor from His beloved Son as He paid the penalty for our sins on the cross. The symbolic rending of the veil of the Temple, which separated the Holy Place from the Holy of Holies, showed that the death of Christ fulfilled the whole law and sacrificial system and made it possible for every saint of God to "come boldly unto the throne of grace" (Hebrews 4:16).

In verses 42-47 Joseph of Arimathaea, a member of the Jewish Sanhedrin who had not voted for His death, made perhaps his first public confession of his faith in Christ by boldly requesting Jesus' body and giving it a tender burial.

But, praise the Lord, the gospel story does not end there, for as the saddened women approach the tomb early on Sunday morning, they discover the greatest truth of Christianity, the truth of "the empty tomb." How those women must have rejoiced at the word from the angel, "He is risen; he is not here: behold the place where they laid him." Note in verse 7 the angel's emphasis on Peter, no doubt to reassure him that the Lord still wanted him as His disciple in spite of his cowardly denial. As a result of the resurrection, Jesus commissions His disciples in 16:15 with the words, "Go ye into all the world, and preach the gospel to every creature."

Verses 17, 18 are difficult verses, but they certainly do not condone the modern cult of snake handling or other daredevil stunts as a proof of faith; it seems rather that these verses are best explained as a promise of protection for the Christian, while in the line of duty, as illustrated by Paul's survival of the bite of the deadly viper in Acts 28:4-6.

Mark closes his Gospel with a brief mention of the ascension and the beginning of Jesus' present ministry at the "right hand of God," applying the power and authority of His kingdom in the work of His servants throughout the whole world.

A SURVEY OF THE GOSPEL OF

Luke

by Charles A. Thigpen

The Gospel of Luke is one of the Synoptic Gospels. The word "synoptic" comes from a Greek word meaning "seeing the whole together, or taking a comprehensive view." We call Matthew, Mark, and Luke "the synoptic Gospels" because they present a similar view of the life and teachings of our Lord. The writer of the Gospel of John takes a different viewpoint in his writing; therefore, the fourth Gospel is not looked upon as one of the synoptics.

Luke wrote to the *Greeks.* He presented Christ as the perfect man. Christ is also seen as the Great Physician and as the Savior of mankind.

Although the author of this book does not identify himself, there has been almost complete agreement that it was Luke. He does not mention his name even once in the Gospel or in the Acts of the Apostles. Only in Paul's epistles do we find Luke's name mentioned. He is spoken of in Colossians 4:14, in 2 Timothy 4:11, and in Philemon 24. Luke was a companion of the Apostle Paul and made missionary trips with him. Paul identifies Luke as a Gentile in Colossians 4:14 when studied in its context.

Paul refers to Luke as the "beloved physician" (Colossians 4:14). The fact that he was a physician can also be well substantiated by his special interest in sickness and the sick, as well as the medical language which he uses in both the Gospel and Acts of the Apostles.

Many authorities agree that Luke wrote this book from Caesarea about the year A.D. 58. This was during Paul's imprisonment in that city. He addresses both of his New Testament books (Luke and Acts) to Theophilus. Some suggest that because this name means "lover of God" or "loved of God" that Luke is really writing to all who love God. The context does not bear this out, however. Theophilus is referred to as "most excellent," which probably signifies that he was a high official.

Luke had a two-fold objective in writing. The first reason was his desire to confirm Theophilus in the faith, and to do the same for all who would read this Gospel account.

Luke is the only Gospel writer who sets the Gospel story within the framework of world history. In many places he refers to emperors, kings, and imperial officials. The longest and most complete list of rulers and the particular offices each held is found in Luke 3:1 and 2. Look at the list: Tiberius Ceasar, Pontius Pilate, Herod, Philip, Lysanias, Annas, and Caiaphas.

Luke also has a more comprehensive view of the complete biography of Christ. He gives greater details of His infancy and boyhood than do the other Gospel writers.

There are several outstanding characteristics of the Gospel according to Luke:

I. HE EMPHASIZES AND GIVES SPECIAL PROMINENCE TO PRAYER

Christ is pictured at prayer 15 times in the four gospels, 11 of which are found in the Gospel according to Luke.

In this Gospel, He taught His disciples to pray with importunity (11:5-10), with perseverance (18:1-7), and with penitence (18:9-14). It is Luke alone who states the following times when our Lord prayed: (1) at His baptism, (2) after cleansing the leper, (3) before calling the twelve apostles, (4) at His transfiguration, (5) on the Cross for His murderers, and (6) with His last breath.

Luke insists on the duty of persistent prayer as he alone presents parables of the Friend at Midnight (11:5-13) and of the Unjust Judge (18:1-8).

II. LUKE MUST BE REGARDED AS THE FIRST CHRISTIAN HYMNOLOGIST

Luke alone gives us the words of five great hymns which were later set to music: the Ave Maria (1:28), the Magnificat or the Song of the Blessed Virgin (1:46-55), the Benedictus or Song of Zacharias (1:68-79), the Gloria in Excelsis (2:14), and the Song of Simeon (2:29-32). Luke records all these songs in his first 2 chapters. The church has been singing them ever since.

III. THE PERFECT HUMANITY OF CHRIST IS PRESENTED BY LUKE

The clearest picture of the birth, childhood, growth, domestic and social life of Christ is given by Luke. It is Luke who states, "And the child grew, and waxed strong in spirit, filled with wisdom: and the grace of God was upon him" (Luke 2:40). Again he states in 2:52, "And Jesus increased in wisdom and stature, and in favour with God and man."

Luke points out that He "rejoiced in spirit" (10:21); He "wept" over Jerusalem (19:41); He "prayed more earnestly . . . " (22:44). Luke even points out that Christ ate a piece of broiled fish before His disciples after His resurrection (24:41-43).

IV. WOMEN AND CHILDREN ARE PROMINENT IN THIS GOSPEL

Luke gives a prominent place to Mary, our Lord's mother. He alone speaks of the widow Anna (2:36). He talks of the eager Martha being cumbered with serving and Mary choosing the better part (10:38-42). A humble band of ministering women followed Jesus (8:1-3). He speaks to a poor, crushed, trembling, humiliated woman the tender name of "daughter" (8:48). He speaks of another as a "daughter of Abraham" (13:16). Luke is the one who tells how Christ consoled and warned the "daughters of Jerusalem" who followed Him to Calvary (23:28). Luke shows our Lord permitting the woman out of whom He had cast seven devils to minister to Him.

Children are referred to with more affection than elsewhere in the New Testament. "Infants" are brought to Christ (18:15). Jairus' daughter was twelve years of age and an "only daughter" (8:41, 42). He presents the birth as well as the events surrounding the birth and early life of Christ.

V. THIS IS ESPECIALLY THE GOSPEL OF THE OUTCAST

Here we see the Samaritan (9:52-56; 17:11-19), the publican, the harlot, and the prodigal. It was Jesus who came "to seek and to save that which was lost" (Luke 19:10), and Luke demonstrates this verse by showing our Lord doing just that. We see such instances as Zacchaeus, Mary of Magdala, the woman with the issue of blood, and the dying robber.

The Gospel according to Luke is the longest and most comprehensive of the four gospels. It is the most literary and beautiful of the gospels.

There are miracles and parables which are peculiar to Luke. The miracles given only by Luke are:

1. The miraculous draught of fishes (5:4-11)
2. The raising of the widow's son at Nain (7:11-18)
3. The woman with the spirit of infirmity (13:11-17)
4. The man with the dropsy (14:1-6)

5. The ten lepers (17:11-19)
6. The healing of Malchus (22:50, 51)

There is an even longer list of parables peculiar to Luke. They are as follows:

1. The two debtors (7:41-43)
2. The good Samaritan (10:25-37)
3. The importunate friend (11:5-8)
4. The rich fool (12:16-21)
5. The barren fig tree (13:6-9)
6. The great supper (14:16-24)
7. The lost sheep (15:3-7)
8. The lost coin (15:8-10)
9. The prodigal son (15:11-32)
10. The unjust steward (16:1-13)
11. The rich man and Lazarus (16:19-31)
12. The unjust judge (18:1-8)
13. The Pharisee and the Publican (18:10-14)

This Gospel record alone records the Samaritan or Gentile ministry of our Lord. It extends from 9:51 through 18:30.

Now, if you will get your Bible in your hand, we will survey together this wonderful Gospel of Luke.

One way to divide or outline the book is in the following seven sections:

I. Preface 1:1-4
II. Birth and Childhood of Christ 1:5—2:52
III. Preparation of Christ for His Ministry 3:1—4:13
IV. Christ's Galilean Ministry 4:14—9:50
V. Christ's Journey toward Jerusalem 9:51—19:27
VI. Closing Ministry 19:28—21:38
VII. Christ's Death, Resurrection, and Ascension 22:1—24:53

And now we will survey the Gospel of Luke. As we go through we will remind ourselves of the overall outline that has already been given. We will look at the book one chapter at a time. Usually we will give only a brief resume of each division of the chapter. There will be some particular portions that we will treat more extensively than others.

It may be well to have a pencil or pen in hand, along with your Bible. You may find some items or verses you would like to mark for future reference.

CHAPTER 1

As you will recall, the first major division of our outline is the

Preface (1:1-4). Even though only four verses in length, this is one of the most interesting and revealing introductions ever written. This is really an account of how the writer did his work. We learn here that Luke was a very careful historian. In the American Standard Version (of 1901) a clearer statement is seen in the translation of verse 3 as it reads, "It seemed good to me also, having traced the course of all things accurately from the first . . . . " This is Luke's statement of his work. He further states that he has written "in order." This means in sequence of time, which means an orderly, chronological approach.

The second major division, the birth and childhood of Christ (1:5—2:52), picks up at this point and continues through the entire second chapter. In chapter 1 we have Gabriel's two announcements. He came first to Zacharias, a priest, whose wife was Elisabeth. They were well along in years and childless. While Zacharias was doing priestly service, Gabriel came and announced that Zacharias and his wife would have a son named John, who would possess the Holy Spirit from birth and would be the forerunner of the Messiah.

Gabriel next appeared to Mary. This is one of the most touching scenes in all the Bible. Gabriel stated that Mary had found favor with God. She was looking forward to the coming of the Messiah without any realization that she would be the instrument that God would use by which His Son would be clothed in human flesh. Mary inquired of the method God would use to bring this to pass. Gabriel told her that it was by the Holy Spirit that this would be performed. Notice verse 37, "For with God nothing shall be impossible"—not even the virgin birth of His Son.

Mary then visited Elisabeth (1:39-56). This was the meeting of two miracle mothers. Elisabeth, though old and beyond child-bearing age, would give birth to John the Baptist, and Mary would give birth to a child in a completely super-natural manner. When they met, Elisabeth was immediately filled with the Holy Spirit, and she began to bestow verbal blessings upon Mary and to the child that Mary would bear. Mary responded by giving that poem which we call The Magnificat. Mary abode here for three months.

To conclude this chapter, John the Baptist was born. Zacharias sang a beautiful song called The Benedictus. It is a great hymn of faith, of hope, and of gratitude. This is a song of the salvation that God has provided for all men. God is spoken of as the Dayspring from on high who has visited us.

CHAPTER 2

This chapter tells of the birth of Jesus. The events that caused Mary and Joseph to go from Nazareth to Bethlehem are related. Luke tells of the trip to Bethlehem and that here in Bethlehem, the baby Jesus was born and laid in a manger for there was no room for them in the inn.

The angel of the Lord announced Christ's birth to lowly shepherds. The angelic host praised God and said, "Glory to God in the highest, and on earth peace, good will toward men." The shepherds arose and made their way to see the One of whom the angel spoke.

When the baby Jesus was carried to Jerusalem to be dedicated in the Temple, two very unusual people appeared to pay special homage to this miracle baby. There was Simeon to whom God had revealed that he would not die until he had seen the Messiah. Also, a very aged woman named Anna came. She gave thanks unto the Lord because in her presence was the One who would provide redemption.

The remaining verses of chapter 2 cover the thirty years that our Lord lived with His parents. In verses 40 and 52, we see the growth and development of Christ as He grew in favor with God and man.

The only specific incident related in these silent years was the family trip to the Temple in Jerusalem when Christ was twelve. While here He stated His intention to be about His Father's business.

CHAPTER 3

The third major division in the outline has to do with the *Preparation of Christ for His ministry (3:1—4:13).* In this chapter we find the ministry of John the Baptist related. The first two verses identify the civil and religious leaders of the time. An emperor, a governor, three tetrarchs, and two high priests are named. The emperor was Tiberius Caesar. Israel had been divided and was ruled by four of Rome's vassals.

It was then that the word of the Lord came to John the Baptist. Even though his preaching was strong, multitudes flocked to be baptized of him. He did not spare them. He insisted on repentance that produced fruit in the life.

Throughout this passage we find John's faithful proclamation concerning the Messiah who would follow him. That One would baptize with the Holy Spirit and with fire.

John was imprisoned by Herod because John exposed Herod's gross sin.

Luke now presents Christ and tells of His baptism by John. The greatest single illustration of the Trinity given in the Bible is the baptismal scene of Christ. As John brought God's Son up out of the water, God the Father spoke approvingly of His Son, and the Holy Spirit as a dove descended and remained upon Christ. We see the Son, the Father, and the Spirit all present in this beautiful event.

CHAPTER 4

The first 13 verses of this chapter speak of the temptation of

Christ. This surely is one of the most important events in the life of our Lord. The three temptations by Satan are stated clearly. Our Lord, in overcoming each of them, used the Word of God.

The perfect and victorious Son of God now set out on His ministry. This begins the fourth major division in our outline: *Christ's Galilean Ministry* (4:14—9:50).

Christ went to His hometown of Nazareth and in reading publicly from Isaiah, He claimed for Himself His Messiahship. Our Lord is seen in several roles at this time as He taught, cast out demons, and healed the sick.

The chapter closes by Christ announcing that He cannot remain in this one area as He stated, "I must preach the kingdom of God to other cities also . . . . "

CHAPTER 5

Four of Christ's disciples are here called to service and soul-winning. After He used a boat from which to speak, Christ commanded that nets be let down for fish. Reluctantly the command was carried out and a great catch was enclosed. Peter confessed his lack of faith, to which Christ said, "Fear not; from henceforth thou shalt catch men."

Jesus was addressed by a man "full of leprosy" who asked to be cleansed. Christ cleansed him with a touch and commanded that he tell no man. Luke adds, however, that "so much the more went there a fame abroad of him: and great multitudes came together to hear . . . . "

Christ made it clear that He possessed power to forgive sins when the palsied man was let down to Him through the roof.

Levi, a tax collector, was called by Christ. He forsook all and followed Christ. Then Levi (Matthew) gave a great feast for Christ and invited many publicans and others to attend. In answer to the scribes' question, "Why do ye eat and drink with publicans and sinners?" Christ answered that the sick, not the well, need the physician and that He had come to call sinners, not the righteous, to repentance.

CHAPTER 6

Christ's ministry in Galilee continues. The Lord further enraged the Pharisees in the two opening paragraphs of this chapter. His treatment of sinners and His claim to forgive sins had already infuriated them, but their hatred was brought to its highest point by His attitude toward Sabbath keeping.

Christ here showed that although the Sabbath is a day designed for rest, it should not be broken except by deeds of necessity or mercy. Our Lord was correct in breaking loose the Sabbath from the burdensome interpretation of tradition that the Pharisees had bound to it. Christ restored it to God's original purpose—that the day should be for rest, worship, and fellowship with God.

The selection of the apostles came next. The importance of this event is greatly underscored by Luke's observation that Christ prayed all night before these choices were made. We do not know how many disciples were now following Him, but He called them together and from among them, chose the twelve apostles.

These men did not realize that they were chosen to be the leaders and organizers of the greatest and most important movement the world has ever known. It certainly had not been revealed to them that their names would be graven on the foundations of the Holy City.

Perhaps on this same occasion, the lengthy sermon (6:20-49) was given. It is referred to by some as the "Sermon on the Plain" to distinguish it from the long "Sermon on the Mount" recorded by Matthew. This, no doubt, is the same sermon, but the Holy Spirit led Matthew to include more than Luke. Each, however, begins with blessings and ends with warnings.

CHAPTER 7

Luke devotes this chapter to four events: the centurion of Capernaum, raising the widow's son, the meeting with John's disciples, and the woman who anointed Christ's feet.

One of the most remarkable displays of faith, and that from a very unlikely source, was that of this Gentile centurion. When his servant was at the point of death, the centurion, who had evidently heard of Christ's miraculous works, sent elders of the Jews to seek help from Christ. He showed faith by sending for Christ—then by sending again and humbly requesting that Christ not come under his roof, because he was unworthy. He asked rather that Christ "say the word" and his servant would be healed. This caused Christ to marvel at such great faith. The servants found the ailing servant "whole" when they returned.

Then Christ raised a young man from the dead. The key word in this passage is the word *compassion.* Two facts seem to have provoked Christ's compassion: The young man was the only son of his mother and she was a widow.

The next incident in Luke 7 shows the discouragement of John the Baptist. He had now been in Herod's jail for some time and he sent two of his disciples to Christ to ask Him, "Art thou he that should come? or look we for another?" Christ answered these messengers by deeds more than by words. Many miracles of healing were performed "in that hour." Christ told John's messengers to return and tell John what they had seen and heard. Perhaps there was a slight reprimand in Christ's last statement, "And blessed is he, whosoever shall not be offended in me."

Just what prompted John to send these questions to Christ, we can only speculate. However, Christ took this occasion to acknowledge John as the greatest person ever to be born of a woman. He clearly stated that John was the forerunner of the Messiah who was prophesied by Malachi.

As Christ was eating a meal in a Pharisee's house, a woman, who perhaps had met and believed on Christ on some previous occasion, came and anointed Christ's feet and wiped them with her hair. Christ knew that the Pharisee was seriously questioning this happening. He was saying in his heart that Christ was no prophet because, if He were, He would know this woman was a sinner.

However, Christ shows that every act of the woman was one of true devotion. Our Lord makes it clear that the woman was providing the ordinary hospitality that should have been provided by the Pharisee, His host. The Pharisee provided no water for His feet, no kiss, no oil for anointing, but this woman had provided all of these.

Then Christ reaffirmed her forgiveness of sins which He had previously given. Her cleansing was publicly announced and Christ bade her to go in peace.

CHAPTER 8

This is another interesting chapter. Luke here records one parable and four miracles. The miracles are: stilling the stormy waters of Galilee, healing the demoniac of Gadara, healing the woman with the issue of blood, and raising Jairus' daughter from the dead.

We are introduced to this chapter by learning about the ministering women who often are found following Jesus. All of these had been the recipients of some special providence of the Lord. Luke summarized the benefits they had received by saying, "And certain women . . . had been healed of evil spirits and infirmities."

The parable of the sower, the seed, and the soils comes next. This is perhaps the most basic and meaningful parable that we have in the entire Gospel record. The fact that our Lord carefully explained this parable's meaning makes it a pattern and a guide for us as we study each of Christ's parables.

One of the most impressive miracles to the disciples was perhaps the one that Luke now records. This is the stilling of the storm. Christ was asleep in the boat, a storm came up rapidly—as they are known to do on Galilee—and the boat was about to sink. Then Christ said the word and all was peaceful. This shows that our Lord is master of the forces of nature.

Healing the demoniac of Gadara shows our Lord's concern for the mentally and emotionally outcast. His healing of this man serves to bring out the value system of the Gadarenes. They placed more value on a herd of swine than on a human life made whole.

The final movement in chapter 8 places two miracles together. As Christ went to help Jairus' daughter, a woman with a serious embarrassing illness touched Him. He stopped, inquired who it was, and after having her to publicly acknowledge her healing, Christ answered that her faith had made her whole.

After this Christ went on to Jairus' house and raised the little twelve-year-old girl from the dead. The parents were thrilled and very amazed. They were charged to tell no man what had been done.

CHAPTER 9

The twelve apostles were next sent out. Christ gave them tremendous power. They would be able to cure diseases and have authority over demons. This unusual ability, although limited to their own day, was to serve as their credentials on this mission. They were to heal the sick and preach the gospel.

Luke now records the feeding of the 5,000. This is the only miracle recorded in all four Gospel accounts. Five loaves and two fish provided enough food for all; and yet, there were twelve basketfulls left over.

Christ stated openly to the disciples that He was to die and arise from the dead. This was followed eight days later by the transfiguration experience. Here, the chief representative of the law, Moses, the chief representative of the prophets, Elijah, and Christ met together and talked of Christ's approaching death at Jerusalem. This, no doubt, was to remind Christ of the necessity of His death to provide an atonement for the sins of the world and to encourage Him. It was also to be, in days to come, a source of inspiration and blessing to the disciples.

The fifth major division in our outline now begins in Luke 9:51, *Christ's Journey Toward Jerusalem.* This continues down through Luke 19:27. Christ was now journeying toward Jerusalem. Luke says of Him, "He stedfastly set his face to go to Jerusalem."

In Luke 9:57-62 the high standards of devotion and sacrifice to which Christ calls His followers are given. Three turned back from following Christ. They had not adequately counted the cost so they were not accepted.

CHAPTER 10

There are three divisions in this chapter: the seventy sent out, the good Samaritan, and Martha and Mary. The seventy are sent forth into the places where Christ was to go on His journey toward Jerusalem. We see also their return and hear their rejoicing at great success.

A certain lawyer engaged Jesus by saying, "Master, what shall I do to inherit eternal life?" Christ turned the question to him and asked what was written in the law. He responded by saying, "Thou shalt love the Lord thy God with all thy heart, and with all thy soul, and with all thy strength, and with all thy mind; and thy neighbour as thyself." Christ commended him for his answer, to which the lawyer said, "Who is my neighbour?" Christ stated that our neighbor is anyone who needs our help. He here gives the parable of the good Samaritan.

The sisters, Mary and Martha, entertained Christ in their home. Martha was the busy one, while Mary sat at Jesus' feet, hearing Jesus' words. Martha complained, but Christ responded by saying that "Mary hath chosen that good part" and He would not take it from her. This should remind all of us that although work for Christ is important, it is also vitally important to sit devotionally at Jesus' feet and worship Him.

CHAPTER 11

One of the greatest passages on prayer in the entire Word of God is found here in Luke 11:1-13. Christ's disciples found Him praying and asked Him to teach them to pray. In answer to this request we find these moving verses.

In the next division of this chapter (11:14-36), Christ severely rebuked unbelief and blasphemy. He accused that generation of being evil and closed by saying that a Greater than Solomon and a Greater than Jonah was there in their very presence.

In the final part of chapter 11 Christ spoke out against the Pharisees, the major religious group in Jesus' day. Here He uttered six solemn woes in condemning their hypocrisy.

CHAPTER 12

Chapter 12 is one of the most interestingly balanced chapters in Luke. Faithfulness to the Lord is encouraged at the first. In the last part of the chapter, Christian watchfulness is insisted upon for believers. Between these divisions, Christ warned against covetousness (12:13-21) and against anxiety (12:22-34).

CHAPTER 13

The first division of chapter 13 finds a group telling Christ of Pilate mingling the blood of certain Galileans with their sacrifices. His question to them was, Were these Galileans greater sinners than other Galileans? In other words, is exceptional suffering a proof of exceptional guilt? Then Christ answered His own questions and admonished them to repent. Everyone who has not repented will suffer. Even a temporary delay in punishment should lead to repentance.

Christ further stressed His call to repentance by illustrating the barren fig tree. The gardener found no fruit for three consecutive years. The entire Jewish nation was in focus here. One more year of mercy was given—for the purpose of repentance. He warned of judgment but yet extended mercy at this time.

We next see our Lord in a synagogue on the Sabbath day. As usual, His compassionate heart is made evident. A woman was present who was severely crippled. She was bowed together and could not lift herself. This condition had prevailed for eighteen years. Christ performed a miracle of healing on her although He knew many of the people present would accuse Him of Sabbath breaking. Christ reminded them that they loosed animals and led them away to water on the Sabbath; therefore, Christ is fully justified in this miracle even on the Sabbath.

This chapter concludes with Jesus' lament over Jerusalem. Here we see again, in a very dramatic way, the compassion of Christ. But also, Christ pronounced a severe judgment on the unbelieving Jews. He said, "Behold, your house is left unto you desolate."

CHAPTER 14

Once again we find our Lord performing miracles on the Sabbath Day. A Pharisee had invited Christ to his home for a meal. A certain man was present who was afflicted with dropsy. Christ healed this man, justifying His action by the fact that any of those present would free an ass or an ox which had fallen into a pit on the Sabbath Day. Why was it not then proper for Christ to set free this man on the Sabbath Day?

This miracle is followed by five parables. The first is a parable of the ambitious guest. The main teaching here is humility which is summarized in Christ's statement, "For whosoever exalteth himself shall be abased; and he that humbleth himself shall be exalted."

The second parable is one of the best known of Christ's parables, the parable of the great supper. Here Christ was showing the refusal of the Pharisees and other leaders of Christ's offer of salvation and its acceptance by Publicans, sinners, and eventually by the Gentiles.

The remainder of the chapter concerns discipleship. True and effective discipleship requires one's supreme love, faithful cross-bearing, and forsaking all for Christ. Christ gave the final three parables to illustrate various aspects of discipleship.

CHAPTER 15

At the beginning of this chapter, the Pharisees and Scribes

accused Christ of receiving sinners and even eating with them.

The remainder of this chapter is Christ's apology or reason for receiving and eating with sinners. Three parables are given, each presenting the dominant character seeking something or someone which was lost. There was the lost sheep and the great shepherd who sought until he found. There was the lost coin and the diligent woman who sought and found that which was lost. Finally, He presented the prodigal son, and the unsympathetic elder son whom the father sought by his great love. His love won the younger but failed to win the older who represented the Pharisees. He was still angry and rebellious as the chapter ends.

CHAPTER 16

This chapter begins with a parable which has presented a problem of interpretation to many. This is perhaps the most perplexing problem Christ ever spoke. A man is pictured who robbed his master and yet was used by Christ as an example to his followers. A careful reading of this passage should disclose that the good qualities of the bad man are pointed out. Christ commended this unjust steward's prudence and foresight. Christ certainly did not commend him for his dishonesty.

This is followed by a brief passage in which Christ again condemned the awful sin of adultery.

The remainder of this chapter is one of the most solemn in the entire Word of God. Here Christ pulled back the curtain of eternity for one brief moment of time. This is no parable. Christ used the proper name, Lazarus, and He never used a proper name in parables. This is definitely a historical event that Christ was depicting. Perhaps the reason He did not give the name of the rich man was in deference to his relatives who perhaps were still living.

Christ shows the afterlife for the one who lives selfishly and for the one who lives for God. The good man, Lazarus, went to the place of comfort called Abraham's bosom. The unbeliever, just after death, found himself in a place of great suffering. The word "torment" is used four times by our Lord in this short passage to describe the pain. The unbeliever possessed all his faculties. He could see, feel, thirst, think, and remember. And, in contrast to this, Lazarus was comforted.

Our Lord intended this to constitute a serious warning to every unbeliever.

CHAPTER 17

This chapter begins by Christ giving the disciples instruction in somewhat unrelated areas. He warned against a lack of love which would manifest itself in an unwillingness to forgive others. The disciples were then chided and gently rebuked for their lack of faith. Finally, Christ rebuked the disciples for their desire for praise and reward.

Ten lepers are reported healed, but only one came back to glorify God and give thanks to Christ, and this one was a lowly Samaritan.

In response to the Pharisees' question as to when the Kingdom of God would come, Christ spoke of the spiritual aspect of His Kingdom. The first place where God's Kingdom manifests itself is in the hearts of men.

In the remainder of this chapter, Christ spoke of His second coming. The judgmental aspect of Christ's return is prefigured by the judgment in Noah's time and in Lot's time.

CHAPTER 18

This chapter opens with the parable of the unjust judge. Christ is once again teaching the necessity of faithfulness and persistence in prayer. Christ drove home the truth that men ought always to pray and not to faint.

Pride and self-righteousness are once again exposed in the parable of the Pharisee and the Publican. It was not the proud, boastful Pharisee who received God's mercy, but the repentant Publican.

All are commanded to suffer little children to come to Christ. He said concerning these little ones, "for of such is the kingdom of God."

We next find the rich young ruler's encounter with Christ. This man's life was outstandingly exemplary, except for one thing. His problem was with the first commandment, "Thou shalt have no other gods before me." The young man's attitude toward riches was the difficulty. He preferred gold to God; he preferred cash to Christ. He found himself completely unwilling to meet Christ's requirements. As someone has said, "Christ must be Lord of all, or he will not be Lord at all."

Christ and those journeying with Him were moving closer and closer toward Jerusalem. It was only natural that Christ began to speak of His death and resurrection. The language is so clear, so plain. Why did His followers not understand? We do not know. Perhaps they were unwilling to believe or had their minds on other things. Luke records the sad statement, "And they understood none of these things . . . . "

A wonderful miracle concludes chapter 18. A blind man near Jericho cried out to Christ to have mercy on him. The restoring of his sight is such a striking example of Christ's miraculous power that each of the synoptics, Matthew, Mark, and Luke, record this event.

CHAPTER 19

One of the dramatic conversions reported by Luke is that of Zacchaeus. Even though he was a Publican and rich, he received Christ and gave a marvelous testimony of his radical change. Christ announced to him that salvation had come to his house that day.

Christ now turned the attention of His disciples toward the truth that the kingdom of God would not immediately appear as they thought. The parable of the ten pounds teaches that believers are to occupy until Christ returns. The kingdom they long for will not be an immediate reality, but there is a faithful stewardship to be administered while waiting for the Master's return.

We now enter another major division in the Book of Luke and in the earthly ministry of our Lord. From chapter nine to the middle of chapter nineteen, Christ was seen moving steadily towards Jerusalem. He arrived and we read of His triumphal entry into the city, His weeping over Jerusalem, and His second (and final) cleansing of the Temple.

We now find the pace rapidly picking up. Only a few days remained before Christ's crucifixion.

CHAPTER 20

During the passion week our Lord spent His days in Jerusalem and His nights in Bethany. We can feel the emotion building up as Christ was questioned first by the chief priests and the scribes and then by the Sadducees. His authority was the focal point of the questioning at the outset of this chapter.

The parable of the vineyard shows us the omniscience of Christ as He related the action of the husbandmen against the true heir of the vineyard. This will be precisely what these very listeners would do in just a few days. They would reject and kill God's Son. Christ summarized this by saying, "The stone which the builders rejected, the same is become the head of the corner."

The chief priests and scribes tried to ensnare Christ as they raised the question of the legality of tribute to Caesar. Then the Sadducees came with their questions about the resurrection. Christ answered each question, and in so doing, drove home the spiritual aspect of the question raised.

CHAPTER 21

Chapter 21 opens with Christ observing the collection plate. Many came and gave, but as Christ was able to see not only their gifts but also their motives, He commended only the widow. And here it was not the amount given but the motive and the fact that she had given all she had. Should we not keep in mind that God sees us, our motives and what we have left, as we give to Him?

The remainder of the chapter relates to future events. The course of this age will be characterized by wars, earthquakes, famines, pestilences, and persecution of believers. Christ said that these things would continue until the consummation of the age and increase with greater intensity.

Jerusalem's destruction was foretold. Christ's personal return is stated. In the light of this He warns us to be alert so that day will not come upon us unawares.

CHAPTER 22

Here we find Judas Iscariot making a deal with the chief priests and captains to betray Christ into their hands. God has so arranged it that every time this man's name appears in the Scriptures, the awful deed which he did of selling the Savior is stated.

Events moved rapidly to the time when Christ instituted the Lord's Supper. He announced that His disciples were to continue this in remembrance of Him.

Christ then announced that one of them would actually betray Him. Luke does not include the fact, as John does, that Christ then sent Judas out to do what he planned to do.

After rebuking them for their strife over who should be greatest, Jesus announced that prominent places of leadership awaited each of them in His service in the future.

After predicting Peter's denial, they all went to the garden at the Mount of Olives where Christ prayed, but the disciples slept. Then Judas came with the arresting party, and planted the betrayal kiss on Christ's cheek.

Christ was arrested and brought to the high priest's house. Peter was with the multitude and was questioned about his relationship to Christ. After his three-fold denial, the cock crowed as Christ had prophesied. Peter then went out and wept bitter tears of repentance.

Christ was then buffeted and taunted before being led away to the Sanhedrin.

CHAPTER 23

Christ was led before Pilate whose verdict was, "I find no fault in this man." Upon learning that Christ was from Galilee he sent Him to Herod who happened to be in Jerusalem at that time. Luke reports that Herod questioned Christ "in many words." Christ remained silent and did not answer Herod.

Then Herod returned Christ to Pilate who finally capitualted and commanded that Christ be crucified.

Luke then relates the crucifixion. He tells about Christ's prayer from the cross for those taking His life, the repentant thief's prayer, and Christ's reponse. Then Christ dismissed His spirit and commended it into the hands of His Father.

CHAPTER 24

This is both the concluding and climactic chapter of Luke. The previous chapter ended with the body of Christ in a tomb and women preparing fragrant spices and ointments which would be carried to the tomb.

This chapter reveals that the women came to the tomb and were greatly surprised to find the body of Christ gone. Their dismay did not last long as two men in shining garments, perhaps angelic beings, announced that Christ had risen just as He promised.

This news was too good to keep to themselves so they rushed back to tell the apostles. The men were so disillusioned and downhearted that Luke says the announcement from the women seemed "as idle tales." However, Peter had enough faith to go and check out this unusual story. He too found the tomb empty except the graveclothes.

The scene then swiftly changes as Luke tells of the walk to Emmaus by two of Christ's followers. As they traveled, Christ joined them. They did not recognize Christ but responded to His inquiry about their conversation by telling Him of the Lord's death and their personal disillusionment. Then Christ opened the Scripture "beginning at Moses and all the prophets," and explained to them that in His life and death all these prophecies were fulfilled.

It was not until He blessed and broke the bread that their eyes were opened, and they realized that this was indeed the risen Christ. Then they rushed back to Jerusalem, found the eleven, and told them of their dramatic meeting with the Lord.

Jesus then met with the eleven and convinced them of His bodily resurrection. He then gave the commission to evangelize all with the message of repentance and remission of sins. After promising the Holy Spirit, Christ was taken up into Heaven.

A SURVEY OF THE GOSPEL OF

John

by Charles A. Thigpen

It is Doctor Philip Schaff who calls the Gospel of John, "the most important literary production ever composed." The synoptics antedate the Gospel of John by about thirty years. During this time certain matters had arisen and certain questions were raised that demanded authoritative attention. Most of these must have centered around the person and work of Christ and the significance of His death.

The earlier three gospels, Matthew, Mark, and Luke are a presentation of Jesus. But the Gospel of John is an interpretation of Jesus. The others show Jesus outwardly while John interprets Him inwardly. Christ's public discourses are stressed by the synoptics, but John gives special attention to His private discourses. John is devoted almost wholly to Christ's Judean ministry, while the others emphasize His Galilean ministry. The first three are quite factual, but John is also doctrinal.

Each of the other three gospels gives a human genealogy of Christ. John, however, begins by asserting that Christ is the eternal One. John gives no account of the Lord's birth or genealogy, no description of His baptism, and no mention of His transfiguration or His ascension.

Each of the synoptics lists far more of the Lord's miracles than does John. Matthew relates twenty miracles, Mark gives eighteen, Luke records twenty, while John gives only eight miracles.

Matthew records sixteen parables; Mark, five parables; and Luke relates twenty parables. John does not record a single parable. The word translated "parable" in John 10:6 should really be translated "allegory" or "proverb."

Even though the author does not name himself in this Gospel, there is no doubt that he is John, the Beloved. His father was Zebedee, and his mother was Salome, who was probably a sister of Mary, the mother of Jesus. John's brother was James. John and

James were engaged in the fishing business with Zebedee, their father, when Christ called them to follow Him (Matthew 4:21 and 22). Both James and John were appointed apostles in Matthew 10:2. The great zeal and drive of these two brothers may have been the reason why Christ surnamed them "Boanerges," which means "sons of thunder" (Mark 3:17).

John was one of the members of Christ's inner circle of disciples along with James and Peter. Although he does not state his own name, yet he claims to have been an eyewitness of many of the events he writes about. For instance, in John 1:14 he says, "And the Word was made flesh, and dwelt among *us*, (and we beheld his glory . . .)." Also consider how he refers to himself in John 21:24, "This is the disciple which testifieth of these things, and wrote these things . . . . "

John is also the author of Revelation and the three epistles that bear his name. The Apostle John states his purpose in writing this book in John 20:30, 31: "And many other signs truly did Jesus in the presence of his disciples, which are not written in this book: But these are written, that ye might believe that Jesus is the Christ, the Son of God; and that believing ye might have life through his name."

The word translated "signs" in this passage refers to some power or meaning in back of the deed and is really of greater significance than the outward event. This is John's characteristic word for each of Christ's miracles.

John here acknowledged that Christ performed many additional miracles, but that these were selected which are most likely to stimulate faith in the reader.

The purpose of this book is that those who receive it will come to believe that Jesus is the Christ, God's Son; so that they may, therefore, have life through Him. This "life" that John speaks of is the grand purpose of the moral creation. To come to personally know God's Son through faith brings eternal life. As Christ says in John 17:3, "And this is life eternal, that they might know thee the only true God, and Jesus Christ, whom thou hast sent."

Many titles of Christ are given in the Gospel of John. Most of these came from the lips of Christ Himself. He is spoken of as the Lamb of God, the Son of God, and the Word. He says of Himself, "I am the way, the truth, and the life," "I am the resurrection, and the life," "I am the living bread," "I am the door of the sheep," "I am the good shepherd," "I am the light of the world," and "I am the true vine."

There is no book in all of God's Word that has more to say about faith than the Gospel of John. The word faith does not occur even once, but John's action word for faith is *believe.* Usually it is written in the present tense, "believeth."

John tells us first of all *the one in whom we are to believe.* In John 12:44 he says, "He that believeth on me, believeth not on me, but on him that sent me." Thus we are to understand that we believe on *God* who sent Christ. The golden text of the Bible, John 3:16, states, "For God so loved the world, that he gave his only begotten Son, that whosoever believeth in him should not perish, but have everlasting life." We are to believe on God, and we are to believe on His *Son* whom He sent.

The reasons for believing on Christ are presented by John. There are six of these given by John:

1. The Testimony of John the Baptist (John 1:6, 7)
2. The Word of Christ (John 4:41, 42; 8:30)
3. The Miracles of Christ (John 2:11; 10:37, 38)
4. The Resurrection of Christ (John 20:8, 29)
5. The Testimony of God (John 5:30-37)
6. The Unity of Believers (John 17:21)

John also presents certain definite *results of believing.* We will have eternal life (John 5:24; 6:47). We will never thirst (John 6:35). And, we will not abide in darkness (John 12:46).

And finally, John shows the serious *results of not believing.* All such are condemned (John 3:18). The unbelievers shall not see life (John 3:36). The wrath of God abideth on unbelievers (John 3:36). John adds that the unbelievers shall die in their sins (John 8:24).

There is a very strong emphasis on prayer in the Gospel of John. Even in the three chapters where the dominant theme is the teaching concerning the Holy Spirit, Christ weaves in many prayer promises. We find in John 14:13, 14, "And whatsoever ye shall ask in my name, that will I do, that the Father may be glorified in the Son. If ye shall ask any thing in my name, I will do it." In the next chapter, Jesus makes the following statements, "If ye abide in me, and my words abide in you, ye shall ask what ye will, and it shall be done unto you." " . . . whatsoever ye shall ask of the Father in my name, he may give it you" (John 15:7 and 16). Also in the concluding chapter on the Holy Spirit, the Lord says in John 16:24, "Hitherto have ye asked nothing in my name: ask, and ye shall receive, that your joy may be full."

And now let us consider the major divisions of the Gospel of John:

I. Prologue, 1:1-18
II. Preparation for Christ's Earthly Ministry, 1:19—2:11
III. Public Ministry of Christ, 2:12—12:50
IV. Private Ministry of Christ, 13:1—17:26
V. Passion of Christ, 18:1—19:42
VI. Power of Christ as Shown in His Resurrection, 20:1-31
VII. Epilogue, 21:1-25

John wrote this Gospel that bears his name probably from Ephesus somewhere around A. D. 90.

One fact of great importance that John makes clear is that

Christ's earthly ministry extended over more than three years. The synoptics tell about only the final visit of our Lord to Jerusalem. John records at least three passovers and possibly four that Christ attended in Jerusalem.

There are eight miracles performed by Christ which are recorded by John. Six of these we find only in this Gospel account. They are changing the water into wine, healing the nobleman's son, healing the impotent man, healing the man born blind, raising Lazarus from the dead, and the miraculous draft of fish.

The final chapter of John centers around Peter who had earlier boasted of his firm loyalty, then thrice denied he knew Christ. While the other Gospel writers do not tell of this personal audience Christ provides for Peter, John does. He does not leave Peter forlorn and dejected as do the others, but rather he tells of his "restoration and recommission."

Now, if you will take your Bible in hand, we will go through the Gospel of John and summarize each chapter.

CHAPTER 1

John does not give Christ's genealogy. He does, however, show that Christ, as the Word, was in the beginning with God.

Christ is presented as the Creator of all things and as the Source of light and life.

The forerunner of Christ, John the Baptist, is also presented in the prologue. His chief duty is declared in John 1:7 and 8. In each of these verses, we learn that he was to bear witness of Christ.

The clearest statement ever given of the incarnation of Christ is found in this prologue, John 1:1-18. John says, "And the Word was made flesh . . . . " The eternal, invisible Son of God, putting on human flesh to provide our redemption, is the true meaning of the incarnation.

At this point, we now leave the prologue and begin the second major division of the book. This deals with the preparation for Christ's earthly ministry, John 1:19—2:11.

The ministry of John the Baptist is now explained. His work created so much attention that priests and Levites were sent to inquire who he was. John made it clear that he was only a voice, a witness. He was preparing the way for the coming of the Messiah.

John gives two great testimonies concerning Christ in this division. John announced that he saw the Holy Spirit as a dove come and abide on Christ. Here he also made that profound declaration, "Behold the Lamb of God, which taketh away the sin of the world."

The chapter concludes with four men coming to know Christ. Andrew, Simon Peter, Philip, and Nathaniel all had life-changing encounters with Christ.

CHAPTER 2

Our Lord's first miracle was at a marriage in Cana of Galilee. In order to prevent an embarrassing situation for the bridegroom, Christ, at His mother's suggestion, miraculously provided the needed wine.

The two-fold purpose of this miracle was to show forth His glory and to cause His disciples to believe on Him.

The third major division starts at this point. Here John relates the public ministry of Christ (2:12—12:50).

Christ's public ministry was begun in Jerusalem at the Temple. John states that Christ went to the Passover in Jerusalem and was enraged at what He found going on in the Temple.

Perhaps it had begun innocently enough, but slowly the sellers and money changers had moved bit by bit into the very court of the Temple. There were noise, arguing, perhaps greed, extortion, and disorder associated with these financial transactions.

It is no wonder that Christ spoke of the Temple as having become "an house of merchandise."

After Christ had cleansed the Temple, the Jews asked Christ for a sign. To this He answered, "Destroy this temple, and in three days I will raise it up." John adds that Christ thus spoke of His body.

Before we go to the next chapter, let us observe one of the major aspects of this division of the Gospel of John. Christ was on display and John tells of many individuals and groups who looked Christ over and evaluated Him. What a list this made. It ranged from the small to the great, from the insignificant to the dignitary. They considered Christ; some believed Him to be the Messiah, but others rejected Him.

CHAPTER 3

Only in the Gospel of John do we learn about Nicodemus. He appears in chapters 3, 7, and 19. He was an outstanding ruler of the Jews and came to Christ one night to discuss spiritual things. Surely he must have been sincere, for to him Christ revealed some of the simplest yet most profound truths ever uttered. The great contrast between physical and spiritual birth is here made clear. Nicodemus felt himself secure because of his physical descent from Abraham, Isaac, and Jacob. Christ informed him that the first birth was not enough, that he must be born again.

This meeting closed with Christ giving very beautiful and meaningful statements to Nicodemus. In the midst of these verses we find John 3:16, the gospel in embryo.

John the Baptist appeared once more and gave a final witness or testimony for Christ. No one ever praised Christ more highly than John did. To show us how completely unselfish John was—and how devoted he was to Christ—he said, "He must increase, but I must decrease."

We cannot tell from the evidence presented in this chapter just what Nicodemus thought of Christ after this meeting. But no one can doubt how John the Baptist regarded Christ. He had carefully evaluated Christ and stated that "He that cometh from above is above all."

CHAPTER 4

Christ is now viewed and evaluated by one whom the Jews would have bypassed. She was a lowly Samaritan woman. Christ met her at Jacob's well and engaged her in conversation. Here was a woman who was almost the exact oppostie of Nicodemus. And yet, our Lord, by leading her to an understanding of Himself, is telling us that she was just as worth saving as was Nicodemus.

This is perhaps the outstanding example of personal evangelism in all the Bible. John, under inspiration, seems to have recorded every word of Christ and of the Samaritan woman. We can learn, therefore, this method of evangelism. Surely any method our Lord used would be proper for us to follow.

It seems that because the woman got so excited about the truth that Christ was the Messiah, she left her waterpot at the well. She had truly accepted Christ as her Savior. One further proof John gives is that she went into the city to give public testimony acknowledging Christ. We conclude that she became that day a follower of Christ.

As a result of the woman's witness, Christ was able to have a fruitful harvest among the Samaritans. In fact, the contrast is very sharp as one considers the cold reception He received in Jerusalem and Judea and the warm hearty reception in Sychar of Samaria.

The second miracle to be recorded in John is found in chapter four. A nobleman from Capernaum came to Cana to ask Christ to heal his son. Jesus' response was, "Go thy way; thy son liveth." Even though the sick child was more than twenty miles away, space did not hinder the miracle-working power of Christ. At that same time when Christ spoke, the child recovered.

CHAPTER 5

This chapter begins with Christ visiting a certain pool in Jerusalem and healing an impotent man. This is the third miracle that John records. The fact that this man had had this infirmity for thirty-eight years was no obstacle to Christ's miracle-working power. Christ convinces us in this, that time is no hindrance to Him.

In the central portion of this chapter, Christ clearly and openly asserts His own deity. Just look at His tremendous claims:

1. He claims that He is equal with God the Father (5:17, 18).

2. He possesses life-giving power (5:21).

3. To Him has been committed all judgment (5:22, 27).

4. He is worthy of the same honor as God the Father (5:23).

5. He shall raise the dead (5:25).

These claims are so tremendous that Christ then presented four witnesses to testify for Him. John the Baptist gave witness to Christ. These Jews had accepted John as a truthful prophet. Logic then demanded that they accept Christ as John had.

Christ pointed to the works which He had performed. These were an even more forceful witness than that of John, for no mere human being could do what Christ had done.

The voice of the Father also gave testimony to Christ's true identity. However, the voice of the Father could mean very little to anyone who was rejecting God's Son.

The final witness Christ spoke of was the one that was most accessible, most available to them; namely the Holy Scriptures. Christ said of them, "They are they which testify of me." Christ is the grand subject of the Word of God. Anyone who accepts the Holy Scriptures as God's Word must therefore accept God's Son, for the Scriptures point to Him.

CHAPTER 6

This chapter opens with Christ performing the miracle of feeding the five thousand people. This is the only miracle performed by Christ which is recorded by Matthew, Mark, Luke, and John. John gives more details. He tells us that it was Andrew who said, "There is a lad here . . . . " Here we learn that it was a little boy who provided the five loaves and two fish. We do not know how many people were present. There were five thousand men. The total number could have been substantially more.

The fifth miracle occurred when Christ set aside natural law and walked on the water. The disciples were in a boat on the sea of Galilee and they saw Christ coming toward them. He spoke to them to allay their fears as He stilled the storm and the turbulent sea.

Christ next presents one of His longest discourses recorded by John. He identified Himself as the bread of life. He is the true source of all spiritual life. He regards the spiritual needs of man more vitally important than the physical. Some have had difficulty with Christ's statement in this chapter, " . . . Except ye eat the flesh of the Son of man, and drink his blood, ye have no life in you."

This statement is to be taken in a figurative sense. Receiving Christ is here likened to taking food, eating it, and the food then becoming a part of you. What an illustration this is for every believer. It is wonderful to know that Christ desires to be completely identified with His children and received into every sphere of life.

As a result of this message on the bread of life, there were many disciples who turned back and followed Christ no more. Christ asked the twelve, "Will ye also go away?" Peter answered, "Lord, to whom shall we go? thou hast the words of eternal life."

CHAPTER 7

The brothers of Jesus urged Him to go to Jerusalem for the celebration of the Feast of Tabernacles. This was one of the major annual observances instituted through Moses. It was an eight-day national festival. Christ's brethren did not believe on Him (see John 7:5) but desired that Christ go and display His deeds before the multitude that would be in Jerusalem.

Christ encouraged them to go, but stated that He would not go just yet to the feast.

The Lord secretly went to Jerusalem about the middle of the week and taught in the Temple. Here Christ stated how serious it is to reject His claims.

Surely the most important event of this week happened on the eighth day. Custom was that on the first seven days during the morning, water was poured in the Temple to remind the children of Israel of the water from the riven rock. The last day this ceremony was not performed. However, at this time, Christ stood and dramatically offered Himself to all who were thirsty. Christ here claimed to be the One who could satisfy thirst even as the riven rock at an earlier time. No greater claim could have been made on this occasion.

There was a division among the people because of Him. Some believed, but others still had doubts.

CHAPTER 8

This was early the next morning. Christ came to the Temple where the scribes and Pharisees brought before Him a woman who was taken in adultery. One wonders why the man was not brought also. They told Christ that Moses commanded stoning as the penalty for such a crime. But they wanted to know what He recommended. Christ knew that they were not really interested in His opinion, but that they sought to find evidence on which to accuse Him to the civil or the religious authorities. Christ tried to ignore them, but John says, "They continued asking him." Then Christ stated, "He that is without sin among you, let him first cast a stone at her."

This brought conviction to their hearts, and they left, from the eldest to the youngest. Christ then admonished the woman to go and sin no more.

While still in the Temple in Jerusalem, Christ declared to the multitude that He was the light of the world. Christ again identified Himself with God the Father.

One of Christ's clearest statements and harshest warnings was now uttered. He stated, " . . . For if ye believe not that I am he, ye shall die in your sins."

In this same great discourse Christ made clear the path to spiritual freedom. "And ye shall know the truth, and the truth shall make you free."

CHAPTER 9

The sixth miracle recorded by John is in chapter 9. This was the healing of the man born blind. In answer to the question of the disciples, "Master, who did sin, this man, or his parents . . . ?" Christ declared, "Neither . . . but that the works of God should be made manifest in him."

Then Christ performed a miracle of healing so that this young man could see.

This chapter reveals for all to see the cruelty and hard-heartedness of the Pharisees. They had already agreed that if anyone confessed that Jesus was the Christ they would put Him out of the synagogue. A great furor was aroused as the Pharisees learned of this miracle and questioned the man's parents. The parents had been made moral cowards by the Pharisees' decree of punishment if one acknowledged Christ. So, the parents refused to answer, only to refer their questions to the young man, who they said was of age.

The young man answered clearly and forthrightly concerning what Christ had done for him and even admitted that He is a prophet. After being subjected to severe questioning, the young man was cast out of the synagogue.

When Christ learned of this He found him and revealed Himself as the Son of God. The young man believed and then worshiped Christ.

CHAPTER 10

Here is a very beautiful and touching allegory told by our Lord. He likens Himself to a shepherd and His followers to sheep. This is not a new figure for it frequently occurs throughout the Old Testament.

This passage may be divided into three parts. The first part may be likened to an early morning scene as the shepherd leads his sheep from the sheepfold. The second part is like a noon-time scene. The sheep have freedom to enter the sheepfold for protection or go out to eat the green grass. Then the final part is a scene at nightfall. The flocks are returning. There is possibly greater danger now, but the shepherd is there to protect even with his life if necessary.

Christ shows Himself to be the true shepherd, the door of the sheep, and the good shepherd. We learn here that not only is Christ willing to lay down His life, but that it is definite that He is to lay down His life. He has received commandment from the Father to lay down His life and take it up again.

John next tells us of Christ's visit to the Temple in Jerusalem at the feast of dedication. The Jews crowded around Jesus and said, "If thou be the Christ, tell us plainly." So, once again Christ revealed His true identity, ending with the statement, "I and my Father are one." At this they accused Him of blasphemy, took up stones to stone Him, and sought to take Christ but He eluded them.

CHAPTER 11

The most far-reaching miracle performed by Christ was the raising of Lazarus from the dead. Lazarus' sisters Mary and Martha sent for Christ because of their brother's serious illness. After abiding where He was for two days, Christ announced to His disciples that Lazarus was dead. John describes in great detail the way in which Martha was the first to come out to Christ. After being comforted by Christ, she sent for Mary who came and was also comforted by the Lord.

Even though Lazarus had been dead for four days, this was no hindrance to Christ as He performed this seventh miracle as told by John.

This miracle caused many to believe on Christ. It had another effect also. The chief priests and Pharisees called a council because they said, " . . . If we let him thus alone, all men will believe on him." The result of this council is stated in John 11:53, "Then from that day forth they took counsel together for to put him to death."

John has written in such a dramatic way that he has present belief and unbelief as the two opposing forces. The turning point of the drama is in the eleventh chapter of John. The forces of unbelief were now committed to take the life of Christ. If wicked men had had their way this book would have ended in tragedy. But they had overlooked the power of God and the glory of the resurrection of Christ.

CHAPTER 12

It was now only six days before Christ's death. Of course, only Christ knew this. Mary and Martha provided a supper to honor Christ to show their gratitude for His having restored their brother Lazarus to life. Mary anointed Jesus with a pound of very precious ointment. Judas Iscariot complained but Christ gave her high praise and stated that this was done "against the day of my burying."

We see Christ the next day entering Jerusalem. This was the triumphant entrance with the shouting, the palm branches, and Christ being acknowledged as the King of Israel.

John closed this division by showing how this grand display served to further incense the Pharisees.

John tells about the wish expressed by the Greeks. These were Greeks who perhaps had become Jewish proselytes. They were in Jerusalem for the Passover. Their desire was, "Sir, we would see Jesus." Christ's answer to them is found in this final discourse which He spoke in the Temple. His response was, "And I, if I be lifted up from the earth, will draw all men unto me."

His answer then was that before His redemption became available to the Gentiles, He must taste death for every man. "All men," without exception and without distinction would be drawn to Him after His death.

In the closing division of this chapter Christ quoted Isaiah to show the hardness of the people's hearts. More had believed in Christ than those who had made it public. Their reticence was because they loved men's glory more than God's glory.

Yet, the majority have remained in unbelief. And with this note, the public ministry of Christ closes. His teachings from this point on were private. From then on He taught only His chosen ones.

CHAPTER 13

The disciples were alone with the Lord now. Christ's public ministry was over. His private teachings begin here. It was now very close to the hour of Christ's departure. They were sharing the last supper and Christ, in the midst of the supper, rose and washed the disciples' feet. He thus taught them the need of daily cleansing and genuine humility. Christ let the disciples know that what He had done was to give them an example to follow. He is very explicit here. He says " . . . Ye also ought to wash one another's feet."

Judas, the traitor, was then dismissed.

Christ then spoke clearly of His own departure. Peter wanted to follow and expressed that he would even lay down his life for Christ. Christ told him that he would deny Him before the rooster crowed that very day.

CHAPTER 14

The structure of this chapter is made clearer to us as we note the questions that were asked and answered. Each question was asked by a disciple; each answer was given by Christ. We need to look into the close of chapter thirteen for the first question. Peter asked, "Lord, whither goest thou?" Christ's answer is given in the first several verses of chapter fourteen where He said, "I go to prepare a place for you."

Thomas then asked how they could know the way. To this Christ responded that He is the way, the truth, and the life. Christ

Himself is the way to the Father.

Philip asked that they be permitted to see the Father. Christ said in answer, "He that hath seen me hath seen the Father."

The one final question in this chapter comes from Jude. He asked how Christ would manifest Himself to His followers and not at the same time show Himself to the world. The answer to this was by the person and ministry of the Holy Spirit.

Chapters 14—16 of John give the most extensive teaching concerning the Holy Spirit than any other portion of the Bible. In the first of these chapters the truth is introduced, then developed more fully in the latter two chapters.

Christ refers to the Holy Spirit as "another Comforter," "the Spirit of truth," and "the Comforter." His duties are to abide with believers, teach them, and bring all things to their remembrance.

CHAPTER 15

Christ used the symbols of the vine and branches to teach a spiritual truth. Christ is the vine, the Father is the husbandman, and believers are the branches. As the branches abide in the vine there will be fruitfulness. The father purges and prunes the abiding branches to stimulate fruitbearing.

The believer's prayer life is stressed in this chapter. The promises are staggering! Consider this in John 15:7, "If ye abide in me, and my words abide in you, ye shall ask what ye will, and it shall be done unto you."

The chapter ends speaking of a two-fold ministry of Christ. The Holy Spirit is to testify to believers of Christ—then the believers are to testify of Christ. God still expects this of us today.

CHAPTER 16

Once again Christ stated that it was necessary for Him to go away. Only in this way would the third person of the Godhead, the Holy Spirit, come. With His coming, He would be assigned a three-fold ministry. He would convict or reprove the unbelievers because of sin, righteousness, and judgment. The inner workings of the Holy Spirit produce conviction.

This chapter concludes as Christ reminded His disciples again of His death and His resurrection. He encouraged them even though He plainly states that they would be scattered because of Him.

CHAPTER 17

Here is the high priestly prayer of Christ. He intercedes for His present and future followers. The main thrust of this prayer is for the unity and protection of those who believe on Christ.

This is the only place in the Bible where eternal life is defined. Note John 17:3, "And this is life eternal, that they might know thee the only true God, and Jesus Christ, whom thou hast sent." Eternal life is a quality of life that comes from knowing God through Christ.

His final petition is that Christ will be able to have His followers with Him. His love is so great, so intense, that He desires the presence of the object of His affections.

This high priestly prayer of Christ will be finally and completely answered.

CHAPTER 18

Christ and His disciples were in the garden of Gethsemane when Judas and the Temple guards arrived. John carefully points out that Judas "knew the place." John records the boldness of Christ. As the soldiers approached, Christ stepped out and inquired whom they sought. When they responded, "Jesus of Nazareth," Christ said, "I am he." The soldiers were so startled at this, that "they went backward, and fell to the ground." Upon regaining their composure they followed through with Christ's arrest.

Peter put up quite a little defense for Christ as he cut off an ear of Malchus, one of the members of the guard. Christ asked him to put up his sword, for this was the cup the Father had given Him and He would drink it.

Christ was taken first before Annas. Annas, though still called the high priest, no longer held the office. He had had four sons to succeed him in this office, and now the office was held by Caiaphas, a son-in-law of Annas. After Annas' death, another of his sons became high priest.

Annas still held tremendous religious power. When his name appears in the Bible with that of Caiaphas, Annas' name is always listed first. Note that Christ was taken *first* to Annas.

After a series of questions, Annas sent Christ to his son-in-law, Caiaphas, the official high priest.

It was in connection with these two trials that Peter was questioned and denied Christ three times. John says concerning Peter's final denial, "Peter then denied again: and immediately the cock crew."

Caiaphas sent Christ to Pilate. It is interesting to note how carefully John describes the hypocrisy and self-righteousness of the Jews who were condemning Jesus. He states that they would not enter the judgment hall lest they be defiled. They had to keep themselves unspotted so they could eat the Passover.

After Pilate examined Christ he reached his initial decision and stated it for all to hear, "I find in him no fault at all." History would have had a different place for him if he had held to this decision.

CHAPTER 19

Pilate had Christ scourged although he had already stated His innocence. The soldiers placed a crown of thorns on Christ's head. This was the only crown placed on the head of our Lord while He was on earth.

A verbal battle ensued between Pilate and the Jews. Pilate wanted to release Christ because he found no fault in Him. The Jews wanted the death sentence imposed. John reveals the Jew's statement that caused Pilate to have Christ killed. It is, "If thou let this man go, thou art not Caesar's friend: whosoever maketh himself a king speaketh against Caesar."

This statement turned the tide. Pilate was fearful of Caesar and wanted to please him. Guilt or innocence was of no concern now, for Pilate felt that he must consider his own job, his own future. So he gave the order for Christ's crucifixion.

John then records the terrible event, the crucifixion of Christ. After Christ's death Joseph of Arimathaea asked Pilate for the body of Christ. He and Nicodemus gave burial to Christ.

CHAPTER 20

Even though chapter 19 is a dark, sorrowful chapter—chapter 20 is just the opposite. It is full of light and hope and joy.

Mary Magdalene found the empty tomb on the first day of the week. She was the first one to whom Christ appeared on this resurrection morning. When she realized that this was Christ, He told her not to touch Him. That is, He admonished her not to cling or hold on to Him. He stated that He was ascending to His Father at that very time. It is logical to believe that Christ, having completed His own sacrifice, was on His way to present His blood in Heaven. Christ told Mary to go and tell His brethren that she had seen the Lord.

Jesus appears twice more in this chapter. He revealed Himself to His disciples, once with Thomas absent and once with Thomas present. He gave them the commission to go. He said, " . . . As my Father hath sent me, even so send I you." He stated to them, "Receive ye the Holy Ghost." Thomas' great exclamation is recorded by John as he says of Christ, "My Lord and my God."

CHAPTER 21

Peter, though still feeling the sting of failing Christ, was yet looked upon as the leader of the disciples. He said to six other disciples, "I go a fishing." They responded, "We also go with thee." So, Thomas, Nathanael, James, John, and two unnamed disciples went fishing with Peter. They fished all night and caught nothing.

Christ, though unrecognized, stood on the shore when morning light came, and shouted to them, "Children, have ye any meat?" When they answered in the negative, He commanded that they cast the net on the right side of the boat. This they did, still not knowing that the man on the shore was Christ. But as soon as their net was filled with a multitude of "great fishes," John exclaimed, "It is the Lord." Peter, eager soul that he was, jumped in the water and swam to the shore where Christ was.

The others soon came to land and found that Christ had already prepared fish and bread. They added some of their fish to the meal, and then the Lord invited them to come and dine.

After the meal, Christ gave Simon Peter a three-fold opportunity to profess his love for the Lord. Christ said, "Simon, son of Jonas, lovest thou me more than these?" To each of these probing questions Peter responded by saying that the Lord knew that he loved Him. And each time, the Lord then reminded Peter that he was to work for Christ. He was to feed the Lord's lambs and sheep.

This was Simon Peter's public reinstatement and recommission. The synoptics did not make this fact clear. But John did not close without clearly revealing that Peter had been fully forgiven and publicly commissioned by Christ Himself to care for the Lord's followers.

The book ends with Christ giving Peter his final orders, which may be applied to present-day disciples of the Lord. Christ said to him, "Follow thou me."

A SURVEY OF THE BOOK OF

Acts Of The Apostles

by Charles A. Thigpen

The Acts of the Apostles is surely one of the most exciting books in all the Word of God. Here we have the actions and reactions of that first group upon whom the Holy Spirit was poured forth. This is the only book of inspired church history in the Bible. It electrifies the imagination and grips the emotions of every serious reader. It is the logical and proper bridge from the Gospel accounts to the Epistles of the New Testament. This book is not only charming, but exceedingly invaluable history of the beginning church from approximately A.D. 30 to 60.

The author of this book is none other than Luke, the beloved physician; although he did not identify himself by name anywhere in these pages. There are four reasons that convince any fair-minded person that Luke is the author of Acts. In the first place there is a definite similarity of style in the Gospel of Luke and Acts. Proofs for Luke as the author of the Gospel that bears his name would serve as additional proof that he also wrote Acts of the Apostles. The second reason is that which is referred to as the "we" sections of Acts. Note carefully in Acts 16:10 and 20:6; the author of these words definitely joined the apostolic team and made it clear from the use of the pronoun "we." We know from Paul's epistles that Luke accompanied Paul on at least two of his missionary journeys. Paul speaks of "Luke, the beloved physician" in Colossians 4:14. In 2 Timothy 4:11 Paul says, "Only Luke is with me." Paul also speaks of Luke as a companion in Philemon 24. The third reason for being assured of Luke's authorship of Acts is that he dedicated both of his New Testament books to the same person—Theophilus. Luke also in Acts refers to a "former treatise" he had written, which certainly points back to the Gospel of Luke. The final reason is that there has been an unbroken line of tradition which has accepted Luke as the author of Acts.

It is generally acknowledged that Luke was a native of Antioch, a Greek by birth, a careful researcher and writer, highly intelligent, modest, patient, and loyal.

Most likely Luke wrote Acts from Rome. He pictures himself as being with Paul near the end of his two-year imprisonment in Rome. If Paul had been tried by Nero, released, re-arrested, or had been martyred, it is almost certain that Luke would have recorded these events. Therefore, we conclude that Paul was very close to the end of his two-year Roman imprisonment when Acts was written. The date, then, was approximately A.D. 61, as Paul arrived in Rome in A.D. 59.

From the contents of Acts we conclude that Luke wrote this book to give clear, authoritative evidence of the activities of Peter and Paul and the founding and early history of the Church. The unity of the Christian Church is set forth as the gospel was received by those in Jerusalem, Judea, Samaria, and unto the uttermost part of the earth, by Jews and by Gentiles. Also, there may have been some misunderstanding as to why Paul had been arrested and imprisoned so often. Luke, as the careful historian and faithful companion, was the logical one to put Paul's activities in proper light.

The outline of the book is stated in Acts 1:8, "But ye shall receive power, after that the Holy Ghost is come upon you: and ye shall be witnesses unto me both in Jerusalem, and in all Judaea, and in Samaria, and unto the uttermost part of the earth." In this verse we see the Divine appointment, the spiritual equipment, and the territorial assignment of God's plan for the ages. The witness in Jerusalem is from Acts 1:1—8:3; the witness in Samaria and Judea, Acts 8:4—12:25; and the witness unto the uttermost part of the earth, Acts 13:52—28:31.

In the first 12 chapters the Apostle Peter is the prominent character. In chapters 13—28, Paul is prominent. The focal point of chapters 1—7 is Jerusalem; chapters 8—12 focus on Judea and Samaria. From chapter 13 on to the end of Acts, the home base of the gospel is Antioch in Syria.

Keep ever in mind the missionary nature and missionary purpose of this book. The gospel reached people from many parts of the civilized world on the day of Pentecost, then reached out through Judea, Samaria, Syria, Asia Minor, Macedonia, Greece, and Rome.

This is a book of public addresses—actually, twenty-four in all. Some are complete, some are not. There are nine messages by Peter, nine by Paul, and one each by Gamaliel, Stephen, James, Demetrius, the townclerk at Ephesus, and Festus.

Acts serves as the historical and geographical background of all of Paul's epistles except his pastoral letters, 1 and 2 Timothy and Titus. Therefore, a clear understanding of Paul's writings demands a thorough understanding of Acts of the Apostles.

All of Paul's visits to Jerusalem after his conversion are recorded in Acts. He made five trips. These are recorded in chapters 9, 11, 15, 18, and 21.

This book rests solidly on the historical events of Luke's times. Luke speaks of Annas the high priest and Caiaphas. Many outstanding Roman officials are named, such as, Sergius Paulus, Gallio, Claudius Lysias, Felix, Festus, Herod Agrippa I, Herod Agrippa II, and Julius. This is just one of the many reasons why Luke is known as a very careful historian.

This book fulfills Joel's prophesy of the coming of the Holy Spirit and our Lord's promise of the advent of the Holy Spirit. It is beautiful to behold how the Holy Spirit does not magnify Himself. Rather, He does precisely that which our Lord said He would. That is, He testifies of Christ. The Lord Jesus Christ is ever the subject of the Spirit's ministry. He takes the things of Christ and makes them real to those who believe. Even though this present age is the dispensation of the Holy Spirit, He does not center attention on Himself, but always on the Christ of God.

Now, please take your Bible in hand, turn to the Book of Acts, and we will consider each chapter in this wonderful book.

Bear in mind that the overall outline is the one suggested in Acts 1:8. Therefore, the first seven chapters tell us of the work of witnessing in Jerusalem; chapters 8—12 present the Christian witness reaching Judea and Samaria; and the remainder of the book, from chapter 13 on, give the witness unto the uttermost part of the earth.

Luke begins chapter 1 by addressing Theophilus and telling him that his former book concerned itself with what Christ began to do and to teach. The implication here is that the present book takes up the story at the point just before Christ's ascension and shows what Christ continued to do through His followers, after He was taken up. Doctor Luke strongly underscores the truth of the resurrection here in his introductory verses. He asserts that Christ showed Himself alive after His passion by "many infallible proofs" over a period of forty days. Christ centers the apostles' attention for this period of fine instruction on "the kingdom of God." It is not strange or unusual then, that their question to Him relates to the time of the setting up of this kingdom. Christ did not rebuke them or even chide them for asking the question, but rather directed their attention to the great missionary task at hand—that of being His witnesses all over the world.

Christ asked that they remain in Jerusalem to receive the "promise of the Father." He assured them that not many days hence, "ye shall be baptized with the Holy Ghost." Earlier Christ had said to them concerning the Holy Spirit (in John 14:17), " . . . He dwelleth with you, and shall be in you."

The other emphasis in Christ's parting words was that His followers were to extend their witness unto the uttermost part of the earth, beginning at Jerusalem, reaching out through Judea and covering Samaria as it moved out. Then, from the Mount of Olives, Christ ascended up and a cloud received Him. A message reached them from two standing nearby. We gather from their raiment and their message that they were angelic beings. It is interesting to note the substance of this message centers on the dear Lord's return. So, even as the Lord was being received into Heaven, His Word to His believing children was, I am coming back again.

When they returned from the Mount of Olives, these followers went to the upper chamber where they were abiding. We do not know the exact location. Perhaps it was the same room where they partook of the Last Supper. Christ's eleven apostles are named. Judas Iscariot's name is not in the list as he had already betrayed Christ and had committed suicide. Note carefully that these apostles along with Mary, our Lord's mother, and other women, now started the prayer vigil. The word "accord," appears here as Luke describes the relationship of this group. This word is a musical term in the original, meaning "without discordant note." It is not believed that all of these people remained in uninterrupted prayer for ten days. Rather, it is supposed that this was a "marathon" of prayer. This was the chief thing they did during these ten days. No doubt someone, or several, were continually in prayer, then others took their places. At least one activity that demanded their attention during this time was the selection of Judas Iscariot's successor. Peter appealed to two passages in the Old Testament as Scriptural authority for their actions (Psalm 69:25; 109:8). It is evident that the apostles reasoned from providential circumstances, sought Scriptural guidance, and submitted themselves to God in prayer as the selection of Matthias was made. The group will now be called "the twelve" as we see in Acts 6:2.

Chapter 2 begins on a Sunday morning, the fiftieth day after the Passover. This is Pentecost. This is one of the three great festivals or feast days of the Old Testament. On these three occasions—Passover, Pentecost, and Feast of Tabernacles—every able-bodied male of the children of Israel was to come to Jerusalem. Pentecost is sometimes called "Feast of Weeks" as it was celebrated seven full weeks after the Passover. It is also called "Feast of Harvest" as it concluded the harvest of later grains. It is spoken of as "the day of first fruits" as loaves made from the new grain were offered on the altar in this celebration.

This chapter does not make clear the place where the apostles and the others were when the Holy Spirit descended. If they were still in the Upper Room, they soon moved out into the streets or to the Temple for their witness to be effective.

The first manifestation was a sound, "as of a rushing mighty wind." This was not wind—but just the sound of wind. Second, there appeared to be tongues of fire. The first sign appeared to the sense of sound—the second to the sense of sight. The second sign looked like flames of fire. Perhaps these tongues of fire are symbolic of the fact that each of them was to be a fervent, Holy Spirit empowered witness. The third manifestation appealed to their feelings—their entire inner beings. The Scripture says, "And they were all filled with the Holy Ghost."

There was another miracle that occurred at this time. Luke says that they "began to speak with other tongues, as the Spirit gave them utterance." How else could this large group of Jews from over the entire Roman Empire hear in his native tongue or dialect the wonderful truth of the Messiah? This was the very practical outworking and purpose of this miracle of "other tongues." In this way, the gospel could be communicated on a single day to hearers from perhaps a score of nations. Luke is clear and explicit here as he says twice, "Every man heard them speak in his own language [or tongue]."

In response to the question of many in the multitude, "What meaneth this?" Peter delivered his first sermon recorded in the Acts of the Apostles.

The introduction to this message shows a great deal of skill used by Peter. Some in the audience had mocked, implying that those who had received the Holy Spirit were actually inebriated on strong drink. Peter began at this point by refuting this allegation in appealing to the custom of the times and the early hour of the day. He immediately went into an explanation of the cause of the believers' behavior. Peter pointed to the prophet Joel and quoted a long passage from his prophecy to explain that this immediate sight was a miraculous event provided by God as He had just poured forth His Holy Spirit on them.

The body of Peter's message is a three-fold presentation—each point centered on Jesus Christ. He argued that Jesus Christ was approved of God by works, wonders, and signs. Then he moved on to show that the greatest miracle of all was Christ's resurrection from the dead. The third sweep of his sermon presented Christ as the ascended Lord and Christ of which the Holy Spirit's present manifestation is an evident witness. In response to the people's grave question, "Brethren, what shall we do?" Peter clearly stated to them that genuine repentance must be experienced by each who desired remission of sins. This was to be followed by publicly following the Lord in baptism as an outward sign of the inward death to the old life and resurrection to the new life. The response was overwhelming. There were three thousand souls who were added to the believers at this time.

One final word as to the significance of Pentecost. This is the birthday of the New Testament Church. The Church is an organism, with believers as the body and Christ as the Head. The Church was in existence embryonically during Christ's earthly ministry. Pentecost is the Church's birthday, Christ the exalted Head is now in the

Heavens, the Holy Spirit has now been poured forth and is forming the earthly body of Christ—the Church.

The first apostolic miracle took place in Acts, chapter 3. Peter and John were going into the Temple at the hour of the afternoon prayer. The Jewish day was divided into twelve equal parts with the times of prayer being the third hour and the ninth hour or, our 9 o'clock in the morning and 3 in the afternoon. A man lame from birth got Peter and John's attention. Peter commanded the man to stand and walk. The miracle took place immediately. This is amazing—the elders of the church were not called for, the apostles offered no prayer—Peter said, "In the name of Jesus Christ of Nazareth rise up and walk."

This miracle served the apostles as Christ's miracles had served Him. This miracle attracted a large crowd. They were filled with "wonder and amazement" at this unusual happening. Thus, the people were gathered and Peter used the occasion to again preach about the crucified, risen Savior who was exceedingly available to everyone. He issued a call to repentance and closed with admonitions and promises from Moses and the prophets.

In chapter 4, Peter and John showed great boldness even though they were arrested, jailed overnight, and tried by the Sanhedrin. The conclusion was that the apostles were commanded to refrain from speaking or teaching in the name of Jesus. The apostles politely refused to accept this command. This experience prompted the church to prayer and praise. Again, they were filled with the Holy Spirit.

Chapter 4 ends with the notable example of Barnabas who sold a field and gave the money to the church. Chapter 5 tells of a similar deed by Ananias and Sapphira, the difference being that they kept back part of the price but pretended to give it all. This is the saddest, darkest chapter in Acts as hypocrisy and sin are found in the membership of the church. God took the life of Ananias, then of his wife, Sapphira. This is a very impressive illustration to show that God expects His Church to be kept pure and holy.

Other exciting events happened in chapter 5. Unusual miracles, "signs and wonders," were performed by Peter and the other apostles. They were imprisoned, but the angel of the Lord opened the prison doors. The apostles were again arrested and reminded that they had been ordered to be silent about Jesus. The response was, "We ought to obey God rather than men." After Gamaliel's imperfect counsel was given, they were released.

Murmuring arose in chapter 6. The Greek speaking Jews complained that their widows were neglected in the daily distribution by the church. The complaint was sufficiently accurate to prompt the apostles to action. The result was that "servers of tables," or deacons, were chosen to take care of the responsibility. This was the first major step providing for organizational structure within the church.

Luke proceeded at this point to deal with the activities of one of these deacons; namely, Stephen. Keep in mind that this was not an ordained preacher but a layman with a message. As Stephen witnessed, serious opposition arose which led to his being brought before the Sanhedrin. Stephen was charged with speaking against Moses, the Law, and the Temple. Stephen was given an opportunity to speak. His defense showed him to be a very thorough student of the Old Testament. His message takes up most of chapter 7 of Acts. Stephen showed he was not guilty of their charges, but that the leaders of the Jews and the Jewish people were guilty of following a path of spiritual conceit and rebellion. The people were so convicted and angry that they stoned Stephen even as he prayed for them and asked the Lord to receive his spirit.

Saul of Tarsus first appears in the Acts at the stoning of Stephen. Saul consented for Stephen's death and gave encouragement, if not assistance, to the murderers. We shall see much more of Saul shortly; but first, chapter 8 addresses itself to the activities of another witnessing deacon. Philip, a layman, was the first to have reached out beyond Jerusalem and Judea. He went to Samaria with the saving message and multitudes responded. Peter and John were sent to give assistance. One of Peter's first duties was to rebuke the erring Simon, who had been a sorcerer. From the city of Samaria the message of the Cross was taken to many villages in Samaria.

Philip left at the command of an angel and was able to win to Christ a very influential government leader from Ethiopia. The last picture of Philip in chapter 8 showed him still preaching the gospel.

Chapter 8 makes it clear that there was a "great persecution" against the church, and that one of the leaders in this was Saul of Tarsus. Acts 8:3 states, "As for Saul, he made havock of the church, entering into every house, and haling men and women committed them to prison."

Chapter 9 of Acts focuses in on Saul as he began one of his tours of persecution. As he journeyed toward Damascus, armed with warrants for the arrest of every Christian in that city, he met the Lord. Saul asked two questions, "Who art thou, Lord?" and "Lord, what wilt thou have me to do?" The Lord answered the first question but commanded Saul to go into Damascus, and there it would be told him what he was to do. Saul was led to Damascus because of his blindness, and three days later a disciple named Ananias came as a messenger from the Lord. Saul received his sight, received the Holy Spirit, was baptized, and "preached Christ in the synagogues, that he is the Son of God."

Saul then visited Jerusalem and was received by Barnabas, who brought him to the apostles. Luke says that here Saul spoke "boldly" in the name of the Lord. Saul's life was endangered, and the brethren brought him to Caesarea and sent him to Tarsus.

Chapter 9 concludes with two miracles performed by Peter. He healed Aeneas of the palsy and raised Dorcas from the dead. This final miracle caused many in Joppa to be saved.

Chapter 10 of Acts of the Apostles is one of the outstanding important chapters in this book. Here, we see Peter's second use of the "keys of the Kingdom," this time opening the doors to Gentile believers. It started with a man named Cornelius who had a vision during prayer which told him to send for Simon Peter and that he would "tell thee what thou oughtest to do."

God was simultaneously preparing Simon Peter's heart for his ministry to these Gentiles. While he was in prayer, God convinced him by means of a vision that "what God hath cleansed, that call not thou common." The vision was given to Peter three times, then God said that there were three men seeking Peter. He was to go with them "doubting nothing." Peter followed this command and was brought to the house of Cornelius in Caesarea. After Peter and Cornelius told each other of God's dealings with them, Peter preached a simple message about the central truth of Christian doctrine. A climax was reached as Peter stated, "To him give all the prophets witness, that through his name whosoever believeth in him shall receive remission of sins." At this point, Luke states that the Holy Ghost immediately came on those in Cornelius' house. Peter conferred with the believers who came with him, and they all agreed that these Gentiles had been saved and were proper candidates for the waters of baptism.

This event set the pattern for the entire age, this Gentile age. From henceforth, the very moment a person believes in Christ with true repentance, that is the moment the Holy Spirit comes into the heart. No waiting, no laying on of the apostles' hands, but the instant of true belief in Christ as Savior, the Holy Spirit comes in to dwell.

Peter found it necessary, in chapter 11, to clearly relate his experience with the Gentiles and defend his action when he went to Jerusalem. A very revealing and enlightening verse is the one which tells how the believers responded to this unusual event. This is Acts 11:18, "When they heard these things, they held their peace, and glorified God, saying, Then hath God also to the Gentiles granted repentance unto life."

Then the message of Christ reached Antioch in Syria. Many were saved. The Jerusalem believers sent Barnabas to assist them. He got Saul to work with him as the opportunities were so great. A point worthy of note is found in Acts 11:26b, "And the disciples were called Christians first in Antioch."

Persecution increased as we learn in chapter 12. Herod Agrippa I, the king, had James, the apostle, brother of John, killed by the sword. Herod had Peter arrested. The church prayed "without ceasing" for him. God sent an angel and miraculously released Peter from prison. Peter joined the prayer meeting after they finally let him in. Someone said that Peter found it easier to get out of jail than to get into a prayer meeting. Instead of judgment falling on Peter, this chapter concludes by telling of the horrible death of Herod.

Now we come to that part of this book which tells the most thrilling and exciting missionary story ever written. Here, in chapter 13, Paul began his first missionary journey. Saul, Barnabas, and John Mark went first to Seleucia and sailed to the island of Cyprus. Here they preached at Salamis and at Paphos. It was here that Saul's name was changed to Paul. The Bible does not give any reason for this change. Sergius Paulus, deputy of the country, was converted. Elymas, the sorcerer, was struck blind for trying to withstand the missionaries and hinder the deputy from being saved.

The missionary party left the island and went north to the mainland. At Perga in Pamphylia, John Mark left them and returned to Jerusalem. Paul and Barnabas went then to Antioch in Pisidia. A lengthy message by Paul is recorded which Paul preached in the synagogue. The theme of this sermon is justification by faith in Christ. There was a large number who responded favorably to Paul, which seemed to be the reason why the Jews were filled with envy, spoke against Paul, and blasphemed. This is the first time that Paul and Barnabas stated that they were turning to the Gentiles. We do not know the length of time the missionaries stayed, but Luke states, "The word of the Lord was published throughout all the region."

Chapter 14 brings the first missionary tour to a close. A great multitude of Jews and Greeks had been saved at Iconium. Opposition finally mounted and Paul and Barnabas went to Lystra. Luke says, "And there they preached the gospel." Paul healed a man who had been born a cripple. For this, the fickle populace wanted to worship them. Paul and Barnabas stopped this, but it was not long until disgruntled Jews from Iconium and Antioch came, stirred up the people against the truth, and caused Paul to be stoned. He was dragged out of the city "supposing he had been dead."

They moved on to Derbe, then made a return trip through the cities of the first missionary journey, ordaining elders in every church and setting the churches in order. From Attalia they sailed to Antioch where they were received with great joy by this great missionary church which had sent them out.

The great church council, which concerned the believer's relationship to the Law of Moses, is presented in chapter 15. Some were still insisting that, in addition to faith in Christ, one must submit to all the Law of Moses including the rite of circumcision for all males. Some had come from Judea to Antioch with the word, "Except ye be circumcised . . . *ye cannot be saved*." The church at Antioch sent Paul and Barnabas to Jerusalem to confer with the apostles and elders about this matter.

Peter was the first to speak on this momentous issue. He declared that he had witnessed Gentile conversions apart from any law observance and even before Christian baptism. He insisted that the law was much too heavy to be borne by Gentiles as it was too heavy for our fathers. He went on to say that the law was also too heavy for them to bear.

Paul and Barnabas then told of their work with Gentiles and the wonders God had wrought. James gave the summary speech which was the final decision. The law could not be a grounds of salvation. This position in liberty, however, should be for the purpose of developing a holy life and not used as a license. This message was to be sent to the Gentile believers in Antioch, Syria, and Cilicia. This was the greatest single victory for grace as opposed to *law-works.* This is indeed a pivotal chapter in Acts and makes clear for the entire age that a person is saved "by grace, through faith, plus nothing."

After returning to Antioch, Paul wanted to leave on another missionary trip. Barnabas again desired to take his nephew, John Mark, along but Paul refused. The Word says they had *sharp contention* over this matter. This should show us that good men can have differences of opinion. Barnabas left with Mark—Paul left with Silas.

Chapter 16 found Paul and Silas well into the second missionary journey. They had visited churches in Syria and Cilicia. After Derbe, they came to Lystra and added young Timothy to their party. After going through Phrygia and Galatia, the Holy Spirit forbade them to preach in Asia. After arriving at Troas, God spoke to Paul in a night vision inviting him to Macedonia. This began the first of the "we" passages, where Luke joined the missionary team. They crossed over to the European mainland. This was a history-making voyage. Suppose the gospel had been sent Eastward rather than Westward. All subsequent history would have been changed. At Philippi they had their first convert on European soil, Lydia, who opened her home to Paul and the others.

Paul commanded the evil spirit to come out of a demon-possessed girl. This enraged her masters, and they assaulted Paul and Silas and had them arrested. The magistrates had them beaten and placed in prison. At midnight the two missionaries prayed and sang when God sent an earthquake which opened every door and loosed everyone's bands. The frightened jailer was about to take his own life, but Paul shouted for him not to harm himself as all the prisoners were still there. The jailer was so overcome that he inquired the way of salvation, to which Paul responded, "Believe on the Lord Jesus Christ, and thou shalt be saved, and thy house." Salvation came to this entire household that night.

The next day, the magistrates, upon learning of the Roman citizenship of Paul and Silas, were greatly disturbed and came personally and urged them to leave Philippi. After comforting the brethren, the missionary team left.

In chapter 17, the Thessalonian church was founded. After Paul preached, there were those who responded in faith and were saved.

Here again, there was opposition by the Jews. Luke says they were moved with envy. Paul and Silas were sent away for their own protection. In Berea many responded to the gospel as preached by Paul. Here again opposition started up when Jews from Thessalonica arrived.

Paul next went to Athens. This was the intellectual as well as the religious center of the ancient world. One may well wonder why Paul did not establish a church at Athens. Upon this point the Bible is silent. The Epicureans and the Stoics encountered Paul and took him to the Areopagus and asked him to speak to them. Paul delivered a masterful message with the theme centering on God, who will judge the world by Jesus Christ. There was a three-fold response—some mocked, some said they would hear him again, but certain ones believed.

Chapter 18 begins with Luke writing, "After these things Paul departed from Athens, and came to Corinth." Here he met Aquila and Priscilla, who were also tentmakers, and stayed with them. Corinth was a very wicked and sinful city. A temple was here that had been erected to the goddess Aphrodite, the goddess of love. The worship here was lewd and licentious, including as a part of their ritual and worship the most degrading acts which wicked minds could imagine.

Paul stayed a year and six months in Corinth and established a large church. He followed his usual approach here, in seeking to reach Jews first, by going to the synagogue. Some Jews and Greeks responded, but other Jews hindered Paul and blasphemed. Paul publicly announced that he would then seek to reach Gentiles. Crispus, Gaius, and the household of Stephanas were converted. Then the Lord appeared in a vision to give Paul assurance of His presence with him. The Jews had Paul arrested and brought before Gallio, but he would not listen to the Jews and drove them away from his judgment seat.

Paul then concluded his second missionary journey as he sailed from Ephesus to Caesarea and over to Jerusalem, which was his fourth visit in Acts to that city, and on to Antioch. After rehearsing to his missionary-minded home church what God had done through him, Paul left again and made a swing through Asia Minor "strengthening the disciples."

There is a brief parenthetical paragraph at the close of chapter 18. Here, Apollos appeared for the first time. This was in Ephesus. He was a Jew, an eloquent man, and mighty in the Scriptures. He knew only the baptism of John until Aquila and Priscilla, after hearing him, called him aside and "expounded unto him the way of God more perfectly." Apollos evidently willingly received the further truth with complete acceptance.

As chapter 19 opens, Paul had come to Ephesus. These disciples whom Paul found here had perplexed many. It is very clear that they were not saved. They had been baptized unto John's baptism, but Paul sensed that they were not true believers. Paul asked them if they had received the Holy Spirit *when* they believed, to which they responded, "We have not so much as heard whether there be any Holy Ghost." Verse 2 is a very misleading verse as translated in the King James Version. The correct translation states, "Did you receive the Holy Spirit when you believed?" The incorrect translation is, "Have ye received the Holy Spirit since ye believed?" It is a pity that entire denominations could follow an incorrect translation, but such is the case. From Acts, chapter 10, right on down to the consummation of the age, the very moment a person genuinely believes Christ to be his Savior, that very moment the Holy Spirit comes in. As Paul states in Romans 8:9, "Now if any man have not the Spirit of Christ, he is none of his."

After Paul led these disciples of John to a clear understanding of Christian truth, and they were saved, Paul entered the synagogue to win others. Paul taught in the school of Tyrannus, also. Paul stayed in Ephesus the greater part of three years during which time, "All they which dwelt in Asia heard the word of the Lord Jesus, both Jews and Greeks."

Luke notes that God wrought "special miracles" by Paul at Ephesus. Seven sons of a Jew named Sceva sought hypocritically to duplicate Paul's miracles. The man who possessed the evil spirit, upon whom they were practicing, jumped on all seven and prevailed against them, wounding them all. This further added momentum to the Christian cause. The gospel had a purifying effect as many brought wicked books and other devices and publicly burned them. Luke in giving the cause of this says, "So mightily grew the word of God and prevailed."

A silversmith at Ephesus, Demetrius, led an uproar against Paul and his party. It turned into a riot and general uproar. Luke tells us that for two hours the people shouted, "Great is Diana of the Ephesians." The uprising was finally quelled by the town clerk as he silenced them and then dismissed the assembly.

Paul, in chapter 20, moved rapidly to close out his third missionary journey. He made a brief three-month trip through Macedonia and returned to Troas, then to Miletus. Here he sent for the Ephesian elders and gave them some parting instructions after recounting his ministry among them. This chapter contains more about Paul's method in soul-winning and church planting than any other chapter in the New Testament. He recalls that he held back nothing that was to their profit, he taught publicly from house to house, he declared the whole counsel of God to them, and he ministered night and day with tears. Therefore, he could say, "I am pure from the blood of all men." He commended them to God and His Word and admonished them that wolves would enter if they were not exceedingly vigilant. Paul departed amidst one of the most moving scenes in Acts as the Ephesians "wept sore" for him.

Chapter 21 covers Paul's return to Jerusalem. In Tyre, Paul was told by disciples "through the Spirit, that he should not go up to Jerusalem." This is the only place where the Holy Spirit forbade Paul; the other places He only warned Paul of the imprisonment and suffering which awaited him if he returned to Jerusalem.

Upon his arrival at Jerusalem, Paul conferred with James and the elders. They further warned Paul of the Jew's harsh attitude toward him. Later, Paul was in the Temple worshiping when Jews of Asia recognized him and led in having him arrested. The chief captain permitted Paul to speak to the people as he stood on the steps of the castle.

The next chapter, chapter 22, gives the record of that speech. Paul spoke in Hebrew. It is mostly a personal testimony of God's dealings with him. He told of his background, his careful training at the feet of Gamaliel, and his conversion on the Damascus road. He spoke of his prior persecution of Christians and that he assisted in the death of Stephen.

When he told of God's commission to him to go to the Gentiles, the crowd listened to him no more. The chief captain brought Paul into the castle at this point and would have had him scourged, but Paul informed him of his Roman citizenship. The chief captain decided he would take Paul before the Sanhedrin the following day.

The entire Sanhedrin gathered as is recorded in chapter 23—even Ananias, the high priest. Paul deliberately sought to divide them as both Pharisees and Sadducees were sitting in judgment against him. He announced that "of the hope and resurrection of the dead I am called in question." It was then necessary for the chief captain to rescue Paul from those who were set on his destruction.

The Lord appeared to Paul and assured him that he would yet witness in Rome. Paul's nephew learned of a conspiracy to kill Paul. He informed the chief captain. Paul, under very heavy guard to protect his life, was brought from Jerusalem to Caesarea. He was now a prisoner of Felix, the governor.

Paul's defense before Felix is give in chapter 24. Paul's accusers, Ananias the high priest, and an orator named Tertullus, arrived and presented their case against Paul. Felix then gave Paul permission to speak in his own defense. Felix did not make a decision at this time but stated that he wanted to hear from Claudius Lysias when he came to Caesarea. So Paul was kept a prisoner.

The second time Paul appeared before Felix was when Drusilla was by Felix's side. Paul spoke not of himself, but preached an evangelistic message. Luke said, "He [Paul] reasoned of righteousness, temperance, and judgment to come." Luke tells us that Felix trembled and promised to call for Paul at a convenient season. Although he called for him often during the next two years, the New Testament does not record that he responded positively to the gospel call. Then Porcius Festus took Felix's place, and Paul was kept a prisoner.

In chapter 25 Paul is about to be sent back to Jerusalem for trial. Because of their intense hatred for Paul and his religious position, the Jews planned to lie in wait to kill Paul on this journey. Therefore, Paul appealed to Caesar. He had this privilege as a Roman citizen. Agrippa and Bernice visited Festus in Caesarea. Festus insisted that they hear Paul so they could help him write the charge to send to Caesar. They agreed to hear Paul.

The entire twenty-sixth chapter is Paul's defense before Agrippa. In reality, it is more than a declaration of his innocence; it is a restatement of the essential tenets of Christian doctrine. This is Paul's last public defense given in this book. Here again as in chapter 22, he gives his Damascus road experience. Everything centers around the person and work of Jesus Christ, especially His resurrection from the dead. Festus accused Paul of being mad. After courteously responding to him, he urged Agrippa to make a decision, to which in irony he stated, "Almost thou persuadest me to be a Christian."

The Biblical record for all to see makes it clear that both Festus and Agrippa agreed to Paul's innocence.

The last two chapters, 27, 28 of Acts, tell of Paul's journey and eventual arrival at Rome. The voyage was hazardous and ended in shipwreck, although because of Paul's advice not a single life was lost. On the island of Melita Paul was miraculously delivered from the bite of a poisonous viper. Paul healed Publius' father of an illness. After three months on this island, they departed for the Italian mainland, and from thence up to Rome.

In Rome he was permitted to dwell in his own hired house for two years. He was a prisoner, but had great liberty to receive people and even to preach to those who came to his home.

We have no way of knowing why the Book of Acts closes so abruptly. This we do know—this book tells of earth's only Savior, the Lord Jesus Christ—this book tells of the greatest organization on earth, the Church—and this book tells of the greatest missionary of the Cross this world has ever known, the Apostle Paul. Thank God for this wonderful book, the Acts of the Apostles.

A SURVEY OF THE BOOK OF

Romans

by Leroy Forlines

Romans is the favorite book of the Bible for many Christians. It is profound in its treatment of the redemptive grace of God. Its treatment is logical and convincing. Its central theme is justification by faith, but its breadth is far-reaching. The scope of its contents includes the depravity of fallen man, the universality of condemnation, the relationship of the race to Adam, atonement, justification, sanctification, law and grace, the bountiful blessings of the believer, the place of the Jews and Gentiles in the plan of God, the gifts of the Holy Spirit, and many aspects of the practical side of the Christian life.

Paul wrote this book while on his third missionary journey. The evidence for this is seen in chapter 15. In 15:25-28, Paul indicates that he is soon to take an offering to the saints at Jerusalem. By a study of the mention of this offering in 1 Corinthians 16:1, 2 and 2 Corinthians 8:1—9:15, we know that this offering was received on Paul's third missionary journey.

It appears that Paul wrote this epistle from Corinth. It was taken to Rome by Phebe who was a servant of the church at Cenchrea. Cenchrea was a seaport of Corinth. Therefore, it is assumed that Paul was likely in Corinth when he wrote the letter to the Roman Christians.

There are different ideas concerning the origin of the church at Rome. Roman Catholics have taught that Peter founded the church and became its first bishop or pope. This does not fit with Paul's caution, " . . . lest I should build upon another man's foundation" (15:20). It also appears very unlikely that Paul would have made no mention of Peter in the letter if Peter had been there serving as its bishop.

Some have said that it was started by Jewish converts who were in Jerusalem on the day of Pentecost. This is unlikely since there is no mention that any of the converts from the day of Pentecost returned to their homes and started churches. It is very possible that some of these converts were involved in the early stages of the church at Rome, but not likely that they were its sole organizer.

It seems more likely that some of Paul's converts founded the church, or at least had a big hand in it. On this basis Paul would feel free to write such an important letter and still feel that he was not building on another man's foundation.

There is some difference of opinion over whether the Jews or the Gentiles made up the majority in the membership of the church. Most commentators are of the opinion that the Gentiles were in the majority. This is based on such verses as 1:13 and 15:16. It is probably true that the Gentiles were in a majority, but the strong attention given to Jews seems to indicate that there were also a good many Jews in the church.

While all of the book logically fits together, it is better to treat it as falling into three parts rather than using one continuous outline for the book. Part I covers 1:1—8:39 and deals with the development of the doctrine of justification by faith and its implications. Part II includes 9:1—11:36 and is taken up with the place of the Jews and Gentiles in the plan of God. Part III concludes the book and includes 12:1—16:27. Its contents are practical and personal.

Before becoming involved in the doctrinal development of the book, Paul makes a few introductory comments in 1:1-17. Paul introduces himself as a servant of God whom God has given the special call to be an apostle. Paul's whole heart and life were taken up with the gospel of God. This gospel was not something that had made a sudden, unannounced appearance into the world. It was firmly rooted in the promises of the holy Scriptures. Jesus was the seed of David in keeping with Old Testament prophecies as it relates to His humanity. He was more than human. He was also Divine. The resurrection from the dead confirmed for all times that Jesus was the Son of God. Paul's gospel centered in Jesus Christ, whom he recognized as Lord.

Having declared his own identity and the gospel that he preached, Paul addresses the Christians at Rome. They are beloved of God and share the calling of all God's people to be saints or to be holy ones. Paul commends them for having a faith that was spoken of throughout the whole world. You may want to compare verse 8 with 16:19.

Paul now shares with the people the yearning that he has to see the Christians at Rome. He had desired to go to Rome but had been hindered until now. In 15:19-23 we learn what had hindered Paul. It was not, in this case, Satan's interference, but the hindrance of an unfinished task. He had now finished his work in the area and the way was clear for his trip to Rome. This he would undertake after taking the offering to the poor saints in Jerusalem (15:25-28).

Paul was strongly motivated. He had something of which he was not ashamed. It was something that everybody needed. It was the gospel of God which would bring salvation to anybody anywhere in the world if they would only come to Christ in faith. This news was too good for Paul to keep to himself. It was based on a righteousness that God had provided through Jesus Christ.

This gospel was not only available; it was needed. Without it all men everywhere are under Divine condemnation. In 1:18—3:20 Paul establishes this fact. He first shows in 1:18-32 that the Gentiles were under condemnation. God's wrath is against ungodliness, unrighteousness, and "holding the truth," or as most commentators understand it, "the suppression of the truth" (verse 18).

Ungodliness means lack of reverence. It refers to that failure to give God the place He deserves as the God of the universe. The failure of the Gentiles to do this is seen in their turning to idolatry instead of giving proper recognition to the true God (1:21-25).

Unrighteousness refers to the failure to measure up to God's moral standard. The guilt of the Gentiles in this area is seen in the abounding unrighteousness among them that Paul talks about in 1:24-32.

The ungodliness and unrighteousness of the Gentiles, Paul argues, cannot be charged to ignorance. He says in 1:20, "They are without excuse." He tells us that there is a revelation of God in the created order. For men to turn to idolatry and immorality, they must suppress the truth that is revealed in the created order. What men call ignorance, Paul calls suppressed truth. The truth instead of being given expression is suppressed. This thought is clear in 1:19-23. It is particularly clear in 1:28 where Paul says of the Gentile pagan, "They did not like to retain God in their knowledge." They resisted the truth of God. They sought to drive it from their consciousness. The finer details of knowledge require Biblical study. According to 1:18-32, the only way that a person can avoid basic knowledge about God as the righteous Judge of the universe is to suppress that knowledge. Suppressed knowledge is not honest ignorance. God says that those who go on in their ungodliness and unrighteousness cannot claim ignorance. They are suppressing the truth. They are under condemnation. Paul speaks of the Gentiles who only have the revelation of God in nature as "knowing the judgment of God, that they which commit such things are worthy of death" (verse 32).

Paul is not saying that redemptive knowledge can be known through the created order. It can be known only through the gospel. However, man's moral and rational constitution along with what he observes in the created order leaves him without any justification for his sins.

In 2:1—3:8, Paul develops his argument against the unbelieving Jew. He, too, is without excuse for his sins (2:1). The Jew could easily see the condemnation of the Gentile, but Paul warns the Jew that he cannot escape judgment when he is guilty of the same sins found among the Gentiles. In verse 2, Paul reminds them that God's judgment is a true judgment. It sees sin as sin no matter whether the one being judged is Jew or Gentile.

In 2:5-16 he reminds them that God's judgment is a righteous judgment. A righteous judgment judges all men by the same principles. Sin brings judgment whether the person be Jew or Gentile. Righteousness brings justification whether the person be Jew or Gentile. The same thing that is required of the Gentile is required of the Jew. The same thing that works for the Jew will work for the Gentile. God uses the same set of principles to judge all men.

The unbelieving Jew talks about the Law and God. He knows the right way and can tell it to others. Nevertheless, Paul makes it clear in 2:17-24 that this is no cover-up for failure to keep the Law. By some piercing questions Paul seeks to get the Jew to see that he really stands before God as a law-breaker.

In 2:25-29 it is made clear that circumcision is to no avail if it is not accompanied by righteousness. Righteousness is the real need of both Jew and Gentile. Nothing else will do. It is sufficient for either Jew or Gentile. The question is not who you are, but do you have righteousness? Paul is trying to make it clear to the Jew that he has no righteousness that will stand before God.

Paul's argument was quite perplexing to the Jew. His argument sounded convincing, but were not the Jews a special people with God? Paul knew the Jewish mind well, so he raised the question that he knew the Jew had in his mind: "What advantage then hath the Jew?" (3:1). There was an advantage, but this would not make up for not having righteousness. They were the ones who had received God's revelation. This certainly increased the possibility that they would believe God and receive His promises. Unbelief would not receive the reward of these promises, but the unbelief of some would not keep God from being faithful to those who did believe.

There is one more argument that is put forth by the unbelieving Jew in desperation. The unrighteousness of the Jews had made God's righteousness shine even brighter in contrast to it. The question is raised: Since God's righteousness is seen to be brighter and, thus, God would receive even greater glory, would it not be unrighteous for God to punish their unrighteousness? Paul gives a quick answer of "No!" If this were the case, God could not judge the world. Even the pagan world furnishes a contrast with God that makes His greatness shine. Nothing but righteousness will suffice before God. The unbelieving Jew does not have it.

In 3:9-20 Paul draws definite and emphatic conclusions. Up to this point he has made it clear that the need of all men to escape God's wrath, whether Jew or Gentile, is to have righteousness. What he has already made clear, he restates in no uncertain terms. "As it is written, There is none righteous, no, not one" (verse 10). It is further made clear in verse 20 that by human effort no one could be justified before God. The verdict of verse 19 stands: " . . . that every mouth may be stopped, and all the world may become guilty before God."

Up to this point the picture has been dark. In 3:21—5:21 the picture changes. Paul talks about a righteousness that has been provided by God to meet the need of man. The basic description of this righteousness is found in 3:21-31. It is apart from personal law-keeping (verse 21). It is witnessed by the Old Testament (verse 21). It is by faith in Christ (verse 22). It is needed by everybody and is offered to everybody (verses 22, 23). It is bestowed without cost as an unmerited favor (verse 24). It is grounded in the atoning or propitiatory work of Christ (verses 24-26). In the propitiatory work of Christ the requirements made by Divine Law upon sinful man are all met by Jesus Christ. For us He lived a righteous life, and by His death He paid the penalty for sin. That was all the Law demanded. This made it possible for God to be just on the one hand because the demands of justice have been met, while on the other hand He can justify the one who believes in Christ because these demands of the Law have been met for him. Justification means that one has been declared in right standing with God. Paul concludes that this is ours on the condition of faith apart from personal law-keeping (verse 28). Whatever difference might have existed at one time between Jews and Gentiles, since the coming of Christ, justification has been made available to both Jews and Gentiles on the same condition; that is, faith in Jesus Christ (verses 29, 30). While this justification is not based on personal law-keeping, it is not intended to make the Law void. Rather, it establishes the Law because it satisfies its every demand (verse 31).

This justification by faith apart from law-keeping sounds so good to a Gentile that he can hardly believe it is true. To a Jew it raises a lot of questions. Therefore, Paul gives a defense of this fact in chapter 4.

The key person in Paul's defense is Abraham. It is important to recognize why Paul makes such a use of Abraham. Abraham was the father of the nation of Israel. It was with him that God made the basic redemptive covenant. Paul lays great stress on the condition for receiving righteousness in this covenant. Neither the Mosaic Covenant of Law nor the New Covenant changes or sets aside the Abrahamic Covenant. They each contribute to its fulfillment. Time does not permit a more thorough discussion of the covenants. This is done in the tape on Galatians. It would be helpful if the listener could listen to that tape in connection with his study of Romans.

In 4:1-8 Paul establishes the fact that justification is by faith apart from works. He makes reference to Genesis 15:6 when he says, "Abraham believed God, and it was counted unto him for righteousness." Faith, then, was the condition for Abraham's receiving righteousness. Paul, then, makes it clear that to be justified by faith is something distinctly different from being justified by works (verses 4, 5). For the one who ceases to try to be righteous before God by works, God gives him righteousness on the condition of faith.

David is also called as a witness to the truth that God considers people righteous on a condition other than works. David is important as a witness because the Messiah was of the lineage of David.

Paul goes back to Abraham again to establish the fact that circumcision is not a condition of justification. This is made clear in verses 9-12 by the fact that God considered Abraham righteous on the condition of faith (Genesis 15:6) before he was circumcised (Genesis 17:23, 24).

In verses 13-25 Paul makes it clear that law-keeping cannot be considered the condition for receiving the inheritance that God is to give to the redeemed. The Abrahamic Covenant was made over 400 years before the Covenant of Law. The condition of being righteous by faith was already established before the Covenant of Law. To make law-keeping the condition for being righteous would change the condition. This could not be. (See Galatians 3:15-18.) To make law-keeping the condition for receiving the inheritance would make the promise "of none effect" (verse 14), because no one could keep it so as to receive the promise.

In order that the promise might be sure to the seed of Abraham, God put it on a condition that they could meet (verse 16). By putting it on the condition of faith it was made possible for both Jews and Gentiles. Anyone could become the seed of Abraham and become an heir of the promises made to Abraham and his seed on the condition of faith. This is in keeping with the fact that Abraham was said to be the father of many nations. This included both Jews and Gentiles.

The nature of Abraham's faith was believing God's promises under most difficult circumstances (verses 18-22). He believed that God would make him a father of a great nation when he and Sarah had no children, and under natural circumstances would never expect to have any. Yet, that was what God promised, and he was sure God could fulfill the promise. God honored his faith by counting it to be the condition for being righteous. This promise was important because it was connected with the birth of the nation that was to give to the world its Redeemer.

In a sense, Abraham is the father of all the redeemed. We are told about how God honored Abraham's faith so we can have assurance that God will honor our faith in Jesus and give us the righteousness of Christ so that we may stand before God.

It is important to observe that the proof that Paul offers dates back before the coming of Christ. Abraham was about 2000 B.C. and David was about 1000 B.C. Salvation has always been by faith. That it was by faith became a lot clearer with the death and resurrection of Christ, but it did not begin then.

In 5:1-11 the tone changes from a strictly doctrinal one to a somewhat devotional one. Paul speaks of the blessings belonging to the one who is justified by faith. He has peace with God (verse 1). He rejoices in hope of the glory of God (verse 2). He rejoices in tribulation because in this tribulation he develops Christian virtues and is made aware in his experience of God's presence (verses 3-5). The incomparable love of God in sending Jesus to die for us while we were sinners and enemies of God gives assurance that Jesus will continue to stand for us on our behalf (verses 5-10). The believer rejoices not only in what the future holds, but also in the fact that he is already in a right relationship with God through Jesus Christ (verse 11).

All that Paul had said about salvation centered in one person, Jesus Christ. It sounds almost incredible that one person could do so much for so many. In 5:12-21 Paul reminds us that on the negative side one person, Adam, had been the cause of sin and condemnation entering into the human race. In view of the fact that God would rather help than to hurt, it is far more reasonable that one could be the source of salvation for many than that one could be the source of sin and condemnation for many. The fact stands that through God's grace one person, Jesus Christ, has provided righteousness for as many members of the human race as will receive it.

In 3:21—5:21 Paul talked about justification. In 6:1—7:6 he shows how justification is related to sanctification. The fact that justification is by faith instead of works does not mean that a saved person can continue to live in sin. That such a conclusion is impossible is seen by the fact that the believer died to sin in Jesus Christ. By a study of verses 3-11 we find that the believer's death to sin is the same kind that Jesus' death to sin was. Jesus' death was a payment for the penalty of sin. By union with Christ, Jesus' death becomes the death of the believer so that he can say, "I died to sin, or paid the penalty of sin in Jesus Christ."

In verse 5, the "likeness of his [Jesus'] death" refers to the benefit of His death. It pays the penalty of sin or brings justification to the believer. Paul points out that those who are "planted together in the likeness of his [Jesus'] death, . . . shall be also in the likeness of his resurrection." The likeness of His resurrection refers to a life of triumphant power over sin. This refers to sanctification. Sanctification changes the believer's experience so he will be like Christ. Justification (related to the likeness of Christ's death) solved the guilt problem for the believer and opened the way for the entrance of God's sanctifying grace (related to the likeness of Christ's resurrection).

To think of a believer continuing in sin would be to say that Jesus' death did not break the power of sin and that God's sanctifying grace does not have the power to change the believer. To think so is to misunderstand the gospel.

In the second step of Paul's argument that we cannot think of the believer as one who continues in sin, he points out that such an idea overlooks the fact that the believer is a servant of righteousness (6:15-23). Before salvation we were servants of sin and showed it by our lives. Paul points out that to serve sin means that sin is our master and will bring death. To serve righteousness means that righteousness is our master and will bring forth holiness and everlasting life.

Paul's third point is that we have been changed from subjection to the Law to subjection to Christ (7:1-6). The Law had no power to change our lives. We were discouraged by our inability to keep it. Christ, as our new Master, forgives our sin and gives us strength by the Holy Spirit. When it is properly understood, it is inconceivable that a believer would continue in sin.

For Paul to point out that the Law could not produce holiness in its subjects and that it was good to be delivered from the Law might make some people think that the Law was sinful. He denies such a thought and points out that the Law is holy, just, good, and spiritual in 7:7-25. In 7:7-13, the Law is seen to be good because it reveals the nature of sin. Sin is seen as being powerful, deceitful, that which brings condemnation, and that which is exceedingly sinful. In 7:14-25, the Law is seen to be good because it makes a person aware that he is in bondage to it, and makes him aware of his need of the deliverance that only Jesus Christ can give. The fault is with sin, not the Law.

So far as the tone is concerned, chapter 8 is the high point in the Book of Romans. Paul writes as one whose cup is full and running over as he calls attention to the glorious blessings of the believer.

In 7:10-13, 24, Paul had emphasized that the Law had passed the death penalty on sin. Man stood in need of deliverance. In 8:1 he sounds the joyful note that there is no condemnation to those who are in Christ Jesus. The death sentence has been removed. The heart of man not only cries out for forgiveness, but man also longs to be someone who is respectable—one who has a good conscience before God as it relates to his life, one who has a healthy self-respect and a good testimony before others. This need, too, is met for him. The Holy Spirit enables him to experience a practical fulfillment of the Law in his life (verse 4).

The unsaved person is one who is in the flesh. His doom is death—not only physical death, but spiritual and eternal death. He cannot please God. The believer is not in the flesh. The indwelling Holy Spirit makes the difference. The end result is life and peace (verses 5-9). Paul is not saying that the believer never sins again, but he is saying that he is not in bondage to the flesh. He may suffer some defeats, but he is primarily a victor.

The Christian is not spared physical death, but the presence of the Holy Spirit guarantees the resurrection of the body (verse 11).

One of the most welcomed fruits of the Holy Spirit in our lives is assurance of salvation (verse 16). This assurance reminds us of the fact that we are heirs of God. Most of us will not inherit a great fortune in this lifetime, but we are heirs of God which is far better than inheriting a fortune in the present phase of our experience. Paul does not stop at saying we are heirs. He goes on to say that we are joint-heirs with Jesus Christ. We will share with Him in His inheritance (verse 17). No wonder Paul said, "For I reckon that the sufferings of this present time are not worthy to be compared with the glory which shall be revealed in us" (verse 18).

The present life for the Christian is a life of victory, but it is not a victory that eliminates all problems and difficulties. This means that there is still an undesirable side of our experience. Paul points out that the whole creation shares with us in this groaning. Nevertheless, our future deliverance will be a great one—so great that even the created order will experience a deliverance in connection with the redemption of our body (verses 19-23).

Another one of the blessings of the Holy Spirit is His work of intercession (verses 26, 27). We do not know how to pray as we ought. We do not always understand our need, and how it could be met. The Holy Spirit has a perfect understanding of these things. This need He perfectly communicates to the Father. When our heart is right, we need not fear because of our inability to tell God exactly what the situation is, or what it will take to meet it. This the Holy Spirit does for us.

When Paul realized what was going for him, no wonder he cried out, "And we know that all things work together for good to them that love God, to them who are the called according to his purpose" (verse 28).

This wonderful plan of God is not something that was a recent development on the part of God. It had been planned by God in eternity past. God had before planned and determined that those who came to believe in His Son would be made in the likeness of His Son (verses 29, 30).

When Paul thought on these things his heart was so filled with joy that he said, "What shall we then say to these things? If God be for us, who can be against us?" (verse 31). If God would give His Son to die for us, does it not follow that He will give us the other things that we need (verse 32)?

God's elect are God's chosen. Paul was convinced that when the chosen ones of God are justified by God, no one can make a charge stick against them as long as they trust in Jesus (verse 33). Who can succeed in condemning us as long as we have the crucified and risen Christ as our defense attorney (verse 34)? The answer is no one.

All of these blessings are not to be interpreted to mean that the Christian life is a bed of roses. A Christian may suffer tribulation, distress, persecution, famine, and other difficulties. None of these mean that he has been separated from the love of Christ. Far from it! Instead, as Paul says, "In all these things we are more than conquerors through him that loved us" (verse 37). The Christian may suffer, but he will not suffer alone.

This brings us to Part II where Paul discusses the place of the Jews and Gentiles in the plan of God. Paul opens this section by expressing the heaviness and continual sorrow in his heart for the many Jews who were not saved. If it could bring their salvation, though he knew it could not, he would have been willing to have been separated from Christ and be lost for them (9:1-5).

Since the Jews were a specially chosen people of God, it was a puzzle for many to even think about a Jew being lost. In 9:6—10:3 Paul explains that God, as Sovereign Ruler of the universe, is right in rejecting Jews who reject Jesus Christ.

In verse 6, Paul explains that not every one who was an Israelite by descent was an Israelite in the full meaning of the word; that is, an Israelite who would receive the covenant promises. The same is true with regard to the seed of Abraham. In one sense, the seed of Abraham included Ishmael and his descendants. However, it is made clear that when the Bible speaks of the covenant made with the seed of Abraham, the reference does not include the descendants of Ishmael. Only those who have descended from Isaac are called the seed of Abraham so far as the covenant is concerned. Also, a further distinction is made in the descendants of Isaac. Esau's descendants did not make up a part of this special people. Only Jacob's descendants made up the seed of Abraham in the special sense (verses 7-13). If one could be the seed of Abraham so far as descent is concerned, and not be the seed of Abraham in the covenant sense, does it not follow that one could be an Israelite so far as descent is concerned, and not inherit the promises of the covenant?

It was true that the covenant promises were made to the seed of Abraham that descended from Jacob. These promises included salvation. The point that many of the Jews missed was the fact that the promise of salvation was conditioned on faith. Instead, they sought to establish it by works (9:32; 10: 3).

The basic thrust of what Paul is saying in 9:14—10:4 is this: God is Sovereign Ruler of the universe. As such, it is His right to set the condition of salvation. A sovereign is to be obeyed, not to be accused or to be argued with. God saves those whom He wills to save. What we need to find out is: Whom does He will to save? He has told us. He wills to save those who believe in His Son. The unbelieving Jew needed to cease depending on his works and listen to God. He needed to come to God in faith. If he did not, he would be lost. The fault did not lie in God, but in the unwillingness of the unbelieving Jew to submit to God on God's terms. God's terms are faith in Jesus Christ. Paul was very concerned that they recognize this and be saved

God's way.

God's sovereignty does not exclude human responsibility. Instead, it determines what human responsibility is. The problem was this. The unbelieving Israelite, though a party to the Abrahamic Covenant, had failed to meet the condition of that covenant for personal salvation. He had not listened to the Sovereign Ruler of the universe. The believing Gentile, though not a party of the Abrahamic Covenant originally, had met the condition of the covenant for salvation. By so doing, he had become by faith in Jesus Christ a party of the Abrahamic Covenant and an heir of salvation.

In further elaborating on this righteousness provided by God on the condition of faith, Paul makes the following observations in 10:5-21. (1) It is easily accessible (verses 6-9). It is simply by believing in the heart and confessing with the mouth Jesus Christ as Lord and Savior. (2) It is offered to all, both Jews and Gentiles (verses 11-13). (3) The universality of the offer of this righteousness by faith calls for an aggressive program of world-wide evangelism (verses 14, 15). (4) The Old Testament should have made it clear to Jews that there was going to be a great ingathering of Gentiles to receive this righteousness. The Jews should not have been caught off guard by it (verses 16-21).

Paul had made it clear that many Israelites were lost. In fact, the majority had rejected Christ. This raised a question: "Hath God cast away his people?" (11:1). His people were the people of Israel as a covenant people. Paul's answer is no. God has not cast Israel away. He offers two points of proof that God has not cast Israel away. (1) Paul himself was an Israelite (verse 1). (2) There was at that time a remnant of Israel that did believe and was saved (verses 3-6). For God to have cast Israel away would have meant that the covenant would have been broken. The covenant remained and there were those who were experiencing its benefits. However, since it was a conditional covenant so far as individual salvation was concerned, there were many who failed to meet the condition and were lost.

In 11:11-35 Paul discusses the meaning that certain happenings among the Israelites have to Gentiles and the relationship of Gentiles to Israel. The unbelief on the part of so many of those in Israel had actually speeded up the evangelization of the Gentiles. Paul went to the Jews in a city first, but when he was rejected by them he then turned to the Gentiles. In a sense, then, the unbelief of the Jews had resulted in a blessing to the Gentiles. If this were the result of their fall, what would it mean if the Jews would return to God in true belief (verses 12, 15)? Many are of the opinion, based on verses 24-26, that there will be such a return in connection with the second coming of Christ. Not all agree with this, but there are those, both amillennialists and premillennialists, who take this position.

The point of greatest interest in chapter 11 is the allegory of the olive tree. The olive tree seems to be Israel. In connection with their unbelief, those who rejected Christ were broken off of the olive tree. The only Israelites left in the olive tree were those who believed in Christ. When Gentiles believed in Christ, they were grafted into the olive tree and became identified with the believing Israelites. They became the seed of Abraham and became heirs of the redemptive promises along with the believing Jews. Those who believe that there will be a mass conversion of Jews in connection with the second coming of Christ believe that verses 24-26 speak of grafting these converts back into the olive tree. This would make them Israelites in the full sense of the word. Whatever opinion one may take, it is clear that no Jew will ever be saved apart from coming to Jesus Christ through faith.

The plan of God as elaborated by Paul in this book is wonderful. Any failures are man's failures. As Paul reflected upon God's grace and His dealings with both Jews and Gentiles, he cried out, "O the depth of the riches both of the wisdom and knowledge of God! how unsearchable are his judgments, and his ways past finding out!" (verse 33).

We now come to Part III which concludes the book and deals with practical matters. In this part there are two basic divisions: (1) Instructions are given in the practical aspects of the Christian life (12:1—15:13). (2) Paul makes some personal remarks (15:14—16:27).

To Paul, doctrine was for life, not just a fascinating experience of the mind. Both mind and heart had been stirred as he had written about the marvelous plan of God. Paul's heart had been so stirred over the mercies of God that he challenged the people to give themselves completely to God in the light of these mercies (12:1, 2). How could anyone do any less when God has been so merciful?

Paul now moves from a general challenge of surrender to a discussion of the specifics such a surrender would involve. In verses 3-8, he points out that our service to God should be in accord with our gifts. These gifts are bestowed by God. There is unity in the body of Christ, but there is also variety. Nowhere is this variety more evident than in the difference in gifts from one person to another. It is our responsibility to discover our gifts and serve God accordingly.

One of the most important aspects of the Christian life is the matter of personal relationships. These are discussed in verses 9-21. We are to love each other and let this love express itself in kindness and concern for others. We share with others in their joys and their sorrows.

We are even to love our enemies. The spirit of getting even has no place in the Christian's life. He must view everyone as one to win and to help even when he is mistreated by that person. He is to treat his enemies with such love that they are made ashamed of the way they have mistreated him. The Christian is not to be a peacemaker at any price, but he is supposed to be a peacemaker if it be reasonably possible.

In 13:1-7 Paul turns his attention to civil authority. Civil authority is ordained of God. It is to be obeyed by Christians, not only to stay out of trouble with the law, but also for conscience' sake. The Christian must obey the law unless it brings him into direct disobedience to God. When laws are unfair or oppressive, we should seek through proper means to change them, but Paul gives no grounds for resorting to civil disobedience to bring about change.

The Christian is to be a good citizen. He is to render to those in authority the respect and honor that is due to them. The basic obligation to others is to love them. This love leads to the fulfillment of the morality of the Ten Commandments. It works no ill to one's neighbor. Instead, it leads to proper concern (verses 8-10).

At this point, Paul inserts a moral challenge. This challenge is based on the fact that the second coming of Christ is nearer than we may think. What we do, we must do now (verses 11-14).

While still in the practical area, chapter 14 takes a different turn. Principles are laid down for the proper approach to questionable matters. (1) Each person must ultimately make up his own mind (verses 1-6). (2) We must guard against critical attitudes toward sincere Christians who do not always agree with us (verses 3, 4, 10, 12). (3) In making moral judgments, we must keep in mind that each of us will stand before God and give an account of our lives (verses 1-12). (4) We are not to do that which would bring serious detriment to others, even though our own conscience may be clear in doing it. Love for others is to be the guiding principle in the exercise of our liberty (verses 13-21). (5) We are not to do things when we are doubtful about whether they are right (verses 22, 23). (6) Those who have a better understanding of right and wrong are to be considerate of those who have over-sensitive consciences (15:1-3).

All through this epistle Paul has stressed proper relationships between Jews and Gentiles. In this practical section, he brings this problem up again (15:4-13). Jews and Gentiles are to receive each other "as Christ also received us to the glory of God" (verse 7).

The remainder of the book beginning with 15:14 is taken up with personal remarks. Paul understood human nature. He praised as well as reprimanded. He pointed out people's strong points as well as their weaknesses. In verse 14, he reminds them that he recognizes them to be competent in their Christian experience. Yet, he felt that he had a responsibility to them as a minister to the Gentiles (verses 15, 16).

Paul had had an effective ministry that had reached from Jerusalem to Illyricum. In three missionary journeys, he had accomplished his work in these areas, and as soon as he had delivered the offering to the poor saints at Jerusalem he would be free to go to Rome (verses 19-29). Paul knew that his conversion to Christianity had not made him very popular among the unbelieving Jews in

Jerusalem. In the light of this, he requested prayer that he would be delivered from those in Judea who did not believe so he would be able to visit Rome (verses 30-33).

Phebe, from the church at Cenchrea, was the bearer of the epistle. In 16:1, 2 Paul commends her to the church at Rome. In verses 3-16, Paul greets a number of his acquaintances who were in Rome. Many of these had labored with him in his ministry. Before bringing this epistle to a close, Paul admonishes the people to be on the alert for those who would divide them by false doctrine (verses 17, 18). Greetings are passed on from some of his fellow-laborers (verse 22). Tertius, who penned the epistle, is allowed to extend a few personal greetings (verses 22, 23). The epistle is closed by a prayer that God would establish the Roman Christians in the gospel (verses 25-27).

A SURVEY OF THE BOOK OF

First Corinthians

by Dr. Robert Picirilli

The purpose of this lecture is to introduce you to the Book of 1 Corinthians. I hope you have your Bible handy, so you can follow along with me as I read portions of this epistle. Let us begin by turning to chapter 1, verses 1, 2. These two verses identify this as a letter written by the Apostle Paul to the Christians in the city of Corinth.

You will recall that the great apostle made three missionary journeys. On the second of those journeys, he and Silas departed from Antioch and passed quickly through Galatia and Asia Minor to Troas, on the seacoast at the eastern end of Asia. During the night, the Lord caused Paul to see a vision of a man across the waters, a man from Greece calling for help. So Paul and his fellow-workers sailed to Greece and carried out an extensive tour there, founding churches in Philippi, Thessalonica, Berea, Athens, and Corinth.

Corinth was in the southern part of Greece and was the capital of its district. In Acts, chapter 18, we have the account of Paul's original visit to this great city on his second missionary journey. In Acts 18:2, 3 you can read how Paul met and lodged with Aquila and Priscilla while he was in Corinth, because they made their living by tent-making, a trade Paul also knew. In Acts 18:8, you will read that many Corinthians believed and were baptized. In verses 9, 10 you will see that the Lord Jesus appeared to Paul and instructed him to stay at Corinth a longer time than usual, because there were many people there who would turn to God.

And so we read in Acts 18:11 that Paul stayed there a year and a half, teaching the Word of God. His ministry at Corinth was very successful, and clearly a large congregation was established there.

We do not know how long it took for problems to arise among the Corinthian Christians; perhaps these problems began to develop soon after Paul moved on to other places. We do know some of the things that contributed to the problems. For one thing, there were large numbers of both Jews and Gentiles in the church. For another thing, many of the Corinthians were converted from a background of heathenism, with its idolatry and immorality; and these were not yet well-trained in Biblical principles. For another thing, another preacher came and ministered at Corinth for a time after Paul left. His name was Apollos, and Acts18:24 describes him as an eloquent and knowledgeable man. Obviously, many of the Corinthians, with their Greek love for wisdom and oratory, found Apollos more appealing than Paul.

So, it is not surprising that problems developed. Paul had gone on home to Antioch for a brief visit, and then started out on his third journey, planning to minister at length in the city of Ephesus, just across the gulf from Corinth. By the time he got to Ephesus, news had already begun to make its way to him, that the Corinthian church was in trouble. Paul wrote them one letter, which we do not now possess. This lost letter is referred to in 1 Corinthians 5:9, where Paul says, "I wrote unto you in an epistle not to company with fornicators."

But even after that letter, reports continued to reach Paul about the Corinthian situation. In 1 Corinthians 1:11, Paul reveals one of his sources of information, saying that he had heard about the contentions there through the household—family—of a woman named Chloe. In 1 Corinthians 16:12 we learn also that Apollos, the preacher I mentioned a moment ago, had now left Corinth and was with Paul at Ephesus. He would certainly have given Paul much insight into the problems at Corinth.

Finally, the situation was evidently so critical, that some of the Corinthians decided to send three men with a letter to Paul. Turn to 1 Corinthians 16:17; there you can read the names of the three men who came to Ephesus: Stephanas, Fortunatus, and Achaicus. Turn also to chapter 7, verse 1, and there you will see clearly that the Corinthians had sent a letter to Paul, for he specifically states that he is going to write "concerning the things whereof ye wrote unto me."

So Paul, because of the urgent problems at Corinth, and in response to the letter and committee from Corinth, sat down to write this letter we call 1 Corinthians. Paul was in Ephesus at the time, as we have already noted, and on the third missionary journey. This means that the year was about A.D. 55. The most serious problem at Corinth was a divisive spirit; as we shall see in a moment, the church was split into several factions. There were other problems, too: The church was tolerating a fornicator in its fellowship; there were lawsuits between some of the members; there was disorder in the observance of the Lord's Supper and in other worship services; and there was a group denying the doctrine of a bodily resurrection. Add to these problems the questions asked in the Corinthians' letter to Paul, and you can certainly understand why Paul needed to write this letter. The serious circumstances there may serve to remind us of some churches *we* have known!

Now, with that bit of historical background, let us turn back to chapter 1 of 1 Corinthians and begin our survey of the book. As we go along, I will try to point up the main parts of the letter by giving you an outline. I do not know whether you are taking any sort of notes, or if you may be writing in your Bible. Perhaps you would like to do that. Anyway, chapter 1, verses 1-9, serve as an introduction to the letter. In this introduction, Paul identifies himself and his readers in verses 1, 2, and greets them in verse 3 with these words: "Grace be unto you, and peace, from God our Father, and from the Lord Jesus Christ."

In this introduction, Paul also expresses thanksgiving for the Corinthians' experience of the grace of God. Notice the things he is thankful for: in verse 4, for the grace they had received; in verse 5, for their spiritual enrichment; in verse 6, for the testimony of Christ that was confirmed at Corinth; and in verse 7, for the spiritual gifts they had received. You see, then, that what Paul was really thankful for was what God had done for the Corinthians.

But now Paul gets down to the business of the main problem at Corinth. You will recall that I have already pointed out that the main problem was a divisive spirit. Paul's treatment of this problem starts at chapter 1, verse 10, and goes to the end of chapter 4.

You will note, in 1:10, that Paul beseeches the Corinthians to "speak the same thing," and "that there be no divisions" among them. Verse 12 gives us more details; let us read it: "Now this I say, that every one of you saith, I am of Paul; and I of Apollos; and I of Cephas; and I of Christ." In other words, there were at least four parties, four factions, into which the Corinthian Christians were divided, and they had divided over which human leader they would follow! Some said, "Paul is our man." Some said, "We like Apollos better." Still others said: "Simon Peter is a better example of apostleship." And a fourth group said: "You are all wrong; we will follow Jesus."

Paul attacks the problem of divisions by exposing to the Corinthians the basic errors that have contributed to their divisions. I think we can see, in these first four chapters, at least five basic mistakes at Corinth which have brought on the strife. First, in chapter 1, verses 13-16, Paul chides them for foolishly choosing one human leader over another. Look at verse 13, for example. There Paul asks them these questions: "Is Christ divided? was Paul crucified for you?" How utterly foolish to make such a big fuss over the human leader one will follow, when Christ is the One Savior of all!

Second, Paul tries to show them the falseness of the confidence they have placed in human, natural wisdom. This exposure occupies a lengthy portion, from chapter 1, verse 17, to chapter 2, verse 16. This false emphasis on natural wisdom was certainly a part of the cause of division. The Greeks loved wisdom and eloquence. Some of the Corinthian Christians evidently liked Apollos much better than Paul on this very account. They were appealed to, in a fleshly way, by his great oratorical ability and his intellectual approach.

Paul's treatment of this problem of natural wisdom is quite interesting. In chapter 1, verse 17, he says that Christ's commission to preach was *not* a commission to preach natural wisdom, but the gospel; and he observes, in verse 18, that the preaching of the Cross may well seem like foolishness to natural man. In verses 19-21, Paul clearly states that natural wisdom does not lead to the knowledge of God. Note verse 21, for example, where Paul says, "The world by wisdom knew not God."

Paul goes on, in 1:26-31, to show that God does not use worldly wisdom as an instrument of His service. Look at verse 27: "God hath chosen the weak things of the world to confound the things which are mighty."

The correcting of the false emphasis on natural wisdom continues in chapter 2. There Paul reminds the Corinthians, in verses 1-8, that his ministry at Corinth had not been based on a display of natural wisdom. Read verses 4, 5, and you will get the point: "My speech and my preaching was not with enticing words of man's wisdom, but in demonstration of the Spirit and of power: That your faith should not stand in the wisdom of men, but in the power of God."

Paul concludes the rebuke of their false confidence in natural wisdom by stressing the fact that spiritual truths are not learned by natural, earthly wisdom. This is seen in chapter 2, verses 9-16. Let us let verse 14 summarize this point; there Paul says: "The natural man receiveth not the things of the Spirit of God: for they are foolishness unto him: neither can he know them, because they are spiritually discerned."

Now you will remember that I have said there were five errors behind the Corinthians' divisions. The third of these is dealt with in chapter 3, verses 1-4. This is the problem of a fettering carnality. A fetter, as you know, is something that hinders, that holds back. Well, the Corinthians were bound and limited by a carnal immaturity. Note verse 1 of chapter 3, for example: "I, brethren, could not speak unto you as unto spiritual, but as unto carnal, even as unto babes in Christ." Paul was distressed by their lack of spiritual progress. In picking and choosing one preacher against another they showed their fleshly childlikeness.

Now, the fourth cause for the Corinthians' divisions is dealt with from chapter 3, verse 5, through chapter 4, verse 5. The point, here, is that the Corinthians had a fallacious concept of the relationship that exists between the servants of the Lord, the preachers like Paul and Apollos. Obviously, the Corinthians more or less conceived of Paul and Apollos and Simon Peter as competitors, with each striving to obtain the largest following. So Paul proceeds to correct this mistaken notion by stressing the unity, the *oneness* of God's servants.

Paul uses three interesting illustrations in this section to prove the oneness of God's workers. First, he uses the illustration of farming. So he says, in chapter 3, verses 6, 7, that one fellow may plant the seed, and another may water the plant, but both are working toward the same objective under the same Master.

Next, he uses the illustration of construction. As he puts it in verse 10, "I have laid the foundation, and another buildeth thereon." It takes a lot of different workmen doing different jobs to construct a building, but all are working for the same objective and for the same Master. So, says Paul in verse 9, he and Apollos and Simon Peter are all laborers together with God.

This same truth is stressed in Paul's third illustration of stewardship. Paul says, Apollos and I and all the rest of God's servants are but stewards. We are not managing our own business, but God's. It is foolish for you to choose between us, for we all represent the same Master. We do not answer to you, but to Him. Note chapter 4, verse 2, where Paul says: "It is required in stewards, that a man be found faithful." Note also, verse 4, where Paul says, "He that judgeth me is the Lord."

We complete, now, the section on the divisions by taking note of the fifth error Paul charged his readers with: They were possessed of a festering conceit. This error is dealt with in chapter 4, verses 6-21. Notice that, in these verses, Paul says three times they are "puffed up." He says this in verse 6, where he urges them *not* to "be puffed up for one against another." He repeats this charge, you will see, in verse 18: "Now some are puffed up." The expression occurs again in verse 19.

The idea of this expression is that they were like balloons, blown up by their notions of their own abilities. This conceit, like an inflamed sore, festered in their souls and threatened to destroy them.

But now we must move on. We have been dealing with the first major portion of 1 Corinthians, the problem of the Corinthians' divisions. The *second* major portion of 1 Corinthians begins at chapter 5, verse 1, and continues through chapter 6, verse 20. These two chapters deal with other internal problems within the church at Corinth.

There are, in fact, three internal problems dealt with in chapters 5, 6, and we will take these briefly. The first of these problems is a specific case of immorality which existed there. This problem takes up all of chapter 5. The particular case involved is defined in verse 1. Look at the last part of the verse, and you will see that one of the Corinthian church members was living in adultery with his own father's wife, not his mother, of course.

Paul's main rebuke is not against the incestuous man, but

against the church for *tolerating* the man in its fellowship. The church might not be able to force the man's repentance, but they could certainly discipline him; instead—and here you want to notice verse 2—their conceit has caused them to ignore the problem.

Some things about chapter 5 may provoke debate, but two things are very clear. One thing is that Paul considers the conduct of this man as so serious that the man must be regarded as a sinner. The other thing is that Paul insists the church should excommunicate the man right away. Note, in verse 11, how Paul pointedly refers to one who is *called* a brother. Note also, in verse 13, that Paul refers to the man as "that wicked person." In verse 7, you see, Paul says definitely: "Purge out therefore the old leaven." And in verse 13, he says specifically: "Put away from among yourselves that wicked person."

The second internal problem dealt with in chapters 5, 6 is found in chapter 6, verses 1-8. The problem was a matter of lawsuits among the members. Obviously, this problem was a carry-over from the problem of division and strife. Some had gone so far as to drag others down to the judge for a hearing. You can see how indignant Paul was about this, by reading verse 1: "Dare any of you, having a matter against another, go to law before the unjust, and not before the saints?" Paul could hardly believe their audacity.

Paul's main concern, of course, is that these lawsuits will bring reproach on the church in at least two ways; for one thing, people will conclude that the church has none wise enough to handle such disputes. You can see this point in verse 5: "I speak to your shame," says Paul: "Is it so, that there is not a wise man among you?" For another thing, the brotherly-love of the church will be doubted. You can see Paul's concern on this point in verse 6, as he stresses the word *brother* and exclaims as though it were beyond his belief, that "*brother* goeth to law with *brother!*"

And now let us look at the third internal problem dealt with in these two chapters. This problem completes chapter 6, beginning with verse 9, and is the problem of a tendency toward moral impurity. Remember that many of the Corinthians had been converted from a background that gave them no moral absolutes, and you will understand why Paul needed to warn them against any tendency toward immorality. The very fact they had tolerated the fornicator described in chapter 5 shows they were not as concerned about purity as they ought to be.

Thus, Paul reminds the Corinthians, in verses 9, 10, that folk who practice any kind of immorality will not inherit the kingdom of God. In verse 11, he reminds them that they have been saved from such sins, washed, and made holy and just. They must not return to this way of life. In verse 15, he reminds them that they are members of Christ. It is unthinkable to defile, by immorality, that which is part of the body of the Lord Jesus! In this connection, verses 19, 20 give us excellent incentive for holy and pure lives. "Your body," says Paul, "is the temple of the Holy Ghost."

Well, we must hurry along. We come now to the third major portion of this letter, and in this section Paul answers some practical questions which the Corinthians had asked him in a letter. Note chapter 7, verse 1, where Paul indicates this: "Now concerning the things whereof ye wrote unto me." We are not quite positive how much of the rest of 1 Corinthians deals with questions they had asked. Perhaps all of it does. But at least the part from 7:1—11:16 does, and for convenience sake I am going to limit this section to these four and one-half chapters. And in these chapters there are three questions they had asked Paul, and which he answers.

The first of these questions concerns marriage, and this involves all of chapter 7. We do not have time, in this one lecture, to treat chapter 7 carefully, but I do want you to see three main lessons which Paul teaches about marriage. First, he insists that marriage is honorable and the normally proper course for people to follow. Evidently, some of the Corinthians had thought that marriage was not good, so Paul corrects this notion. Notice verse 2, for example, where Paul says: "Let every man have his own wife, and let every woman have her own husband." Then Paul proceeds to make it clear that the sexual side of marriage is also wholesome and right. You will see, in verse 4, that the body of one marriage partner belongs to the other. Indeed, according to verse 5, a mate who withholds his or her body from the other is actually defrauding the other. Paul can certainly not be put on the side of those who teach against marriage.

The second lesson taught about marriage in chapter 7 is that some may remain unmarried in order to be of greater service to the Lord. We hasten to note, however, that Paul does not regard this as the usual thing. In verse 7, for example, you will see that he refers to this fact: "Every man hath his proper gift." Therefore, the only ones who should consider celibacy would be those possessing this unique ability by special gift. Particularly, Paul thinks some widows or widowers might consider this, as you will see in verse 8.

Now let us look at the third lesson Paul teaches about marriage in chapter 7, and it is one that is sorely needed in our day. The lesson is this: Divorce is wrong. Notice with me verse 10, for example: "Let not the wife depart from her husband." Notice also the last part of verse 11: "Let not the husband put away his wife." Evidently some of the Corinthians who were converted figured this rule did not apply if one's mate was not a Christian, but Paul makes it plain in verses 12-14 that a believing mate has no right to divorce an unbelieving husband or wife so long as the unbelieving partner is willing to remain.

Paul does allow one exception to his rules. Notice verse 15: "If the unbelieving depart, let him depart. A brother or a sister is not under bondage in such cases." In other words, in case of desertion, the mate left behind is no longer bound to the marriage; divorce may take place without any guilt attached to the one deserted. I personally think that Paul is assuming the deserter will take up with another partner; therefore, this grounds for divorce is really the same as the one given by Jesus. There can *never* be divorce and remarriage without at least one partner being guilty of adultery in one way or another.

Now we move on to chapters 8, 9, and 10. All three of these chapters deal with one subject, the second question that the Corinthians had asked in their letter to Paul. This question deals with eating food that had been offered to idols. You may find it difficult to understand this question, so allow me to offer a brief explanation. In Paul's day, and even now in many parts of the world, the worship of idols included placing food in front of the idol as a sacrifice. Well, naturally the idol did not consume the food, and it was a shame to waste good food, so the people took the food back, after the prescribed length of time, and ate it themselves. Sometimes such food was sold in the market, and often at a lower price. Often the unconverted served such food at their tables.

You can see, then, how a question would arise about their food. Could a Christian eat such food? If one ate food that had previously been offered to an idol, did that make him guilty of idolatry? The question had come up at Corinth, and evidently some felt one way and some another. So they asked Paul.

Again, time does not permit a detailed treatment of chapters 8–10 in which Paul answers the question. But we do need a summary of the way in which Paul deals with the problem. Even though you and I are not faced with this particular problem, we are faced with similar ones, and we can apply to our problems the principles Paul used.

Specifically, Paul observes that the food has not been harmed by the idol; and therefore, there is technically nothing wrong with eating it. Notice chapter 8, verse 4, for example, in which Paul says, "We know that an idol is nothing." For this reason, Paul advises them, in chapter 10, verse 25: "Whatsoever is sold in the shambles [that is, the market place], that eat, asking no question." Notice also chapter 10, verse 27, where Paul advises that if they go home to eat with an unbeliever, eat "whatsoever is set before you" without asking questions.

But, he continues, there are times and situations and circumstances when the eating of such food *will* cause a problem, and then it will be best to abstain. In chapter 8, for example, Paul mentions the fact that some weaker brethren just cannot rid their minds of the idea that this food is associated with an *idol*, so he warns against offending those brethren. Notice chapter 8, verse 9: "Take heed lest by any means this liberty of yours become a stumblingblock to them that are weak." Now this does not mean, simply, that the weaker brother will not *like* what the other fellow does. The word "offend" means "cause to stumble." So Paul says, in verse 13, that if eating the food will risk causing a Christian brother to stumble into sin, we must abstain from eating.

In chapter 10, Paul gives another caution. He reminds the Corinthians that many Israelites, as he says in verse 5, "were overthrown in the wilderness" and thus did not make it to Canaan. In verse 12 he notes that we, too, must take heed against falling into sin and falling short of Heaven. The point here is that too much exercise of liberty may open the door of our own lives to sin. We must not only watch out for our brethren, but for ourselves.

Another caution appears in chapter 10, verses 16-22. Here, Paul warns against provoking the Lord's jealousy, as you see in 10:22. The point is this: The Lord wants His children's lives and actions to show that they belong to Him, not to the devil and the devil's crowd. One way in which food offered to idols was often eaten was in a feast in the idol's temple as a part of the worship of that idol. Paul notes, in verse 20, that in reality the heathen worship the devil; and therefore, we cannot afford to be identified and associated with such devilish doings. Thus, we cannot eat this food in any circumstances where doubt might be created as to which God we serve!

Finally, Paul offers one more caution in chapter 10, verses 27, 28, when he talks about dining in the home of an unbeliever. As long as the unsaved fellow says nothing about the food he serves, eat without worrying. But if he specifically mentions that the food has been offered to idols, do not eat it. The fact that the sinner mentions the matter shows that *he* is not sure a Christian should eat food offered to idols, and so the Christian must abstain because of the *sinner's* conscience.

And so we see that, even though Paul regarded the food as undefiled and permissible to eat when no problem was created, yet he gives five good reasons for abstaining. A Christian must be concerned about himself, not risking openness to sin. A Christian must be concerned about his identification and associations, not risking God's jealousy. A Christian must be concerned about his brother in Christ, not risking causing him to stumble. A Christian must be concerned about the sinner, not risking a violation of the sinner's conscience. A Christian must be concerned about his service in the gospel, not risking any hindrance to his effectiveness in witnessing to and winning others. This last principle is particularly discussed in chapter 9. Notice there, verse 22, where Paul says: "I am made all things to all men, that I might by all means save some." The mature Christian worker is willing to deny himself and his liberties in order to win men to Christ.

Now let us go to chapter 11. You will recall that I have said that this third major portion of 1 Corinthians deals with three questions the Corinthians asked Paul. We have looked at the first two of these questions. The third one is covered in chapter 11, verses 1-16, and the question concerns whether the women should wear the customary head-covering in public worship. In order to understand this question, you need to realize that all women, in those days, were expected to wear a large veil that covered the head and face out in public. Only their own husbands were to see their unveiled faces. Evidently, some of the Corinthians had figured that their salvation freed them from such a custom.

But Paul insists that they continue to wear the head-covering. In verse 5, for example, you see that he says, a woman praying or prophesying with uncovered head dishonors her head. In verse 13, notice, that he indicates it is "uncomely," which means "improper."

You may wonder whether this teaching of Paul's applies to women in our day. In one way it does not, but in another way it does. Literally, the instruction no longer applies, because the meaning of the veil is not the same in our culture as it was in Paul's. But the *principle* is still valid: Christian women must still conduct themselves in such a manner that their faithfulness and submission to their husbands will not be questioned.

And now we come to the fourth major division of 1 Corinthians, which begins at chapter 11 and extends through the end of chapter 14. This section deals with certain worship disorders that existed at Corinth.

There are, in fact, *two* worship problems dealt with from 11:17 to 14:40. The first of these is taken up in the rest of chapter 11, and the problem concerns the observance of the Lord's Supper. The disorder at the Lord's table was two-fold: For one thing, the Corinthians were allowing their divisions to be brought to this sacred ordinance and were partaking in little groups rather than as one body. For another thing, they were taking communion in connection with a fellowship meal, and some were over-indulging, while others were being left out. Look at verse 18, and you will see Paul's reference to the divisions. Then in verse 21 you will find a reference to the fact that some went hungry while others got drunk. Paul is so horrified at this sacrilegious treatment of the ordinance that he affirms, in verse 20: "This is not to eat the *Lord's* supper!" In order to correct their abuse, Paul reminds them, in verses 23-26 how the Lord Jesus instituted this sacred ordinance. The key is found in verse 26: "Ye do shew the Lord's death."

The other worship disorder at Corinth was an abuse of spiritual gifts. This abuse is corrected in chapters 12, 13, and 14. Obviously, the Corinthians' divisiveness and strife were carried over into this area, too. Some thought their gift was more important than that of others. Many looked down their noses at others who did not possess their gift. Perhaps each faction exalted certain gifts. Clearly, many of them preferred the more spectacular gifts like speaking in tongues.

The first thing Paul does in attacking this problem is to prove the unity of all the spiritual gifts. The Corinthians' sense of competitiveness over the gifts was entirely unwarranted, because the spiritual gifts are all for one ultimate purpose. Paul proves this in chapter 12 by explaining that all spiritual gifts are from the one Holy Spirit, and so it is folly to think that the Spirit competes with Himself. Notice chapter 12, verse 4, which says: "There are diversities of gifts, but the same Spirit." Paul gives further proof by comparing the various spiritual gifts to the different parts of the human body. Notice verse 12: "As the body is one, and hath many members . . . so also is Christ." In verse 15 he mentions the foot; in verse 16 the eye and the ear. Each of these has a different function, but all work together for the one body. Thus, it is with the various individuals in the church; each has his own gift, his own part to play; but all work together in one accord.

Clearly, the main thing the Corinthians lacked was love for one another. So Paul goes on, in that wonderful chapter 13, to say that love is the one absolutely essential ingredient, the spirit in which all the gifts must be exercised. One may be a prophet, speak in tongues, or perform great miracles of faith; but if these gifts are not exercised in love, they profit him nothing.

Finally, in chapter 14, Paul proceeds to explain what he meant in chapter 12, verse 31, when he said: "Covet earnestly the *best* gifts." Which are the best gifts? According to chapter 14, they are the ones that do the most to edify the church. As I pointed out above, the Corinthians evidently preferred gifts like the tongues, but Paul wants them to see that tongues do not do much in the way of edifying Christians. Prophecy on the other hand—and in our day we call this preaching or testifying—does edify one's fellow-believers. Notice verse 26: "Let all things be done unto edifying."

Indeed, Paul does not compliment the gift of tongues very much. In verses 14, 15 he says he prefers to pray in a language he understands. In verse 15, he prefers to sing in a language he understands. In verse 16 he prefers to hear praise in a language he understands. Verse 19 summarizes Paul's opinion quite well: "In the church I had rather speak five words with my understanding . . .than ten thousand words in an unknown tongue."

Time does not permit further treatment of this interesting subject. For now, let me just say that I do not doubt there was, in the apostles' days, a miraculous gift of speaking in foreign languages. Personally, I do not think this gift is still given; but even if it is, we have in this chapter God's own evaluation of the gift. It was not given for the purpose of edifying anyone, but—as is indicated in verses 21, 22—for a sign against the unbelief of Israel, and a testimony that the gospel was for all nations. This is certainly the significance of Pentecost.

Now, we come to the last major part of 1 Corinthians, chapter 15, commonly known as the resurrection chapter. Notice verse 12 with me, and you will see what the problem was: "How say some among you that there is no resurrection of the dead?" Some at Corinth were denying the idea of our bodily resurrection, and verse 35 gives us their reason: "Some man will say, How are the dead raised up? and with what body do they come?" In other words, they could not explain how or what sort of resurrection body could exist, so they denied the idea altogether.

Paul deals with this denial in several ways. First, in verses 1-11, he shows that Christ's resurrection is an essential part of the saving gospel, and that Christ's resurrection was plainly witnessed by many people. Then Paul argues that Christ's resurrection is a guarantee of our own bodily resurrection. See this is verse 20, for example: "Now is Christ risen from the dead, and become the firstfruits of them that slept."

The objection that the Corinthians have offered, that they cannot explain what sort of body the resurrection body will be, is answered by Paul beginning at verse 36. He shows that God has created all sorts of bodies already; why, then, is it incredible that God can make yet another kind of body we do not know about? At least we do know that it will be, as Paul observes in verse 44, a *spiritual* body; and, according to verse 49, it will be in the image and likeness of Christ's glorified body.

The last chapter of 1 Corinthians is more or less a conclusion to the letter. In it Paul mentions several lesser matters not directly related to the major problems at Corinth. In verses 1-4 he urges them to give liberally toward an offering he is collecting for the poorer saints in Jerusalem. In verses 5-12 he speaks of the plans of himself, of Timothy, and of Apollos. In verses 13-16 he offers a few final exhortations. In verses 17, 18 he expresses appreciation for the committee which had come to him. In verses 19-21 we find the final salutations, and in verses 22-24 the benediction. I can think of no better words with which to close this lecture on First Corinthians than the Aramaic word Paul uses in verses 22, "Maranatha." It means, "Our Lord is coming."

A SURVEY OF THE BOOK OF

Second Corinthians

by Dr. Robert Picirilli

I trust you have your Bibles handy. If so, please turn to the Book of 2 Corinthians. I hope you have already listened to the lecture on the other side of this tape, which served to introduce you to Paul's *first* Epistle to the Corinthians. If not, I would strongly suggest that you do, *before* you listen to this one, since considerable background material was explained in that lecture. You will understand 2 Corinthians much better if you already have a good understanding of 1 Corinthians.

You will remember that Paul visited Corinth, for the first time, on the second of his three missionary journeys. He spent a year and one-half in this great city, and his ministry met with considerable success. A large church was established there, before Paul moved on to other places. But by the time Paul got back to Ephesus, on the third missionary journey, he began to hear reports about problems at Corinth. In particular, the church suffered from divisions and strife. There were at least four factions: One group followed Paul; another group said they preferred the leadership of Apollos; still another group followed Simon Peter; and yet others said they followed *no* human being, but Jesus only. Paul had written First Corinthians in order to try to deal with the problems he had heard about, as well as to answer some questions which had been raised in a letter from the Corinthians.

By the time 2 Corinthians was written, a year had probably passed since the writing of First Corinthians. Paul was still in the city of Ephesus, on the third missionary journey. But many things had happened between the writing of 1 and 2 Corinthians. In order for us to understand 2 Corinthians better, it is necessary that we spend a few minutes discussing some of the things that happened in Paul's relationship with the Corinthian Christians after 1 Corinthians was written. There were, in fact, *two* very important things that happened between 1 and 2 Corinthians. The *first* of these was a visit made by Paul to Corinth. This visit is not mentioned in the Book of Acts, but there is no doubt Paul made such a visit. You will remember that Paul had only visited Corinth *once* when he wrote 1 Corinthians. But when he wrote 2 Corinthians, he mentioned that he was about to visit them for the *third* time. Obviously, then, Paul must have paid Corinth a visit between these two epistles. Turn with me to 2 Corinthians, chapter 12, verse 14. Here Paul says, "Behold, the *third* time I am ready to come to you." Look also at chapter 13, verse 1, where Paul says: "This is the *third* time I am coming to you." As I have said, then, Paul's second visit to Corinth came between 1 and 2 Corinthians. Turn to 2 Corinthians, chapter 1, verse 15. In this verse Paul says: "And in this confidence I was minded to come unto you before, that ye might have a *second* benefit." Here, you see, Paul is referring to this second visit he had made to Corinth.

Now, the *second* thing of importance that took place between the writing of 1 and 2 Corinthians was the writing of another letter by Paul. This letter no longer exists, but we know one thing it said. In that letter Paul told the Corinthians he was never coming back to visit them again under the grievous circumstances of his latest visit. If you want to know how I know Paul told the Corinthians this in a letter, turn to 2 Corinthians, chapter 2, verse 1. Paul says, "I determined this . . . that I would not come again to you in heaviness." Then in verse 3, Paul says, "I wrote this same unto you."

It is clear, then, that Paul is referring to a letter we do not possess, because there is nothing like this in 1 Corinthians. The letter Paul wrote between 1 and 2 Corinthians must have been written under a burdened heart. Notice 2 Corinthians, chapter 2, verse 4, where Paul says: "Out of much affliction and anguish of heart I wrote unto you with many tears." Now turn to 2 Corinthians, chapter 7, and you will see this same letter referred to again. In verse 8, Paul says, "Though I made you sorry with a letter, I do not repent, though I did repent."

From reading these verses, and the rest of 2 Corinthians, we get the feeling that something very serious had happened with respect to Paul's relationship with the Corinthians. Putting it all together, and reading a little between the lines, we come to a reasonably clear understanding of what happened. Paul received word that, even in spite of his first epistle, the Corinthian church problems had not been settled. Therefore, he must have decided to make a brief and unannounced visit to the Corinthians. He probably sailed directly across the Aegean gulf from Ephesus to Corinth. Evidently, however, the opposition to Paul was so strong that his efforts at making peace were sternly rebuffed. It is clear that there was one individual at Corinth who served as the leader of the opposition to Paul. Evidently, this man personally rebuked Paul and insulted him. As a result, Paul had to leave Corinth under a grievous burden. He returned to Ephesus and wrote the letter that I have referred to previously. This letter is often called the severe letter, because Paul obviously was very bold and frank concerning the Corinthians' problem.

Paul sent the letter to the Corinthians by his helper, Titus, and instructed Titus what route to follow in returning to him. When the time began to draw near for Titus to return and report whether the letter had been successful, Paul became so impatient that he would not wait at Ephesus for Titus to come back. Instead, he left Ephesus and went along the usual route to Troas. He did not find Titus at Troas; and even though there was a marvelous opportunity for him to preach there, he was so eager to hear of the results of the severe letter, that he went on into Macedonia seeking for Titus. Turn with me to 2 Corinthians, chapter 2, verses 12, 13, and there you will see these things stated. Paul says: "Furthermore, when I came to Troas to preach Christ's gospel, and a door was opened unto me of the Lord, I had no rest in my spirit, because I found not Titus my brother: but taking my leave of them, I went from thence into Macedonia."

When Paul arrived in Macedonia, he located Titus and was greatly relieved to learn that most of the Corinthian church had repented and were now eager for Paul to come back. You will see this indicated in chapter 7 of 2 Corinthians. Notice chapter 7, verse 5: "When we were come into Macedonia, our flesh had no rest"; then look at verses 6, 7: "Nevertheless God, that comforteth those that are cast down, comforted us by the coming of Titus; And not by his coming only but by the consolation wherewith he was comforted in you, when he told us your earnest desire, your mourning, your fervent mind toward me; so that I rejoiced the more." And in verses 8, 9 Paul observes specifically that his severe letter had brought them to repentance. And yet, because there was still a small group at Corinth who had not repented and were not yet reconciled to Paul, Paul decided to write one more letter before he personally went to Corinth again. That letter is our 2 Corinthians.

We may say, then, that Paul's purposes in writing 2 Corinthians are four. First, he wrote to express his rejoicing that the majority of the Corinthians had repented of their sinful resistance and were ready to follow his leadership again. You cannot read 2 Corinthians without realizing that Paul had been under a terrific burden about Corinth, and that Titus's happy report had greatly relieved him. Second, Paul wrote in order to urge the unrepentant minority to lay down their antagonism toward him and prepare to receive him when he would come again soon. Third, Paul was concerned about the disciples which the church at Corinth had administered to the leader of the opposition. As we shall see later, Paul felt that the discipline was sufficient and should now stop; and he wrote to tell them this. Paul's fourth purpose for writing 2 Corinthians concerned the collection which he was in the process of taking up, for the poverty-stricken saints in Jerusalem. He wanted the Corinthians to participate liberally in this collection, and he urged them to do this in chapters 8, 9.

And now, with your Bibles open, let us survey the Book of 2 Corinthians. In chapter 1, the first 7 verses serve as an introduction to the book. In verses 1, 2 you will see the same opening that Paul uses in most of his letters. He identifies himself, as well as the ones to whom he is writing; and he pronounces upon them the familiar blessing: "Grace be to you and peace from God our Father, and from the Lord Jesus Christ." But look more closely at verses 3-7; can you tell what was especially on Paul's mind? Well, if you will glance over these verses, you will notice that there is *one* word that keeps appearing over and over. Look in verse 3: The word is "comfort." In verse 4, note the words "comforteth," "comfort," and "comforted." In verse 5, the word is "consolation." In verse 6, the word "consolation" occurs twice and "comforted" once. Again in verse 7, you see the word "consolation." It is clear, is it not? Paul is praising God for the comfort and consolation which the Lord has brought to his soul. He had been through a period of real anxiety and doubt because of the situation at Corinth. The report of Titus about their repentance brought to him a new peace and joy in the ministry. "The God of all comfort" proved Himself again!

Now, at the start of the main content of this epistle, let us take a few minutes to glance quickly through it. I want you to get a bird's-eye view of what we will find in 2 Corinthians, and what the main divisions are. If you want to jot down these main outline points, you may do so. Actually, there are four main sections in 2 Corinthians. In the first section, from 1:8 to 2:13, Paul explains the preceding events. I have already read several of these verses to you, and you will recall that Paul explains about his visit and letter. The second major portion of 2 Corinthians begins at 2:14 and goes through 7:16. This section can be called "The Glory of the Ministry." You will notice, in 2:14, that Paul begins this section by saying, "Now thanks be unto God." Notice in chapter 4, verse 5, Paul says, "We preach not ourselves, but Christ Jesus." In chapter 5, verse 18, Paul rejoices that God has given him "the ministry of reconciliation." If Paul had been down in the dumps awhile, the repentance of Corinth has put him on cloud nine; he is glad to be a preacher of the gospel. The third section of 2 Corinthians covers chapters 8, 9, and the subject is the collection to which I have already referred. Paul wants to tell the Corinthians, as he put it in chapter 9, verse 7: "God loveth a cheerful giver." The fourth and final part of 2 Corinthians covers the last four chapters, 10-13; and in this part, Paul defends himself against the accusations of the minority who still rejected his leadership. This is one of the most personal sections in all of Paul's letters.

And now, if you have turned through 2 Corinthians with me, for this bird's-eye view, turn back to chapter 1, and let us look more closely at each one of these four main sections. As I have already pointed out, the first section covers the material from 1:8 to 2:13.

In this section Paul explains to the Corinthians some of the things that have just previously taken place. There are at least five things which Paul undertakes to explain in this section. Number one: He explains the period of suffering which he has just undergone in Asia. In chapter 1, verse 8, Paul says: "We would not, brethren, have you ignorant of our trouble which came to us in Asia, that we were pressed out of measure, above strength, insomuch that we despaired even of life." We do not know what particular type of suffering Paul had been exposed to, but we do know, according to verse 10, that the Lord delivered Paul from death.

Number two: Paul explains his change of plans. In chapter 1, verse 15, he mentions the plan he had made to come to Corinth for a second benefit. Then, in verse 16, he says that he had planned to leave them, go into Macedonia, and then come again from Macedonia back to the Corinthians. Obviously, Paul has not done this, and he recognizes that they will be wondering why. So he explains, in verse 23, that he has not come back to Corinth, as originally planned, because he had determined in his soul that he wanted to spare the Corinthians. And in chapter 2, verse 1, he says, "I determined this with myself, that I would not come again to you in heaviness." He had made up his mind he would not go back to Corinth until the situation was different.

Number three: Paul explains the severe letter he had written to them. In chapter 2, as I have already pointed out to you, Paul mentions this letter. Notice verse 4 with me. Paul says, "Out of much affliction and anguish of heart I wrote unto you with many tears; not that ye should be grieved, but that ye might know the love which I have more abundantly unto you." Paul wants the Corinthians to understand that he had not written the severe letter just to rebuke them, but because he wanted them to repent.

Number four: Paul explains concerning the punishment of the person who had offended him. Obviously, Titus had reported to Paul that, when the Corinthians had repented, they had determined to discipline the man who had led the opposition to Paul. So Paul says, in 2 Corinthians, chapter 2, verses 6, 7: "Sufficient to such a man is this punishment, which was inflicted of many. So that contrariwise ye ought rather to forgive him, and comfort him, lest perhaps such a one should be swallowed up with overmuch sorrow." In verse 10, he adds: "To whom ye forgive any thing, I forgive also."

Number five: Paul explains the turmoil that had existed in his soul, when he had left Ephesus searching for Titus, eager to find out the results of the letter which he had sent to Corinth. In 2:13 Paul says, "I had no rest in my spirit, because I found not Titus my brother: but taking my leave of them [that is them at Troas], I went from thence into Macedonia." This brings the first section of 2 Corinthians to a close.

The second major portion of this letter begins, as I have already indicated, at chapter 2, verse 14, and extends on to chapter 7, verse 16. This lengthy section is often called, "The Glory of the Ministry." Paul had been through deep grief because of the Corinthian situation, but the report of Titus filled his heart with rejoicing. He is glad to be a preacher of the gospel, and he proceeds in this section to talk about the ministry and service of the Lord Jesus Christ in which he is engaged. This is one of the finest treatments of the ministry to be found anywhere.

I want to sub-divide this section into six parts, so that I can share it with you better. In these six parts, Paul speaks first about the *triumphs* of the ministry; second, about the *superiority* of the ministry; third, about the *boldness* of the ministry; fourth, about the *sufferings* of the ministry; fifth, about the *motives* of the ministry; and sixth, about the *appeals* of the ministry. Let us look at each one of these briefly in turn.

The first part of this section on the glory of the ministry is chapter 2, verses 14-17. Here, Paul speaks about the triumph he experiences as a minister of the Lord Jesus Christ. Look at verse 14. Paul says, "Now thanks be unto God, which always causeth us to triumph in Christ, and maketh manifest the saviour of his knowledge by us in every place." Paul understood that the minister of the gospel does not win everybody he contacts to Christ, but he also understood that the preacher of the gospel is always on the winning side.

The second part of this section on the glory of the ministry is chapter 3, verses 1-11, and here Paul speaks about the superiority of the ministry of the gospel. In particular, Paul compares the service of the Lord in *Old* Testament times with the service of the Lord in New Testament times. There is *quite* a difference! Follow along with me in verses 6-11 of chapter 3. In verse 6, the Old Testament is the *letter*, while the New Testament is the *spirit*. Also in verse 6, the Old Testament *kills*, while the New Testament *gives life*. In verse 9, the Old Testament brings condemnation, whereas the New Testament ministry brings a person to righteousness. In verse 11, notice that the Old Testament was done away—that is, was *temporary*—whereas the New Testament remaineth—in other words, is *permanent*. You see, then, that Paul regarded it a glorious thing to be a minister of the gospel. Oh, it was glorious for a man like Moses to minister the Law. Paul points this out in verse 7. But, as he says in verse 8, the ministry of the gospel is far more glorious than the ministry of the Law.

Now, the third part of this wonderful section on the glory of the ministry begins at chapter 3, verse 12, and extends through chapter 4, verse 6. This part concerns the *boldness* of the minister of the gospel. Look at chapter 3, verse 12, for example, and you see that Paul bases this boldness on the superiority that he has just discussed in the previous verses. He says this: "Seeing then that we have such hope, we use great plainness [or boldness] of speech." In verse 17, Paul says, "Where the Spirit of the Lord is there is liberty." In chapter 4, verse 2, Paul says, "But have renounced the hidden things of dishonesty, not walking in craftiness, nor handling the word of God deceitfully; but by manifestation of the truth commending ourselves to every man's conscience in the sight of God." The preacher of the gospel is bold because he knows he is delivering the *truth!*

But now to the fourth part of this section, which begins at chapter 4, verse 7, and extends through chapter 5, verse 8. This section deals with the *suffering* of the minister, and the section is an excellent help for us in understanding the problem of human suffering. Perhaps the best way to deal with this section is to present it in question and answer form. The first question would be, "Why is the preacher of the gospel still subject to suffering?" Paul answers this question in verse 7. He says, "We have this treasure [that is the gospel ministry] in earthen vessels." In other words, the bodies in which we live are still bodies of clay; and, as imperfect vessels, we are subject to suffering.

The next question would be this: "Why are we still left with earthen vessels?" The answer to this question is also given in verse 7: "That the excellency of the power may be of God, and not of us." God uses weak human instruments to accomplish His work so that *He* will get the glory and credit for that which is accomplished.

A third question about suffering would be this: "What *kind* of suffering must we endure?" The answer to this question is found in chapter 4, verses 8-12. Paul says in verses 8, 9, "We are troubled on every side, yet not distressed; we are perplexed, but not in despair; Persecuted, but not forsaken; cast down, but not destroyed." In other words, the kind of suffering a preacher of the gospel is subject to is a suffering that is still mingled with hope.

That raises the next question: "What is the *source* of this hope which the servant of the Lord has in the midst of his suffering?" The answer to this question is found beginning in chapter 4, verse 14, and is a two-fold answer. First of all, Paul says in verse 14: "Knowing that he which raised up the Lord Jesus shall raise up us also by Jesus." We have hope because of the promise of the resurrection of our bodies. The second basis for hope in the midst of our suffering is found in what Paul says in chapter 5. We not only have promise of resurrection, but we have promise of a new body! Look at verse 1 of chapter 5: "We know that if our earthly house of this tabernacle were dissolved, we have a building of God, an house not made with hands, eternal in the heavens."

And now we come to what may be the most important part of

this entire section on the glory of the ministry. This part begins in chapter 5 and runs from verses 9 through 19. It concerns the *motives* of the minister. Why does a preacher serve God? Indeed, why does anyone serve God? There are three reasons Paul lists in this section. Notice with me chapter 5, verses 9, 10, and you will see the first reason. Paul says: "We labour, that, whether present or absent, we may be accepted of him. For we must all appear before the judgment seat of Christ; that every one may receive the things done in his body." One motive for serving God is to be found in the fact that we are going to have to stand before Christ and give an account of our service. The second motive is found in chapter 5, verse 11. Paul says: "Knowing therefore the terror of the Lord, we persuade men." Those who are unsaved are going to have to face the terrible judgment of the Lord. Our hearts should be moved by compassion to persuade unsaved men to turn to God and avoid this awful terror of the final judgment. The third motive for serving the Lord is perhaps the most important one of all, and is found in verse 14 where Paul says: "The love of Christ constraineth us." Some people wrongly interpret that phrase. The love of Christ, in this verse, does not mean our love for Christ. It means the love Christ showed us when He died for us. You will notice that verse 14 refers to Christ's death, and verse 15 says that those for whom He died "should not henceforth live unto themselves, but unto him which died for them." The judgment seat of Christ, the terror of the Lord on the unsaved, and the great love of our Savior in dying for us on the Cross; these things should motivate us to serve the Lord. They are the things that motivated Paul.

Now, the final sub-division of this lengthy section on the glory of the ministry begins at chapter 5, verse 20, and continues on through the end of chapter 7. This part concerns the *appeals* which the minister must make in his dealing with men. What is the preacher of the gospel trying to get men to do? There are several things. First, the preacher tries to get men to be reconciled to God: that is, to be saved. In chapter 5, verse 20, this appeal is stated. Paul says: "We are ambassadors for Christ, as though God did beseech you by us: we pray you in Christ's stead, be ye reconciled to God." The second appeal the preacher of the gospel must make to people comes after the individual has been converted. This appeal is found in chapter 6, verse 1: "We then, as workers together with him, beseech you also that ye receive not the grace of God in vain." To receive the grace of God in vain means to turn back from God after one has been saved. So, the preacher of the gospel must urge his converts to be careful, and go on, and make progress in the grace of God, rather than to let their experience become empty and vain. The third appeal which the preacher of the gospel must make, to those with whom he deals, is the appeal for separation. This appeal is found in chapter 6, beginning at verse 14, and continuing on through chapter 7, verse 1.

In particular, notice verse 14 of chapter 6: "Be ye not unequally yoked together with unbelievers." And note verse 17: "Wherefore come out from among them, and be ye separate, saith the Lord." The lives of God's children are supposed to be different from the lives of the unsaved. The preacher of the gospel must work diligently to get his converts to lead clean and separated lives. The final appeal which Paul makes to the Corinthians is found in chapter 7, verse 2, where he says simply: "Receive us; we have wronged no man." This appeal reflects the fact that many of the Corinthians had resisted Paul. And, although most of the Corinthians had repented, yet there was at least one group holding out. Paul urges all of his people at Corinth to follow him, to receive him as one who loves them and as one whose very life is wrapped up in their own success and happiness. In chapter 7, verse 3, Paul says: "Ye are in our hearts to die and live with you." With these four appeals the section on the glory of the ministry closes.

Now, we move on to the third major section of 2 Corinthians. This particular section covers all of chapters 8, 9 and deals with one very specific subject. That subject is the collection which Paul was receiving for the poverty-stricken believers in Jerusalem. These chapters provide an interesting insight into Paul's attitude toward the matter of liberal giving. Paul urges the folks at Corinth to give liberally. Indeed, these chapters help us understand some of the reasons Christians ought always to give liberally in response to the needs of their brethren.

Paul begins his words to the Corinthians by telling them how liberally the folks up in Macedonia have given. Notice in chapter 8, verse 2, where Paul observes that the Macedonians have "abounded into the riches of their liberality." In verse 3 he says the Macedonians have given *beyond* their ability! And in verse 5 he tells us exactly why: because they "first gave their own selves to the Lord." People will always give liberally to others, when they have first given themselves to the Lord. Paul expects the liberal example of the Macedonians to serve as an incentive for the Corinthians.

Starting in verse 7, Paul mentions several things which ought to encourage the Corinthians to give. For one thing, the Lord has blessed them so bountifully with other things. In verse 7, notice: "As ye abound in every thing, in faith, and utterance, and knowledge, and in all diligence, and in your love to us, see that ye abound in this grace also." In verse 9, Paul gives another challenge, the example of the Lord Jesus Christ. Even though He was rich, He became poor that we through His poverty might be rich. If the Lord Jesus Christ gave everything, we ought to be able to give a little. Then there is another challenge in verse 11: Paul tells them they need to live up to the *promises* they have made. Paul does not count *promises;* it is what folks *do* that counts.

In verses 13, 14 of chapter 8, Paul gives still another reason the

Corinthians ought to give liberally. He says, "I mean not that other men be eased, and ye burdened: But by an equality, that now at this time your abundance may be a supply for their want." In other words, the saints in Jerusalem were in need. The Corinthians had the means whereby some of these needs could be fulfilled. Why should they not give liberally?

Now look in chapter 9, and you will find more things Paul used as means by which to prod the Corinthians to give. In verse 2 of chapter 9 Paul tells the Corinthians that he has been boasting about them to the folks up in Macedonia. And in verse 4 he says he would certainly be ashamed and embarrassed if the folks of Macedonia came with him to Corinth and found the Corinthians had not lived up to his boasting. Then look down in verse 6: Paul says, "He which soweth sparingly shall reap also sparingly; and he which soweth bountifully shall reap also bountifully." In other words, God will bless those who give liberally. Then, another reason for liberal giving is found in verse 12 of chapter 9. Paul says, "The administration of this service not only supplieth the want of the saints, but is abundant also by many thanksgivings unto God." What Paul means is that the Corinthians can expect that those who receive their liberality will give great thanksgiving and praise to God for them. And in verse 14 Paul says the folks in Jerusalem who receive these offerings will themselves offer prayers to God on behalf of those who have given. It is interesting the way Paul closes this section about liberal giving, by reminding us in chapter 9, verse 15, of God's unspeakable gift of the Lord Jesus Christ. Having been reminded of that, how can we consider holding back ourselves and our goods from the needs of others?

And now we come to the fourth and final major division of the letter called 2 Corinthians. This division begins in chapter 10, and continues on through chapter 13, verse 10. This section is usually called "Paul's Defense." Most of the rest of this letter was written because the majority of the Corinthians had repented concerning their resistance to the leadership of Paul. But, as I have already pointed out, some of the Corinthians did *not* repent, and still had accusations to offer against Paul, and objections to following his leadership. These last four chapters, 10—13, are written by Paul to defend himself against these accusations.

In chapter 10, verses 1-12, Paul answers the main criticism against him. It is quite clear that the Corinthians who resisted Paul had accused him of being two-faced. They said that when he was present with them in person, he was ever so meek and mild; but when he was away writing to them, he wrote very stern and powerful letters. They said he was not consistent. Notice that Paul quotes their criticism in chapter 10, verse 1: "Now I Paul myself beseech you by the meekness and gentleness of Christ, who in presence am base among you, but being absent am bold toward you." That is what some Corinthians had accused him of. This same accusation is also quoted by Paul in verse 10: "His letters, say they, are weighty and powerful; but his bodily presence is weak, and his speech contemptible." Evidently, this minority would have accepted the leadership of Paul if he had been as powerful and authoritative when he was present, as he was in the letters he wrote.

Paul's answer for their criticism is found in chapter 10, verse 4: "The weapons of our warfare are not carnal." Paul deliberately refrained from being domineering; he deliberately followed meekness, because he depended on the power of the Spirit of God more than on the power of his own personality. As Paul implies in verse 7, the stubborn ones at Corinth were judging too much by outward appearance.

Then, beginning at verse 13 of chapter 10, and going on through chapter 12, verse 18, Paul opens his heart to these rebellious Corinthians, and speaks about his personal experiences in the ministry. As you will notice in chapter 10, verse 13, he calls this boasting. But he is really boasting about what Christ has done for and through him, not about any personal accomplishments. Briefly, let me point out to you some of the things Paul mentions about himself and his ministry. In 10:14, notice how he refers to the fact that he had reached out with the gospel. Indeed, he was the one who had preached Christ to the Corinthians. In chapter 11, verse 7, Paul mentions the fact that he had preached the gospel to them without cost. As he says in verse 9: "When I was present with you, and wanted, I was chargeable to no man."

Then notice chapter 11, verses 23-27. Here, Paul tells us much about his sufferings as a missionary preacher: in labors, in stripes, in prisons . . . five times I received 40 stripes . . . three times beaten with rods, once stoned, three times shipwrecked . . . in journeyings, in all sorts of perils . . . weary, in pain, hungry, thirsty, cold, and without proper clothing. If the rebellious Corinthians had any heart at all, they must have been pricked in conscience by these words, to recall how much Paul had suffered for the likes of them. And in verse 28 of this same chapter 11, Paul mentions an inward burden that must be added to all these external sufferings, "the care of all the churches." The Corinthians had added a great deal to that burden.

In chapter 12, Paul mentions some other personal items. For one thing, he had received some unusual revelations and visions from the Lord. In verse 2, he speaks of one who was "caught up to the third heaven." In verse 4, he says this one "heard unspeakable words, which it is not lawful for a man to utter." It may not sound like it, but Paul is definitely talking about himself. This is proved by the next thing Paul mentions about himself in 12:7: "Lest I should be exalted above measure through the abundance of the revelations, there was given to me a thorn in the flesh, the messenger of Satan to buffet me." We do not know what this physical malady was, but it was clearly God's will for Paul to experience this, and God did not deliver Paul. God used Paul in spite of it.

Paul concludes this final section, in defense of himself, with a warning to the Corinthians. Notice chapter 13, verse 1: "This is the third time I am coming to you." Now notice verse 2, the latter part: "If I come again, I will not spare." Paul wants even the reluctant minority to repent so that he will not have to use the rod of discipline.

The letter has only a brief conclusion, chapter 13, verses 11-14. Paul has poured out his heart, and there is not much more to say. Anyway, he expects to see them soon. Meanwhile, he leaves them in the care of the grace of the Lord Jesus, the love of God, and the fellowship of the Holy Spirit. Nor can I think of any better benediction with which to leave you.

A SURVEY OF THE BOOK OF

Galatians

by Leroy Forlines

In the Book of Galatians, one sees the earnestness and deep concern of Paul for the Galatian Christians. In his absence some false teachers had zealously sought to get them to submit to circumcision and add law-keeping to their faith in Christ. It appears that they did everything possible to destroy the confidence of the people in Paul and the gospel of justification by faith alone which he preached. This called for a letter from Paul in which he spared no effort in establishing the people's confidence in his independent authority as an apostle and their confidence in the gospel he preached.

The occasion which called for the writing of this epistle gave rise to a highly developed logical defense of: (1) Paul's independent authority as an apostle; (2) the fact that justification is by faith apart from works; and (3) the fact that the New Covenant believer is delivered from the Old Covenant Law as an approach to a God-directed life.

The strong teaching of this epistle on justification by faith apart from works helped shape Martin Luther's conviction on this subject. Thus, the Book of Galatians became a powerful influence in bringing about the Protestant Reformation. To this day it has remained a powerful weapon against the doctrine of justification by works.

Galatia was used in two ways: (1) It was used geographically of the area where the Gauls had settled in the third century B.C. (2) It was used politically of the Roman province of Galatia. The political province included the area settled by the Gauls in addition to an area to the south which the Romans added in 25 B.C. The cities of Antioch, Iconium, Lystra, and Derbe were located in the southern part which was added by the Romans.

Many have advocated the theory that Paul was writing to churches in the North Galatia area that was settled by the Gauls. The position that is more commonly held now, however, is that Paul was writing to the churches in the South Galatia area. This fits in with the fact that we know that Paul established churches in Antioch, Iconium, Lystra, and Derbe on his first missionary journey. We are not positive that Paul established any churches in the North Galatia area.

It is impossible to settle with certainty the time of the writing of this epistle. It is obvious that it would have been written sometime after the first missionary journey, but how much later is difficult to decide. Part of the problem centers around the question of which visit to Jerusalem Paul referred to in 2:1-10. Some are of the opinion that the reference is to a visit made by Paul and Barnabas to take relief to the brethren in Judea mentioned in Acts 11:30.

Others are of the opinion that the reference is to the Jerusalem Council of Acts 15 where the question of the Gentiles' responsibility to the Mosaic Law was settled. If the reference was to the Acts 11:30 visit, Galatians would have most likely been written after the first missionary journey but before the Jerusalem Council. If the reference is to the Jerusalem Council, it is obvious that Galatians would have been written after the Jerusalem Council; but it is difficult to decide just how much later it would have been written. Opinions vary from soon after the Council to a date sometime on Paul's third missionary journey.

Studies on the destination and date of the epistle are interesting, but it is not necessary to arrive at a definite conclusion before one can get the basic message of the book. This is made clear in the book by the argument Paul develops.

We do not know as much about the error of the false teachers referred to as we would like to know. All we know is what we can gather from the answers that Paul gives to their criticisms of him and his doctrine. However, this is adequate for us to see the danger of having a false view of works and to see the importance of developing a true doctrine of justification by faith apart from works and a true doctrine of Christian liberty.

In our study of the contents of the book, we will use the following outline: I. Greeting (1:1-5); II. The Occasion of the Epistle (1:6-9); III. Paul's Independent Authority (1:10—2:21); IV. Justification By Faith Defended (3:1-18); V. The Inferiority of the Covenant of Law and the Superiority of the New Covenant (3:19—4:31); VI. Practical Exhortations (5:1—6:18).

Let us now turn to a study of the book. In 1:1-5 Paul greets the Galatian Christians.

At the very beginning of this letter Paul declares that he owes his apostleship not to man but to God. He also sends greetings from those who were with him at the time he was writing.

In verse 3 he wished God's presence and blessings to be with them. The thought is like it is when we say to someone: "May God's richest blessing be upon you."

At the very beginning, he makes it clear that he believes in Jesus Christ and His sacrificial death for our sins (verse 4).

In 1:6-9 Paul hastens to the purpose of his writing. False teachers had come in and were seeking to lead them away from the gospel. These teachers claimed to be teaching a different gospel. Paul said that what they were preaching was not really a gospel but was a perversion of the gospel.

In no uncertain terms Paul made it clear that they were not to follow these teachers. Instead, they were to let them be accursed.

In the remaining part of this letter, Paul seeks to establish the Galatian Christians to keep them from being led astray by these false teachers.

It seems apparent from the epistle that the false teachers had, as a means of turning the people from Paul, tried to undermine the people's confidence in Paul's authority which, of course, would destroy their faith in his gospel. This is evidenced by the fact that Paul goes into such an elaborate proof in 1:10—2:21 of his independence of other apostles in the receiving of his gospel which he says came to him by revelation.

In verses 11, 12 Paul emphatically states that his gospel is not after man; (that is, it was not a human production), it was not taught to him by someone else, but it was revealed to him from Jesus Christ. Its authority rests on the fact that it came from the very author of salvation.

Having made such a claim he proceeds to substantiate his claim with evidence. His first point is that prior to his conversion he was a zealous devotee of the Jewish religion. He was not sympathetic at all to the Christian gospel; therefore, he could not have been taught it by Christians at that time (verses 13, 14).

His next point is that there was no consultation with others immediately following his conversion (verses 15, 16). In fact, three years elapsed before he had personal contact with any of the apostles. Even on this occasion he stayed only fifteen days and saw only Peter and James (verses 17-19). He further adds that for another period of time he was away from Judea (verses 21-24).

Up to this point Paul has shown that his life before his conversion, and the very limited contacts with the apostles following it for several years, are evidence of the fact that circumstances made it impossible for him to have received his gospel from the other apostles.

His next step in proving his independent authority is to point out that in a contact with the apostles about this very question of circumcision, instead of his being there as a learner, he was an active spokesman defending his own position (2:1-10).

As has already been mentioned, there is some debate over whether this passage refers to the trip to Jerusalem mentioned in Acts 11:30 or to the Jerusalem Council spoken of in Acts 15. It seems more likely that it was the Jerusalem Council since he implies in verses 2-5 that the purpose of his going to Jerusalem was in connection with the matter of circumcision. The one in Acts 11:30 was to take relief to the brethren in Judea. The Jerusalem Council took place between Paul's first and second missionary journeys. This would very well fit the case in Galatians 2 since Barnabas accompanied him, and verse 2 implies that Paul had already done some of his work prior to this trip. The work referred to was probably his first missionary journey.

As evidence of his independence on this occasion Paul mentions how he succeeded in keeping them from circumcising Titus (verses 3, 4). Also, he won the recognition from Peter, James, and John that the gospel of the uncircumcision had been committed by God to him.

Paul concludes this part of his argument by pointing out that on one occasion, which involved the very question of the Gentiles' relationship to the Law, he rebuked Peter to his face for an act of hypocrisy. This hypocrisy involved a refusal to eat with the Gentiles which was, by example, telling the Gentiles that they must take up the Jewish way of living prescribed by the Law. The fact that Paul withstood Peter makes it clear that he was neither dependent upon him nor inferior to him.

In verses 15, 16 Paul introduces as an emphatic fact what he will defend later in the epistle: Justification is by faith in Jesus Christ, not by works of the Law.

In verses 19, 20, Paul describes his own relationship to the Law as having died to the Law. This death was accomplished by identification with Christ in His death. Christ's death paid the penalty of the Law for sin. This death was also Paul's death. Therefore, the penal claims of the Law has been settled, and the Law had no further claims on Paul. Not only did he share in the death of Christ but also in the life of Christ. In Christ he has new life. As a concluding statement for this section Paul points out that if righteousness were through Law, Christ died without a cause. There would have been no justifiable reason for Christ to have died if a person could have been made righteous through Law-keeping.

Paul now addresses the Galatians directly and takes up the most elaborate defense of justification by faith apart from works to be found in the New Testament (3:1-18).

Paul's first approach is to present some very thought-provoking questions which were to be answered by the Galatians. The implied answer was to direct them to see the fallacy of the position of the false teachers. Not only were these questions thought-provoking, they were jolting as well.

These questions were centered around their relationship to the Holy Spirit. Was it in connection with Law or faith that they received the Holy Spirit? Will they finish in the energy of the flesh (as suggested by circumcision and law-keeping) what was begun in the energy of the Spirit? Were the miracles worked by the Holy Spirit worked in connection with one who relied on works of the Law or on faith (verses 1-4)?

Having arrested their attention by questions he now proceeds to argue for justification by faith alone. This he does by calling attention to the example of Abraham and the covenant God made with him. The example of Abraham was that he "believed God, and it was accounted to him for righteousness" (verse 6).

It is important for us to see why Paul is referring back to Abraham. Abraham was the father of the nation of Israel. The call of Abraham by God and the covenant that God made with Abraham marks a major point in the history of redemption. Up to this point the distinctions that we now know as Jew and Gentile did not exist. In the formal sense, Israel came into existence as a nation at Mount Sinai with the giving of the Law which served as its national laws. The roots of the nation go back to Abraham.

God called a special nation into existence through Abraham. This nation came to be known as Israel. It was through this nation that God revealed Himself, His plan, and gave to the world the Redeemer. It was with this nation that God made His redemptive covenants (see Romans 9:5).

The word "Gentiles" means nations. Israel was *the nation.* Israel was the nation with whom God had a covenant relationship. All other nations were outside this covenant relationship (see Ephesians 2:12). Israel, when true to its calling, worshiped the true God. The other nations worshiped false gods.

Abraham was important not only because he was the father of the nation of Israel but also because the basic redemptive covenant was made with him and his seed. In the Abrahamic Covenant the promise of everlasting life is implied when God promised the everlasting possession of the land to Abraham and his seed (Genesis 13:14, 15; 17:8). This promise was to find ultimate fulfillment in the resurrection of the body and everlasting life. The remaining part of the Biblical story of redemption is dealing with this promise, the enlargement of this promise, and the fulfillment of this promise through Jesus Christ and the redeemed.

It was important for Paul to go back to Abraham because the original covenant with the seed of Abraham was made with Abraham. It was important to observe that the original condition for righteousness, so as to be right with God, was faith. Paul refers to the statement of this fact in Genesis 15:6. To be right with God by faith makes one an heir of the promise of everlasting life found in God's covenant with Abraham. Having nailed this down, Paul will develop the proof of the fact that being righteous on the condition of faith has not and cannot be changed.

In verses 10-13, he points out that to be under the works of the

Law is to be under the curse of the Law which makes it impossible to be justified by Law. The ways of Law and faith exclude each other. It is either one or the other. The Scripture settles the question in favor of faith. This redemption from the curse of the Law has been brought about by Christ who took the curse upon Himself when He died on the cross. In doing so He paid the penalty for man's sins.

Since the redemptive covenant was made with Abraham and his seed, a very important question is: What about the Gentiles? God had designed that in Jesus Christ the blessing of Abraham which involved everlasting life might come to the Gentiles as well as to the Jews (verse 14). The manner in which this was done will be shown as Paul continues to develop his argument.

Having connected the redemptive work of Christ with the fulfillment of the covenant of God to Abraham, Paul turns to the nature of that covenant (verses 17, 18). Sometimes the word testament is used instead of covenant. This is the case when our Bible is spoken of as Old and New Testaments. The Old Testament is a reference to the Covenant of Law that was made with Israel at Mount Sinai. It is used as the name of the first 39 books of our Bible since almost all of them were written while the Covenant of Law (or Mosaic Law) was in force. The New Testament is the New Covenant that was established by Christ. The Old Covenant is called Old because it is set aside by the New Covenant. The New Covenant is called New because it sets aside the Covenant of Law. The last 27 books of our Bible are called the New Testament because the events and writings were in connection with the introduction, establishment, and living under the New Covenant. Most prefer the word *covenant* to the word *testament*. Covenant is the term that we will use in this study.

What Paul says about the nature of a covenant finds no parallel in our society. We have contracts which resemble covenants in many respects, but the covenant of which Paul spoke was irrevocable and could not be added to. This was the nature of a covenant in the society of which Paul spoke. It was true he says even of human covenants. By the consent of both parties our contracts can be changed. It is not so with the covenant of which Paul spoke.

The redemptive covenant with Abraham had been established on the condition of faith long before the entrance of the Covenant of Law. The very nature of a covenant meant that the entrance of the Covenant of Law could not make law-keeping the condition of salvation. That would change the covenant. Covenants do not allow such a change. Salvation must continue on the condition of faith even during the ministry of the Covenant of Law.

The point of verse 16 is that the covenant embraced Christ. The promises were made to Him as the seed of Abraham. The argument made over the singular use of the word *seed* seems to be that the promise is really in a sense made with Christ, but through Him others partake of the promise. It is by union with Him that a believer partakes of the promise. Christ does not stand as one among many as an heir, but He is the heir in whom the many inherit.

The redemptive work of Christ is pictured as the ground of the fulfillment of the Abrahamic Covenant, which was irrevocably and unalterably made on the condition of faith so far as individual participation in the promises is concerned.

If the giving of the Law did not in any way alter the Abrahamic Covenant, and thereby cannot contribute to one's justification, the question might be raised: What was the purpose of the Law? Paul's answer serves a double purpose. He shows the true purpose of the Law, but at the same time he brings out the inferiority of the Law. Beginning with 3:19 and going through 4:31 Paul points out the inferiority of the Covenant of Law (Old Covenant) and the superiority of the New Covenant.

In verses 19, 20, three things about the Law are pointed out. First, is that, "It was added because of transgressions." Many commentators think that in this context "for the sake of" is preferred over "because" to translate the Greek. This seems to be correct. The meaning would be to bring out the true nature of sin by making it a transgression. Transgression has reference to the over-stepping of a stated law. Sin was wrong before the Law, but it did not have the character of over-stepping fixed revealed laws, but when the Law was given, it did take on this character when the individual violated the Law. This gave a greater insight into the true nature and seriousness of sin. This is one of the purposes of Law: to reveal sin and its true nature.

The second thing pointed out in these verses is the temporary nature of the Law, "till the seed [Christ] should come." Thus, the Law was not intended to be a permanent arrangement.

The third observation is that the Law came from the hand of a mediator. The point of this observation is brought out in verse 20. A mediator implies more than one. This is, there is not a direct relationship involved. In the case of the Law it was given through Moses, not directly from God. There was no direct relationship between God and the people. "*But*," Paul says, "God is one." In the context it seems to have this meaning. God is one; that is, to receive something directly from God is to receive it from one, not from a mediator which implies more than one. The promise that Abraham received came directly from God, whereas the Law came through a mediator. Thus, the Abrahamic Covenant is seen to be superior to the Covenant of Law.

Now the question is raised: "Is the Law then against the promises of God?" Paul denies that it is and states that if it could have been an effective instrument to give life, it would have been used (verse 21).

In verse 22, "*scripture*" seems to be used for *law* and shows that the purpose of the Law in condemning is that, all being condemned, they are in position to receive the offer of mercy through Christ. The Law presents the message of judgment so the gospel can present the good news of redemption.

A word of explanation needs to be made here about the relationship between the Covenant of Law and the Abrahamic Covenant. The Abrahamic Covenant was the basic redemptive covenant. It is permanent and unchangeable. The Covenant of Law came in as a temporary aid in the fulfillment of the Abrahamic Covenant. Its ministry was from the giving of the Law at Mount Sinai until the coming of Christ and the establishment of the New Covenant. During this time it served as a means of moral and spiritual instruction and discipline for the nation of Israel. It prepared the way for the coming of the Messiah. In the verses that follow, Paul sheds light on the nature of the ministry of the Law.

Verses 23, 24 are very important verses in our understanding of the ministry of the Law prior to the coming of Christ. "Before faith came" must be interpreted to mean before the New Covenant revelation of faith came. These verses do not speak of a present ministry of the Law in leading people to Christ. Rather, they must be interpreted historically. Verse 24 sheds light on verse 23. The word translated *schoolmaster* means *child-conductor.* It refers to a slave who had charge of Greek and Roman boys of wealthy families from about 6 to 7 to about 16 or 17 years of age. The ministry of the child-conductor was protective and corrective. He was needed because of the immaturity of the young boy. The reference to being kept and shut up must be viewed in the light of verse 24 as being protective rather than holding under condemnation.

It will be noticed that the words "to bring us" in verse 24 are in italics which indicate that they do not appear in the Greek. The translators at times felt that it was necessary to add words not found in the Greek in order to give the meaning. Most of the time these are helpful. In this instance it appears to be better to omit them. It is better to translate, "The law was our schoolmaster [child-conductor] *unto* Christ." *Unto* has a temporal significance and means *until.* The Law served as the child-conductor; that is, to protect and correct God's people until Christ came.

Verse 25 points out the end of the ministry of the Law. "But after that faith is come [the New Covenant revelation of faith, or the faith which should afterwards be revealed of verse 23], we are no longer under a schoolmaster [child-conductor]."

Verse 26 gives the reason for the termination of the ministry of the Law: "For ye are all the children of God by faith in Christ Jesus." The word translated "children" in this verse, according to many commentators when used of believers, means *adult sons.* This is in keeping with the context. The ministry of the Law (child-conductor) is terminated because in connection with the New

Covenant revelation of faith which came with Christ, all believers have been placed in the position of adult sons, and thus delivered from the child-conductor.

The believer is said to be baptized into Christ; that is, in union with Christ. In this union he partakes of the benefits of Christ. There is the erasing of lines of distinction, so far as spiritual benefits are concerned, between Jews and Gentiles.

Verse 29 states a very important truth. The Abrahamic Covenant was made with Abraham and his seed. Therefore, the promise of eternal life was made to the seed of Abraham on the condition of faith. Gentiles are not naturally the seed of Abraham. The question is raised: How then do they become heirs to eternal life since that promise is only to the seed of Abraham? The answer is found in Christ. Christ is the natural seed of Abraham. Through Him we become seed of Abraham. Paul says: "And if ye be Christ's, then are ye Abraham's seed, and heirs according to the promise." The true seed of Abraham are made up of those who are natural seed and believe in Christ and those who, though not natural seed, by belonging to Christ by faith have become seed and belong to the family of Abraham.

A word of explanation about the New Covenant would be in order at this time. The New Covenant like the Old Covenant (Covenant of Law) is related to the Abrahamic Covenant. Yet, there are important differences. The Old Covenant was temporary. The New Covenant is permanent. The Old Covenant prepared the way for the fulfillment of the Abrahamic Covenant. The New Covenant is the *means* of fulfilling the Abrahamic Covenant. In the New Covenant Jesus Christ came, paid our penalty for sin, and gave us a better understanding of God, His promises, and what He expects of us. The New Covenant is established in this life but continues in fulfilled promises in the life to come. In every way, the New Covenant is the superior covenant.

Chapter 4:1-7 is very much like 3:23-29 except for a different emphasis. In 3:23, 24 the emphasis is on the fact that the Law fulfilled a temporary need, while in 4:1-7, the emphasis is on the inferiority of the Law as compared with the New Covenant.

It is pointed out in verses 1, 2 that as long as the heir is a child (not a legal age) he is very much like a bondservant in that he is not free but is under tutors (of his person) and governors (of his estate) until the day appointed of the father.

In verse 3, Paul compares the condition of God's children under the Law with that of the child-heir. He says that we "were in bondage under the elements of the world." The elements of the world refer to an elementary system of instruction which made great use of the tangible, the visible, and the external. The fact that it was for children means that it multiplied the list of *do's* and *don'ts.* This system had a binding effect, not the bondage of condemnation, but bondage in contrast with liberty. This emphasizes the inferiority of the Law.

In verses 4-7, the higher position of the New Covenant is brought out. First, Paul shows how the ministry of Christ brought this new relationship. He says, "But when the fulness of the time was come [compare verse 2, the day appointed of the Father], God sent forth his Son . . . " (verse 4). This was the time in history which God had set for the freeing of His children from the Law (child-conductor). The purpose of this coming was to "redeem them that were under the law, that we might receive the adoption of sons" (verse 5). The adoption here is not taking an alien and making him a member of the family, but rather the placing of the one who is a child into the position of an adult. So with the coming of Christ God placed His children into the position of adulthood (compare 3:26).

Verses 6, 7 point out the privileges of this new position. The first is the reception of the Holy Spirit who produces the consciousness in us of a father-son relationship with God. The second is the believer is no more a bondservant. That is, he is not like the child-heir who is under the ministry of guardians and stewards, or the child-conductor. This, of course, means that he is free from the Law and its elementary system of instruction with its binding effects.

The third privilege is, "Thou art no more a servant, but a son." The *son* of verse 7 is contrasted with the *child* of verse 1, who is a servant because he is a child. The son of verse 7 is no longer a servant in view of the fact that he is a son. This makes sense only when a distinction is made between child and son. The son is in the position of maturity and no longer a servant because he has been delivered from the tutor and governor.

The fourth privilege is, "If a son, then an heir of God through Christ." The use of *heir* here must be seen in contrast with the heir of verse 1. It is the heir who is in the position of adulthood. He is now ready to receive his inheritance. Lack of legal age does not stand in the way. This being true he has received the earnest of his inheritance which is the Holy Spirit. He enters into many of the blessings of God now and will receive his full inheritance when it is time for it to be given.

Before going on with verse 8, let us sum up the major observations made in 3:19—4:7. (1) The Old Covenant believer was viewed by God as being immature. The first proof of this is seen in the meaning of the Greek word which is translated *schoolmaster* (3:24). It refers to a child-conductor who was over Greek and Roman boys from the age of 6 or 7 to the age of 16 or 17. To call the Law a child-conductor is to tell us that God viewed His people at that time as being children and thus immature. The second proof is found in 4:3 where Paul, in referring to the time when God's people were under the Law, says, "When we were children."

(2) In the New Covenant God views His people as being

adults—thus being mature. The first point of proof is found in the fact that we are no longer under a child-conductor (3:25). This implies that we are viewed as being adults. The second point of proof is found in the meaning of the word *adoption* in 4:5. In the light of the illustration of verses 1, 2, it is clear that adoption is related to the time appointed of the father when the child will no longer be under tutors and governors. He will be of legal age. He will be mature. The third point of proof is found in the meaning of the Greek word for *son.* In 4:7, Paul says of the New Covenant believer, "Thou art no more a servant, but a son." In the illustration given in verses 1, 2, the "child differeth nothing from a servant." He is like a servant because he is not in control of himself or his inheritance. The son is no longer a servant, which implies that the son is viewed as being of legal age or mature.

God viewed His people as being immature in the Old Covenant, and the Law was adapted to this immaturity. Children are given detailed instruction. A reading of the civil laws in Exodus through Deuteronomy indicates that the Law gave detailed instructions. These detailed instructions deprived them of the liberty that we enjoy. For that reason they are spoken of as having been in bondage (4:3). In teaching children, extensive use is made of object lessons. The Law with its priesthood and sacrificial system made extensive use of object lessons. Thus, the Law is seen, in this regard, as being adapted to immaturity.

The treatment of God's people in the New Covenant is seen to be adapted to maturity. Basic moral laws and principles are given in the New Covenant, but no extensive set of laws is given. There is more responsibility left up to the believer in making decisions. He has liberty as contrasted with the detailed instruction of the Covenant of Law. The only divinely instituted object lessons are the ordinances. What a reduction as compared with the sacrifices and ritual of the Law!

The Law was good in view of the immaturity of God's people. However, for us as God's adult sons the New Covenant is far superior. To go back to the Law would be trading the superior for the inferior.

In verses 8-10 Paul addresses the Galatians with another question. He says words to this effect: Before your conversion, you served other gods which in reality were not even gods. They were nothing. From that background you were converted and came into this blessed relationship with God of which I have just spoken. Now, "... How turn ye again to the weak and beggarly elements, whereunto ye desire again to be in bondage?" In other words, if you choose to go back under Law as these teachers are suggesting, you will actually be leaving the superior position of an adult for the position of a bondservant. This is true since the Law as a system adapted to childhood is very binding upon those under it. This whole matter of a system of days, and months, and years belongs to an inferior system.

Paul now turns to personal appeal. He reminds them of the danger they are in. He reminds them of how it was through infirmity of the flesh (bodily sickness) he had preached to them and how graciously they had received him. He reminds them of the fact that the effects of these false teachers upon them are evil. Then, he again expresses his great concern for them and his fear concerning them (verses 11-20).

In verse 21 Paul says words to this effect: You who desire to be under Law do not understand exactly what this implies. Listen to this allegory about Isaac and Ishmael, and then answer if you want to place yourself under Law. He points out in this allegory that to go back under the Law would mean to be excluded from the promises (verses 21-31).

The point of this section in Paul's argument is that for them to go back to Law would be a backward step. It would be to leave the superior for the inferior. It would actually mean an exclusion from the promise of grace.

Up to this point in the book Paul has defended his position. His position is that justification is by faith in contrast to works. The believer has been delivered from the Law to a much higher system. To exchange the New Covenant for Law would be to exchange the superior for the inferior.

In 5:1, Paul leaves the argumentative part of the book and turns to practical exhortations for the remainder of the book.

In verses 1-15 there are three main lines of thought. The first is to stand fast in the liberty which is theirs, and be not entangled again in the yoke of bondage. This views the believer as being freed from the system of Law which was adapted to childhood. He is under a higher system which is in keeping with adulthood. However, the believer is reminded that he must not make a misuse of his liberty but should exercise it only as love would direct. The second line of thought deals with the warning of the severity of the results in the event anyone should make the final departure to Law. The third is a warning against, and the expression of his attitude toward, the false teachers.

In verses 16-26, he takes further precautionary steps to be sure that the liberty of which he spoke was not abused.

First, he points out that the ways of the flesh and the Spirit (Holy Spirit) are contrary. To walk by the Spirit is not to fulfill the lusts of the flesh. He points out that the Holy Spirit is fighting against the flesh and that because of this the believer is not the same that he would be without the Holy Spirit. Lest anyone should receive a mistaken idea about this liberty, he makes it clear that those who are characterized by gross sin will not inherit the kingdom of God. Such things give evidence that one is not possessed of the presence of the indwelling Holy Spirit. Then, he points out the true fruits of the Holy Spirit which should characterize those who are partakers of this wonderful liberty.

Second, he declares that a basic change has taken place in those who belong to Christ. They have crucified the flesh. That is, at the time of their conversion they made a decisive break with sin. It does not follow that they will never sin again, but this point is always looked back to as a definite turning point in one's relation to sin.

Third, he exhorts them to a life of living in the Spirit and one free from envy.

In 6:1-5, he speaks of the Christian's relationship to the weaker brother. He should restore him. In their general relations they should bear one another's burdens (the loads of life too heavy to bear alone). But there are some burdens (things of less magnitude) which each person should bear alone.

In verse 6 he points out the obligation of the one being taught to the one who teaches. Some interpret, " . . . communicate unto him . . . in all good things" with reference to the learner sharing his material substance with his teacher.

In verses 7-9, Paul warns against anyone's mistaking Christian liberty to mean that the Christian is free to live after the flesh. To live after the flesh means that one will reap corruption. The redeemed person is one who sows to the Spirit. He will reap life everlasting.

Verse 10 ties very well into the thoughts of verses 1-6 and stands as a final reminder of the responsibility of fellow Christians to each other.

Verse 11 seems to indicate that Paul wrote this letter in his own hand. Some say the emphasis given to "large letters" indicates that Paul's eyesight was not good.

He makes one final mention of the false teachers and accuses them of having wrong motives. One was to avoid persecution. The other was that they might glory in the flesh of the Galatians (verses 12, 13).

As for himself, his glorying was centered in the cross of Christ, through which the world was crucified unto him and he unto the world (verse 14).

In closing Paul reminds the Galatians of the scars which he bears in his body because of his stand for Christ, which should testify to them, and pronounces the blessings of God upon them (verses 16-18).

A SURVEY OF THE BOOK OF

Ephesians

by Dr. Robert Picirilli

Of all the writings of Paul, I think Ephesians is my favorite. When I read this letter I feel like I am entering into a treasure room that holds all sorts of precious goods. Then I am told that these treasures are all mine! That is exactly what happens when we read it as Christians. We are ushered into the treasure-house of God's spiritual blessings and told that all of these belong to us!

There is so much to be told about Ephesians that it is difficult to decide just what to present in this short survey. Probably, the best place to begin is by giving you an introduction to this letter. A book of the Bible is always easier to understand if you have a clear picture of its historical background: the people to whom it was written, the time it was written, the problems in the church, and the purposes Paul had for writing. Knowing such facts as these makes the meaning of a book much clearer.

So let us start by opening our Bibles to the first chapter of the letter of Paul to the Ephesians. Look at the first verse of this letter: "Paul, an apostle of Jesus Christ by the will of God, to the saints which are at Ephesus, and to the faithful in Christ Jesus."

Turn, now, to Acts 19, and we will review the story how Paul laid the foundation of the church in Ephesus. You will recall that Paul made three missionary journeys. He visited the city of Ephesus during the last of these three journeys, and this history is recorded in Acts 19. We will not take time to go over this in detail, but I especially want you to take note of verse 10 of Acts 19 which tells us that the ministry of Paul in Ephesus continued two years. That is the longest time Paul ever ministered in any city at one time, as far as we know.

Note also in Acts 19:10 that "all they which dwelt in Asia heard the word of the Lord Jesus" while Paul ministered in Ephesus. Now the word "Asia" here does not mean the continent of Asia as we know it. "Asia" was the name of a small Roman district on the western end of the peninsula we now call Turkey or Asia Minor.

Anyway, the point of Acts 19:10 is that Paul's ministry in Ephesus was not just a ministry to that one city, but to the entire district of Asia, of which Ephesus was the capital. Throughout the whole district, the gospel was preached: by Paul, by his co-workers, and by converts traveling back and forth. People were saved in many towns in the area. New churches were, no doubt, organized in every city and village in the district.

I have emphasized this in order to make an important point about the letter we call Ephesians: No doubt Paul intended this letter to go to *all* the churches in Asia and not just to Ephesus. Turn back to Ephesians 1:1, and let us notice the way it is worded. You see that there is an "and" after the word Ephesus. Not only are those at Ephesus addressed, but so are "the faithful in Christ Jesus." Furthermore, the Greek words translated "at Ephesus" can easily mean in the area of Ephesus.

In addition to this, turn to the last chapter of Ephesians, and you will note something a little unusual about this letter. In chapter 6, in fact in the whole letter, not one single Christian is greeted by name. Paul greets at least a few people in almost all his letters; then why not at Ephesus? Again, the reason may be that he wanted it to be less personal so that *all* the churches in the district around Ephesus would feel equally included.

Maybe you would also find it interesting to know that several very old Greek manuscripts of this book do not have the words "at Ephesus" in chapter 1, verse 1. I would not be surprised to learn that Paul himself had several copies of this letter made, and that only the copy that went to Ephesus itself included the words "at Ephesus." The other copies would have been sent to the other influential churches in Asia.

In my opinion, then, Ephesians was originally intended by Paul to be sent to various churches in Ephesus and the surrounding area. His main purpose in writing this letter was to fortify the Christians there against a particular form of false doctrine that had got started in the city of Colosse, another city in Asia, not far from Ephesus.

This explains, by the way, why Ephesians and Colossians are so similar. If you have ever read one of these right after the other, you have probably noticed that they both cover very similar subject matter. The false teaching existed at Colosse, and Paul wrote Colossians to combat that heresy. At the same time, he decided to send another letter to several churches in the district where Colosse was located. That district was Asia, and Ephesus was its capital and the location of its strongest church. Paul's purpose for this epistle was to keep the error at Colosse from spreading to other churches nearby.

What was the false doctrine at Colosse? We will not take time to explain this now. Perhaps you can get the cassette on Colossians and learn more about the problem there. What you need to know now is that the Book of Colossians deals with these errors directly, while the Book of Ephesians takes a more indirect approach, trying to strengthen the spiritual insights of the Christians in the area so they will not fall prey to any false teachings.

There is not any doubt that Ephesians will clarify a Christian's spiritual insights. This letter will open your eyes to the wonderful privileges and possessions which are yours in Christ. The spiritual development and maturing that come from studying Ephesians will help any Christian withstand false teachings. That is exactly what Paul means when he says, in Ephesians 4:14: "That we henceforth be no more children, tossed to and fro, and carried about with every wind of docrtine."

One more thing, now, you need to understand about the background of Ephesians. Paul was in prison in Rome at the time he wrote this letter. You may recall that Paul was arrested in Jerusalem at the close of the third missionary journey and spent the next four years in jail: two in Caesarea and two in Rome. All this is related in the closing chapters of the Book of Acts. Well, while Paul was in prison in Rome, the heresy at Colosse got started, and Paul could not go in person to deal with the situation. So he did the next best thing, he wrote letters. Three of Paul's New Testament letters were written, by the way, on exactly this same occasion and sent to the same general area by the same messengers. These were Colossians, Ephesians, and Philemon. These three epistles, then, can be very helpfully studied together. They along with Philippians, which was written a few months later, make up the group we call the Prison Epistles.

Ephesians, Colossians, and Philemon were all written in about the year 60, then, while Paul was in prison in Rome. We can summarize Paul's main purposes for writing Ephesians as four-fold: (1) to help the young Christians in the area to obtain deeper spiritual insight into the nature of their relationship with Christ; (2) to fortify these Christians, in this way, against the false teaching at Colosse; (3) to deepen their understanding of the basis of Christian victory in daily living; and (4) to remind them of their obligations to one another in family relationships. There are other purposes, of course, which we will try to clarify as we look through the book.

And now we begin our survey of Ephesians. There is more than one way of outlining this book. Perhaps the easiest way is to start by dividing it into two equal halves. If you want to do this, you can say that the first three chapters make up the *doctrinal* part of the letter, and the last three chapters make up the *practical* part.

Let us look at the Book of Ephesians a minute or two with this in mind. Notice chapter 1, verse 18, for example. There you see that Paul wants us to be enlightened, and that we "may know what is the hope of his calling." This is certainly a doctrinal matter; Paul wants to improve our understanding of the spiritual riches we possess in the Lord Jesus Christ. Look also in chapter 2, verse 1, where Paul reminds us that we were dead in trespasses and sins but have now been quickened. He spends the whole chapter explaining what has happened to us in salvation and how it happened. Look at chapter 3, verse 18, where again Paul expresses a desire that we may *comprehend* the marvelous love of Christ. That, too, is a doctrinal purpose. The whole first three chapters are aimed at deepening our understanding of the wonderful plan and nature of salvation.

But now look at chapter 4, verse 1, where Paul begins by saying, "Therefore, . . . *walk* worthy of the vocation wherewith ye are called." You see, then, that from here on Paul is interested in how the doctrine affects our *lives.* What he has explained in the first three chapters surely has a practical effect on our day-by-day walk. So the last three chapters talk about conduct and behavior. You will notice this in chapter 4, verses 25, 26, and 28, where Paul talks about lying, anger, and stealing. You will notice this in chapter 5, verse 4, where he warns against foolish talking; or in verse 22: "Wives, submit yourselves unto your own husbands." These practical instructions continue in chapter 6; notice verse 5: "Servants, be obedient" to your masters. You can easily see, then, that Ephesians logically divides itself into these two great halves, with the first three chapters aimed at our *minds*, and the last three at our *lives;* the first half doctrinal, the last half practical.

Long ago, someone invented a nice, neat outline of Ephesians that I think is a very good and helpful one. I do not know who started it, but it is easy to remember. It catches the true spirit of Ephesians even if it does divide the book into three parts rather than two. Those three parts are: the wealth, walk, and warfare of the believer. I will repeat that in a moment, but let me first suggest that you may want to jot this down in your Bible's margin or in your notebook, because this is the overall outline which I am going to follow in this lecture.

Once again, now, the overall outline is as follows. Part one of Ephesians starts at chapter 1, verse 3, and goes to the end of chapter 3; and it is called the WEALTH of the believer. In this section Paul tells us about all the wonderful spiritual treasures we possess in Christ as children of God.

Part two of Ephesians begins at chapter 4, verse 1, and extends through chapter 6, verse 9; and this is called the WALK of the believer. In this part Paul talks about applying spiritual truths to our daily lives.

Part three of Ephesians begins at 6:10 and goes through 6:20 and is called the WARFARE of the believer. As you may remember, that is the concluding part of the letter in which Paul describes the armor of God that is available to us in our fight with spiritual wickedness.

Surely you will want to remember this three-fold division of Ephesians. As I said earlier, I think it catches well the main themes and emphases of this letter: the wealth, walk, and warfare of the believer. I hope this whets your appetite to read more about this great little book as we proceed now to look at it more closely with this outline in mind.

First, let us study chapter 1 a few minutes. The first two verses are about the same as in all of Paul's epistles, so we will pass them by without further attention and go right to verse 3. Let us read that verse: "Blessed be the God and Father of our Lord Jesus Christ, who hath blessed us with all spiritual blessings in heavenly places in Christ." You can see, right off, that Paul is talking about the spiritual riches that are ours, the WEALTH of the believer.

Let me give you a title for chapter 1; here it is: "The Predestinated Position of the Believer in Christ." Now you may not like that title, but just stay with me a few minutes; and I think you will like it better. You will notice that verse 5 uses the word "predestinated," and so does verse 11. We will look at these more closely in a moment, but at least you can see *I am* not the one who invented that word; and maybe that will help you understand why I want to call this chapter "The Predestinated Position of the Believer in Christ."

First, let us make sure we realize that this predestination does *not* mean that some have been eternally predestined to go to Heaven, and others to Hell, against their wills. That does not have anything to do with this chapter. But this chapter *does* tell us that there is a predestined purpose for the one who *is* a Christian. God has not predestinated a person to be a believer, but He has predestinated some blessings as possessions of one who is a believer. That is what we will see here.

Let us read verses 3-14: "Blessed be the God and Father of our Lord Jesus Christ, who hath blessed us with all spiritual blessings in heavenly places in Christ: According as he hath chosen us in him before the foundation of the world, that we should be holy and without blame before him in love: Having predestinated us unto the adoption of children by Jesus Christ to himself, according to the good pleasure of his will, To the praise of the glory of his grace, wherein he hath made us accepted in the beloved. In whom we have redemption through his blood, the forgiveness of sins, according to the riches of his grace; Wherein he hath abounded toward us in all wisdom and prudence; Having made known unto us the mystery of his will, according to his good pleasure which he hath purposed in himself: That in the dispensation of the fulness of times he might gather together in one all things in Christ, both which are in heaven, and which are on earth; even in him: In whom also we have obtained an inheritance, being predestinated according to the purpose of him who worketh all things after the counsel of his own will: That we should be to the praise of his glory, who first trusted in Christ. In whom ye also trusted, after that ye heard the word of truth, the gospel of your salvation: in whom also after that ye believed, ye were sealed with that holy Spirit of promise, Which is the earnest of our inheritance until the redemption of the purchased possession, unto the praise of his glory."

The first thing I want you to notice in this passage about the predestinated position of the believer in Christ is the *method* of that predestination, the matter of *how*. In order to see this, all you have to do is watch how often the little word "in" occurs in these verses. Look at verse 1: "in Christ"; verse 4: "in him"; verse 6: "in the beloved"; verse 7: "in whom"; verse 10: "in Christ . . . even in him"; verse 11: "in whom"; verse 12: "in Christ"; verse 13: "in whom." Over and over this little phrase is repeated to burn in our minds the important truth that all that we possess we possess in Christ! God did not predestinate you or me to *be* in Christ, but God has predestinated that all those who *are in Christ* possess certain marvelous spiritual treasures.

The second thing you need to see here is the *content* of the predestinated position of the believer in Christ. This is the matter of *what*. Of course we possess many things in Christ, but there are five particular ones clearly mentioned in these verses. One is in verse 4: "holy and without blame before him." We stand clothed in the righteousness, the purity, the innocence, the sinlessness of Christ! Another is in verse 5, called "adoption." In Christ we are placed as full-fledged, adult, responsible sons in the family of God Himself! A third is in verse 7: "redemption." In Christ we are freed completely from the penalty of our sins. The fourth thing is seen in verse 10: "oneness." In Christ we are as one with all the family of God of all times, all races, all classes. Finally, in Christ we also have *inheritance* as noted in verse 11. We are assigned a place in God's family as His sons, slated to inherit that which is His. These five treasures—holiness, adoption, redemption, oneness, and inheritance—are all yours, if you are a Christian, whether you like it or not! I do not know about you, but I like it.

The third thing to notice about this predestinated position of the believer in Christ is the *basis*, the *reason*, for the predestination. This is the *why* question. And to answer this question, I want you to notice a phrase that is repeated three times in these verses. First, verse 5: "according to the good pleasure of his will." Then, verse 9: "according to his good pleasure which he hath purposed in himself." Then again, in verse 11: "according to the purpose of him who worketh all things after the counsel of his own will." In other words, dear friend, God has not planned these marvelous blessings for you and me because of any goodness or deserving of our own, but simply because He was pleased to do so. The basis, then, is found in His own sovereign will, not in our works.

The fourth and last thing to find in these verses is the *purpose* or *intended result* of this predestination. This is the matter of *what for.* What does God want to see accomplished by predestinating such treasures for the believer in Christ? Well, again the answer can be found in a phrase repeated three times in the passage. Look at verse 6: "To the praise of the glory of his grace." Now verse 12: "That we should be to the praise of his glory." And then verse 14: "Unto the praise of his glory." See, God has done all this for us so that we will, in turn, praise and glorify Him and His grace. If your salvation, and mine, have not resulted in the unending glorification of God by our lips and lives, then something is wrong.

We do not have any more time for chapter 1. But before we leave it behind, take one look at verses 15-23. If you will look closely at this, you will see it is a prayer of Paul's for his readers. And surely that includes us. And you will also see, upon closer study, that his prayer is that we will come to a fuller *understanding* of this wonderful salvation which he has just been explaining to us.

Now let us move on to chapter 2. Again I want to give you a title for the chapter; this time, the title is: "God's Before and After Pictures of Salvation." If you do not quite catch what I mean, read verses 1-10, and maybe you will: "And you hath he quickened, who were dead in trespasses and sins; Wherein in time past ye walked according to the course of this world, according to the prince of the power of the air, the spirit that now worketh in the children of disobedience: Among whom also we all had our conversation in times past in the lusts of our flesh, fulfilling the desires of the flesh and of the mind; and were by nature the children of wrath, even as others. But God, who is rich in mercy, for his great love wherewith he loved us, Even when we were dead in sins, hath quickened us together with Christ, (by grace ye are saved;) And hath raised us up together, and made us sit together in heavenly places in Christ Jesus: That in the ages to come he might shew the exceeding riches of his grace in his kindness toward us through Christ Jesus. For by grace are ye saved through faith; and that not of yourselves: it is the gift of God: Not of works, lest any man should boast. For we are his workmanship, created in Christ Jesus unto good works, which God hath before ordained that we should walk in them."

You know what a before and after picture is, surely. You see them in all sorts of advertisements. For instance, you may see a before picture of someone very fat, who then uses a certain product or diet and the result is an after picture that is entirely different. Well, that is exactly what we have here in Ephesians 2:1-10. God's before and after picture about our salvation.

Look at verses 1-3 again. Every verb is past tense. These three verses give us the *before* picture. If you will study them closely, you will find *three* words that God uses to describe what we were *before* we were saved. The first is in verse 1, and it is the word "dead." We were spiritually dead, separated from God. The second is in verse 2, and it is the word "disobedience." We did not obey Him who created us. By the way, verses 2, 3 tell us exactly how we were disobedient: We followed the world, the devil, and the flesh instead of God.

The third word in the before picture is in verse 3, and it is the word "wrath." As sinners we found ourselves under the wrath of God. You see, then, that the before picture is not a very pretty one: dead in sins; disobediently following the world, the flesh and the devil; and under God's wrath. It is a picture of utter hopelessness and helplessness.

Thank the Lord that is only the before picture. There is also an after picture, and this one is developed for us in verses 4-10. In fact, for all three of the words found in verses 1-3, opposites are found in verses 4-10. The opposite of death is life, and that is why verse 5 says that even when we were dead we were "quickened." And verse 6 says we were "raised up" together with Christ. In other words, a Christian has been raised from the dead, made alive spiritually.

There is an opposite for disobedience, too. It is found in verse 10: "Created in Christ Jesus *unto good works.*" Instead of disobeying God, we now walk in good works, not as the *means* of salvation, but as the *result.*

And what was the third word we found in the before picture? It was wrath, was it not? Well, now we find that there are several words in the after picture that provide opposites to wrath: In verse 4, notice "mercy"; also in verse 4, "love"; in verse 5, "grace"; in verse 7, "kindness." You see? Now we are under the mercy, love, grace, and kindness of God instead of His wrath. Before, the sinner looked to Heaven and saw the red face of an angry God; now, we look and behold the smile of His kindness. What a wonderful change!

But wait! How has all this happened? The passage answers this question, too. For one thing, note verse 8: "It is the gift of God." For another thing, note verse 5: "with Christ"; verse 6: "in Christ"; verse 7: "through Christ." It is the work of Christ, then. Finally, note verse 8 again: "through faith." Man's part is to believe, to receive. Man's works or goodness get no credit here. God's grace and Christ's work must receive the glory. Man can only accept by faith and then glorify his God and Savior.

Now we move on to verses 11-22, which I am not going to take time to quote. But here is another before and after picture, only a slightly different one. If the first ten verses of chapter 2 were a before and after contrast in reference to our *individual* salvation, then verses 11-22 provide the same kind of contrast in reference to our salvation as a *people*, in other words, as Gentiles.

Once again, you can see the difference between the past and the present. Verse 11 speaks of "time past"; verse 13 says "now." And what is the past picture? What was our place as a people before

Christ came and saved us? Verses 11, 12 tell us: We *were*, as Gentiles, of the uncircumcision, without Christ, aliens, strangers, having no hope, without God. Verse 13 says "far off." Verse 14 refers to a middle wall of partition that was between us and God's people. Verse 19 speaks of us as formerly being strangers and foreigners.

But now notice the after picture: verse 13, "made nigh"; verse 14, "made . . . one"; verse 16, "reconciled"; verse 18, "access": and all of this was done for us by Christ! Perhaps verse 19 summarizes it best: "Now therefore ye are no more strangers and foreigners, but fellowcitizens with the saints, and of the household of God." We have been made, even as Gentiles, full-fledged members of the family of God! No wonder this section of Ephesians is called the Wealth of the believer!

Now, we just do not have much time for chapter 3. At least I can give you a title for the chapter, and it is this: "Paul's Part in Sharing the Wealth." If these first three chapters tell us of the wealth of the believer, this third chapter points up the place filled by Paul, and all who serve God, in carrying the news of the wonderful salvation found in Christ.

Notice verse 9, for example, where Paul says his goal is "to make all men see" what marvelous things are available for men in Jesus Christ. You and I ought to share Paul's commitment to this task. Once we have seen what wealth we possess in Christ, we should want to share it with others.

Perhaps the most intriguing part of chapter 3 is Paul's prayer with which he closes this first part of Ephesians. That prayer begins in verse 14 and continues through verse 21. Like the prayer which concluded chapter 1, this prayer also expresses primarily a desire that God will help the readers understand more fully the spiritual treasures Christians possess in Christ. Without taking time for all of them, read verses 17-19: "That Christ may dwell in your hearts by faith; that ye, being rooted and grounded in love, May be able to comprehend with all saints what is the breadth, and length, and depth, and height; And to know the love of Christ, which passeth knowledge, that ye might be filled with all the fulness of God."

The part of this that catches my attention is the four dimensions Paul puts on "the love of Christ": breadth, and length, and depth, and height! I think this little piece of poetry is an excellent summary of the whole first three chapters, of the whole provision of salvation to be found in the Lord Jesus.

Take breadth, for example, and remember chapter 2, verses 11-21, where Paul reminded us how Christ's love has reached out and brought us *all* in, whether Jew or Gentile.

Look also at the dimension of length, and recall chapter 1, verse 4, where God chose us "before the foundation of the world." Remember also chapter 2, verse 7, which promises that God is going to be showing kindness to us throughout the ages to come! From before the foundation of the world, throughout the ages to come: That is how long Christ's love is!

Now consider the depth. This reminds me of chapter 2, verses 1-3, where Paul described our former state in the despairing depths of sin. That is how deep Christ had to reach to save us!

Finally, what about height? Well, do not forget chapter 2, verse 6: We who were in the depths of spiritual death have been raised up together and made to sit in heavenly places in Christ! That is height for you!

Now when we leave chapter 3 and come to chapter 4, verse one, we enter an entirely new portion of this epistle to the Ephesians. The first three chapters of Ephesians, you remember, describe the *wealth* of the believer. From chapter 4:1 through 6:9 Paul describes the *walk* of the believer.

In this part of the epistle there is far too much for one brief lecture. Therefore, I want to select some of the main themes that are involved in this section and make sure you see how these themes are developed. To begin with, one of the most important words in these chapters is the word "walk." This word occurs five times. You may want to underline the word in the following verses. First, look at 4:1: "*Walk* worthy of the vocation wherewith ye are called." Now look at verse 17: "*Walk* not as other Gentiles *walk*, in the vanity of their mind." Now turn to chapter 5, verse 2: "*Walk* in love, as Christ also hath loved us." Now down to verse 8: "*Walk* as children of light." Finally, in chapter 5, verse 15, Paul says, "*Walk* circumspectly, not as fools, but as wise."

Let us look at each one of these, briefly, to get Paul's picture of the Christian's walk: First, chapter 4, verse 1. Paul says, "Walk worthy of the vocation wherewith ye are called." What Paul is saying here is that we need to be conscious of the wonderful position we enjoy as Christians in the Lord Jesus Christ and walk *worthy* of this position. The Lord has called us into His family and given us the wonderful privileges of sonship in His family. We are identified with Him and with the Lord Jesus Christ. The precious Holy Spirit lives in our hearts. We are holy in the Lord Jesus Christ. We have been redeemed from our sins, and we are expecting the wonderful inheritance that has been promised to us. Now Paul says, live up to that wonderful position which you have been called to in the Lord Jesus Christ. As Christians we are really "somebodies," and we must live in keeping with our identity as children of God.

Now look at 4:17, which is the second occurrence of the word "walk." Paul says, "Walk not as other Gentiles walk, in the vanity of their mind." What Paul means here is that we have been saved from the kind of life we used to live before we came to know the Lord Jesus Christ. And now, because we have been saved, we are new creatures and we want to make sure that our walk reflects this change. In the next few verses Paul talks about the old man and the new man. In verse 22, he says for us to "put off concerning the former conversation the old man, which is corrupt according to the deceitful lusts." In verse 24 he says, "Put on the new man, which after God is created in righteousness and true holiness." The Christian life is a matter of putting off the old and putting on the new.

Now turn to chapter 5, verse 2, which is the third occurrence of the word "walk" in this section. Paul says, "Walk in love." One of the most important aspects of the Christian life is for us to realize that we are brought into a new relationship with other people. We become part of the Christian community. We have brothers and sisters in the Lord. I am going to mention more about this in a few minutes, so now the important thing is to remember that in order to live successful Christian lives we must walk in love.

The fourth occurrence of the word "walk" is in chapter 5, verse 8. Here Paul says: "Ye were sometimes darkness, but now are ye light in the Lord: walk as children of light." It is reasonably easy to grasp what Paul means. You know, there are some folks who love darkness, as Jesus said, because their deeds are evil. They want to hide what they do. But Christians should walk as children of light, because we are in the light of God. He sees everything we do. We must live in such a way as to be unashamed for the Lord or others to see all we do.

Now the last verse in which the word "walk" appears is in chapter 5, verse 15. Paul says, "Walk circumspectly, not as fools, but as wise." "Circumspectly" means *looking all around.* Paul is saying that we Christians face many dangers and temptations. Satan hides himself and his methods as well as he can. He is always watching to trip us up. He sets ambushes and stumblingblocks in our paths. If we walk carelessly and half asleep, we will be sure to stumble and fall, or turn aside from the way. Paul says we must be wise, with our eyes open, looking all around, making sure that we are aware of what is going on around us.

Well, I think these five verses make up a very interesting picture of the Christian life: not crawling, not stumbling; not spurting or jumping; but *walking.* Walking is steady, deliberate progress toward a goal. As Christians we realize what a wonderful, privileged position the Lord Jesus has brought us into, so we walk with shoulders erect, realizing who we are, and worthy of that wonderful position. We realize we are new creatures, delivered from the emptiness and death and wickedness in which we once lived under the wrath of God. We walk as new persons, putting aside the old ways. We walk shoulder to shoulder in love and fellowship with others, helping one another make progress. We walk as children of light, on inspection all the time, unashamed of our deeds. We walk alertly, with our eyes open, aware of the traps and tricks Satan sets to hinder us. And so we walk on, making consistent progress towards spiritual maturity.

Now let us turn our attention to another of the important themes that stand out in this particular section of Ephesians. As you have realized, a lot of folks seem to want to walk straight but never seem to be able to succeed. Well, Paul gives us some very important suggestions about the method of such a Christian walk, just exactly how we can accomplish this. And I think the part Paul wants to emphasize *most* is that the secret of success in living for the Lord Jesus lies in our relationship with the Holy Spirit. You will find several references to the Holy Spirit in these chapters of Ephesians. I want to point these out to you. Again, you may want to underline them. First, look at Ephesians chapter 4, verse 3. Paul says, "Endeavouring to keep the *unity* of the Spirit." Now look at chapter 4, verse 30, "And *grieve* not the holy Spirit of God." Now look down in chapter 5, verse 9, "For the *fruit* of the Spirit is in all goodness and righteousness and truth." Finally, look at chapter 5, verse 18, "Be *filled* with the Spirit." There just is not any doubt that a believer's relationship with the Holy Spirit is the thing that determines whether he is going to walk like Christ wants him to.

Let us look at each one of these individually for a minute. Ephesians 4:3: "Keep the unity of the Spirit." What does Paul mean? Well, if you will look at the next two or three verses, you will find that Paul says the Holy Spirit has brought us all together in one body in the Lord Jesus Christ. Keeping the unity in the Spirit means that we preserve the fellowship that we have with one another in the body of the Lord Jesus Christ. You see, we *need* one another in the Christian life. The right relationship with the Spirit means that we will be in the right relationship with one another. Then we will have the help of one another for a successful Christian life.

Paul's second reference to the Holy Spirit is 4:30, where he says, "Grieve not the holy Spirit of God." We must realize that the Holy Spirit lives within us, and that He is a person with sensitive feelings. Any sin in our lives will grieve the Holy Spirit. Look at the verses right above verse 30, you will notice that Paul talks about specific sins. For instance, in verse 25, he talks about lying. In verse 26, he talks about anger and wrath. In verse 28, about stealing. In verse 29, corrupt communication. In verse 31, bitterness, wrath, anger, clamor, and evil speaking. All such things are put away from us because all of these will grieve the Holy Spirit of God. When we stay conscious of this, it helps us make sure our lives are kept clean.

The third reference to the Holy Spirit is in chapter 5, verse 9, where Paul talks about bearing the fruit of the Spirit. I remind you that in John, chapter 15, Jesus compared Himself to a vine; all of us who are His disciples are branches of that vine. The branches bear fruit, and the Holy Spirit produces the fruits in the lives of the believers. Here in Ephesians 5:9, Paul talks about three fruits in particular—goodness, righteousness, and truth. If we will be submissive to the Holy Spirit, if we will allow Him, He will produce these wonderful supernatural fruits in our lives.

Paul's last reference to the Holy Spirit in this particular section of Ephesians is in chapter 5, verse 18. Perhaps this is the most difficult verse of the four, but it certainly is an especially important one. Paul says, "Be filled with the Spirit." All sorts of false and confused doctrines are based upon this verse. We need to know what it really means. It seems to me Paul is using this expression as a *summary* of everything else he has taught about the Holy Spirit. If we preserve the unity of the Holy Spirit in our fellowship with one another; if we walk making sure our lives do not grieve the Holy Spirit; if we submit to the Holy Spirit and let Him produce in us goodness, and righteousness, and truth; that will be the fullness of the Holy Spirit. We often use the word *full* to describe the domination of a person. For instance, if I say someone is filled with hate, full of envy, or filled with joy, I simply mean that he is dominated by that characteristic. Well, when someone is filled with the Holy Spirit, he is completely controlled by the Holy Spirit rather than by any of his own selfish interests. The fullness of the Holy Spirit consists in our complete submission to Him and to His control.

And now there is one more theme in this section about the walk of the believer that I want to emphasize. It concerns our relationship with one another. Some of the things that I have already said have laid a good foundation for this. Of the five different occurrences of the word *walk*, one teaches us to walk in love. Of the four different references to the Holy Spirit, one says we must keep the unity of the Spirit. Throughout this section Paul puts great stress on our relationship to one another.

First, look in chapter 4, verse 2. Paul says, "forbearing one another." Then look over in chapter 4, verse 25. Paul says, "Speak every man truth with his neighbour: for we are members one of another." Then to chapter 4, verse 32. Paul says, "Be ye kind one to another, tenderhearted, forgiving one another, even as God for Christ's sake hath forgiven you." Now look at chapter 5, verse 19, where Paul says, "Speaking to yourselves," which means "speaking to *one another* in psalms and hymns and spiritual songs." Finally, chapter 5, verse 21: "Submitting yourselves one to another in the fear of God." In all five of these places you can see the importance Paul is placing upon the proper Christian relationship to one another. As I mentioned previously, we need one another in the Christian life.

This emphasis on our relationship to one another is the one that leads Paul, starting in chapter 5, verse 21, to talk about the Christian's family relationships. In chapter 5, verse 21, he says, "Submitting yourselves one to another in the fear of God." Immediately following that, Paul speaks of family obligations. The Christian not only has duties to fellow-believers, but to his own family. First, Paul speaks concerning the relationship between Christian wives and their husbands; then between Christian children and their parents; and finally, Christian servants and their masters. We do not have space to study these sections in this brief survey, but you need to note that Paul addresses some very important instructions both to wives and husbands, both to children and to parents, both to servants and to masters. And Ephesians 5:21 is the key to understanding all the responsibilities of all these groups of people: "Submitting yourselves one to another in the fear of God."

And now when we leave chapter 6, verse 9, and move into verse 10, we come to the third and final portion of the Book of Ephesians. We have already seen that the first three chapters describe the wealth of the believer. Chapters 4:1—6:9 describe the walk of the believer. Paul concludes the epistle with a few brief words concerning the warfare of the believer. First, he reminds us that we need to "be strong in the Lord, and in the power of his might"—note verse 11, "that ye may be able to stand against the wiles of the devil." The point of all of this is explained in verse 12: "We wrestle not against flesh and blood, but against principalities, against powers, against the rulers of the darkness of this world, against spiritual wickedness in high places." In other words, we are involved in a spiritual conflict with unseen forces. Obviously, we are not equipped naturally to deal with such a warfare. We cannot combat such an enemy without supernatural help. So Paul describes the equipment God has provided for us; he calls it "the whole armour of God" in verse 13, using the analogy of a soldier. Various pieces of this armor are listed in verses 14-17 including truth, righteousness, the preparation of the gospel of peace, salvation, and the Word of God. When we equip ourselves with these things, we will be able to withstand satanic attacks. We will be able to carry on warfare with demonic forces and be victorious.

Verse 18 also has something to do with this. As you know, any army needs supplies. Verse 18 talks about the Christian's supply line in his spiritual warfare with satanic forces; "Praying always with all prayer and supplication in the Spirit." The Lord will answer our prayers and provide for us the strength that we need with which to withstand Satan.

Now when Paul finishes discussing this Christian warfare, he is ready to close the letter. This he does in verses 19-24. Verses 19, 20 contain a request that the Christians in Asia pray for Paul in his bonds, that he may still speak boldly. Verses 21, 22 tell that Tychichus will bring this letter to them and inform them more fully about Paul's situation. And the last two verses provide the benediction. I trust that studying this wonderful letter will help open your eyes to the tremendous spiritual blessings and obligations that are yours in the Lord Jesus Christ.

A SURVEY OF THE BOOK OF

Philippians

by Dr. Robert Picirilli

The purpose of this study is to cover the letter to the Philippians as thoroughly as possible in a short time. Since this is a rather short book, we ought to be able to get pretty well acquainted with it before we are through. I certainly hope so, because Philippians is well worth getting acquainted with. It may be one of the most neglected books in the New Testament, but it certainly ought not to be. There are some sparkling gems of truth in this little book.

As you already know, Philippians is one of Paul's letters to a church he had personally founded. Let us begin our study of this letter by reviewing, briefly, the story of the founding of the church. I am sure you recall that the Book of Acts describes three missionary journeys which the Apostle Paul made, along with various ones of his companions in travel. The Philippian church was founded on the second of those three journeys, and the story is contained in Acts 16.

Like all the others, the second missionary journey began at Antioch in Syria. Silas was Paul's fellow-missionary at the start of this journey. The two men moved from Antioch, first, through Syria and Cilicia, into Galatia, where they visited the churches in Iconium, Lystra, and Derbe. In Lystra, a young man named Timothy attached himself to them, and so the gospel team now numbered three.

After touring Galatia, Paul was of a mind to evangelize the district of Asia, of which Ephesus was capital; but the Lord said, "No." So the team moved northward, thinking that perhaps they should enter Bithynia. Again, the Lord said, "No." Consequently, they came to Troas, as far as they could go by land, wondering exactly what to do next. The Lord did not leave them in doubt. That night Paul received the Macedonian vision, as we call it, described in Acts 16:9. So the next day they boarded a ship and headed for Macedonia. By the way, the fact that Acts 16:10 is the first time the pronoun "we" occurs in the Book of Acts means that Luke—the author of Acts—had joined the gospel evangelistic team in Troas. So now there were four.

When Paul and his companions left Troas by ship, they were headed for Philippi, one of the most important towns in Macedonia. Acts 16:12 tells of their arrival there. Notice in Acts 16:13 that Paul's first action in Philippi was to attend a prayer meeting with some women of the Jewish faith. The fact that no synagogue is mentioned means that there were not many Jews in Philippi.

At this prayer meeting Paul won his first convert in Macedonia, a woman named Lydia. Lydia was not Jewish by race, but had evidently become a proselyte to the Jewish faith. She was a businesswoman, obviously prosperous, and her home became headquarters for Paul and the others while they were in Philippi. Verses 14, 15 tell about this.

Acts 16:16-18 tell about another interesting thing that happened while Paul was first in Philippi. A young girl, who was a slave, was possessed by a demon which gave her unusual fortune-telling powers. After several days Paul cast the demon from her. And this got Paul in trouble, for the next verses tell how the men who were the masters of this little slave girl became very angry. After all, the girl's unusual powers had brought them a very nice income, and now they could expect to use her this way no longer. Like so many, they would rather line their pockets with money and keep others under the devil's hand.

So they had Paul and Silas seized and dragged down to the city rulers. Without any sort of trial, Paul and Silas were beaten and put in the local jail with their feet locked in the stocks.

Is it not interesting that Paul and Silas did not mourn and complain, but—according to Acts 16:25—prayed and sang! Then God sent an earthquake, their bonds were loosed, the jailer awakened, Paul stopped him from attempted suicide, the jailer was converted, so was his family, he washed the backs of Paul and Silas, and they baptized him! What an inspiring account of the power of God! The next day, Paul and Silas were released and stayed on in Philippi until they had finished their ministry there..

Such is the story of the founding of the church to which the letter called Philippians was written. Obviously, Paul's ministry there was very successful. There is not any doubt that the church at Philippi was one of Paul's finest. Two things in particular stand out about them: the fact that the church was evidently more free of problems than were most of the early churches, and the fact that they regularly contributed to Paul's ministry. We will look at these two facts more closely in a few minutes. For the time being remember that there was an especially close bond of fellowship between Paul and the Christians in Philippi.

Now, let us get a little historical background for the writing of this letter. Actually, the Philippian church was founded in about the year A.D. 50. But the letter to the Philippians was not written until about A.D. 61, some eleven years later. And many things happened in between. Paul completed the second missionary journey, on which he founded the Philippian church; then he made the third missionary journey, after which he went to Jerusalem. There he was arrested and spent the next two years in jail in Caesarea. Then, he appealed to Caesar and spent two more years in prison in Rome. These last two years were probably the years 60 and 61. And it was toward the end of this second year that Paul wrote Philippians from his prison quarters.

In Philippians 1:13 notice that Paul says: "My bonds in Christ are manifest in all the palace." He mentions his bonds several times in this letter, making it clear he was in prison. Then notice in chapter 4, verse 22, he sends greetings to the Philippians from the Christians who live in the city where he is imprisoned, and he particularly mentions "they that are of Caesar's household." This confirms the belief that Paul was in Rome at this time.

Now, turn to Philippians 2:23, and there you will see that Paul tells the Philippians he is planning to send Timothy to them, as soon as he sees how it will go with him. That statement indicates that Paul expects to find out soon what the outcome of his case before Caesar will be. And that is the reason we say that Philippians was written toward the end of the two-year Roman imprisonment.

You also need to understand that a certain chain of events had taken place after Paul got to Rome, and before this epistle was written to the Philippians. First, the Philippians learned that Paul had been sent to prison in Rome. Next, the Philippians decided to send some gifts to Paul. They sent these gifts by a man named Epaphroditus, and you will find this mentioned in Philippians 4:18. There Paul says: " . . . having received of Epaphroditus the things which were sent from you . . . . " Then, after Epaphroditus arrived in Rome with the gifts which the Philippians sent, he fell sick. He was so seriously ill that he was near death. The news of his illness got back to the Philippians, and they were worried. The fact that they were worried over him got back to Epaphroditus. All this is said in Philippians 2:26, 27.

When Paul writes Philippians, however, Epaphroditus has recovered from his illness, a fact which Paul attributes to the mercy of God in Philippians 2:27. Now Epaphroditus is ready to return home to the Philippians, as Paul notes in 2:28. This is a wonderful opportunity for Paul to send the Philippians a letter. Furthermore, they had sent the gifts, and Paul wants to express his appreciation for those gifts. Too, Paul recognized they would be concerned over his own lengthy imprisonment, and he wants to reassure them that he is confident God's will is being done. Paul also wants to warn them against the Judaizers, who were causing trouble in the churches everywhere they could. Finally, Paul had learned that two of the leading women in the church at Philippi had fallen out and were creating a disturbance, and he wants to urge them to settle their differences.

Now, we are ready to look at Philippians more closely. I remind you that there was a very close spirit of fellowship between Paul and the Christians in Philippi. I also remind you that this letter was written, more than for any other reason, to express gratitude for gifts which the Philippians had sent to Paul. Surely, then, you can see that Philippians is going to be a very personal letter. As you read the epistle, you will feel the affection Paul felt for these people. You will also notice that there is no direct reference to any internal problems within the church at Philippi except for the strife between the two women. Paul must have been happy to be able to write a letter to a group who were relatively free from problems. You will also note there is not much time spent in doctrinal discussion in the letter. Evidently, the Philippians were well taught.

So I say, again, that Philippians is a very personal letter. As you read it, I think you will agree with many interpreters who have observed that the theme of Philippians is Christian *joy.* You may wonder how Paul could express such joy when he was in jail and uncertain about his future. But I think you will agree that joy is the characteristic of Paul's spirit that is most prominent in this letter. And when you stop to think about it, there were many things for him to rejoice about. He was glad about the spiritual maturity of the Philippians, and we learned long ago that the thing that made Paul happiest was for his converts to be stable and mature. He was glad for their generous gifts; their attitude showed they wanted to participate in his ministry. Furthermore, even though he was bound, he was glad that the gospel was not bound, that the preaching of the gospel was, in fact, being *helped* by his imprisonment. And that is all that mattered to Paul. Finally, he knew Christ, and he had learned to be content in any sort of external circumstances so the joy of the Lord was not gone from his soul. You just cannot read Philippians without finding a new sense of joy. No wonder Paul says, in Philippians 4:4: "Rejoice in the Lord alway: and again I say, Rejoice."

And now let us turn to verse 1, chapter 1 and begin our survey of Philippians. Perhaps you will want to take notes, or even to make notes in your Bible. Anyway, I am not going to start by giving an outline for the entire book. Instead, we will simply examine it one section at a time. You may find it helpful, however, to notice that the first two chapters are primarily personal matters, dealing with the relationship between Paul and the Philippians; while the last two chapters are mostly instructional, containing some words of warning and exhortation.

The first part of the letter is the opening salutation. This is in chapter 1, verses 1, 2. This is much the same as the opening few verses in all of Paul's letters, and so detailed comments are not needed here.

The first main portion of this letter to the Philippians is chapter 1, verses 3-11. We need to look at this part closely, because it expresses so well the spirit of fellowship and joy that existed in the relationship between Paul and the Philippian believers. Let us call this section, 1:3-11, "Paul's Joyful Relationship with the Philippians." Note verses 3-8: "I thank my God upon every remembrance of you, Always in every prayer of mine for you all making request with joy, For your fellowship in the gospel from the first day until now; Being confident of this very thing, that he which hath begun a good work in you will perform it until the day of Jesus Christ: Even as it is meet for me to think this of you all, because I have you in my heart; inasmuch as both in my bonds, and in the defence and confirmation of the gospel, ye all are partakers of my grace. For God is my record, how greatly I long after you all in the bowels of Jesus Christ."

You certainly cannot miss the *joy* here, can you? Notice the different things Paul says about his feelings for the Philippians. In verse 3, thanks; in verse 4, prayers; in verse 5, fellowship; in verse 6, confidence; in verse 7, Paul's heart; and in verse 8, he longs after them. You might want to underline those key words that express just how dear the Philippians were to Paul. I am always impressed and amazed, when I read any of Paul's letters, at the depth of his feelings for those to whom he ministered. He wanted to see them grow and prosper spiritually, and he constantly prayed for them. That is the reason he can say, in verse 8: "For God is my record, how greatly I long after you . . . . "

As we have already seen, one of the things that prompted Paul's letter was the gift which the Philippians had sent to minister to him in his imprisonment. I want you to take note of the interesting way Paul refers to this gift in verse 5. He calls it "fellowship in the gospel." Again, in verse 7, he says the Philippians are "partakers" of his grace. The word fellowship and the word partakers are the same, and they are both the same as the word "communicate" over in Philippians 4:15, where Paul specifically speaks of giving and receiving. What Paul means here in Philippians 1:5 and 7 is that the Philippians' gifts made them partners in his ministry. And verse 5 means that the Philippians had been such partners all along, ever since Paul first made their acquaintance when he established the church in their city some eleven years previously. When Paul presents his souls to the Lord on judgment day, the Philippians will receive part of the credit for the work that won them.

Paul closes this first section with a prayer for the Philippians, contained in verses 9-11: "And this I pray, that your love may abound yet more and more in knowledge and in all judgment; That ye may approve things that are excellent; that ye may be sincere and without offence till the day of Christ; Being filled with the fruits of righteousness, which are by Jesus Christ, unto the glory and praise of God." You will not find it difficult to break this prayer up into its separate petitions, and I think you will find that ought to be desired by us for all Christians: abounding love, spiritual discernment, blameless behavior, and fullness of righteous deeds that glorify God.

And now we move on to the second major portion of the letter to the Philippians which starts in chapter 1, verse 12, and goes on through verse 26. The first part we entitled "Paul's Joyful Relationship with the Philippians." This second part let us call "Paul's Joy in His Suffering." No doubt the Philippians had sent word to Paul that they were much grieved by the fact that he was bound. Paul wants to reassure them that he is not in despair because of his condition. Instead, he still has joy and confidence that God's will is being accomplished.

Now I am not going to take time to cite all of this passage from 1:12-26, but I do want to point out to you that "Paul's Joy in His Suffering" was based on at least two very important factors. First, he could still be joyful in jail because he felt that his imprisonment was actually contributing to the spread of the gospel. He was bound, but the gospel was not bound. Indeed, the gospel was progressing more rapidly as a result of his imprisonment, and so Paul was willing to be bound if the gospel could gain ground. You can see this point made by Paul in verse 12, for example: "the things which happened unto me have fallen out rather unto the futherance of the gospel." In verse 14, he tells one reason this is true: "Many of the brethren in the Lord, waxing confident by my bonds, are much more bold to speak the word without fear." In other words, some had been challenged by Paul's example to speak out more boldly.

The second reason Paul could rejoice in the midst of imprisonment is to be found down in verses 21-23. There Paul explains that the threat of death cannot rob him of his joy, simply because death will only serve to bring him into the presence of the Lord whom he loves! How can you threaten a man who says, "Kill me if you will; I have been wanting to go on and leave this world anyway!" That is exactly what Paul means in verse 21: "To die is gain." Or in verse 23: "Having a desire to depart, and to be with Christ; which is far better." He hastens to add, however, that he knows that there is a ministry he must perform on earth, and that he cannot leave until that is finished. You see, then, that Paul could have joy in suffering because he loved the Lord and was submitted to the Lord's will for him.

We come now to the third major portion of Philippians, which begins at chapter 1, verse 27, and extends through chapter 2, verse 18. This part of Philippians we can entitle "Paul's Joy in the Philippians' Spiritual Progress." In this section of the letter, Paul indicates the thing that determines his joy is not whether he is in jail or free, but the success of his converts. Paul's joy is dependent on their lives. And he wants to tell them some of the things that will particularly please him. You will see, then, as you read this part of Philippians that it contains some exhortations about their attitudes and behavior. If the Philippians will heed these exhortations, they will make Paul happy. As he puts it in 2:2: "Fulfil ye my joy." Futhermore, these things will also make the Philippians happy; and so Paul says in 2:18: "For the same cause also do ye joy, and rejoice with me."

There are too many things in this part of Philippians for us to be able to look at every one in detail. So we shall have to select some of the most typical exhortations that Paul addresses to his readers. Notice 1:27: "Let your conversation be as it becometh the gospel of Christ." That is the kind of thing Paul will be happy about. Conversation, as you know, means manner of life. Paul wants his readers, and us, to live in such a way as will bring credit to the gospel. Notice also 2:2: "Fulfil ye my joy, that ye be likeminded, having the same love, being of one accord, of one mind." In this exhortation Paul expresses a concern that was always important to him, that there be a spirit of fellowship, love, and harmony among believers. That need is just as important today as ever; we need one another.

Another thing Paul was concerned about is seen in 2:15, 16: "Be blameless and harmless, the sons of God, without rebuke, in the midst of a crooked and perverse nation, among whom ye shine as lights in the world; Holding forth the word of life." You see, Paul was concerned about the Philippians' testimony in the world. He recognized what Jesus meant when He called His disciples "the light of the world." Paul's heart would be made especially glad by reports that his converts were letting their lights shine, both by the uprightness of their lives and by the declaration of the Word.

Perhaps the most important exhortation which Paul addresses to the Philippians in this section is found in 2:3-8. In verse 3, Paul says: "Let each esteem other better than themselves." He goes on in verse 4 to say: "Look not every man on his own things, but every man also on the things of others." In these verses, then, Paul is urging the Philippians to humbleness of mind and the service of one another. This is true Christian love by which each of us considers the needs of his fellow-Christians as more important than his own needs. When that is our attitude, we gladly serve one another. You will note that Paul gives us a very challenging example for this kind of attitude. In verse 5 he reminds us that this was the attitude of Christ Himself. And look at what Christ did, as is seen in verses 7, 8: "Made himself of no reputation, and took upon him the form of a servant, and was made in the likeness of men: And being found in fashion as a man, he humbled himself, and became obedient unto death."

Christ certainly served others' needs rather than selfish considerations. That is what Paul wants the Philippians to do, and by which he will rejoice.

But now we must move on to the next section of Philippians. This is a brief section, from 2:19-30. In this section Paul talks about his immediate plans both for himself and his co-workers. Perhaps we can fit this part into the theme of the whole letter by entitling it: "Paul's Joy in His Co-Workers." Two of Paul's fellow-servants are mentioned in particular. The first is Timothy, a young man with whom we are already familiar. Paul speaks of him in 2:19-24. He indicates that he is planning to send Timothy to Philippi in the near future, as he states in verse 19. In verse 23, he says he will wait until he sees how it is going to go with him, and then Timothy will be able to tell the Philippians what has been learned about Paul's case.

The other man Paul talks about in these verses is Epaphroditus, who had come to Rome to bring the Philippians' gifts. As I explained earlier, Epaphroditus had become sick and was ready to go back to Philippi. He will carry this letter to the Philippians. Note what Paul says about him in verses 29, 30: "Hold such in reputation: Because for the work of Christ he was nigh unto death, not regarding his life." Like Paul himself, Epaphroditus lived only for the service of Christ.

When we come to chapter 3, we move into the fifth part of this letter to the Philippians. This part we can call "Paul's Joy in Christ's Righteousness." This section begins at 3:1 and goes through 3:21, and most of this chapter consists of a mild warning to the Philippians against those false teachers who try to substitute self-righteousness for Christ's righteousness. Notice in verse 2, to begin with, that Paul says: "Beware of dogs." And he does not mean bulldogs, either! He is talking about those who attempt to base righteousness on the keeping of the Law. As you know, the Jews did this, and they were the very ones who had caused Paul to be jailed. Even worse, some of the professing Christians with a Jewish background taught that justification required that the Law of Moses be kept.

Paul's view is that such a false doctrine is based on the works of the flesh. He reminds the Philippians, in verses 4-6, that he personally was a Jew and had rigorously observed Jewish ritual. But, as he puts it in verse 7: "What things were gain to me, those I counted loss for Christ." Then in verse 9, Paul reaches the climax of the discussion: "Not having mine own righteousness, which is of the law, but that which is through the faith of Christ, the righteousness which is of God by faith." This verse makes plain the difference between those who try to save themselves by their own works and merit, and those who recognize their sinfulness and cast themselves on the mercy of God for the righteousness of Christ. Paul's confidence rested entirely on Christ's righteousness, and so should ours.

We do not have space to cover the rest of the chapter in great detail, but there is at least one more thing about this section of which I want you to take note. The joy that Paul had because his confidence was in Christ's righteousness created a real hope in him which served as a goal toward which he always pressed. Note how Paul expresses this in verses 12-14: "Not as though I had already attained . . . I follow after . . . Brethren, I count not myself to have apprehended: but this one thing I do, forgetting those things which are behind, and reaching forth unto those things which are before, I press toward the mark for the prize of the high calling of God in Christ Jesus."

No doubt these are some of the most memorable words of Philippians. Paul's hope in Christ caused him never to swerve from what God had given him to do. Living for Christ is the greatest purpose for which any person can live. Notice also verses 20, 21, where this same hope is expressed: "Our conversation is in heaven; from whence also we look for the Saviour, the Lord Jesus Christ: Who shall change our vile body, that it may be fashioned like unto his glorious body." If that kind of confidence and hope in Christ, looking especially to His return, does not give a Christian joy, then nothing can!

Now, at last, we come to the sixth and final part of Philippians. This section covers all of chapter 4, except for the last few verses, which provide the parting words. This chapter we can call "Paul's Joy in a Christ-like Church." In these verses Paul more or less concludes the letter with a few brief exhortations to the Philippians about their church life and about their attitudes as Christians. Paul will be glad to see his children walking in such order and Christ-likeness.

First, he mentions in verses 2, 3, the matter of the two women, Euodias and Syntyche, who had become involved in some sort of disagreement. They were good women, as clearly indicated in verse 3. We do not know anything more about them or their argument. But harmony among the believers is an essential part of a Christ-like church.

In verse 5 Paul mentions another Christ-like quality: moderation. This word actually means gentleness. In verse 6, another quality is mentioned: freedom from care. The words "Be careful for nothing" simply mean that a Christian ought not be worried or anxious over any of the concerns of life. Instead, as Paul indicates, one's needs should be made known to God in prayer; and then one can rest easy in the peace that God gives.

Perhaps verse 8 is the finest summary of Christ-likeness to be found anywhere: "Finally, brethren, whatsoever things are true, . . . honest, . . . just, . . . pure, . . . lovely, . . . of good report; . . . any virtue, . . . any praise, think on these things." Men have often said that a person becomes what he thinks about. No doubt our lives are strongly influenced by the things we let occupy our minds. We will be most Christ-like if we occupy our minds with such things as are listed in this verse. And our lives will bring joy both to ourselves and to others who observe us.

Most of the rest of chapter 4 of Philippians is by way of conclusion. In verse 10, Paul brings up again the subject of the gifts which the Philippians had sent. He is particularly glad for their concern. He commends them for this in verse 14, and recalls warmly that the Philippians have been the most faithful of all his churches to respond to his material needs. But we cannot pass this part by so quickly without noting the wonderful expression of attitude which Paul gives in verses 11-13. In verse 11 he says: "I have learned, in whatsoever state I am, therewith to be content." And in verse 13: "I can do all things through Christ which strengtheneth me." Paul wanted the Philippians to know that, even though he sincerely appreciated their material gifts, his joy did not depend on his physical condition. Whether hungry or full, well or ill, bound or free, he had satisfaction in the Lord. There is the secret of real joy.

Perhaps there is no better thought with which to close our examination of this book. Paul himself concludes shortly after these words with the important assurance of verse 19: "My God shall supply all your need according to his riches in glory by Christ Jesus." That promise is for us all. Paul's benediction in the letter will be mine upon you: "The grace of our Lord Jesus Christ be with you all. Amen."

A SURVEY OF THE BOOK OF

Colossians

by Dr. Robert Picirilli

Once again, it is a privilege to be able to speak to you by cassette recording. I trust you have your Bible handy and are ready to give your undivided attention, for the next thirty minutes, to a survey of the Book of Colossians.

You are already aware that this is one of Paul's letters. But there is much more about the historical background of Colossians that is especially important. So let us devote our attention, for about the first ten minutes of the time, to background information using a question and answer approach.

Question number one is this: When was the church at Colosse founded, and was it founded by Paul? In order to answer this question, we have to think back to the record given us in the Book of Acts, where Paul's missionary journeys are described. I want to direct your attention to the *third* missionary journey, so turn to Acts, chapter 18, verse 23, where the record of the third journey begins.

In Acts 18:23, you will see that Paul started his journey by revisiting the churches he had established earlier in Galatia and Phrygia. He probably did not tarry there long, for he was eager to get to Ephesus, the capital of the Roman province of Asia. Acts 19:1 tells about his soon arrival in that important city. If you have a map of New Testament times handy, you will quickly be able to locate Ephesus. The province of Asia was the westernmost district on the peninsula we call Asia Minor, and Ephesus, the capital city, was located in the western side of Asia, on the coast.

Now look at Acts 19:8, where the description of Paul's ministry at Ephesus is given. First, you see, he was permitted to speak regularly in the synagogue for about three months. But then, as usual, the Jews who did not believe became antagonistic. Therefore, as Acts 19:9 indicates, Paul began teaching daily in the school of a man named Tyrannus. We really do not know anything else about this fellow or about his school. But the thing about this ministry at Ephesus that I really want you to notice is said in verse 10 of Acts 19: "And this continued by the space of two years; so that all they which dwelt in Asia heard the word of the Lord Jesus, both Jews and Greeks."

You see, in this verse, one especially important fact: Paul's ministry was extensive. While he was in Ephesus the gospel reached out and covered the whole district of which Ephesus was capital.

That is not surprising, after all. For one thing, Paul had many co-workers. No doubt he sent them out into the various cities of Asia. For another thing, Ephesus was the district capital; and many people would have been traveling back and forth regularly, in and out of Ephesus, from the other cities and towns of the district. Therefore, even though Paul himself probably did not *personally* go around the district and visit the other towns, his gospel did.

We conclude, therefore, that Paul did not personally found the church at Colosse. However, he obviously considered that it was one of *his* churches! Else he would not have felt free to write them. He always said that he did not try to build on another man's foundation. But if the church at Colosse were founded by Paul's converts and co-workers, under his own supervision, while he himself was in Ephesus, then he certainly had a right to consider it one of his churches. Colosse, by the way, was only about 100 miles east of Ephesus, in the district of Asia; and do not forget that Acts says that *all* Asia heard the gospel under the impetus of Paul's ministry in Ephesus. The answer to our first question, then, is that the church at Colosse was founded by Paul's converts and co-workers, while he ministered at Ephesus on his third missionary journey in about the year A.D. 54 or 55.

Now let us go to question number two: When was the letter to the Colossians written, and where was Paul at the time? The answer to this question is pretty well agreed upon by most interpreters. Paul was in prison at Rome when he wrote the Colossians, and the year was about A.D. 60. You may recall that at the end of Paul's third missionary journey, most of which was spent in Ephesus, he went down to Jerusalem. There he was seized by the unsaved Jews and jailed. He spent two years in prison in Caesarea, and then was sent to Rome where he continued in jail for two more years. Thus, about five years elapsed between the founding of the church in Colosse, and the writing of the letter to the Colossians. And Paul spent a solid three years of this time in jail, assuming that he wrote Colossians in the *first* year of his two years in Rome.

You will see some references in the letter to the Colossians to Paul's imprisonment. Look at chapter 4, verse 3, for example, where Paul says: "I am also in bonds." Look also at verse 10 of chapter 4, where Paul refers to Aristarchus his "*fellowprisoner.*" Again, look at the closing verse of the letter, Colossians 4:18. Paul says: "Remember my bonds."

Now let us come to the third and final question about the historical background of Colossians. This is the most important question of all: Why was the letter to the Colossians written? Or, put it another way: What was the problem at Colosse?

One thing is clear: Whatever the problem, it was reported to Paul by a man named Epaphras. Look at Colossians 1:7; here Paul says the Colossians had learned about the grace of God from Epaphras, which probably means that Epaphras was the very one who had founded, under Paul's supervision, the church at Colosse. Now turn to Colossians 4:12, where Paul says that Epaphras is now with Paul in Rome sending greetings to the Colossians. All this makes it quite clear that Epaphras had recently come to Paul in Rome, from Colosse.

But back to the main question: What was the problem? There was a very definite false doctrine being taught in Colosse, a dangerous doctrine which threatened the spiritual life of the church there. Time does not permit us to explore all the philosophical ideas involved in the error at Colosse, but the main points are these. First, the heretics at Colosse taught that Jesus was not fully God, that He was a Divine being of some lesser importance than God the Father. They said Christ was not eternal but owed His existence to the activity of God the Father.

Of course, the false teachers said Jesus was to be worshiped, but not with the full honor He deserves. Furthermore, they also believed that there were various other divine beings of different levels who might be worshiped too. These included several different ranks of angelic beings.

And there were still other things wrong. In particular, the false teachers at Colosse held the Greek philosophical view that all matter is evil. And, since the human body is made of matter, they said the body is evil. Consequently, some of them believed that Christians ought to deprive the body of as many things as possible; so they adopted the strange practices of self-denial which we often associate with hermits. On the other hand, some of them said that whatever the evil body wants, let it have; it cannot affect the spirit in any way. So they practiced or tolerated all sorts of moral wickedness.

Now let me summarize the answer to question number three by listing the four main things involved in the heresy at Colosse: (1) a wrong view of Christ as a lesser god; (2) a misguided notion of angel-worship; (3) an extreme form of self-denial based on the doctrine that physical things are evil; and (4) a wicked permission of immorality, based on the same doctrine. Paul felt he must write immediately in order to try to set things straight.

I trust you have been helped with this rather lengthy introduction to Colossians. Surely you can see that an understanding of these things will help us understand the letter itself much better. And now it is time for us to turn to the letter, and survey its contents.

To begin with, take a moment to turn the pages of Colossians in your Bible, and notice that there are but four chapters. If you will take time after a while to read through the epistle from start to finish, I am sure you will agree that the book just naturally divides itself into two equal halves. In this two-fold division, the first two chapters give doctrinal instruction, while the last two give practical teachings. You might say that chapters 1, 2 deal with doctrine, and chapters 3, 4 deal with deeds. That is a pretty good balance, and it reflects Paul's usual concern both for what we need to know and for how we live.

Verses 1-14 of chapter 1 provide a personal introduction to the letter. As usual, the first two verses are Paul's opening salutation: Paul identifies himself as the writer, the Colossians, to whom he is writing, and blesses them with the customary grace and peace. The next part of the introduction covers verses 3-8 and is an expression of thanksgiving for the faith of the Colossians. Let us read some of these verses: "We give thanks to God and the Father of our Lord Jesus Christ, praying always for you, Since we heard of your faith in Christ Jesus, and of the love which ye have to all the saints, For the hope which is laid up for you in heaven, whereof ye heard before in the word of the truth of the gospel; Which is come unto you, as it is in all the world; and bringeth forth fruit, as it doth also in you, since the day ye heard of it, and knew the grace of God in truth" (Colossians 1:3-6).

You will not find it difficult to go through these verses and pick out the things Paul is thankful for in reference to the Colossians. One thing in particular I want to point out to you, though, is the grouping together of faith, love, and hope, in verses 4, 5. Paul often groups together these three graces in his writings. They provide a pretty good summary of Christian experience, and Paul is thankful for the Christian experience of the Colossians. Notice, too, how he refers, in verse 6, to the time when the gospel came to the Colossians; and they came to the knowledge of God's grace. You will also see, in verse 7, that Epaphras, whom I have mentioned to you already, was the one who evidently first taught the Colossians about the grace of God; and Paul is thankful for his ministry there. Verse 8 makes it clear that Epaphras had come to Rome, where Paul was, and reported to Paul about the spiritual condition of the Colossians.

Now, starting in verse 9, Paul concludes the personal introduction to this letter with an interesting prayer. Again, let us read: "For this cause we also, since the day we heard it, do not cease to pray for you, and to desire that ye might be filled with the knowledge of his will in all wisdom and spiritual understanding; That ye might walk worthy of the Lord unto all pleasing, being fruitful in every good work, and increasing in the knowledge of God; Strengthened with all might, according to his glorious power, unto all patience and longsuffering with joyfulness; Giving thanks unto the Father" (1:9-12). First, Paul is interested in their *knowledge.* In verse 9 you see the words knowledge, wisdom, and spiritual understanding. In verse 10 note the emphasis on increasing in the knowledge of God. Second, Paul is interested in their *daily lives,* and this is the reason he prays, in verse 10, that they may walk worthy of the Lord and please the Lord in everything. Verse 10 also mentions good works which need to be manifested publicly in their lives, like fruit on a tree. Third, Paul is concerned about their need for *spiritual strength* as you can plainly see in verse 11. He prays that they may be strengthened so that they can persevere. Fourth, and finally, Paul prays that the Colossians may have *joy and thankfulness.* Note the reference to joy in verse 11 and to thanksgiving in verse 12.

It seems to me that this prayer of Paul's is an excellent expression of the needs that all of us Christians have. I think you will find it well worth your while to mull over this prayer in verses 9-14, often, and make Paul's prayer for the Colossians your own prayer for yourself and your fellow-believers.

We move on, now, to verse 15 of chapter 1; at this point we enter into the main lessons of the letter to the Colossians. As I have already pointed out most of the first two chapters deal with matters of doctrine; and that is exactly what is involved here. I hope you will remember that one of the main doctrinal problems at Colosse grew out of the fact that some false teachers were denying that Jesus was truly God. So the very first thing Paul does in his letter is lay down the truth about Jesus Christ. This part of the letter extends from 1:15 through 23, in which Paul deals with *who* Jesus is, and then explains *what* Jesus has done. Let us take this one part at a time, and first let us read verses 15 through 19. See if you can pick out the things Paul says about who Jesus is. "Who is the image of the invisible God, the firstborn of every creature: For by him were all things created, that are in heaven, and that are in earth, visible and invisible, whether they be thrones, or dominions, or principalities, or powers: all things were created by him, and for him: And he is before all things, and by him all things consist. And he is the head of the body, the church: who is the beginning, the firstborn from the dead; that in all things he might have the preeminence. For it pleased the Father that in him should all fulness dwell."

Perhaps we can understand this section best by listing the important facts. Number one: Paul defines the relationship between Jesus and God. In verse 15, Paul says Christ is the image of the invisible God. This means that Jesus Christ is God Himself expressed in visible form; verse 19 says that all the fullness of God dwells in Him. This teaching of Paul's was in direct contradiction to the heresy at Colosse which taught that Jesus was a second-rate Divine being.

Number two: Paul defines the relationship between Jesus and creation. The false teachers said Jesus was a creature Himself, but what Paul means in verse 15 is that Jesus is before all that creation, and thus is not a part of the creation. In verse 16, he reminds us that Jesus Himself was the Creator of all things. Paul takes another step in verse 17, showing that Jesus is the One who upholds all the material things that exist even now. Nothing ever came into existence without His work, nor does anything ever continue to exist without Him.

Now number three: Paul defines the relationship between Jesus and the Church. This you find in verse 18 where Jesus is described as the head of the Church. The heretics at Colosse had failed to give Jesus the preeminence He so properly deserves.

Now at this point look at verses 20 through 22 in which Paul summarizes the *work* of Christ: "And, having made peace through the blood of his cross, by him to reconcile all things unto himself; by him, I say, whether they be things in earth, or things in heaven. And you, that were sometime alienated and enemies in your mind by wicked works, yet now hath he reconciled In the body of his flesh through death, to present you holy and unblameable and unreproveable in his sight."

Paul speaks primarily of Christ's death in these verses. The death of Christ is certainly the heart of the gospel and the chief act of Christ's redemptive work. And notice the wonderful word Paul chooses to express the effect of that atoning death: "reconcile." There was an enmity between men and God that separated them; but Jesus, by His death, accomplished the reconciliation of God and men.

I think it is especially interesting the way Paul closes this summary of Christ's work. Notice verse 22 which refers to the purpose of the work of Christ to present us, in the end, to God as holy beings. Yet take note of verse 23 which begins with that biggest of little words "if." Jesus will not be able to realize the finally-intended purpose of His redemptive work *unless* the believer continues in his faith in Christ. Paul feared that the false doctrine at Colosse would turn some from their saving faith.

Once more, now, before we leave behind verses 15 through 23, I remind you how important this section is in presenting to us a clear and concise summary of the doctrine of the person and work of Christ. You will do well to restudy these words often. Our very salvation is based on the truths found here and upon our personal appropriation of these truths by faith.

But we must move on. The next section of Colossians finishes up chapter 1, beginning at verse 24. In these verses you will notice that Paul is describing his own personal part in the ministry of redemption. As already explained in the preceding verses, redemption was the work of Christ. But the *servant* of Christ also has a part to play in the application of redemption to other human beings. We will not take time to read all this, but I especially want you to notice verses 28, 29, in which we have something of a summary of Paul's view of his own ministry. Here is what he says: "Whom we preach, warning every man, and teaching every man in all wisdom; that we may present every man perfect in Christ Jesus: Whereunto I also labour."

You can see, in this, how Paul conceives of his work. His task is to present perfect, mature Christians to the Lord Jesus at His return. In order to carry out that task, Paul both warns and teaches. In other words, he both evangelizes, winning men to Christ, and then teaches his converts, building them up toward that goal of mature believers. Sometimes you hear people argue about the supreme task of the Church, whether it is to evangelize the lost or edify the saints. That is a foolish argument, at least as Paul views it, because both are absolutely necessary to the goal of presenting mature believers to Christ.

Now when we move into chapter 2, we change gears only slightly. As I have already said, the first 2 chapters are doctrinal: and we have been seeing the positive side of doctrinal instruction in chapter 1. In chapter 2 we see the negative side. Paul warns the Colossians about the false philosophies and practices that might tempt them.

Without our taking time to read a great deal of chapter 2 right now, let me point out to you some of the most prominent things Paul warns against in this chapter. First, Paul warns them against fancy philosophies that are not built on the true doctrine of Jesus Christ. You can see this in verse 4, for example, where he cautions them about "enticing words." Note also verse 8, where he warns about "philosophy," a word that means love of wisdom. As Paul puts it in verse 3, all the treasures of true wisdom are to be found in Christ; and what they need is indicated in verse 5, a steadfast faith in Christ.

The second wrong emphasis Paul warns against is found in verses 9-17. Here Paul cautions them about Jewish ceremonialism. The heresy at Colosse had a Jewish flavor. Some were putting too much emphasis on the ritual and tradition of Mosaic Law. Thus, in verse 14, Paul reminds the Colossians that the Law was nailed to the Cross and is no longer in force. This is the reason he says in verses 16, 17: "Let no man therefore judge you in meat, or in drink, or in respect of an holyday, or of the new moon, or of the sabbath days: Which are a shadow of things to come; but the body is of Christ."

The third thing Paul warns the Colossians against is angel-worship. You should remember that I pointed out earlier that the doctrine of angel-worship was part of the false teaching at Colosse. This, then, is the reason verse 18 says: "Let no man beguile you of your reward in a voluntary humility and worshipping of angels."

Finally, chapter 2 warns the Colossians against the false separation some were practicing at Colosse. This is seen in verses 20-23. By the way, you really need to understand these verses, since verse 21, in particular, is often wrongly interpreted. Notice that this verse says, "Touch not; taste not; handle not." And a lot of people quote this as something we ought to follow. But this verse is a quotation of what the *false teachers* said. Paul calls this the commandments and doctrines of men. Verse 23 explains that this teaching was based on the idea that the fleshly body ought to be neglected. Remember, as I pointed out earlier, they had the foolish notion that physical things, including the human body, were evil. And they practiced what we call asceticism, the denying of anything which the human body might enjoy except the barest minimum of food, clothing, and shelter.

Now look back over chapter 2, one more time, before we leave it. I find it extremely interesting to note that Paul presents Christ as the answer to all these false doctrines. In the first eight verses, where the warning is against fancy philosophy, Paul says that all the treasures of real wisdom are in Christ. In verses 9-17, where the danger is in Jewish ritual, Paul reminds us that the rituals were mere shadows, and the substance is in Christ. In verses 18, 19, where he warns against angel-worship, the answer is to be found in seeing Christ as the Head of the Church, the only One to whom worship is properly given. Finally, in verses 20-23, where he cautions against too much subjection to man-made rules about bodily denial, the answer is to be found in remembering that we are dead with Christ to such ordinances. All this causes me to remember that the proper view and understanding of Christ and His work will solve most of the problems of false doctrine any time.

Now we must hurry on to chapters 3 and 4, the last half of Colossians, which we will have to survey somewhat more briefly. I have already pointed out to you the fact that the last two chapters are practical rather than doctrinal. The first two chapters give the doctrinal foundation, and the last two talk about the kind of life a Christian builds on this foundation. One is a matter of understanding, the other practice. The two must not ever be separated.

This is the truth about which Paul reminds us in chapter 3, verses 1-3: "If ye then be risen with Christ, seek those things which are above . . . . Set your affection on things above, not on things on the earth. For ye are dead, and your life is hid with Christ in God." In other words, we have a certain position in Christ. We are accounted as having died with Him and as having arisen from the dead with Him. This basis is the right one on which to build the requirements of Christian behavior.

The first main part of this section on Christian living extends from 3:5-17 and is built around an analogy with one's clothing. Paul says there is an "old man" and a "new man." And we should put off the old man as we would put off dirty clothing. We should put on the new man like a clean garment.

Look at verse 9, for example, where you see the reference to the putting off of the old man. Then verse 10 starts talking about putting on the new man. You need to understand what Paul means by these two terms. The *old* man is simply the person before he is saved: in other words, the way of life of the sinner. The *new* man is the person after conversion, the way of life of a believer. Paul's point is very plain: The Christian should not continue to practice the kind of deeds which he practiced before salvation. He lists many examples in verses 5-9: "fornication, uncleanness, inordinate affection, evil concupiscence, and covetousness." The list continues in verses 8, 9: "anger, wrath, malice, blasphemy, filthy communication." As verse 6 says, this is the way the sinner lives; and this is why God's wrath is upon the sinner. What ugly clothes these are!

And how much more attractive are the clothes of the new man as listed from verse 10 on. Look at verses 12, 13, for example: "bowels of mercies, kindness, humbleness of mind, meekness, longsuffering; Forbearing one another," and so on. Then in verse 14 Paul mentions the most important of all: charity. Furthermore, as seen in verse 15, there is the peace of God which should rule our hearts; and verse 16 speaks of our acceptance of the responsbility to teach one another in spiritual things. I do not know about you, but I like the garments of the new man a whole lot better than those of the old man. On second thought, I *do* know about you if you are *really* a Christian. You like the new man's way better, too. I urge you to spend a lot of time with Colossians 3:5-17.

The next section of this letter is the part that begins with chapter 3, verse 18, and goes on through chapter 4, verse 1. This section deals with the Christian's family responsibilities; and these, too, concern the way of life of the new man. In these verses there are three pairs of family relationships. The first is the husband-wife relationship; the second, the parent-child relationship; and the third, the master-servant relationship. By the way, these are treated in exactly the same way in Ephesians.

You will notice that Paul addresses some instructions to each member of each of the three pairs, and that he lists the less authoritative member of each pair first. We do not have time to examine each of these closely, but I think you will find some help here for your own Christian family relationships. And, even though we do not now have slaves in our households, there are some good points in Paul's teaching about these that you can apply to your own job situation and to the employer-employee relationship.

Now that we have reached verse 2 of chapter 4, you will find that most of the remainder of the chapter is in the way of closing words. In verses 2-6, Paul urges the Colossians to be faithful in prayer, and particularly to pray for him. Is it not interesting that Paul does not ask them, in verse 3, to pray that he may be released from his bonds; but that he may find opportunity, even in his bonds, to preach the gospel?

In verses 7-9, Paul mentions Tychichus and Onesimus, who will be bringing this very letter to the Colossians, and who will inform the Colossians in more detail about the circumstances in which Paul presently finds himself.

In verses 10-14, Paul sends the Colossians greetings from several fellow-workers who are presently with him in Rome. Aristarchus, in fact, is in jail with him; the others are probably not. They include John Mark, mentioned in verse 10; Jesus Justus, in verse 11; Epaphras, mentioned in verses 12, 13; and Luke and Demas, mentioned in verse 14.

In verse 15, Paul asks the Colossians to greet the Christians in nearby Laodicea for him. In verse 16, Paul suggests that the Colossians exchange letters with the Laodiceans. By the way, this "epistle from Laodicea" may have been a copy of the letter to the Ephesians; but we cannot be positive about this. In verse 17, Paul gives some special words of exhortation for Archippus who was probably the pastor at Colosse. Finally, in verse 18, Paul takes the pen from his scribe and writes the closing words himself. His one last prayer is especially moving: "Remember my bonds." And his parting words are both simple and wonderful: "Grace be with you." I trust that you have grown in grace as a result of this study of Colossians.

A SURVEY OF THE BOOK OF

First Thessalonians

by Dr. Robert Picirilli

It is time now for us to survey 1 Thessalonians. I trust you have your Bible handy, and maybe even a pen you can make notes with.

First Thessalonians is short, but interesting, and has as much to say to us as to those Christians who first read it. But before we begin a close examination of the *contents* of this letter, let us first pay attention to some background facts. We will understand the message of this book better if we also understand the historical circumstances behind it.

Turn to Acts, chapter 17, for a minute. You remember Paul made three great missionary journeys in his ministry. Acts 17 is in the middle of the second of these three journeys. Paul had started out, as usual, from Antioch in Syria. He went through Galatia and came finally to Troas, on the western end of Asia Minor, uncertain where to go next. That night God gave Paul a vision of a man in Macedonia calling for help. And so he and his companions—Silas, Timothy, and Luke—boarded ship for Macedonia.

They first preached in Philippi, and a good church was established. And then Paul, Silas, and Timothy left Philippi and headed down the highway. This is where we take up in Acts 17, reading verse 1: "Now when they had passed through Amphipolis and Apollonia, they came to Thessalonica."

In verses 1-3 you will see that Paul followed his usual method, going first to the Jewish synagogue and continuing to preach there as long as the Jews would allow it. According to verse 2, they tolerated him three weeks in the synagogue at Thessalonica.

The response in Thessalonica was typical. Some believed and some did not. Notice Acts 17, verse 4: "And some of them believed, and consorted with Paul and Silas; and of the devout Greeks a great multitude." In other words, there were both Jews and Gentiles who put saving faith in Jesus Christ.

Now notice verse 5: "But the Jews which believed not, moved with envy, took unto them certain lewd fellows of the baser sort, and gathered a company, and set all the city on an uproar, and assaulted the house of Jason, and sought to bring them out to the people."

The Jews who refused to accept Paul's preaching were extremely aroused against him. They gathered a mob to seize Paul and his friends but had to settle for Paul's host, a man named Jason, and some other believers. These young Christians were taken to the judge, and he made them post a bond guaranteeing the peace of the city as is indicated in verse 9.

So, because these believers' material possessions were in jeopardy, the decision was made that the gospel team should travel on. Remember, then, that Paul's ministry at Thessalonica was cut short because of the opposition of the unbelieving Jews. The feeling we get from these few verses in Acts 17 is that Paul and the others were not able to stay in Thessalonica much longer than the three weeks mentioned in verse 2. Paul was not able to teach and train the young converts as he would have liked.

First Thessalonians shows that Paul was quite concerned about this. He was apprehensive about their spiritual condition. He knew they were not well-established. Turn with me to 1 Thessalonians, now, and we will notice this. First, look at 1 Thessalonians, chapter 2, verse 17: "But we, brethren, being taken from you for a short time in presence, not in heart, endeavoured the more abundantly to see your face with great desire." Paul had a strong desire to get back to the Thessalonians.

Look also at chapter 3, verse 2. Here Paul says he " . . . sent Timotheus, our brother, and minister of God, and our fellowlabourer in the gospel of Christ, to establish you." Now look at verse 5 of chapter 3: "For this cause, when I could no longer forbear, I sent to know your faith, lest by some means the tempter have tempted you, and our labour be in vain." This is what I meant when I said Paul was apprehensive. He had not been able to teach them thoroughly, and so he feared Satan would turn them aside from faith in Christ.

One more verse, now: notice verse 10. Here Paul says he is "praying exceedingly that we might see your face, and might perfect that which is lacking in your faith." Paul recognized there were areas where their understanding had gaps, and he wanted to fill in those gaps.

All this teaches us something important about the man Paul. He loved his converts. He longed for them to mature in the faith. This concern of Paul is the key element in the background of First Thessalonians.

Let us pause long enough to list briefly the events that took place between the time Paul left Thessalonica, after founding the church, and the time he wrote this first epistle to the Thessalonians. Some of these events are indicated in the Book of Acts, but keep your Bible open to 1 Thessalonians.

First, Paul and his co-workers went to Berea, and from there to Athens, in southern Greece. During this time Paul made two attempts to get back to Thessalonica. He mentions this in 1 Thessalonians 2:18: "Wherefore we would have come unto you, even I Paul, once and again; but Satan hindered us." We do not know any details about this, but we can see that Paul earnestly wanted to get back to teach the Thessalonians.

But he could not go, and so he did the next best thing: He sent a helper. Notice chapter 3, verses 1,2a: "Wherefore when we could no longer forbear, we thought it good to be left at Athens alone; And sent Timotheus." Paul had probably sent Silas somewhere else, and if Timothy went he would be by himself. But he could not stand the suspense, and so he sent Timothy to see how the young converts in Thessalonica were doing. Then he personally moved on over to Corinth to begin a church there.

We can imagine Paul's impatience while he waited for Timothy. Finally he came back, and the news filled Paul with joy. Notice chapter 3, verses 6,7a: "But now when Timotheus came from you untc us, and brought us good tidings of your faith and charity, and that ye have good remembrance of us always, desiring greatly to see us, as we also to see you: Therefore, brethren, we were comforted over you."

To picture Paul's joy is not hard. He had been greatly concerned. But Timothy informed him that the Thessalonians were standing firm, growing in the faith. He rejoiced and renewed his prayerful desires that he would be allowed to return to Thessalonica to build on the solid foundation he had laid there!

But God's will was not for him to go now. The work in Corinth was progressing well and demanded that he stay. So Paul decided—obviously under the direct impression of the Holy Spirit—to write a letter to the Thessalonians. That letter is 1 Thessalonians, written from Corinth, on Paul's second journey. The date was about the year 50.

Without further ado, then, let us begin our survey of the message of this book. To start with, glance quickly through the Book of 1 Thessalonians. I want to point out the main divisions. This epistle just naturally divides itself into two main parts. Part One includes chapters 1—3. Part Two includes chapters 4, 5. Part One is personal and historical. Part Two is practical and doctrinal. In chapters 1—3 Paul recalls the past, reviewing the story of his ministry in Thessalonica. In chapters 4, 5 Paul instructs the Thessalonians in areas where they have needs. No doubt Timothy had explained some of the Thessalonians' problems to Paul, and Paul deals with these needs in chapters 4, 5.

With that preview of the epistle, we need now to give each of these two parts a more careful survey. Turn back to chapter 1. Read verse 1: "Paul, and Silvanus, and Timotheus, unto the church of the Thessalonians which is in God the Father and in the Lord Jesus Christ: Grace be unto you, and peace, from God our Father, and the Lord Jesus Christ."

This verse is what we usually call the salutation or introduction to the letter. All ordinary letters in Paul's day had such an opening as this. These introductions always included three things, and you can find these three things in this verse. First was the name of the writer. That is Paul; and he includes his two co-workers with him, Silas and Timothy.

Second was an identification of the person or persons being written. That is the church of the Thessalonians.

The third thing in most letter openings in Paul's day was some greeting, wishing the readers well. Paul has such a wish for the *spiritual* well-being of his readers: "Grace be unto you, and peace, from God our Father, and the Lord Jesus Christ."

Now, then, the first main part of this letter really begins in verse 2. I have already mentioned that Part One covers chapters 1—3 and is a historical review. I want to subdivide this first part into four smaller sections. I will list these now, and then we will come back and look at each one more closely. If you will identify the first main part with a Roman Numeral I, then you can use A, B, C, and D to identify these four smaller subsections.

Section A is an expression of *confidence* in the Thessalonians. This is chapter 1, verses 2-5. Section B under part I is a *commendation* of the Thessalonians, and includes verses 6-10 of chapter 1. Section C is a review of Paul's *original ministry* at Thessalonica. This applies to chapter 2, verses 1-16. And, finally, section D is a record of Paul's *follow-up efforts* on behalf of the Thessalonians, and this runs from 2:17 to 3:13. These are the four sections of part I, and now we will look at each of these, one at a time.

Read chapter 1, verses 2-5: "We give thanks to God always for you all, making mention of you in our prayers; Remembering without ceasing your work of faith, and labour of love, and patience of hope in our Lord Jesus Christ, in the sight of God and our Father; Knowing, brethren beloved, your election of God. For our gospel came not unto you in word only, but also in power, and in the Holy Ghost, and in much assurance; as ye know what manner of men we were among you for your sake."

As I have already pointed out, these verses make up section A under part I, and this section is an expression of confidence in the Thessalonians' spiritual situation. As you glance through these verses, you can see at least three things that contribute to Paul's confidence. First, he remembers the commitment the Thessalonians made. Verse 4 calls this their election of God. They chose God—that is what this means. In verse 3 Paul speaks of their work of faith; they had put faith in Jesus Christ.

Second, Paul is confident because he is aware of the part God has played. Note the word "beloved" in verse 4: This means the Thessalonians were objects of God's love. Note also verse 5: Paul refers to the power of the Holy Spirit that was displayed when he preached at Thessalonica. Paul's successful ministry did not depend on tricks or self-promotion; the *Spirit's* work was clearly manifested.

Third, Paul is confident because he remembers the ministry of himself and his co-workers. This is what he means in the last part of verse 5 when he refers to what sort of men they were at Thessalonica. Paul has assurance about the Thessalonians' spiritual situation, then, because he remembers what *they* did, what *God* did, and what *he* did. *His* work was what it ought to be and his motives pure. *The Lord* worked for all to see. And *the Thessalonians* made their choice and put faith in Christ. That was a solid beginning.

Now let us turn to section B under part I. This section covers verses 6-10 of chapter 1; here Paul expresses commendation or appreciation for the Thessalonians. Read these verses yourself, and I will point out four of the things Paul commends them for.

First, in verse 6, he commends them because they became followers of the Lord in spite of the opposition they experienced. You will remember that the Thessalonians did experience active opposition from the unbelieving Jews. By the way, the Greek word translated "followers" means *imitators.* That is a right good word to describe Christians: imitators of the Lord.

Second, in verse 7, Paul commends the Thessalonians because they became examples for other believers. The Thessalonian Christians set a challenging standard for other Christians to follow. That is what happens when one becomes an imitator of the Lord!

Third, in verse 8, Paul appreciates the Thessalonian believers because they talked around about their faith. When they got saved, they did not keep mum. They excitedly spread the news.

Fourth, and last, Paul commends his readers, in verses 9, 10, for their changed lives. In verse 9 he says, "Ye turned to God from idols to serve the living and true God." The Thessalonians' lives had been turned around!

I like verse 10; it shows us that waiting for Christ to return is part of the very essence of Christianity. The early Christians had a clearer awareness of this than we do. Expectant eagerness for the Lord's return ought to be part of what it means to be a Christian.

And now to section C under part I of this letter. This section is a review of Paul's original ministry at Thessalonica; and this is verses 1-16 of chapter 2. Follow along from verse to verse as I point out the basic elements involved.

In verse 1, Paul refers to his "entrance in" to the Thessalonians, his original visit there. He says his entrance has not proved vain. His ministry has produced fruit. In the rest of this section Paul lists various characteristics of his ministry there. I think these characteristics account for the success of Paul's ministry. There are ten of them. We could call these the ten commandments of a successful ministry.

Number one: He was bold, as you see in verse 2. He did not let the shameful treatment at Philippi stop him. You remember the beating and jailing. He spoke out boldly, anyway.

Number two: He was honest and open. In verse 3 he emphasizes that he was not deceitful or tricky in his preaching.

Number three: He pleased God rather than men. Verse 4 shows this. Notice that he tried to please God for two reasons: both because God was the One who entrusted the gospel to him, and because God tries the hearts. Paul would give answer to God, not to men.

Number four: Paul was selfless. You see this in verses 5, 6. He did not flatter men nor seek their glorification of himself. He was not covetous, self-seeking. Verse 6 mentions he could have required that they support him, because he was an apostle. But he felt this would burden them, and so he did not.

Number five: He was gentle. Maybe "tender" would be a better word. Anyway, verse 7 does not refer to a hospital nurse, but a mother nursing her own baby. Paul had that kind of tender concern for the Thessalonians.

Number six: He was compassionate. The affectionate desire mentioned in verse 8 indicates Paul was moved by their situation.

Number seven: Paul worked hard. This is what verse 9 means, in speaking of his night and day labors.

Number eight: His behavior was above reproach. Verse 10 indicates this. Paul sensed that his conduct must set an example for the rest.

Number nine: He gave faithful instruction in right living, as seen in verses 11, 12. Paul exhorted them, like a father, to walk worthy of the Lord.

And now number ten: The Thessalonians received his message as the word of the Lord Himself. This is indicated in verse 13. I cannot pass up this opportunity to observe that all the first nine things would have failed had not this tenth been true. And yet I believe people will usually receive the message of one who practices all those first nine characteristics.

But I do not have time to comment on this now, so we proceed to section D, the last section under part I. This section extends from 2:17—3:13, and in these verses Paul outlines his follow-up with the Thessalonians. Most of these verses we have already given attention to a few minutes ago, as we examined the circumstances that led up to the writing of this letter. For now, then, let us just look over this section briefly and take note of the efforts Paul made in following up his original ministry at Thessalonica.

First, he attempted to return to Thessalonica himself. Notice the last part of 2:17; here, Paul mentions his great desire to revisit the Thessalonians in person. In verse 18, the words "once and again" refer to two specific occasions when he planned to return but could not do so.

Second, since he could not go, he sent his fellow-worker Timothy. This is mentioned in chapter 3, verses 1, 2.

Third, Timothy returned to Paul with a good report. Notice 3:6. This report greatly encouraged Paul, as he indicates in verse 7. Paul had been anxious and uncertain about the Thessalonians as you can see in verse 5.

Fourth, and finally, Paul mentions his prayers for the Thessalonians. This was a key part of his follow-up program. Such a prayer is contained in 3:10-13. Notice that he prays for several things: that he may see them again, verses 10, 11; that he may perfect their faith, verse 10; that they will increase in Christian love, verse 12; and that they will be established in holy lives in preparation for the return of Christ, verse 13.

I want to make one more observation about this section on the follow-up ministry of Paul. We learn here that Paul was not satisfied to get men saved and then leave them. He was intensely concerned about the spiritual progress of his converts. Notice 2:20: "Ye are our glory and joy." Notice also 3:8: "Now we live, if ye stand fast in the Lord." Paul's very happiness, his own sense of well-being, was tied up in the success of those he won to the Lord.

Now we turn our attention to the last part of 1 Thessalonians. We have identified the first three chapters as part I and given four sub-sections in that part. That part dealt with the past, with a historical review of what had happened up to the time Paul wrote the letter. The last two chapters are in part II, and in this part Paul gives instructions that speak to the present needs of the Thessalonians.

In covering this second part, I am going to list three sub-sections. Section A is chapter 4, verses 1-12, and gives ethical instructions about the Christian's walk. Section B extends from 4:13 to 5:11 and gives doctrinal instruction about the return of Christ. Section C is chapter 5, verses 12-22. This section gives practical instructions about the Christian's inner-church relationships. Again, we want to look at each of these three sections more closely.

So pay heed now to chapter 4, verses 1-12, where Paul gives ethical instructions about the Christian's walk. You see, in verse 1, that he wants us to walk and please God. Well, there are three specific areas Paul deals with here, three particular matters he wants us to be careful about in our walk.

First, he speaks of moral purity. In verse 3 he mentions abstaining from fornication. This is the subject of verses 3-8. There is an interesting interpretive problem in verse 4: What does Paul mean by possessing our *vessels?* Some interpreters think vessel, here, is a metaphor for wife; and Paul means each one should have his own wife and be faithful to her alone. But I think vessel, in this verse, is a metaphor for one's own body, and Paul is teaching the need for self-control. Either way, the main truth is the same. The Christian must be morally pure, avoiding fornication and lust, as mentioned in verse 5. Any kind of fornication is, after all, cheating someone else, as seen in verse 6. Notice in verses 7, 8, the emphasis on holiness. Christians possess the *Holy* Spirit, so their calling is to holy lives. Anything else is a resistance to God Himself, and not just a man's instructions.

The second area Paul deals with, in his instructions about the Christian's walk, is the need for brotherly love. This is the subject of verses 9, 10. He commends his readers, as you see in verse 10; but he exhorts them to increase in brotherly love, just as he prayed for them back in chapter 2, verse 12.

The third element of the Christian walk is the need for honest, gainful toil. Verses 11, 12 treat this matter. Paul says he wants them to tend to their own business, to work for their own living, so that their material needs will be supplied and their reputation for honesty will be upheld, even in the eyes of the sinners. These verses are included because there was a problem at Thessalonica caused by some who would not work. This problem is dealt with at greater length in 2 Thessalonians, and so I am going to wait for most of my comments on this for the survey on 2 Thessalonians. For now, though, let me observe that it is dishonest to sponge off others when you could earn your own way. And it is not *Christian!* By the way, some think these people had quit work because of an overemphasis on the nearness of the Lord's return. I do not think so. I think they were trifling and taking advantage of the good-heartedness of the other Christians.

Anyway, we have to move on now to section B under part II. This section is a lengthy one, running from 4:13 to 5:11, and it deals with the Second Coming. This is the climax of 1 Thessalonians, and these words serve to sharpen the edge of our anticipation for Christ's return. Paul taught the Thessalonians to live with one eye on the sky, so to speak, expecting the Lord to come back soon. All Christians of every period of history ought to live like that.

Paul deals with two particular aspects of Second Coming doctrine. The first is in 4:13-18. Here he comforts those whose believing loved ones had died. Evidently there was misunderstanding about this at Thessalonica. Perhaps they had expected the Lord to return so immediately that they were not prepared for any of their number to die first. Remember that Paul had not had time to teach them thoroughly in his brief stay there. Anyway, some were grieved and wondered about the fate of those who died in the faith before Christ returned.

Paul hastens to reassure them. They should not sorrow overmuch, according to verse 13. Those who have died in Christ will come with Him when He returns, says verse 14. In verse 15, Paul indicates that we who live until His return will not in any way dispossess those who have died. Indeed, when Christ returns, the dead will rise first (verse 16). Then we will join them and meet the Lord in the sky (verse 17). So we need not be grieved by the loss of believing loved ones.

The other aspect of Second Coming doctrine Paul deals with is watchfulness for the Lord's return. This is the subject of 5:1-11. We can summarize these verses with three observations. First, the time of Christ's return is unknown. That is the reason Paul says, in verse 1, there is no need to write about times and seasons. And that is why he emphasizes, in verse 2, "the thief in the night" truth.

But, says Paul—and this is the second observation—we *can* be prepared. Do not ever read verse 2 and stop without reading verse 4. We do not have to be caught off guard as by a thief. We can be prepared. How? Paul answers this in verses 5-8: by watchfulness every day, by spiritual alertness, and by wearing the helmet of hope all the time. We may not know when He is coming, but we can be ready.

The third observation to make is this: We can have peace of mind while we wait. Verses 9-11 reassure us about this. Whatever happens while Christ delays His coming, we know that God has purposed salvation for us, not wrath. So if some die, if catastrophe strikes, or if wars come, we await Christ's return with quiet confidence and trust.

And now just enough time remains for us to give attention to section C of part II. This section is 5:12-22, and includes various practical instructions for the Christian, mostly about relationships to each other within the church. Let us survey these verses briefly.

First, Paul speaks of respect for church leaders, in verses 12, 13. This is what he means by those "over you in the Lord." He wants us to "know" them; that is, give them due recognition. He wants us to esteem them and love them. And this will contribute much toward peace in the church.

Next, in verses 14, 15, Paul urges us to respond to each other's needs. We must help those that have problems. The unruly are those who get out of line; we admonish them. The feebleminded are those who are discouraged, about to give up; we encourage them. The weak are those lacking spiritual health; we hold them up. And we are patient toward all; when mistreated, we do not strike back, but maintain good works.

Third, in verses 16-18, Paul deals with Christian attitudes, and these instructions are both congregational and personal. Three constant attitudes should be manifested by Christians: verse 16, rejoicing; verse 17, praying; and verse 18, thanksgiving.

Fourth, Paul speaks of spiritual manifestations in verses 19-22. These verses are tied together more closely than you might think at first reading. There are often many conflicting claims about ways in which the Holy Spirit's work is manifested. The temptation is to ignore them all. But Paul says that is not the solution to the problem. What we must do is *test* the spirits. This is what "prove all things," in verse 21, means. Then, when testing shows the work to be truly that of God's Spirit, we hold fast to it, as seen in verse 21. We will then not quench the Spirit, as reminded in verse 19. Nor will we resist genuine prophecy, as taught in verse 20. But when testing exposes evil, we will reject it. That is what verse 22 means: "Abstain from evil, every time it appears."

This brings us to the conclusion to this letter, in 5:23-28. Paul begins with a prayer, in verse 23, for the Thessalonians' spiritual preservation. Verse 24 shows his confidence that the prayer will be answered. Then he asks for prayer in verse 25 and sends his greetings to all the brethren in verse 26. In verse 27 Paul charges that this letter be read aloud to the church. He concludes, in verse 28, with a brief benediction.

I am going to conclude this lesson with that same benediction: May "The grace of our Lord Jesus Christ be with *you.* Amen."

A SURVEY OF THE BOOK OF

Second Thessalonians

by Dr. Robert Picirilli

I expect you have already studied the lesson on 1 Thessalonians. If not, you should do so before you study this lesson on 2 Thessalonians. This second letter to the believers at Thessalonica followed closely after the first one. Many of the problems are the same, and you will understand them better with the content of the first epistle well in mind. Furthermore, the historical background of the letters is the same, since both were sent to the same group of Christians.

To refresh your memory, I am going to review that historical background briefly. You will remember Paul founded the Thessalonian church on his second missionary tour, as recorded in chapter 17 of Acts.

His ministry at Thessalonica was successful, but short. He was not able to remain in town long, probably not much longer than the three weeks referred to in Acts 17:2. The earthly possessions of several of the believers at Thessalonica were put in jeopardy because of intense Jewish opposition. No doubt the lives and safety of Paul and his companions were threatened, too.

So the gospel team traveled on to other places: Berea, Athens, and Corinth. But Paul was not at all satisfied about the Thessalonian situation. He knew the young Christians were not well taught in spiritual matters. The suggestion of 1 Thessalonians 3:5 and 7 is that he agonized over the problem.

Consequently, he tried twice to return to Thessalonica personally. Reference is made to these attempts in 1 Thessalonians 2:18. On both occasions, though, Paul says, "Satan hindered us."

Since Paul could not get back to Thessalonica personally, he sent one of his team, the young man Timothy. Timothy was to instruct the believers awhile and then return to Paul with word about their situation. These things Timothy did, and brought the news to

Paul at Corinth on the second missionary journey. The news was good. The Thessalonian believers were standing firm in the faith. Paul greatly rejoiced over this report.

Naturally Timothy also had some problems to report. The Thessalonians needed instruction in certain areas. So Paul decided to write them. That letter is 1 Thessalonians, perhaps Paul's first to any church. In 1 Thessalonians Paul reviewed his ministry with the believers at Thessalonica and instructed them in the areas where the need was greatest.

We are not told, in the record, exactly what happened next. But we can make an educated guess. Paul probably sent 1 Thessalonians to its intended destination by Timothy. Timothy had been Paul's messenger to Thessalonica before, and he would certainly have the best understanding of the situation there. He would be the logical choice. And, after delivering the letter, Timothy would stay to minister personally in Thessalonica for another period of time. We do not know how long, exactly, but it is reasonably clear that the time was not longer than some months. Then, finally, Timothy would have returned to Paul, who was still in Corinth on that same second missionary journey.

The news was still good, as a whole. Some of the problems at Thessalonica had increased, however, and this would trouble Paul considerably. His concern would be intensified by the fact that he still could find no opportunity to return personally to Thessalonica.

Consequently, there was but one thing Paul could do, and that was to write the Thessalonians yet another letter. So the Holy Spirit put it in Paul's heart to write again. And so it came to pass that Paul wrote 2 Thessalonians, several months after the first letter. He was still in Corinth at the time, and the year was still A.D. 50 or 51.

The problems that made this letter necessary were similar to those dealt with in 1 Thessalonians. To be specific, there were three primary problems at Thessalonica, and Paul spent the entire letter dealing with almost nothing but these three problems. The first problem resulted from growing persecution, and there was probably discouragement among the believers as a result. This problem occupied Paul's attention in most of chapter 1.

The second problem in the background of 2 Thessalonians was a false doctrine related to the subject of the Second Coming. This problem provided the subject matter for chapter 2.

The third problem that made 2 Thessalonians needed was one that carried over exactly from 1 Thessalonians. This was the disorder caused by those who were idle, not working for their own needs but sponging off their brethren in the church. This subject took up most of chapter 3. You remember Paul had written briefly about this in 1 Thessalonians 4:11, 12.

Paul's purpose for writing 2 Thessalonians was to deal with three problems. As I have already observed, almost nothing else claims his attention in this epistle. With this preview in mind, let us begin a closer examination of 2 Thessalonians. I expect you have your Bible with you. Open it to 2 Thessalonians. You also need something to write with if you want to take notes.

I am going to outline this letter a little differently, since each chapter is almost wholly taken up with a single subject. I want to give each chapter a title. The title of chapter 1 is "Promises for the Persecuted." Chapter 2 is "Teaching for the Troubled." And chapter 3 is "Discipline for the Disorderly." Now we will look at each chapter closely, with these titles in mind.

Chapter 1, I have called Promises for the Persecuted. In this chapter Paul's main purpose is to comfort and encourage the Thessalonian believers who were suffering persecution for their faith. More about this in a moment.

First, in chapter 1 is the usual salutation. This is in verses 1, 2: "Paul, and Silvanus, and Timotheus, unto the church of the Thessalonians in God our Father and the Lord Jesus Christ: Grace unto you, and peace, from God our Father and the Lord Jesus Christ." You may have noticed that the wording of this is almost exactly identical with the opening in 1 Thessalonians 1:1. I will not repeat here what I said there.

Next, chapter 1 contains thanksgiving for the Thessalonians, in verses 3, 4: "We are bound to thank God always for you, brethren, as it is meet, because that your faith groweth exceedingly, and the charity of every one of you all toward each other aboundeth; So that we ourselves glory in you in the churches of God for your patience and faith in all your persecutions and tribulations that ye endure."

Notice that Paul speaks of three characteristics of the Thessalonians for which he thanks God: their faith, their love, and their patience. If you will turn back to 1 Thessalonians 1:3 for a minute, you will see these same three there: "work of faith, and labour of love, and patience of hope." These three—faith, love, and hope—Paul often mentioned together. Evidently, he felt that these three make up the essence of Christianity. And he is grateful that the Thessalonians are growing in all three areas.

The manifestation of their patience has taken a very specific form! The Thessalonians are under persecution for their faith, and Paul is grateful they are enduring these troubles with patience. He desires to give these persecuted believers some promises. He begins in verse 5 and continues with this subject in mind throughout the rest of chapter 1.

I think a question and answer method is the best way to survey this section on persecution. Question No. 1 is this: What two truths does Paul use to encourage the persecuted Christians? The answer is: First, Paul tells them it is an honor to suffer for Christ's sake. Second, he tells them God will pay back.

Look at verses 5, 6 closely and I think you will see these two answers. In verse 5 Paul refers to being counted "worthy of the kingdom of God, for which ye also suffer." Compare verse 11, where Paul prays that God will count them "worthy of this calling." Paul wants us to realize it is an honor to be counted by God *worthy* to suffer persecution in the name of His Son. This is the first truth he emphasizes as an encouragement to those under persecution.

The other truth is clear in verse 6. Paul says God will "recompense." The word recompense means pay back. God is going to pay off one day; this truth also sustains and encourages us in time of persecution.

But this second answer raises another question, Question No. 2: In what two ways will God pay back for persecution? To find the two answers to this question, all you have to do is realize that the verb "recompense," in verse 6, has two direct objects. The first is the noun "tribulation" in verse 6; the second is the noun "rest" in verse 7.

The first thing God will do in squaring accounts, then, is pay back tribulation to those who persecute His children. Now you may not think it is good to take comfort in the knowledge God will punish the wicked who oppress us for Christ's sake, but the Bible reassures us with just this truth. *We* must not strike back, but God will take vengeance, and that knowledge is encouraging.

The second thing God will do is pay back rest to His persecuted children. God will give release—relaxation—to those who endure persecution for His name. These are wonderful promises for the persecuted.

But another question just automatically pops up. Question No. 3 is this: When will God pay off? The answer to that question is given in verse 7: " . . . when the Lord Jesus shall be revealed from heaven with his mighty angels." God will straighten everything out when Jesus comes back. Therefore, it is our hope for the Second Coming that gives us patience in persecution.

And now one more question, Question No. 4: What will Jesus do when He returns? There are two answers to this. The first thing Jesus will do, at His return, is indicated in verses 8, 9: He will take vengeance on the wicked.

These two verses cause us no rejoicing. The picture is a tragic one, speaking of vengeance and punishment and destruction and flaming fire. Those under this judgment will be eternally removed from the presence of the Lord Jesus, forever beyond the reach of His power to save. But at least the responsibility is theirs: Their ignorance of God stems from their rejection of the gospel of our Lord Jesus. Such is the destiny of the lost. That destiny will be sealed at Christ's return. That is when the persecutors will be punished for their oppression of the saints.

The second thing Jesus will do at His coming is indicated in verse 10: He will "be glorified in his saints." This presents the other side of the coin. In this picture we can rejoice.

Note that *Jesus* will be glorified. The implication, however, is that we will somehow participate in that glorification. Our own greatest happiness and welfare will result from His crowning and exaltation. So here is yet another glorious promise for the persecuted. Get this chapter out when you have been reproached for Jesus' sake. It will give you great comfort.

Paul concludes the chapter with a prayer for these persecuted believers, in verses 11, 12. This prayer involves several requests, all of them closely related: that God will count them worthy of this calling—that is, the call to suffer; that God will fulfill His good pleasure and intended work in them—that is, that God's power will sustain them so that His purpose for them may be accomplished in this trial of their faith; and that Christ will be glorified through it all. Such a prayer as this will be appropriate for any of us in a time of testing.

But we must not tarry too long on chapter 1, so I direct your attention now to chapter 2. The title of this chapter is Teaching for the Troubled. In verse 2, you see the word "troubled." The Thessalonian believers were being troubled by a false teaching about the Lord's return. Paul proceeds to give the truth and thus to correct both the error and the upsetment that had resulted.

The false teaching that had created such confusion is quoted directly in verse 2: Some taught that "the day of Christ is at hand." The Greek word translated "at hand" really means "present," or "here." Somebody at Thessalonica was teaching that the day of the Lord had already come! I wish we knew more of the details of their teaching, but we do not. You can easily imagine the confusion and consternation that were caused by this notion. The believers were all shook up as a result of this doctrine. Paul refers, in verse 2, to their being "shaken in mind."

Note also, in verse 2, that he refers to a "letter as from us" which was evidently being used to support this false doctrine. This seems to mean that some false teacher had written a letter containing the false doctrine and presented it to the church as though Paul had sent it! That piece of dishonesty obviously added to the excitement. So Paul proceeds to give them the truth of the matter to straighten them out and settle their troubled minds.

In summary, Paul corrects the false teaching by reminding the Thessalonians of two events that had not happened yet, thus proving that the day of the Lord had not already come. The first of these two events is mentioned in verse 3. The King James reads "a falling away," but in Greek the definite article is used here, and so it means "*the* falling away." People often refer to this as "the great apostasy."

There is some difference of opinion among interpreters as to the exact nature of this great falling away. Personally, I think Paul refers to this again when he writes Timothy of the time when men will not endure sound doctrine and will turn away their ears from the truth. Peter also predicts there will be scoffers in the last days. Jesus warned that the love of many shall wax cold. All these passages appear to suggest that there will be a wholesale turning away from the truth, within the professing Church, before Jesus comes back. No doubt that work has already begun, and proceeds rapidly. We do not know when its fullness will be reached, although it seems to us there is not much farther to go.

The second event Paul speaks about is also mentioned in verse 3: "that man of sin be revealed." The meaning of this predicted unveiling of the man of sin is a source of great disagreement. You are probably aware that all Christians do not agree about prophetic details related to the return of Christ and the day of the Lord. Because of the differences, there are two basic views about "the man of sin" referred to here.

Some believe this man of sin was future when Paul wrote the Thessalonians in A.D. 50 or 51, but that this man of sin was revealed later on in the history of the early Church. If so, the revealing of the man of sin is in the *past* as far as *we* are concerned. Some of these identify him with the Roman Emperor Titus who destroyed Jerusalem in A.D. 70, thus twenty years after Paul wrote this letter. Those who take this view are also sure that the "great tribulation" Jesus spoke of in Matthew 24:21 referred to this same Roman invasion of Israel.

Others who think the man of sin is now in the past identify him with some later Roman emperor who severely persecuted the Christians. The Emperor Domitian is a favorite candidate, for example. He ruled from A.D. 81-96, thus about 30 or 40 years after Paul wrote 2 Thessalonians. Those who take this view think that the Book of Revelation also describes mostly the early church under Roman persecution, and they identify the "beast" described in Revelation 13 as being the same person as Paul's predicted man of sin.

Generally speaking, those who identify Paul's man of sin as Titus or Domitian, or some similar figure, are amillennialists. They do not believe there will be a millennial kingdom on earth in the future, over which a returned Jesus will reign. They do not think anything yet remains to take place before the Lord's return. They believe that Jesus will raise all the dead at once when He comes back, the saved and the lost. They believe Jesus will judge between the saved and the lost in one general judgment, committing the lost to Hell and the saved to Heaven, with nothing to follow this judgment but the unchanging, eternal state.

On the other side of this question are premillennialists, who think the prophetic future is much more complicated. They believe Jesus can return any time, but only to catch away the saints. Following this rapture, a great tribulation will occupy the world.

Then Jesus will come to the earth, to intervene in men's affairs, put down all open opposition to righteousness, and establish a kingdom on earth for a millennium—a thousand years. Only after that will come the final judgment of the wicked and the eternal state.

In this premillennial scheme of things, a specific person will head up the wicked nations' rebellion against God during the great tribulation. That person is generally called Antichrist. Naturally, those who take this view believe Paul is speaking of the Antichrist of the last days here in 2 Thessalonians. They also believe the Book of Revelation deals mainly with the future great tribulation, and they agree that the "beast" in Revelation 13 is the same as Paul's man of sin.

Time does not permit us to argue the pros and cons of this matter here. You will have to decide whether you think Paul was speaking of a character in the near future for his day, or of a character still future even today.

But we do want to take note of the details of Paul's description of this man of sin, this "son of perdition" as he calls him in verse 3. Several characteristics are mentioned.

First, he tries to put himself in the place of God. Notice verse 4: "he *as* God sitteth in the temple of God, shewing himself that *he* is God."

Second, he is hindered for a while, before his full revelation, by some force not named. In verse 6, something withholds this man's revelation. In verse 7, the word letteth means hinders. When Paul writes, then, he recognizes that some power restrains, for a while, the revelation of the man of sin. According to verse 6, the Thessalonians already knew the identity of this hinderer, but today's interpreters do not know. Some say this hinderer is the Holy Spirit; others the presence of the church; others the force of law and order; and so on. Whatever the view, the ultimate truth on which all would agree is that God's power and providence will not or did not allow this revelation until His own time.

Third, the Wicked One is revealed after the hindrance is removed. This is indicated in verse 8a, and this is the event Paul has already spoken of in verse 3.

Fourth, that Wicked One will only finally and fully be destroyed at Christ's return, according to verse 8. This refers back to the same eternal destruction of all the wicked mentioned in 1:8, 9.

Fifth, the man of sin actually manifests the supernatural power of Satan himself. Verses 9, 10 show this.

Sixth, this man of sin strongly deceives those who follow him. Verse 10 refers to deceivableness of unrighteousness. Verse 11 refers to a strong delusion and to believing a lie.

Seventh, and finally, this deception caused by the Satanic power of the man of sin is allowed by God as part of His punishment of those who reject Him. Verses 10-12 make this clear. We ought to be sobered by this truth. God sometimes reaches a point where He allows deception to overcome those who have willfully resisted the truth.

The rest of chapter 2 completes this section of teaching for those troubled by false doctrine about Christ's return. Paul expresses thanks for the Thessalonians' commitment to the truth, in contrast with those just referred to, who "receive not the love of the truth." Notice this emphasis on the "belief of the truth" in verse 13. Where did the Thessalonians learn the truth? From Paul's preaching of course. He reminds them of this in verse 14.

And for this reason, in verse 15, he exhorts his readers to hold on to the truth he has taught them, whether when he was there—in word—or when he has written letters. This challenge then prompts Paul to pray for his readers once again, and verses 16, 17 contain this prayer. He prays for their comfort and for their establishment.

We come, now, to the third and final chapter of 2 Thessalonians. The title I have already given to this chapter is Discipline for the Disorderly. Most of this chapter is devoted to the problem created by those at Thessalonica who were not working and earning their own living. But before we come to this, let us look first at verses 1-5. Notice Paul begins with the word "Finally," and verse 5 sounds almost like a benediction. So verses 1-5 give us the impression Paul was about to conclude. Verses 6-15, then, seem almost like an afterthought or a P.S. added to the main letter. Maybe Paul did it that way in order to get more attention for the section on discipline.

Anyway, verses 1-5 contain three things. First is a request for the Thessalonians' prayers, in verses 1, 2. Paul wants the Thessalonians to pray for him and his workers, with two particular requests. He desires that God's Word may have freedom and honor to move about unhindered. And he desires that the opposition of unreasonable, wicked men will not stop their preaching. Again we can see that Paul's whole life and happiness were tied up in the success of the gospel cause to which he was completely devoted.

Second, in verses 3, 4, Paul expresses his confidence in the Thessalonians' situation. This confidence is based on two things: first, the Lord's faithfulness to those who have been saved; and second, his expectation of the Thessalonians' obedience.

Third, in verse 5, Paul prays for his readers. He wants them to love God and wait with patience—perseverance—for the Lord's return. Just as in the first epistle, Paul sees eager anticipation for Christ's coming as part of the very essence of Christianity.

And now, when we come to verse 6, we reach the heart of chapter 3. Verses 6-15 all deal with the confusion created by those who lazily refused to work and sponged off their compassionate brethren. Mostly these verses do not speak to the lazy ones, but to the church. Paul is instructing the church to discipline these brethren who are causing such disorder by their inexcusable behavior.

This is exactly what you find in verse 6: Paul urges the Thessalonians to separate, to withdraw from the disorderly ones.

In verses 7, 8, and 9, Paul reminds the Thessalonians of the example he and his co-workers had personally set when they were in Thessalonica. They did not act disorderly at all, according to verse 7. They did not eat the food of others without working, says verse 8. They labored hard to earn their own wages and support, says verse 8, even though it meant they had to put in a double shift, both preaching and working on the job. As verse 9 makes clear, Paul *could* have demanded their support, as an apostle. But he refrained from exercising that power, that authority, in order to set the proper example.

The principle behind all this Paul lays down in verse 10: Any person who can work but will not should not be fed!

Note verse 11 closely: Those who were not working to pay their own way were left free to meddle in the affairs of others. You can always count on it: If one does not keep busy, he will wind up as a busybody! And so the disorder and confusion were only increased.

Consequently, Paul speaks directly to these idle brethren in verse 12: Go to work and feed yourselves—that is the essence of it. This is basically what Paul had already told the same people in 1 Thessalonians, chapter 4, verses 11, 12. Now since they have not obeyed, it is time for the church to discipline them.

You may not catch the point of verse 13 at first glance. You see, the compassionate brethren at Thessalonica probably had a benevolent program that included providing food for the needy. The lazy believers had taken advantage of this program. Consequently, the believers were irritated and tempted to stop their benevolence altogether. Paul is encouraging them here: Do not stop your good deeds to those who are really needy just because some trifling ingrates have taken advantage of your kindness.

Still, the church should discipline these disorderly brethren. So Paul repeats his instruction in verse 14: Any who persist in this wrong-doing should be withdrawn from. Yet, says Paul in verse 15, do not treat these as enemies, but admonish them as brothers. Here is a case when some within the fellowship were creating disruption by their conduct. They were not in open sin, and thus should still be regarded as Christians; yet they needed discipline. Maybe we ought to have some form of discipline like this in our churches today.

But now we have reached the end of the epistle. Remember that Paul more or less gave his conclusion in verses 1-5, so now the actual ending is rather abrupt and brief. Verse 16 contains a closing prayer for the peace and presence of the Lord Jesus to be with the Thessalonians. Verse 17 is the concluding salutation in Paul's handwriting. At this point he took the pen from the scribe and wrote the last words himself to serve as a token of genuineness. Finally, verse 18 is the benediction, practically identical to that which concluded 1 Thessalonians. I trust the study of these two letters has been a help to you, and especially that the return of our Lord Jesus Christ is more real to you now.

A SURVEY OF THE BOOKS OF

First & Second Timothy

by Dr. Robert Picirilli

The two letters from the Apostle Paul to Timothy are the first ones in the New Testament addressed to individuals rather than to churches. Romans, Corinthians, Galatians, Ephesians, Philippians, Colossians, Thessalonians—all these were churches which Paul or his co-workers had established. But 1 and 2 Timothy were sent to one person. That person was obviously one of Paul's closest fellow workers.

Turn to Acts 16 if you have your Bible handy. Before we survey the letters to Timothy, we want to find out more about Timothy himself. He first appears in the New Testament in Acts 16, on Paul's second missionary journey. That journey had begun in Antioch, in Acts 15:40, where we read that Paul and Silas departed and went through Syria and Cilicia first.

Now let us read Acts 16:1-3: "Then came he to Derbe and Lystra: and, behold, a certain disciple was there, named Timotheus, the son of a certain woman, which was a Jewess, and believed; but his father was a Greek: Which was well reported of by the brethren that were at Lystra and Iconium. Him would Paul have to go forth with him; and took and circumcised him because of the Jews which were in those quarters: for they knew all that his father was a Greek."

These verses serve as our introduction to Timothy. Clearly he was a young man at the time. He is called a disciple, and we are told his mother was also a believer. You need not turn to 2 Timothy just yet, but there we learn that Timothy's mother was named Eunice and his grandmother Lois. In fact, these women had put faith in Jesus before Timothy had. No doubt they influenced him to believe. Probably the first members of this family had been saved when Paul had preached in this same region on his first missionary journey, just a few years before he came back through on the second journey and

Timothy joined his gospel team.

Lystra was Timothy's hometown. This city was in southern Galatia. Timothy's mother was Jewish, but she had married a Gentile. No matter, the Jews still considered one a Jew if his mother was. The time of Paul's passage through Lystra on the second journey was about the year A.D. 50. Let us make a guess and estimate that Timothy was about 25 years old at the time. There is no way to be sure: some think he was 20 or less; others as much as 30. Anyway, he was clearly a lot younger than Paul, who regarded Timothy as his son in the ministry. Paul himself was about 50 at this time.

Here was a young man, then, who must have been quite excited to be chosen to travel with Paul and Silas in the work of preaching and establishing churches. Timothy was to prove a faithful companion throughout the rest of Paul's ministry. He was obviously a capable evangelist, and Paul could depend on him to go from one place to another, under his direction, in the work.

Timothy is next mentioned in Acts 17:14, 15: Paul left him and Silas behind in Berea but sent for them to come to Athens. Then in Acts 18:5: Timothy and Silas came to him in Corinth from Macedonia, where they had been sent. Next in Acts 19:22 on the third journey: Timothy and Erastus were sent from Ephesus into Macedonia. Then in Acts 20, verse 4: Timothy was one of a large group accompanying Paul to Jerusalem at the end of the third journey. These references in Acts give you an idea of the kind of busy ministry Timothy had.

We are not surprised, then, that Timothy gets mentioned often in Paul's letters. Check these references with me if you wish. In Romans 16:21, Timothy joins Paul in sending greetings to the Christians at Rome. Paul calls him a "workfellow." In 1 Corinthians 4:17 Paul says, "For this cause have I sent unto you Timotheus, who is my beloved son, and faithful in the Lord." Timothy is mentioned again in 1 Corinthians 16:10: Paul says, "He worketh the work of the Lord, as I also do."

In 2 Corinthians 1:1 Paul includes Timothy with him in the beginning of the letter, calling him a "brother." Timothy is likewise included in the opening of the letters to the Philippians, the Colossians, 1 and 2 Thessalonians, and Philemon. In Philippians 2:19 Paul says he plans to send Timothy to Philippi soon. In 1 Thessalonians 3:2, Paul indicates he sent Timothy to Thessalonica when he personally could not go. Here he calls Timothy a brother, a minister of God, and fellow laborer in the gospel. Timothy is mentioned once more, in Hebrews 13:23, but my own personal opinion is that this was written after Paul himself was dead.

Anyway, the picture is clear. Beginning with the second missionary journey, Timothy was one of Paul's most faithful and dear fellow workers. He was with Paul going out and coming in, we might say. No doubt he labored as tirelessly as Paul himself.

I hope this sketch has prepared you for a more meaningful survey of the two letters Paul wrote to Timothy. Turn now to 1 Timothy, and we will begin our examination of this letter. First, however, we ought to consider briefly the particular background of this epistle. I must admit we cannot be very dogmatic about the exact time and place when this letter was written. There is considerable debate as to where this letter fits into the historical outline of Paul's life as given in the Book of Acts.

We get only one hint in 1 Timothy 1:3, where Paul says: "I besought thee to abide still at Ephesus, when I went into Macedonia." But, so far as we can tell in the Book of Acts, there was no occasion on which Paul could have left Timothy in Ephesus while he personally headed for Macedonia. My opinion, then, is that this letter to Timothy was written *after* the events described in Acts. You know Acts closes with Paul in jail in Rome. We call that the first Roman imprisonment. I believe Paul was released at the end of the two years referred to in Acts 28, and that he continued his missionary travels for four or five years more. There are many ancient traditions that support this view. I think this letter to Timothy was written during that period.

The time for writing 1 Timothy, therefore, would be about the year A.D. 65. If Timothy had been about 25 at the time he joined Paul's traveling team, he is about 40 now, still a young man according to Jewish standards. Clearly he and Paul had been ministering together at Ephesus, when Paul decided to go on over into Macedonia and leave him there to continue the work. Many interpreters think Timothy was actually serving as a pastor in Ephesus at this time. I rather doubt that myself, but it does not make much difference. Either way, he had duties as a leader in the growth and organization of the work in Ephesus, and Paul wrote him to instruct and encourage him in that place of responsibility. I think it is clear that there were many congregations of believers in Ephesus, not just one. And probably new ones were being organized frequently.

So even though Timothy was not a pastor himself, he had to help the pastors with church teaching and organization. This is the reason the two letters to Timothy and the letter to Titus—which is quite similar—are often called the pastoral epistles.

So now let us survey the contents of 1 Timothy. First, glance through the epistle. You see 6 chapters. We will consider this letter in five parts. Part I is chapter 1, an exhortation to war against unsound doctrine. Part II is chapter 2, instruction about prayer and orderliness in the church. Part III is chapter 3, the qualifications of pastors and deacons. Part IV is chapter 4, warnings against false teachers. Part V is chapters 5, 6, with instructions about various church responsibilities.

First, then, we turn to chapter 1. The first two verses are the customary letter-opening. Note that Paul calls Timothy—as he often did—his *son* in the faith.

This first chapter is part I. It is an exhortation to war against unsound doctrine. There was false doctrine at Ephesus. There always is, sooner or later. One of Timothy's responsibilities was to face, expose, and counter any false teaching. Notice verse 3: Paul says the very reason he left Timothy at Ephesus was that he should "charge some that they teach no other doctrine."

Some interpreters think Timothy may have been discouraged and intimidated by the false teachers and needed these urgings to stiffen his resistance. Others suggest that Paul wrote these words so Timothy could show others that he had Paul's own authority behind his resistance to the false doctrine. I like this second theory better.

Now we do not know all the details about the false doctrines at Ephesus. Verse 4 mentions fables and genealogies. Verse 7 says some desired to be teachers of the law but were without understanding. According to verse 9, they evidently failed to understand that the purpose of the law is to condemn and expose sin, rather than to make men righteous. These references indicate the false doctrine at Ephesus, which Timothy was to face, had a strong Jewish flavor. Other things in 1 and 2 Timothy indicate there was an early Gnostic flavor, too, much like the false teaching which Paul wrote against in Colossians.

But though we do not have time to analyze the false doctrine itself, Paul's point is quite clear: Timothy is to make war against anything—as he says in the latter part of verse 10—that is contrary to sound doctrine. And, as verse 11 indicates, Timothy's standard is to be the very gospel he had learned so well from Paul, the gospel which the Lord Himself had entrusted in Paul's hands.

Saying this leads Paul to give his own testimony in verses 12-17. And a moving testimony it is. Paul is especially conscious of how great a sinner he had been, as you see in verse 13 and in verse 15: He was chief of sinners. And a keen consciousness of sin makes one especially aware of God's mercy. Twice, in verses 13 and 16, Paul marvels that he had obtained mercy. Consequently, Paul knows that *God* is the one who had put him in the ministry. So Paul had great confidence in the gospel he preached. Timothy can confidently rely on that gospel as a standard by which to measure and expose false teaching.

In this spirit Paul repeats his charge in verses 18-20: "Timothy," he says, "make war on unsound doctrine." Paul mentions two false teachers by name, Hymenaeus and Alexander. These two Paul had already exposed and disciplined. They had made shipwreck of faith. That expression certainly means apostasy, by the way.

Part II of 1 Timothy is chapter 2. And this chapter contains instruction about prayer and orderliness in the church. In a special way, this chapter seems to deal with the worship services themselves, though there are implications for the private Christian life as well. We can easily divide this chapter into two subsections. Verses 1-8 deal with prayer in the life of the church.

We see, first, some special objects of prayer: In verse 1, all men are to be included, and verse 4 tells us why we are to be interested in all men. God wants all men to be saved. As verses 5, 6 show, the salvation of all men was the purpose of Christ's death as a ransom, and is the purpose of His mediatorhood between God and man. Furthermore, according to verse 7, the salvation of all men is the purpose behind Paul's ministry. So Paul wants the church to pray for all men.

In verse 2 we see another special object of prayer: kings and all who are in authority. Why do we pray for these? So that we may lead a godly life without hindrance or oppression. So verse 8 concludes this section: "I will therefore that men pray every where." The word for men, here, means particularly *the* men rather than the women. The men should take the lead in this in the church.

The second section of chapter 2 is verses 9-15, and this section speaks particularly to the women in the church services. First, Paul speaks of their external behavior. They should be more concerned to dress up their lives with good works, according to verse 10, rather than with the jewelry and fancy hair styles referred to in verse 9. Furthermore, as verses 11-15 teach, the Christian women ought to manifest submission to the men in church life rather than trying to seize the role of leadership for themselves. Even in our modern times, the basic principle taught here still applies, though publicly active women will not hinder their testimonies today as severely as was true in the times and culture of Paul's day. The Divine order remains the same, though, and Paul reminds us of this in verses 13-15.

But we have to move on. Part III is chapter 3. Here Paul gives qualifications for pastors and deacons. As I have already suggested, congregations were no doubt multiplying in Ephesus and the area around. Timothy was responsible for leadership in organization, and that included guidance in screening candidates for ordination.

Verses 1-7 give the qualifications for the pastor—the bishop, as Paul calls him. We do not have time now to examine every single one of these words and phrases closely, so I am going to summarize. These verses suggest at least five areas in which the pastor must be qualified. First is his moral character. Most of verses 2, 3 speak of this. The pastor must be blameless—above reproach—in all aspects of his moral character: in marriage, in behavior, in drink, in financial dealings, in controlling his emotions.

Second, the qualified pastor must be able to teach. Note this at the end of verse 2. This extremely important qualification included both knowledge of the Scriptures and ability to communicate that knowledge to others.

Third, he must have respect and control in his own household. Verses 4, 5 assert this and give the reason for its importance.

Fourth, he must have maturity and experience before he is ordained. "Novice," in verse 6, means one who is new and untried.

Fifth, the pastor's qualifications include a good reputation in the eyes of the unsaved. In verse 7, "them which are without" means the world outside the church.

Now, then, the deacon's qualifications are given in verses 8-13. If you will notice these closely, you will find that the standard is very similar to that required of the pastor. The deacon, too, must be morally upright, mature, and in control at home. Aptitude for teaching is not mentioned, and perhaps this is the most significant difference.

Time does not permit us, in this brief survey, to examine all the questions that arise about these offices. My opinion is that the first New Testament churches began organizing by a pattern similar to that of the Jewish synagogue. They ordained several "elders" in each local church, with perhaps one of these the chief elder—like the "chief ruler" of a synagogue. Gradually this elder came to be known as pastor which means Shepherd or Bishop (which means overseer). The other elders came to be known as deacons (which means ministers).

One lesson is clear, here in chapter 3: ordination of pastors and deacons should be undertaken with great care. They should measure up well against these qualifications *before* they are ordained.

But again we have to move on. Chapter 4 is part IV of 1 Timothy. Here we have warnings against false teachers. In verses 1-5 Paul affirms that false doctrine will snatch some away from faith in Christ in the latter days. We had better recognize how serious false doctrine is. Beginning in verse 6, Paul urges Timothy to face up to his own responsibility in withstanding false doctrine. He must do two things to meet this responsibility. First, as verse 6 shows, he must teach the brethren the truth. Good doctrine is the best counterattack against false doctrine. But, second, he must expose the errors. Verse 7 indicates this.

Perhaps the most important part of chapter 4 begins in the latter part of verse 7. Timothy is exhorted to set the right example in his own behavior. This is the best way to offset false doctrine, after all. In verses 7, 8, Timothy is exhorted to practice godliness, and in verse 11 to teach such godliness. In verse 12, he is to set an example for all believers in every aspect of life: conduct, attitude, speech, emotions, and faith. As spiritual leader of those who follow him, the responsibility rests squarely on his shoulders. Thus, if he takes heed, as verse 16 says, both to himself and to his teaching, he will save both himself and his hearers.

And now we come to the final part of 1 Timothy. Chapters 5 and 6 form part V, and this section gives instruction about a wide variety of pastoral responsibilities in the church. We will have time only to glance at each of these briefly.

First, notice chapter 5, verses 1, 2. Paul speaks of the pastor's attitude toward all parts of his congregation: the older men and the younger men, the older women and the younger women.

Next, notice verses 3-16. Here Paul discusses care for widows, and he gives three instructions. Widows with family should be cared for by that family. Verses 4, 8, and 16 say this. Younger widows should remarry. Verse 14 indicates this. Older widows without family, and of good character, should be supported by the church, in return for service to the church. Verses 3, 5, 9, and 10 establish this.

Next, Paul instructs Timothy about his relationships to the ordained elders. As I have already said, I think this word included both the pastors and deacons. Verses 17, 18 speak of the elders' pay. Verses 19-21 speak of care and impartiality in considering charges lodged against elders. Verse 22 warns against hasty ordination. Then chapter 5 concludes with more reminders about Timothy's own personal purity.

Chapter 6 begins, in verses 1, 2, with instructions for servants and their masters. Both are responsible to maintain a good Christian testimony.

Following this Paul speaks again about false doctrine, this time particularly against false doctrine that is self-seeking, that seeks to acquire material gain. Note this, in verse 5: They suppose that gain is godliness. So Paul warns Timothy to withdraw from such false teachers. He also warns him, in verses 6-10, against covetousness: The love of money is a root from which all sorts of evils grow, says verse 10. Man's real gain is godliness, says verse 6.

This warning against lust for material things follows on through to the conclusion of the epistle. Timothy should seek righteousness and spiritual graces instead of pursuing material things, according to verse 11. This is the commandment, in verse 14, he should carefully keep. In verse 17, he should warn the wealthy against trusting in their riches. According to verses 18, 19, all believers should be more interested in good works and a heavenly store than in earthly treasures.

Paul fittingly concludes the epistle—if somewhat abruptly—by reminding Timothy again: Keep that which is committed to your trust. The final warning against erring from the faith will ring in Timothy's ears for a long time, perhaps even until Timothy will receive another letter from Paul.

Indeed, Timothy did receive a second letter from Paul some time later. This is 2 Timothy in our Bibles, and we must now give that epistle brief attention before this study closes.

First, a few words about the time and place. You may recall that I said, earlier, that Paul was probably released from the first Roman imprisonment described in the last chapter of Acts. Then he would have carried out further evangelistic travels in Asia Minor, Greece, and perhaps even Spain, as ancient traditions say. Thus, I have already suggested that 1 Timothy was written in about A.D. 65 during that period of Paul's ministry.

The ancient historical tradition indicates that this final period of Paul's ministry closed when the emperor Nero had Paul arrested and put in the dungeons at Rome. Paul's first Roman imprisonment had come about because of Jewish opposition. But toward the latter years of Nero's reign, he became insanely antagonistic toward the Christians and persecuted them relentlessly and cruelly. Since Paul was the leading preacher of the Christian faith, it was inevitable that Nero would fasten his attention on Paul. Thus, in about the year A.D. 66 Paul was arrested and put in the dungeon. Then in early A.D. 67 Paul was beheaded on Nero's orders.

If this tradition is correct—and I see no reason to dispute it—then 2 Timothy was written while Paul was in prison, shortly before his death. You can tell Paul knew his ministry was done when you read this letter. Therefore, 2 Timothy was written in about 66 or 67 from Rome, to Timothy, who was still in Ephesus. Paul was nearly 70; Timothy was nearly 50. The letter is a farewell message. This will be the great apostle's last written words to his son in the ministry.

First, let us glance through this brief letter. There are four chapters. The first two include mostly personal exhortations to Timothy. Chapter 1 is a call to faithfulness. Chapter 2 is an exhortation to service. In chapter 3 Paul warns Timothy about false doctrine. Chapter 4 is a concluding charge to Timothy. We will go back, now, and look at each of these chapters more carefully.

The letter opens, of course, with the usual Pauline salutation in verses 1, 2. Is it reading too much into Paul's words to see an unusual reference to "the promise of life" in verse 1 and recall how near he was to death? I do not think so.

Anyway, as I have already said, chapter 1 is a "Call to Faithfulness." In verses 3, 4, Paul begins this call to faithfulness by reminding Timothy of his prayers and of his desire to see Timothy face to face once again. Timothy's tears were being shed, no doubt, because of Paul's situation.

Then, in verse 5, Paul reminds Timothy of his heritage of faith, and in verse 6 urges him to stir up the gift he possessed, another way of saying: "Be faithful to your calling." The implication of verses 7, 8 is that Timothy may have been discouraged and intimidated because of what had happened to Paul. But he should not be ashamed, nor even reluctant to suffer for Christ's sake. As Paul reminds Timothy in verses 9, 10, the Lord has done too much for us that we should be ashamed of Him. In verses 11, 12 Paul speaks of his own calling and bold confidence in the ministry. Timothy knew this well and should be encouraged to be faithful by remembering

Paul's example.

Consequently, Paul concludes this call to faithfulness in verses 13-18 by directly urging Timothy to "hold fast" the sound, wholesome doctrine he had learned from Paul; and to "keep" that which had been committed to him. He has the help of the Holy Spirit. Some others have not stood by Paul in this dark hour: men like Phygellus and Hermogenes have disowned him. Onesiphorus was a glad exception and was not ashamed by Paul's chain. These examples should stir Timothy to remain faithful, both to God and to Paul.

And now to chapter 2, which we call an "Exhortation to Service." Time will not permit us to analyze this chapter closely, but what Paul does here is challenge Timothy to serve the Lord effectively and efficiently. He does this mostly by illustrations. He uses different kinds of persons as examples to teach principles of Christian service. There are five main illustrations.

Number one: the soldier. Verses 3, 4 use this illustration, reminding us that a good soldier must both endure hardness and be free of entanglements with other things in life. So must a good servant of the Lord.

Number two: the athlete. Verse 5 speaks of the athlete as one who strives for excellence and who observes the rules of the game. An effective Christian worker must do these things, too.

Number three: a farmer. Verse 6 reminds us that a farmer must labor faithfully at all seasons before partaking of the harvest. So must the servant of Christ.

Number four: a skilled worker, a craftsman. Verse 15 speaks of this, reminding us how we as servants of the Lord must be skilled in handling the Word of God as the tools of our trade.

Number five: a clean vessel. Verses 20, 21 speak of two classes of vessels. Some are put to honorable uses, like dishes for cooking or eating. Others—like trash cans—are put to dirty, dishonorable uses. A Christian servant must be a clean vessel.

There is obviously much more we could glean from chapter 2, but this is sufficient to make the main point: Paul wanted Timothy to be an effective servant of Christ.

In chapter 3 Paul warns about the perilous times that are ahead. Timothy is urged to be prepared to stand against the invasion of false doctrine. You will remember that there was much of this in 1 Timothy. All of Paul's last letters were much occupied with the danger of false doctrine.

The nature of this threatening doctrine is outlined in verses 1-13. Verses 14-17 remind Timothy of the resources he has to meet the threat: The inspired Scriptures will give him the weapons of his warfare against false doctrine.

And now we come to the final chapter of 2 Timothy, a concluding charge to Timothy. These words are especially moving when we remember they were the last to come from Paul's pen.

First, Paul charges Timothy to faithfully preach the truth. This charge extends from verse 1 through verse 5, and includes another reminder that many will not hear the truth.

Then Paul gives his own final testimony. He has completed his course without swerving from that which God gave him to do. He expects, confidently, the promised reward. What a challenge this should be to Timothy, or to any of us!

Verses 9-22 conclude the letter with various personal observations about people and present circumstances. Both in verses 9 and 21, Timothy should try to come to Paul soon. He should bring Mark along, according to verse 11, and pick up Paul's cloak and scrolls at Troas on the way, according to verse 13. Many have deserted Paul, like Demas in verse 10 and others in verses 14-16. Luke has not deserted him, as verse 11 says, nor has the Lord Himself, as verses 17, 18 show. Greetings and a benediction conclude the letter in verses 19-22. I conclude this study with a heartfelt thanksgiving to God for the example of a man like Paul, faithful in serving Christ through every adversity and even unto death. May God help us to follow his example.

A SURVEY OF THE BOOKS OF

Titus & Philemon

by Dr. Robert Picirilli

When we come to Titus and Philemon, we come to the last two epistles of Paul in our New Testament order. That is, unless Hebrews was written by Paul. I personally do not think so.

Get your Bible, if you do not already have it handy, and be ready to follow along as we survey these two short epistles. They were written at two entirely different times and places, so I will not try to relate them in any special way.

First, let us get a clear picture just who Titus was. I hope you have already studied the lesson on 1 Timothy, because the epistle to Titus was written at about the same time as 1 Timothy, and for nearly identical purposes. Timothy was one of Paul's younger co-workers who had been left at Ephesus with pastoral responsibilities. Titus was another helper of Paul. He had been left at Crete in a position similar to Timothy's. Paul wrote a letter to each of them under those circumstances.

Titus, therefore, had a relationship to Paul similar to that of Timothy, even though we do not know quite as much about him as we do about Timothy.

The very first time we met Titus was when Paul was at the Jerusalem Council in about A.D. 48 or 49, shortly before Timothy became a companion of Paul. Turn to Galatians a minute, and you will see Titus' name. Galatians 2 describes the Jerusalem Council from Paul's viewpoint. In Galatians 2:1 Paul says he took Titus with him to the council. In verse 3 he says Titus, being a Greek, was not forced to submit to circumcision.

That is what the Jerusalem Council was all about, you remember. Some thought that even the Gentile converts should be circumcised and live under the Mosaic system. Paul did not think so, and he went up to Jerusalem, from Antioch, to try to settle the matter. He took Titus along as a test case, and won his point convincingly.

Titus was a Gentile, then, and not a Jew like Timothy. He was probably a young convert at the time of the Jerusalem Council, and his home was either in Antioch or somewhere along the route of the first missionary journey, which had just been completed before the Jerusalem Council. We cannot be positive about Titus' hometown. I would guess he was about Timothy's age, or a little older.

The name of Titus is not mentioned at all by Luke in the Book of Acts. That omission may not mean much, since we know Luke never pretended to tell us everything. Or, the silence may imply that Titus did not travel as much with Paul as Timothy did.

We do know, however, that Titus was with Paul during an extensive period on the third missionary journey, when Paul was in Ephesus in about A.D. 53 or 54. This we learn from 2 Corinthians. Turn to 2 Corinthians, chapter 2, for a minute. In 2 Corinthians 2:3 Paul refers to a letter he had earlier written to the Corinthians. Evidently he had sent that letter to Corinth by Titus, from Ephesus. In verse 12 of 2 Corinthians 2, Paul indicates he went looking for Titus, hoping to meet him and learn of the Corinthians' response to his letter. He did not find Titus in Troas and went to Macedonia to seek him. Then in 2 Corinthians, chapter 7, verses 5, 6, we see that Paul did meet Titus in Macedonia and was greatly comforted by the report Titus gave him about the situation at Corinth.

In 2 Corinthians 8:6, Titus' name occurs again. Notice verse 16 also. If you will read chapter 8 carefully sometime, you will see that Paul sent Titus back to Corinth, probably with 2 Corinthians, with instructions to lead the Corinthians in raising funds for an offering Paul was sponsoring.

Obviously, then, Titus was a trusted co-worker, even though he may not have been as active as Timothy. For all we know, he may have stayed in one place for several years as a pastor. Titus is not mentioned elsewhere in Paul's writings except at the end of 2 Timothy. In 2 Timothy 4:10, Paul says Demas had forsaken him and gone to Thessalonica. He adds that Crescens had gone to Galatia and Titus had gone to Dalmatia. This probably does not mean that Titus had forsaken Paul, but that he had gone there in the ministry he performed under Paul's general supervision.

Now let us spend a minute or two examining the specific circumstances under which Paul wrote this inspired letter to Titus. I want to remind you, briefly, of what I have already said about the historical background of 1 Timothy.

As I said, I feel confident Paul was released from the first Roman imprisonment described in the last chapter of Acts. This would mean that he had a period of ministry after that first imprisonment, and that this period is not described in the Book of Acts at all. My opinion is that Paul was released from the first Roman imprisonment in about A.D. 61, that he ministered in Asia

Minor, Europe, and even perhaps as far west as Spain for about five years, and that he was reimprisoned on order of the Roman emperor Nero in about A.D. 66 or 67 and executed shortly thereafter.

According to this view, Titus was written during that period between the two Roman imprisonments, between A.D. 61 and 66. The best date seems to be about A.D. 65, at about the same time as 1 Timothy. Indeed, I think Paul wrote both these co-workers at the very same time and place.

If you read Titus carefully, you will see that he is in Crete when Paul writes. Crete is an island southeast of Greece, in the Mediterranean. Titus 1:5 says Paul had left Titus in Crete. There was no circumstance recorded in the Book of Acts when Paul could have left Titus in Crete. Look also at Titus 3:12: Paul says he will soon send Artemas or Tychicus to Crete to relieve Titus. Then Titus should come to him at Nicopolis, where Paul had planned to stay during the worst winter months. Nicopolis was in mainland Greece. We may surmise, then, that Paul, Titus, and Timothy had been traveling together. Titus had been left at Crete while the other two moved on to Ephesus. Then Timothy was left at Ephesus and Paul moved on over into Macedonia, which was in northern Greece. Then Paul wrote both his younger companions, from Macedonia, to encourage them in the faithful performance of their duties.

With this historical background in mind, then, we begin our survey of the contents of the letter to Titus. If you want to make some notes I will try to give you an outline for the epistle as we go along.

Part I of Titus is chapter 1, verses 1-4; this is the introduction. These four verses contain the usual letter-opening that is typical of all Paul's letters. The only difference is that this is a little longer than usual. Let us notice these first four verses more closely.

First, Paul identifies himself, as usual: "Paul, a servant of God, and an apostle of Jesus Christ." Then Paul does what is not usual for him and goes into a parenthetical extension that lasts through verse 3. Basically, this extension explains the apostolic ministry which had been committed to Paul by Jesus Christ. In verse 1, he speaks of "the faith of God's elect," God's chosen. The purpose of Paul's preaching was to produce faith. Also in verse 1, Paul speaks of "the acknowledging of the truth which is after"—or according to—"godliness," which means godly living. Paul preached the truth that insisted on godly lives.

Verse 2 speaks of the eternal life that God, who cannot lie, promised before the earth's foundations were laid. Verse 3 expands on this: Paul's apostleship consists of a commission to preach openly the Word of God that makes this eternal life known to men.

Now notice verse 4. Paul has identified himself and described his ministry. Now he identifies the one to whom he sends the letter, Titus. Note that Titus, like Timothy, is Paul's son in the ministry.

Verse 4 concludes the introduction with Paul's usual greeting: "Grace, mercy, and peace, from God the Father and the Lord Jesus Christ our Saviour."

Part II of Titus begins at verse 5 of chapter 1 and goes through verse 9. In this part Paul gives instructions for church organization, particularly for the ordination of elders. Notice verse 5: Paul says he left Titus in Crete for this very reason, to help the churches there with their organizational structure.

If you studied the lesson on 1 Timothy, you will remember that I expressed an opinion in that study about early church organization. My view is that the early churches followed, at first, the pattern of organization already in use in the Jewish synagogue. According to that pattern they would elect several elders as leaders of the congregation, and one elder would be the chief ruler, so to speak. I believe that this office of chief elder gradually became known as pastor or bishop, and the other elders became deacons.

You remember, in 1 Timothy, chapter 3, Paul first gave the qualifications for the bishop, and then gave the qualifications for the deacons. Well, here in Titus 1 he speaks of the ordaining of all elders in verses 5, 6, and then of the bishop in particular in verses 7-9. All the elders would include both the bishop and deacons, if my view is correct.

Therefore, verse 6 gives qualifications for either a pastor or a deacon. "Blameless" means he should be above reproach in moral character. "The husband of one wife" refers to his proper marriage. "Having faithful children not accused of riot or unruly" suggests an orderly, Christian home, with the elder in control.

Verses 7-9 go on and add further specific qualifications that the bishop, in particular, must possess. Remember, "bishop" means "overseer," and this is the same office as "pastor," which means "shepherd." He, especially, must be blameless in moral character, recognizing himself as a steward—a servant—of God. He must be gentle, not easily provoked, in good control of himself at all times, hospitable, and dignified. He must be, as verse 9 says, well taught in sound doctrine and able to teach sound doctrine convincingly to others.

I want to pause here long enough to say that this passage, and the similar one in 1 Timothy, convince me that those whose responsibility it is to ordain men ought to be very cautious in the exercise of that solemn responsibility. It is not enough to hear a man say he has been "called." We should make sure the men we ordain as spiritual leaders are the kind of men who will have the respect both of the church and of sinners. That is the reason Paul carefully defined these qualifications, both in 1 Timothy and in Titus.

Now, part III of Titus is the rest of chapter 1: verses 10-16. In this section Paul warns about false teachers. You remember Paul warned Timothy at length about false doctrine. He does the same for

Titus. Evidently his mind was quite occupied in his later years with this danger; he could see what was ahead, and he wanted these men who were to follow after him to be well prepared to resist and expose false doctrine.

These verses show us, first, the nature of false teachers. Note, in verse 10, that they are unruly. "Vain talk" means empty talk. They deceive. Verse 11 says they "subvert"—corrupt—whole houses. They teach things they ought not. And their own selfish desire for personal gain is their basic motivation. Verse 16 indicates that their works show the emptiness of their hypocritical profession. Disobedience never goes with the truth.

Next, these verses show the Biblical attitude one should have toward such false teachers. Verse 11 says their mouths must be stopped. Verse 13 says, "Rebuke them sharply." Paul wants Titus to expose and resist false teachers with strength and courage. Their poisonous doctrine cannot be tolerated, because the spiritual welfare of the believers is at stake.

But now we move on to part IV of Titus, which is chapter 2, verses 1-8. In this part Paul speaks of the pastor's duty to all segments of his congregation. As verse 1 implies, this is a matter of sound doctrine. First, the pastor has a duty to the older men. Verse 2 speaks of the teaching that should be given them. They should be serious minded, dignified, self-controlled, healthy in faith, love, and patience.

Next, the pastor has teaching for the older women: Their conduct should be holy, their words true, their bodies under their own control, and their teaching sound.

Further, the older women should help the pastor with his teaching for the younger women. They, in turn, should be serious minded, love their families, be pure, and be good homemakers.

Finally, the pastor should also teach the younger men to be serious minded. In particular, verses 7, 8 show that the main method of the pastor's teaching must be by the example of his own behavior. He must be a pattern in teaching, behavior, works, and speech.

Part V of Titus is next. This part begins at chapter 2, verse 9, and continues on through chapter 3, verse 11. In this section Paul speaks of particular teachings that Titus, as pastor, must give to those who are under his influence. We will go through these verses in survey fashion, taking note of the various particular subjects Paul deals with.

First is teaching for slaves: 2:9, 10 contain this teaching. Servants—slaves—should obey their masters, try to please them, not talk back, not purloin—or steal—from them, but show fidelity—that is, faithful loyalty. Notice that such conduct by a Christian slave will adorn the doctrine of God.

Next, Paul speaks of the general teaching of the pastor that Christians ought to be holy. Verses 11-15 present this truth. Verse 11 speaks of the grace of God. But notice that verse 12 says the grace of God *teaches* us something. What does God's grace teach us? That we should live holy lives in this present world. Salvation by grace is no excuse for impure lives. Notice also the place of Second Coming doctrine as an impetus to holy living. Verse 13 mentions the blessed hope. Living in hope of Christ's return will help us be the pure and peculiar people spoken of in verse 14. So Paul repeats for Titus, in verse 15, the need that he instruct the church in these principles of holy living. "Let no man despise thee" means that Titus' own conduct and teaching ought to be such that no one *would* reject him or his teaching.

The next subject Paul deals with in part V is Christian submission. Chapter 3, verses 1, 2 touch briefly on this subject. First, this submission is to be exercised in reference to civil authorities. Verse 1 makes this clear. Then, this submission is to be manifested in meekness toward all men, even those that mistreat us. Verse 2 indicates this.

Following this, in verses 3-8, Paul reminds Titus and all of us of the nature and basis of our salvation. We will be more submissive toward sinners if we simply recall how God has saved us from sins ourselves. In verse 3 we have a description of our past, our unsaved condition. In verses 4-6 we have a description of the plan by which we were saved. In verse 7 we have the promise given to those who are saved, a promise of eternal life. And in verse 8 we have the present obligation of the saved, to maintain good works.

Notice, especially, the plan, the method of our salvation in verses 4-6. We were not saved by our works, but by the kind provision of God in Christ, by the new birth of the Holy Spirit of God.

Part V of Titus concludes, in 3:9-11, with one more warning against false teachers. You see, again, that this problem occupied Paul's mind a great deal. Paul tells Titus to avoid any false teaching, and to discipline false teachers after one or two conscientious efforts to rescue them from their heresy. The welfare of the congregation is too important to risk by prolonged exposure to false doctrine.

And now we come to part VI of Titus. This is the last part, from 3:12-15, and it is the conclusion to this brief epistle. First, Paul promises to send either Artemas or Tychichus to Crete to relieve Titus. Then Titus should come meet Paul in Nicopolis, a city in Greece, where Paul planned to spend the worst winter weeks.

In verse 13, Paul speaks of Zenas and Apollos in such a way as to suggest they were bringing this letter to Titus. Titus should send them on their journey with needs supplied.

In verse 14 Paul gives one last urging that Titus teach the Christians to do works of kindness and good deeds. And in verse 15 Paul concludes quickly with a general salutation from all and words of greeting, for those under Titus' leadership. Thus concludes the letter to Titus.

So now we must turn the page to Philemon, the shortest of all Paul's letters. It follows Titus in your New Testament, and has but one chapter. But though it is brief, this little epistle to Philemon has some important lessons for us.

As usual, we ought to cover some background information first. I always find it helpful to understand the historical circumstances under which any Bible book was written. Philemon is no exception. To begin with, you need to change gears completely, and get in an entirely different frame of mind. The background of Philemon is not at all similar to that of the epistles to Timothy and Titus, which we have just been studying.

In fact, Philemon was written at the very same time as Colossians and Ephesians. So it would be helpful if you would review the background of those two epistles before studying Philemon. We will not take time to repeat all that background now; a brief review will have to do.

First, remember that Colossians and Ephesians were written during Paul's *first* imprisonment at Rome. The last chapter of Acts says that first Roman imprisonment lasted two years. Colosse and Ephesus were both located in the same Roman province called Asia. Asia was on the western end of what we now call Asia Minor or Turkey. Paul had done his major work in that area on the third missionary journey, when he spent well over two years in Ephesus. Churches had been established in many cities in the province of Asia during that ministry.

As I have just said, Paul was in prison at Rome when he wrote Colossians and Ephesians and Philemon. The year was about A.D. 60, and there were serious doctrinal problems threatening the churches in Asia. No doubt Paul would have preferred to go in person, but his imprisonment made him have to settle for a letter. The doctrinal problems in Asia had nothing to do with Philemon's letter, however, so we will not review those problems now.

Perhaps you are asking whether I can prove Philemon was written at the same time as Colossians. I think I can. Turn with me to Colossians, chapter 4. At the same time, keep your place at Philemon. Now note Colossians 4:7: "All my state shall Tychicus declare unto you." In verse 8 Paul says he has sent Tychicus to Colosse. And now note especially verse 9. Here Paul says he has sent Onesimus with Tychicus, and he identifies Onesimus as one of the Colossians. Keep this place and turn back to Philemon, verse 10, where you will see that Onesimus was the very one about whom Philemon was being written. Verse 12 of Philemon mentions Paul's having sent Onesimus home, and this agrees exactly with Colossians 4:9, as we just read.

Furthermore, notice Philemon, verse 2, where the name Archippus is mentioned. Now compare Colossians 4:17, where

Archippus is particularly spoken to in the Colossian epistle. And if all that is not enough, notice one more thing. In Philemon, verses 23, 24, you will see that Paul sends greetings from Epaphras, Marcus, Aristarchus, Demas, and Luke. And what do you know: In Colossians 4, verses 10-14, the very same five people send their greetings to the Colossians!

All this makes clear that Philemon lived in Colosse, and since Paul was sending a letter and messenger to Colosse, he took advantage of the opportunity to write Philemon a personal note and send Philemon's runaway slave, Onesimus, back home.

Let us summarize, then. Philemon was a Christian who lived in Colosse. One of his slaves, named Onesimus, had run away and evidently made his way to Rome. In some way—we are not told how—Onesimus came under Paul's influence at Rome and was saved. Since Paul was confined to the prison grounds, he could not go out into Rome. So my guess is that some of Paul's co-workers, who were free to roam the city, spotted Onesimus and recognized him. There would have been several Christians in Rome who were originally from Asia and would have known Philemon and his servants. For that matter, Onesimus may have become conscience striken and sought out Paul himself. We just do not know.

But no matter how, Onesimus was converted. And then the right thing for him to do was return to Philemon, his master. He probably did not need much urging from Paul to recognize this obligation. At the same time, as Providence would have it, Paul was writing the Colossian and Ephesian letters he would send to Asia by Tychicus. Onesimus could go with Tychicus. This plan was adopted, and Paul wrote our short little letter to Philemon to explain and to suggest that Philemon show mercy. The basic purpose of this letter, therefore, was to urge Philemon to receive the converted runaway without severe punishment. As we shall see in a minute, Paul may have even wished to imply that Philemon should free Onesimus, or at least send Onesimus back to Rome to minister to Paul in prison.

So now, with the letter to Philemon before us, let us survey its contents, part by part.

The first part of Philemon is verses 1-3, and this is the usual letter-opening, the introduction. Remember that all ancient letters included three things in the opening. Always first was the writer's name. Note verse 1: "Paul, a prisoner of Jesus Christ"—thus reminding us of his prison status, a situation he was in because he was also gladly Christ's prisoner. Note also in verse 1 that he includes Timothy with him.

The second thing in all letter-openings was the identification of the person or persons being written. The primary receiver, here, is indicated in verse 1 as Philemon. But two other Christians are mentioned by name. Apphia is a feminine name; she was probably Philemon's wife. Archippus was probably pastor of the congregation, as is implied in Colossians 4:17. Some think he was Philemon's son, and that is possible. Notice also in verse 2 that the congregation that met in Philemon's house—over which Archippus was pastor, we suppose—is also greeted.

The third thing in typical letter-openings of Paul's day was some special greeting. This is verse 3: "Grace to you, and peace, from God our Father and the Lord Jesus Christ."

Now the second part of Philemon is verses 4-7. We can call this "Appreciation for Philemon." Philemon was obviously a fine Christian man, and Paul was grateful. He would not mind so much asking a big favor of Philemon after recalling these good things about Philemon's Christian character.

Let us notice these things quickly. In verse 4, notice Paul's thanks and regular prayers for Philemon. In verse 5, he mentions especially Philemon's faith in Christ and love for all the saints. In verse 6, the word communication means fellowship, sharing. Paul prays that Philemon will keep on sharing his faith. In verse 7, note Paul's joy over Philemon's love. The unusual expression in the last half of verse 7 probably means that Philemon was habitually hospitable and benevolent toward other believers, especially toward traveling evangelists who stopped over for rest at Philemon's home.

Anyway, Paul gets down to business in verse 8, where part three of Philemon begins, going on through verse 21. Let us survey these verses briefly, commenting where necessary to explain the significance. Verse 8: Paul *could* boldly charge Philemon to do what he is about to ask of him. Verse 9: Paul would rather, as an old man and one who loved Philemon, ask him than tell him. Verse 10: The request concerns Onesimus, whom Paul had led to Christ from his prison cell.

Verse 11: Previously Onesimus had been no good. All that has changed. Verse 12: Paul has sent Onesimus home. Philemon should receive him as Paul's own son. Verse 13: Paul would have liked to keep Onesimus to minister to him in prison in Rome. Verse 14: But Paul would not do this unless it came voluntarily and knowingly from Philemon. These verses suggest that Paul would like for Philemon to send Onesimus back to Rome.

Verse 15: Onesimus' flight has turned out for good after all. Philemon should receive him not for time alone but for eternity, because he has become a brother in Christ. Verse 16: Philemon should recognize that brotherhood.

Verse 17: Philemon should receive Onesimus as he would receive Paul himself. Verse 18: If Onesimus owes Philemon anything, charge it to Paul. Verse 19: Paul will repay whatever Onesimus owes, even though Philemon owes his very soul to Paul. Obviously Onesimus had stolen some things when he ran away, at least food and clothing. Paul does not want Philemon to hold this against him.

Verse 20: Paul expects Philemon's actions to give him joy.

Verse 21: Paul is confident Philemon will do even more than he has asked. This is a pretty clear hint that Paul hopes Philemon will set Onesimus free and send him back to Paul. I have an idea Philemon did just that, after so moving an appeal.

Part four is verses 22-25 and forms the conclusion to the letter. Paul asks for prayers that he will be released, and preparations for lodgings at Philemon's house when that happens. Then, in verses 23, 24 he sends greetings from the five co-workers we already mentioned. Verse 25 is a benediction.

This little epistle teaches us a valuable lesson. Most of all it makes clear that Onesimus should be a Christian and do right even as a slave. Likewise Philemon, though a master, should be a Christian and do right. We can always be Christians and do right regardless what circumstances we are in. That is the lesson I leave with you in concluding this lecture. God bless you.

A SURVEY OF THE EPISTLE TO THE

Hebrews

by Dr. Stanley Outlaw

Perhaps the most controversial point in regard to the Book of Hebrews is the question of authorship. An early tradition in the eastern part of the church ascribed authorship of the epistle to Paul. By the fourth century this tradition had been accepted in the western part of the church. However, all during this time there was no unanimous agreement about authorship; and after the Protestant Reformation in the 16th century fresh doubts arose as to Pauline authorship, and new theories were formulated. Perhaps the most classic analysis of the problem is still that of the church father, Origen, who in the fourth century wrote, "As to who actually wrote the epistle, God knows the truth of the matter."

Several points argue strongly against Pauline authorship of the epistle: (1) The Greek style and vocabulary in the letter are not at all similar to those of Paul's known epistles. (2) The absence of Paul's name at the beginning of the epistle is entirely unique if the epistle should belong to him. (3) The author seems to imply in 2:3, 4 that he was a second generation Christian which does not seem to coincide with Paul's declaration in Galatians 1, 2 concerning the originality of his message. (4) The fact that Paul was the apostle to the Gentiles would place some uniqueness upon this letter, if indeed it be Pauline, though it must be admitted that he did have a deep concern for his own people (Romans 9:1-3; 10:1). (5) A final factor which would seem to argue against Pauline authorship of the epistle is the strange way in which he refers to Timothy as "our brother" in 13:23, in contrast to Paul's usual reference to Timothy as "my . . . son" (1 Timothy 1:2). If Paul did not write the epistle, other possible authors who have been suggested down through the history of the church are Barnabas, Luke, Clement of Rome, and Apollos. Although there has not been agreement within the church about authorship of the epistle, from early times all have agreed that the letter is inspired by God and is an authoritative part of the body of God's revelation to man which we call "the Holy Scriptures."

The theme of the Book of Hebrews is quite fascinating, for it concerns the superiority of Christ in His person and His work to the Old Testament dispensation. It is the only book of the New Testament which so thoroughly emphasizes the work of Christ as High Priest. A secondary theme of the epistle is the emphasis on the necessity of Christian progress toward maturity.

Several factors seem to have led up to the writing of the Book of Hebrews. The early church, which was primarily Jewish, did not immediately separate itself from the synagogue, the Temple, or Judaism in general. Gradually, however, it became clearer to the preachers of the New Testament that the old doctrines of the law had no place in this new dispensation which found its basis in the blood of Christ. From the accusations which were made against Stephen in Acts 6:11-14, it seems that he was a pioneer in pointing toward the changes which must, of necessity, take place.

The first great church conference between the mother church in Jerusalem and the predominately Gentile church at Antioch was convened to decide the question of the obligation of Gentile converts to the Law of Moses. The Book of Galatians was written by Paul just a little later to combat the false teachings of the Judaizers who said that faith was not sufficient for salvation, but that it must be supplemented by the ceremonies and works of the law to ensure salvation. In connection with this same basic problem, the Book of Hebrews was written to Jewish Christians who seem to have been considering the possibility of returning to Judaism, and particularly the sacrifices of Judaism, as a way of salvation.

It seems that a lack of spiritual growth, which contributed to a lack of spiritual discernment, as well as the increasing amount of suffering and persecution which Christians were having to face, were likely factors in causing the Jewish Christians to even consider such an awesome retreat from the sacrifice of Christ. It is in the light of these facts that the writer of Hebrews launches into his eloquent arguments pointing toward the superiority and sufficiency of Christ in order to put a halt to the downward road toward irretrievable apostasy which these Hebrew Christians were traveling.

Following the theme of the superiority of Christ, the writer of Hebrews, in chapters 1, 2, points toward the superiority of the New Testament revelation concerning God's Son to the Old Testament revelation which came through the instrumentality of the prophets and the angels. The phrase "sundry times and in divers manners" in 1:1 may be better translated "in many parts and in many ways." Thus, in verses 1, 2 the contrast is made between the Old Testament revelation which came in a somewhat piecemeal fashion, scattered over a long period of time. It was manifested by varying methods, such as dreams, visions, direct conversations, etc. All of this came through the prophets as the human instrument, with the New Testament revelation which was manifested by God's own Son. He was His sole heir and the mediating member of the Trinity through whom the creation took place.

Chapter 1, verse 3, gives a summary of the person and work of Christ as it is to be presented in the Book of Hebrews. From eternity the Son has radiated the Divine glory and has manifested in His person the essential character of the Divine essence. This is one of the greatest affirmations of the deity of Christ in the New Testament, in the category with such verses as John 1:1-3 and Philippians 2:5-11. In summary fashion Hebrews 1:3 says that Jesus was and is Divine, as is manifested by His constant sustaining of all things by His powerful word, and that His redemptive ministry involved a making of purification for sins, after which He showed the completed status of His redemptive work by taking His authoritative and intercessory position at the right hand of God.

In 1:4 through 2:18 the writer turns to the subject of Jesus' superiority to the other instrument of the Old Testament revelation, the angels. The fact that angelic messengers were used in delivering the law is also taught in Acts 7:53 and Galatians 3:19. The proof that the Son is superior to these angelic messengers is drawn from a series of seven Old Testament quotations. Note that the writer seems to be referring to the superiority which was earned by the Son through His redemptive work rather than the superiority which He naturally had as the Second Person of the Trinity, for it was "by inheritance" that He "obtained" this more excellent name.

In verses 5-7 he shows the Son's superiority to angels in their mutual relationships to the Father. In doing this he quotes from Psalm 2:7, a Messianic psalm; from 2 Samuel 7:14, a promise originally made to David about his son Solomon; and from the Septuagint Version (the Greek Version of the Old Testament) of Deuteronomy 32:43. This last quotation is also found indirectly in Psalm 97:7. Then in 1:8-14 the superiority of the Son to angels is presented in relation to the authoritative position which He holds. In quoting Psalm 104:4, he shows that the role of angels is that of ministering and delivering God's messages. Then he quotes Psalms 45:6, 7; 102:25-27; and 110:1 to show the complete superiority of the Son's position on the throne of God, a position more permanent than His own creation in which He will manifest ultimate victory over all his enemies.

In 2:1-4 the first warning of the epistle is issued by contrasting the severity which was involved in disobedience to the Law of Moses, which was delivered by angels, and the much greater severity which must, of necessity, be involved in the disobedience of that Word of God which came through His own Son and His immediate disciples.

In passing it should be observed that 2:4 might suggest that certain of those extra special apostolic gifts were intended only for a specific time and purpose, to give Divine attestation to the message which the early disciples preached, and were not intended to continue throughout the history of the church after the New Testament with its authoritative record had been completed. In 2:5-18 the process of the humiliation of Christ, in which He took a position lower than the angels by becoming man, is described.

In verses 5-9 the author quotes Psalm 8:4-6 where David wonders at the exalted position which God has given to man to have dominion over His creation. But he points to the result of the fall of Adam when he suggests that this dominion has not been realized by man. Thus, Jesus Himself took the form of a man, that He, as the second Adam, might do for man what man had been unable to do for himself, and the ordained method by which He should accomplish this goal was "that he by the grace of God should taste death for every man" (verse 9).

Verses 10-18 point out the fittingness, the appropriateness of Jesus' participation in our humanity to equip Him for His redemptive office. If He was to become the "captain of our salvation," He must become one with us in our human nature, and He did this even to the extent of being able to address us as "brethren." However, the heart of this redemptive identification is in verse 14 where His victory over death is proclaimed through the destruction of Satan. John 12:31, 32 emphasizes the Cross as the place where this victory was accomplished. Chapter 2, verse 16, should be translated, "For assuredly he does not give help to angels, but he gives help to the seed of Abraham"; that is, Jesus, in His redemptive work, made no provision for the salvation of angels, but only for men who become the spiritual seed of Abraham by faith. By this full participation in humanity, He by His work becomes superior again to angels and is able to offer help to us when we are tried.

In chapters 3, 4 the writer of Hebrews shows how Christ is superior to both Moses and Joshua, the great initial leaders of God's covenant people. In 3:1-6 he discusses Christ's superiority to Moses. According to verses 3, 4, this is a two-fold superiority; first, Christ is superior to Moses as a builder is to a house, and, second, He is superior to Moses as a Son is superior to a servant. Jesus, as God, was the creator and builder of the Old Testament economy of Israel, God's chosen people, while Moses was himself a part of that economy. Furthermore, Moses' relation to God in his position of leadership, as great as it was, was still that of a servant, while Jesus' relationship is that of a Son. Note that in 3:1 Jesus is called our "Apostle" and "High Priest." As the Apostle of our profession He was sent by God to minister to us and for us, and as our High Priest He appears for us before God to make intercession for us.

In 3:7 through 4:16 the author of Hebrews makes a lengthy warning to the Hebrews concerning the possibility of their falling short of Heaven, their eternal rest, like Israel fell short of Canaan, their earthly rest, by their rebellion and unbelief in the wilderness. In 3:7-19 basic reasons and results of Israel's wilderness rebellion are examined. In verses 7-11 the writer quotes from Psalm 95:7-11 where God warns the Israelites during the psalmist's day concerning the hardening of their hearts in unbelief, lest he should swear about them, like He did Israel in the wilderness, "They shall not enter into my rest." Note that in verse 7 the authorship of the passage from Psalm 95 is directly ascribed to the Holy Spirit, regardless who the human author might have been. Although God used human instruments to deliver His Word to man, He, through His Spirit, is the ultimate source of all the Scriptures.

In commenting on the quotation from the Psalm, the writer of Hebrews observes in verse 12 that the sin involved "an evil heart of unbelief, in departing from the living God." The sin of Israel was not merely an outward sin of passion or impetuousness but was a basic and inward sin involving totally perverted motive and will. Stephen observes the rebellion of these same Israelites against God in Acts 7:39 when he says that they "thrust him from them, and in their hearts turned back again into Egypt."

In Hebrews 3:13 our writer emphasizes the word "to day" from the quotation in Psalms to encourage the Hebrews to immediately make their decision to turn from this downward road toward apostasy. In 3:14 the need to continuously "hold the beginning of our confidence" is stressed. A Christian should never lose the vitality and excitement of that initial profession of faith, but instead he should keep building upon it as his faith grows toward maturity. Note that in verse 19 the ultimate reason that Israel did not enter into the promised land was "because of unbelief." Just as faith is the only door to salvation, unbelief is ultimately the door which leads to apostasy. In 4:1, 2 the writer of Hebrews definitely applies this quotation from Psalms to the Hebrews. Just as Israel fell short of Canaan, they too may fall short of Heaven through their unbelief. Though the preaching of the "gospel" is usually associated with the New Testament and the message of Christ, it is interesting that here it is said that the "gospel," the good news of salvation, was also preached to Israel. God's promise of salvation and deliverance has always been "good news," and His promise has also always pointed ultimately toward Christ, from the first promise made in Genesis 3:15 right down to the last.

In 4:3-10 our author advances three basic arguments to the Hebrews as to why a rest is still available to them if they will persevere in faith: (1) God first mentioned the rest and made it available to man when He rested on the seventh day after His creative activity. (2) He suggested the continuing availability of the rest for God's people because Israel failed to enter into that rest, and that generation of rebels died in the wilderness. But someone might suggest that Joshua, after the death of Moses, did take the next generation of Israelites into the land. The writer of Hebrews argues, however, that the fact that David, in his day, in Psalm 95, declared that the rest was still available implies that Joshua's taking Israel into the land did not completely satisfy God's promise of a rest for His people. Therefore, he concludes in verse 9, "There remaineth therefore a rest to the people of God." The name "Jesus" in 4:8 should here be translated "Joshua," since it is referring to the Old Testament leader.

The translation problem developed from the fact that the Hebrew word "Joshua" is the equivalent to the Greek word "Jesus." This same problem occurs in Acts 7:45. Chapter 4, verses 11-16, give four aids which the Hebrews, as well as us today, could use to see that they enter into God's rest. These aids are the example of Israel's unbelief and their failure to enter (4:11), the power and conviction of the Word of God (4:12), the omniscient, all-seeing eye of God (4:13), and finally, the continual intercession of our sympathetic High Priest who, in His position at the right hand of the Father, is ever willing and able to meet our every need (4:14-16). Christian songwriters and poets have down through the years made great use of Israel's trip to Canaan as symbolic of the Christian's trip toward Heaven. As an example, we sing in an old familiar hymn:

On Jordan's stormy banks I stand, And cast a wishful eye
To Canaan's fair and happy land, Where my possessions lie.

When shall I reach that happy place, And be forever blest?
When shall I see my Father's face, And in His bosom rest?

I am bound for the promised land, I am bound for the promised land;
O who will come and go with me? I am bound for the promised land.

In chapters 5—10 the writer discusses the superior intercession of the Son as our High Priest. In chapters 5—7 he points out that the priesthood of Christ is an entirely new and different type of priesthood. In 5:1-4 four different qualifications or characteristics of the Old Testament priesthood are mentioned: (1) The priest must be taken from among men, a true man himself. (2) He offers service for the benefit of man before God. (3) He is able to sympathize with sinners who come to him because of his own infirmity and sin. (4) He cannot call himself to the office of priest; he must be appointed to it by someone else. Beginning in reverse order, the writer in 5:5-10 shows how Jesus met each one of these qualifications.

The authoritative call of Jesus as High Priest of a different order is based on the quotation from Psalm 110:4, "Thou art a priest for ever after the order of Melchizedek." He was indeed a true man who came in the flesh (verse 7), and though He had no sin Himself, as the

Old Testament priest did, He became sympathetic with us by the terrible human sufferings which He endured in the process of ministering to men and going to the Cross for them (verses 7, 8). Verse 7 seems to emphasize Jesus' experience in the Garden of Gethsemane. When the plan of redemption was completed, "made perfect," Jesus became our representative before God as "the author of eternal salvation," but only for those who follow Him in obedience and faith (verse 9).

One of the most crucial warnings in the entire book, and for that matter in the entire Bible, occurs in the passage in 5:11—6:20. It is interesting to notice that the problem with the Hebrews has been caused by the fact that they have not grown in the Lord as they should. This fact is brought out in 5:11-14. I can safely say that the danger of apostasy will be no problem for the Christian who continues to maintain a living, growing, vital relationship with the Lord. It is only the Christian who has become cold and stagnant who will soon begin to drift backwards toward that dangerous abyss of no return. Note also that lack of growth and exercise in spiritual things results in an inability "to discern both good and evil," and thus makes it easy for such a Christian to be swept away by any variety of false religious movements. In 6:1-8 the writer emphasizes and describes in detail the possibility of renouncing the true faith because of lack of progress.

The six foundation principles in 6:1, 2 may be placed in three groups: Repentance and faith are the conditions which form the *basis* of the Christian life; baptism and laying on of hands were, from the time of the early church, associated with the *initiation* into the Christian life, while resurrection and eternal judgment will become the consummation of the Christian life. It is the opinion of this writer that the five characteristics which describe these potential apostates in verses 4, 5 most certainly describe people who have truly been saved. If you can have all these experiences and still not be a Christian, I would say, as did the disciples on one occasion, "Who then can be saved?"

It also seems to me that when the author of Hebrews says, "It is impossible . . . If they shall fall away, to renew them again unto repentance," he intends to say that this sin of apostasy is entirely without remedy. Since there is only one sin which cannot be forgiven, the sin of blasphemy against the Holy Spirit (Matthew 12:31, 32), this must be identified with that sin. It should be pointed out that some Arminians prefer to believe that there is a remedy for this apostasy; and they would translate this phrase, "It is impossible . . . to renew them again unto repentance, *while* they are crucifying the son of God afresh." In other words, if and when they will quit doing this, they can be renewed to repentance. Although it must be admitted that such a translation is possible, it does not seem to me that this interpretation fits the gravity and seriousness of the warning and of the general context; for, after all, if this sin can be repented of like any other, though serious it is not as bad as we first thought.

Those who hold to the doctrine of eternal security usually attempt to explain away these verses either by saying that they do indeed warn true Christians against the possibility of apostasy, but that this is only a hypothetical warning. It could, they say, actually never happen, or they say that these were not true Christians who were about to abandon the faith, but only professors of salvation who were never really saved at all. It seems that the illustration of the burned off and rejected land in verses 6, 7 would also suggest total and final abandonment of the apostate by God.

However, the writer of Hebrews is quick to encourage the Hebrews by pointing out that he has confidence that they will change their course and will never become apostates. He encourages them first in 6:9-11 by reminding them of their past diligent work and suffering for the cause of Christ. Then in 6:12-18 he encourages by pointing to the example of Abraham's patience toward God's promise and God's double assurance to him by giving him both His word and then sealing it with an oath. Finally, in 6:19, 20 he further encourages by pointing the Hebrews to Jesus who had gone before them as their priestly forerunner.

Although our author has expressed doubts that the Hebrews would understand and take advantage of Christ's priesthood after the order of Melchisedec back in 5:11, 12 yet in hopes that they would soon follow his admonition and show a change of course, he goes on in chapter 7 to discuss the details of Christ's priestly order. The writer establishes the basis of the Melchisedecian priesthood on a two-fold superiority; first, in 7:1-8, he shows the superiority of Melchisedec to Abraham, the father of Israel, and then, in 7:9-28, he follows by demonstrating the superiority of the priestly order of Melchisedec to the priestly order of Aaron.

In 7:1-8 Melchisedec's superiority to Abraham is shown by the fact that Melchisedec blessed Abraham, and in turn Abraham paid tithes of the spoils of battle to him; both of these acts imply and acknowledge Abraham's subjection to Melchisedec. In 7:9, 10 our author next shows that Melchisedec was also superior to Levi, the father of the priestly tribe, inasmuch as Levi paid tithes representatively through his great grandfather, Abraham. In 7:11-19 he argues that the very idea of a need for a new priestly order implies that the Levitical priesthood failed to attain "perfection" for the worshipers; that is, it failed to bring the sinner to an entirely satisfactory position before God inasmuch as the consciousness of sin still remained. These verses also point out that the priesthood and the law are essentially one institution and must stand or fall together.

In 7:20-28 he points out the superiority of Jesus' priesthood after the order of Melchisedec because of the permanence of this priesthood in contrast to temporariness of the Levitical priesthood. In contrast to the ever changing priest and the often repeated sacrifice under the Levitical order, in Hebrews 7:25 he declares about Jesus, "He is able also to save them to the uttermost that come unto God by him, seeing he ever liveth to make intercession for them."

Chapters 8—10 describe Jesus' work as our great High Priest. In 8:1-5 it is pointed out that the Old Testament tabernacle and priesthood typified Christ's work as High Priest, but 8:6-13 emphasizes that His priesthood was based on an entirely new covenant which had been prophesied in Jeremiah 31:31-34.

In 9:1—10:18 our author contrasts the old and the new covenants. In the first twenty-four verses of chapter 9, he describes in greater detail the typical significance of the Old Testament tabernacle and its services in pointing toward Christ, and he especially emphasizes the importance of blood sacrifices in connection with this tabernacle. He sums it up in 9:22 when he says, "And almost all things are by the law purged with blood; and without shedding of blood is no remission." However, as 9:24 points out, while the Levitical priests performed these services and sacrifices in relation to an earthly tabernacle, Christ has taken His supreme sacrifice into the heavenly tabernacle itself "now to appear in the presence of God for us."

In 9:25—10:18 the writer moves into the area of the priesthood and its sacrifices in contrasting the old and the new covenants. In this area he points out two major contrasts; first, in that the benefits of the sacrifices under the old covenant were temporary and had to be repeated annually, year after year (at this point it is clear that he refers to the day of atonement), while the sacrifice of Christ was made once for all time and will prove eternally sufficient; and second, in that the old covenant was imperfect in its inability to remove the consciousness of sin caused by the guilt of the sinner, while the sacrifice of Christ under the new covenant took care of the sin problem forever by an inward purification of the sinner which totally removed even the guilt consciousness of sin.

In 10:19-39 the writer of Hebrews discusses the application of Christ's word as High Priest. In verses 19-25 he exhorts the Hebrews to continued progress in depending on Christ's priestly ministry by constantly drawing nearer through the sanctification process, by continuing to hold steadfast to the faith, and by constantly encouraging each other, especially as they are faithful to meet together in their church assemblies.

But the question might arise, "What would happen if one does not follow these important admonitions of dependence upon Christ's priesthood and its provisions?" In 10:26-31 the writer answers this with a strong warning against the possibility of apostasy in the same vein as the earlier warning in 6:4-6. There are two important characteristics of this apostasy here. One of these is not clear in the

King James Version, but in the original 10:26 should read, "If we *continue* sinning wilfully"; that is, this apostasy is first characterized by habitual sin. The other key word here is "wilfully," an act of rebellion in the face of God's chastisement and long-suffering. Thus, this act of apostasy after one has come to the full knowledge of the truth is an act of habitual, willful, stubborn rebellion against God, involving an outrage toward the blood of Christ and an insult to the Holy Spirit. Such a rejection of Christ's once-for-all sacrifice leaves no further remedy for sin and places the blasphemer in a hopeless state of condemnation. In verses 32-39 the writer again encourages the Hebrews to patiently endure as they look toward the Second Coming of Christ.

In chapters 11—13 the author of Hebrews gives a final exhortation to faithful perseverance in order to obtain the promises of God. He does this first in chapter 11 by giving several examples of faithful perseverance under the old dispensation. In 11:1, 2 he defines faith as that which gives substance and reality to that which is invisible and unrealized. Of the great leaders in faith from the Old Testament to which he refers, he dwells mostly on Abraham and Moses. In 12:1—13:17 his second means of encouragement toward faithful perseverance is in looking to Jesus as the author and finisher of our faith. In chapter 12 the author urges the Hebrews to depend on Jesus during their persecutions and trials. In 13:1-8 he becomes the example and model to emulate in principles of conduct. In 13:9-14 the Hebrews are exhorted to follow him in separation and to bear his reproach; and in 13:15-17 they are to follow his example in an attitude of praise and submission.

A SURVEY OF THE EPISTLE OF

James

by Dr. Stanley Outlaw

The Epistle of James is located in that section of our English Bibles called the General Epistles, which includes, in addition to James, 1 and 2 Peter, 1, 2, and 3 John, and Jude. These books are called the General Epistles because they are addressed more to the church at large, rather than to some specific church or individual. The writer was one of the earthly brothers of Jesus, a son born to Mary and Joseph after the virgin birth of Christ. In the Book of Acts, especially in the first church conference in Acts 15 and in Galatians 2:12, it appears that James was the most prominent leader in the church at Jerusalem.

Early church tradition pictures James as an austere person. He was so much a man of prayer that his knees were said to have become hardened like a camel's. Tradition also says that he died as a martyr for Christ in the city of Jerusalem. What a contrast this devotion offers to the incident in John 7 where James and his brothers ridiculed Jesus' claims of Messiahship! But it seems that after Jesus' resurrection one of His early appearances, according to 1 Corinthians 15:7, was to His brother James. As a result James became a believer and one of the most loyal followers of the Lord Jesus Christ.

Because of the primitive nature of the church organization which appears in the Epistle of James, most commentators feel that it is likely one of the earliest books of the New Testament. Some would date it as early as A.D. 45. The content of the book is almost entirely practical, rather than doctrinal. James is not so much concerned about the content of faith as he is about the conduct of faith. The nature of the content can especially be compared to that of the Book of Proverbs in the Old Testament and to the Sermon on the Mount in Matthew 5—7. In fact, several observations throughout the epistle are obviously based on the teachings of Jesus in the

Sermon on the Mount. Some have gone so far as to refer to James as a commentary on the Sermon on the Mount. With these introductory comments, we now turn our attention to the contents of the book itself.

James gives a very brief introduction and salutation in 1:1. He says nothing about being the earthly brother of Jesus but confesses rather that he is "a servant of God and of the Lord Jesus Christ." His letter is addressed to Jewish Christians who were scattered in all parts of the Roman Empire. He uses the word *diaspora*, the technical Greek term which referred to these scattered Jews away from their homeland. The references to James in Acts and Galatians reveal that he had a strong religious loyalty to the Law of Moses and a strong racial loyalty to the Jewish people, though he also apparently had an honest and open mind toward Gentile converts as well.

In verses 2-18 of chapter 1 James encourages these Jewish Christians toward proper attitudes regarding trials and temptations which they were then undergoing. In verses 2-4 he boldly admonishes them to even rejoice in these trials since the testing of a Christian's faith produces patience and maturity in his Christian life. Paul also observed in Romans 5:3 that "tribulation worketh patience." This does not mean that in an effort to obtain patience we should pray for God to send us trials and tribulations. It would be totally unnatural to have a martyr complex in attempting to create opportunities for suffering. Besides this, if I asked God to send trials or tried to create them for myself, I would probably ask for them at the wrong time. We should leave this up to the Lord, who, in His infinite wisdom, will allow tests of faith to come our way to strengthen us with the right timing and the right degree. He has promised that He will be faithful in not allowing us to be tested beyond that which we can bear, and that He will supply a route of escape from each test (1 Corinthians 10:13).

In 1:5-8 James promises that wisdom is available for understanding trials through unwavering prayer. Since James is basing his observation on a general truth, it is permissible to infer from this statement that wisdom in relation to the totality of the Christian life is always available for the asking. But it should be emphasized that the request for wisdom here is specifically for understanding and bearing up under the present trials. In discussing wisdom, James is reminiscent of the theme of Proverbs. Wisdom here, as elsewhere in the Scriptures, is more that mere factual knowledge, though it may include that. It is the ability to go beyond mere surface knowledge to discernment and understanding. Knowledge may be merely passive, while wisdom produces convictions and actions.

In 1:9-11 James points out to both the poor and the rich Christians that they each have their reasons for rejoicing in the Lord, even in the face of trials and persecution. Someone has said, "All ground is level ground at the foot of the Cross." There are no big

"I's" and little "yous" when we stand before God, but each one must stand as a sinner; and each one, regardless of social status, race, or wealth, must obtain salvation by the same method. James points out, however, that a poor brother can rejoice in the elevated position which he now has in Christ. The words of an old hymn reflect the attitude when it says:

> A tent or a cottage, why should I care?
> They're building a palace for me over there;
> Tho' exiled from home, yet, still I may sing:
> All glory to God, I'm a child of the King.

Oh, the wealth to which we became heir when we were adopted as sons of God through our Lord Jesus Christ! But James also points out that the Christian rich man has something to rejoice about. He can rejoice in that God gave him true spiritual eyesight to see that his earthly wealth was so fleeting, so temporary, so perishable, and that the only real treasure which he had was that which was stored up in Heaven. Not many rich men will get to Heaven because of their proneness to trust in their earthly riches, but all who do will come by abandoning that corruptible trust for the incorruptible one in Christ Jesus.

James 1:12 promises "the crown of life" for those who remain faithful under trial. The crown of life here probably means "a crown which is life," the fact that the one who perseveres will be crowned with the reward of life eternal for his faithfulness. Jesus made a similar promise when He said, "He that shall endure unto the end, the same shall be saved," or as Jesus said to the church at Ephesus, "To him that overcometh will I give to eat of the tree of life, which is in the midst of the paradise of God."

In 1:13-18 James admonishes these Jewish Christians to have the proper attitude toward God in realizing that He is never the source of evil but of good. In James 1:13 our author declares outrightly that God does not tempt men. At this point we must note that the same Greek word may be translated into English either as "to test" or "to tempt," depending upon the context in which it is used. This may at times be confusing. However, the difference between the two translations is entirely one of motive. God never tempts men; that is, His motive is never to trap them or to get them to fall into sin. God may at times test men, or allow them to be tested, but His motive is to strengthen and increase their faith. In light of this it would be better to translate a passage like Genesis 22:1, "God did *test* Abraham," in commanding him to offer Isaac. God's purpose was clearly to test and strengthen Abraham's faith, not to place an insurpassable barrier in front of him.

A good illustration of the difference between these two actions is in the example of Job. When the devil attacked Job by first destroying his property and his children and later attacking Job's person with severe physical affliction, he was tempting Job; his motive was evil; he wanted to destroy Job's faith. But God, in allowing Satan to take these actions against Job, intended by them to strengthen and to prove Job's faith; and at the conclusion He rewarded Job with a double portion of His richest blessings. Here then is a case where one act is from God's standpoint a test of faith meant to strengthen, but from Satan's standpoint it is a temptation intended to drive Job to despair and destruction. No doubt these trials which these Jewish Christians were now experiencing could come under the same double category, as well as many trials which we as Christians face day by day. But God's promise is that He, in His sovereign will, will always make "all things work together for good to them that love God" (Romans 8:28).

Perhaps James offers somewhat of a surprise in 1:14, 15 when he suggests that the source of most of our temptations is not the devil, but our yielding to our own sinful natures. One of today's most prominent slogans is, "The devil made me do it." Men try to excuse their sin by blaming it on the devil, thus salving their own consciences. But James will not permit us to alleviate the guilt of our sin so easily. James is not declaring Satan innocent, for indeed he has the worst desires for every saint of God. But the Scriptures do not teach that the devil is omnipresent. He cannot be everywhere at once, so he must concentrate his effort in his most important fields. Even his numerous demonic assistants cannot cover all the territory. James is simply declaring frankly that most of our trouble with sin comes from a problem within rather than one without.

In contrast with accusing God with evil motives in placing temptations in our paths, James wants us to realize, in 1:16-18, that all of God's gifts are good. He does not want us to be in error at this important point. And certainly the greatest gift which God has ever given to any of us is the new birth which we received by means of "the word of truth."

The mention of the "word of truth" in verse 18 led James, in 1:19-27, to discuss the proper application of the Word of God to the Christian life. In verses 19-21 we are admonished to apply the Word in gaining self-control and holiness of character. One who is always "spouting off" and losing his temper cannot possibly be a good hearer and applier of the Word of God. Verse 21 teaches that the Word which has been planted must be permitted to take root, else it cannot produce the desired effects which will result in our eternal salvation. The difference between a hearer and a doer of the word is illustrated and defined in 1:22-25. The illustration which James uses of one who is only a hearer is that of a man who glances at his image in the mirror, then quickly goes on his way doing nothing to change the way he looks. A mirror only reveals. It does not change, and neither does the Word of God when it is only heard and not applied.

It is like the seed sowed by the wayside in Jesus' parable of the sower. But what a contrast in the one who both hears and does; he "looketh into the perfect law of liberty, and *continueth* therein." The Word of God can and will change any life when it is heard or read, and then specifically applied.

James goes on to point out in 1:26, 27 that a man with an unbridled tongue cannot possess true religion, but that it is instead manifested by an outward concern for others and an inward concern for holiness and separation from the world.

In chapter 2 James discusses faith in relation to two important subjects in the church, partiality and works. He discusses partiality in 2:1-13. The word translated "respect of persons" in 2:1 literally means "receiving a face"; that is, one who shows partiality is one who looks to see who you are (your friendship to him, your social status, your wealth, etc.). Sometimes it is said in relation to the world, "It is not what you know, but whom you know." Politicians have always had a notorious reputation for favoritism. It should never be this way in the church. James gives a specific example of this favoritism in verses 2, 3. In 2:5-7 he points out that the ironic thing is that some in the church would choose to give special honor to the wealthy while ignoring or berating the poor, when the exact opposite of these social statuses is usually true in God's kingdom. It is the poor who are "rich in faith," while the rich have often been guilty of persecuting Christians and of blaspheming the name of the Lord whom they serve. In 2:8-11 James charges that those who are guilty of partiality are guilty of violating one of the two basic commandments of the law, "Thou shalt love thy neighbour as thyself."

The parable of the Good Samaritan in Luke 10 defined our neighbor as anyone who is in need and whom I have the ability and opportunity to help. Loving my neighbor as myself may mean that I will at times have to minister to those who are, in some ways, humanly repulsive—the drunkard, the harlot, the crude, the vulgar, the sick, and the poor. But part of Jesus' Messianic mission was "to preach the gospel to the poor." In this era of the bus ministry and of rapidly changing urban neighborhoods, many churches have faced the very problem about which James is speaking. Some church leaders and church members have resented a lower social class of people other than themselves being introduced into their congregation. That is the very attitude which James is condemning in this passage. I cannot see Scriptural justification for some of the gimmickry and the circus atmosphere with which the bus ministry is sometimes conducted; but I am always whole-heartedly for going out and bringing lost men, women, boys, and girls, of whatever social class, into the church to hear the gospel and be saved.

Again reminiscent of the Sermon on the Mount, James, in 2:12, 13 reminds us that the basis of judgment which we use in judging others will also be exercised against us when we stand before our Judge one day. If I want mercy in the day of judgment, I must be willing to exercise mercy and kindness toward others here in this life.

One of the most important passages in this entire epistle is the passage in 2:14-26 where James discusses the relationship of faith and works. It was especially this passage which led Martin Luther to denounce James as "a right strawy epistle" and to declare that it should not be included in the canon of the Scriptures. Unfortunately, Luther totally misunderstood the message of James. He saw James' teaching about faith and works as being in conflict with the beloved doctrine of justification by faith alone as seen especially in Paul's epistles to the Romans and to the churches of Galatia. But, when properly understood, James is not teaching anything with which Paul would not fully agree. Any apparent conflict arises from the fact that they are dealing with two different problems. When Paul, in Ephesians 2:8, 9, says, "For by grace are ye saved through faith . . . . Not of works," he is talking about the basis of salvation. No good deed that you ever did before you were saved, no matter how great, could add one iota toward your salvation.

Multitudes of good moral men will lift up their eyes in Hell in eternity. And then that day when you finally realized that you were a sinner, a sinner on the inside as well as on the outside, and knelt at a church altar, or in your home, or wherever, and asked the Lord to save you, you were just as saved at that moment as you ever will be. The basis of salvation is totally by faith; it is a gift of God and not something you have earned or deserved. The thief on the cross was not permitted to work for his salvation, but Jesus promised him that that day he would be with Him in Paradise.

James, on the other hand, is dealing with an entirely different problem. Some people might maintain that they were saved simply because they believed the facts of the Bible to be true, although their lives in no way reflect that a change has taken place. James maintains that saving faith does not work like that. He too agrees that faith saves, but he argues that the existence of faith in an individual's life can only be evidenced or demonstrated by works. In 2:14-17 he points out that faith is demonstrated by helping a brother or sister who has a need. Real faith makes a Christian take action rather than piously saying, "Well, I'll pray for you." In 2:18-20 James emphasizes the impossibility of demonstrating faith apart from works. Just saying that you have faith is not sufficient, for even the devil himself believes for sure that God exists, and that he will give an account to Him one day. Believing in Christ must go beyond mere intellectual assent.

John the Baptist said to the hypocritical Pharisees who came to his baptism, "Bring forth therefore fruits meet for repentance." Second Corinthians 5:17 declares, "If any man be in Christ, he is a new creature: old things are passed away; behold, all things are become new." A man who has been saved will most certainly manifest this salvation by a change both in conviction and in conduct. In 2:21-26 James illustrates the principle that faith is proved by works by pointing to two Old Testament characters. First, he mentions the faith of Abraham which was demonstrated by his offering of his only son, Isaac. It is interesting to notice that in 2:23 James quotes Genesis 15:6, the famous Old Testament verse which declares that God placed righteousness on Abraham's account with Him because of his faith. This is the same verse which Paul quotes in Romans 4:3 and Galatians 3:6 to back up the doctrine of salvation by faith alone. James quotes the same verse in agreement with Paul, but simply adds that Abraham proved his faith by his works.

The second illustration which James uses from the Old Testament is that of Rahab the harlot on the occasion when she by faith hid the Israelite spies and sent them out in another direction. While James uses these illustrations to show how these characters proved their faith by their works, the writer of Hebrews in Hebrews 11 uses these same two characters and these same incidents from their lives to show that they were great examples of faith. The point is simply this: Faith and works must always maintain a close and vital relationship in the doctrine of salvation; they can never be entirely separated, but they must never be mixed or confused. Faith, and faith alone, is the basis of salvation; but the evidence, the demonstration, the proof of true saving faith will always be works or fruit in the life of the Christian. Serious false doctrine can result from a lack of perception of this relationship in either direction. Notice in closing this section that Paul agrees with James about the importance of works as an evidence of faith. After his statement about salvation by faith alone in Ephesians 2:8, 9, he adds in verse 10, "For we are his workmanship, created in Christ Jesus unto good works, which God hath before ordained that we should walk in them."

In 3:1-12 James discusses a problem which is certainly prominent in many of our churches today, the danger and destruction involved in the improper use of the tongue, the gift of speech. James introduces the subject in 3:1 by giving a warning to those who might be overly anxious to claim the position of teacher or preacher because of the glory they supposed to be involved. To stand to teach or preach the Word of God is a grave responsibility which must not be considered lightly. God told Ezekiel in Ezekiel 33 that he was the watchman set on the wall of Israel. If he warned them of their sins, and they yet stubbornly refused to turn from them, he was free from the responsibility of their condemnation. But if he shirked his duty and failed to properly warn them of their sin, then he would be held accountable not just for his own sins, but also for the blood of the souls whom he failed to warn which will drip guiltily from his hands.

This is not to discourage young men who honestly and sincerely feel that God is directing them into the ministry, but it does sound a stern warning to those who would seek the office for some improper motive. God knows that we need many more ministers and teachers of the Word, but every young man should answer the call with a full understanding of the awesome responsibility involved. In 3:2 James states the central point of his argument about the tongue; that is, if a man can gain control of his tongue, it is an accurate indication that he has control of his entire body. In 3:3-6 he gives three illustrations of the principle that the tongue, though one of the smallest members of the body, possesses a very unproportionate role in the control of the body. It is first compared to the small bit which is put into the mouth of a very large horse to perfectly control him. The tongue in our body is also like a small helm which guides a large, multi-tonned ship; and finally, it is compared to a small spark which can start such a great fire. In 3:7, 8 James, almost in despair, declares the human impossibility of taming the tongue.

At least by implication, he is clearly directing us to God as the only source which will be successful in controlling the tongue. He closes this discussion in 3:9-12 by pointing out the frequent hypocritical inconsistency in the use of the tongue. Nature itself never creates such a mongrel monstrosity as a confused fig tree which bears olives, a grapevine which produces figs, or a fountain which yields both salt and fresh water. But I am sorry to say that such vile inconsistency is often manifested in the use of the human tongue unsanctified and undedicated to God. Oh, the damage to the cause of Christ that has been done through the malicious use of the tongue, the friendships that have been broken, the churches which have been divided, and the souls which have been driven away from the kingdom of God! No wonder James declares so strongly, "The tongue is a fire, a world of iniquity: so is the tongue among our members, that it defileth the whole body, and setteth on fire the course of nature; and it is set on fire of hell." May God help each one of us as Christians to examine the control we have exercised on our tongue recently through the grace of God.

In 3:13—4:17 James speaks of several attitudes and relationships which can help or hinder true spirituality. First, in 3:13-18 he shows how earthly and heavenly wisdom are illustrated and contrasted in attitudes and conduct. The words "good conversation" in 3:13 would be better translated "good conduct," for the Greek word used here refers not merely to speech but to the whole behavior of the individual. The kind of wisdom which produces feelings of strife and jealousy cannot claim Heaven as its origin. Such attitudes are worldly and carnal, so much like this age. What a contrast the heavenly wisdom offers when it is described as being "pure, then peaceable, gentle, and easy to be intreated, full of mercy and good fruits, without partiality, and without hypocrisy."

In 4:1-3 James states that improper attitudes and improper motives can produce an absence of God's blessings and unanswered prayer. Those who manifest the earthly wisdom mentioned back in 3:14, 15 cannot possibly expect God's favor. James points out the two main causes for unanswered prayer: First, we simply do not pray; and, second, when we do pray, we often ask for the wrong motives, and thus our prayers go unanswered. Every request in prayer should be made ultimately for God's glory, never for our own selfish ambitions. In my opinion one of the greatest explanations for lack of power in the church today lies in the lack of sincere prayer in the church as a whole and in the lives of most individual Christians.

In 4:4-10 James explains that spiritual victory comes through separation from the world and submission to God. One who would be separated from the world apart from submission to God becomes a mere legalist. One who would claim submission to God without separation from the world is denying James's basic argument about the correlation of faith and works. The world has never been a friend to Jesus, and it will not be the friend of those who live consecrated lives in His service. John states that the love of the world (that is, this world system) and the love of God cannot exist together (1 John 2:15-17). James again points to the balance of Christian action when he commands us to resist the devil to discourage his assaults while at the same time drawing near to God to promote spiritual intimacy. The positive action of drawing near to God will make the negative action of giving resistance to the devil much less difficult.

Verses 9, 10 emphasize the need for times of soberness and humility in the Christian life to promote true spirituality. This is in sharp contrast to the typical lightness and hilarity associated with so much of our modern Christianity. Again turning toward the Sermon on the Mount, in 4:11, 12 James condemns the critical spirit. God is the only lawgiver; therefore, we should be satisfied to relinquish most acts of judgment to Him. A final mistake which hinders true spirituality is the failure to constantly plan our future activities in light of the primary consideration of God's will. He illustrates this in 4:13-17 by describing the man who makes all of his plans about what he is going to do tomorrow, and the next day, and the next, but he completely omits considering God's will through prayer, reading God's Word, and seeking the counsel and guidance of Christian friends. Humanly speaking, life is so uncertain, and it is only by putting God and God's perfect will in the center of our lives that we can live from day to day with the blessed assurance that tomorrow is taken care of by being committed to Him.

In 5:1-6 James gives a severe warning to wicked rich men. In verses 1-3 he reminds these rich men of the coming day of judgment when their riches will rust and vanish away in God's presence. This too is a reminder of Jesus' teaching in the Sermon on the Mount in Matthew 6:19-21 about laying up treasure in Heaven. In 5:4-6 James points out to these rich men that one of the things for which God will hold them most accountable is the unjust wages which they have paid their poor laborers. Many wicked rich men will face grave judgment when they stand before God because of the way they have treated poor, helpless, laboring people.

James closes his book in 5:7-20 with some words of encouragement and admonition to these suffering Jewish Christians. One of the greatest sources of consolation for suffering saints has always been the blessed hope of the return of our Lord to take us to be with Him. In 5:7-9 James points these Christians toward that hope. Jesus purposely taught about His second coming in such a way that every generation could look expectantly for it, knowing full well that He will soon return. In 5:10, 11 James calls their attention to the examples of the Old Testament prophets and of Job who persevered and were rewarded for their suffering. In 5:12, in light of the pressure which they were under, he warns them against swearing and profane speech.

In 5:13-18 James reminds them that God has provided for the needs of His people. There is an appropriate act of worship in every situation of life: if afflicted, we can pray; if we feel happy, we can rejoice in praise and song. In 5:14-18 prayer is especially admonished in behalf of sin and sickness, for the former may at times be the cause of the latter. The action of the sick person in calling for the elders of the church is a great act of faith in itself. The oil is probably symbolic of the presence and power of the Holy Spirit. This is a method of Divine healing which is certainly still available for the church today. James closes his epistle in 5:19, 20 by reminding us of the tremendous work which is accomplished when we succeed in turning a brother away from the error which has been leading his soul toward ultimate destruction. There is never any greater work than the work of conversion, whether it is the conversion of a lost sinner to Christ or the conversion, the turning about, of a saint of God who has wandered for a period of time in perilous error.

A SURVEY OF THE EPISTLE OF

First Peter

by Rev. Milton Worthington

The author was Simon Peter, one of the "inner circle" of three of our Lord's disciples (two of the three in the "inner circle" wrote books of the New Testament). His name was originally "Simon." Jesus changed his name to "Peter . . .Cephas" (Greek and Aramaic, respectively), meaning "a rock . . . stone." He was the son of John (John 1:42; 21:15-17). He was the brother of Andrew, who introduced Peter to Jesus, and a fisherman who lived at Capernaum on the shores of the Sea of Galilee. Peter received three separate calls from his Master: (1) to become His disciple (John 1:40); (2) to become His constant companion (Matthew 4:19; Mark 1:17; Luke 5:10); and (3) to be His apostle (Matthew 10:2; Mark 3:14-16; Luke 6:13, 14). He was the leader of the apostles and is always listed first in the lists of the apostles (Matthew 10:2; Mark 3:16; Luke 6:14; Acts 1:13). His name is also named first in the list of the "inner circle" of disciples (Matthew 17:1; Mark 5:37; 9:2; 13:3; 14:33; Luke 8:51; 9:28). Peter was the natural spokesman of the apostolic group. He was the first to confess that Christ was the "Christ" of God (Matthew 16:16; Mark 8:29). Peter's life naturally divides itself into three parts: (1) The period of training and preparation . . . recorded in the four gospels. (2) The period of leadership . . . Acts 1—12. (3) The period of humble retirement, when Paul took the leadership of the church . . . this period is represented by 1 and 2 Peter. "He was eager, ardent, impulsive—a man of action—self-confident, true, loving and faithful." Jesus predicted Peter's martydom in John 21:19. Tradition says that he was martyred in Rome, crucified with his head downward, because he would not die with his head upward, since his Master had died in that manner and he was not worthy of the Lord's death.

The Roman Catholic Church calls Peter its first "Pope." The following interesting contrasts are drawn between Peter and the Pope of Rome: (1) Peter had no temporal power; the Pope of Rome has much temporal power. (2) Peter was a poor fisherman. He said, "Silver and gold have I none." The Pope is very wealthy. It has been estimated that the annual income of the Vatican is over two hundred million dollars. (3) Peter was a married man (Mark 1:29, 30). The Pope believes in the celibacy of the clergy. (4) Peter called himself a "fellow-elder" (1 Peter 5:1). The Pope considers himself far above all others in authority and prestige. (5) Peter, when he spoke officially, was reproved by Paul (Galatians 2); the Pope claims to be infallible when he speaks "ex cathedra." (6) Peter was primarily God's servant to the Jews; the Pope has almost nothing to do with the Jews. Peter was himself a Jew; no Jew has ever been Pope throughout history. (7) Peter believed strongly in the priesthood of all believers (1 Peter 2:5-9). The Pope believes that all believers generally are far below the Priest and the Pope. (8) Peter kept referring to Christ as the rock; the Pope, practically speaking, believes that he is the rock on which the church is founded.

The addressees were the Christians in the northeast part of Asia Minor (Pontus, Galatia, Cappadocia, Asia, and Bithynia). Most of those addressed were Jewish Christians of the Dispersion, but there were also Gentiles as well (2:10). The Church was undergoing its "first world trial" and needed comfort and strength to undergo such a trial. These Jews were suffering no less than those who were addressed in Hebrews, although they do not seem to have had the same danger of apostasy to Judaism. On the whole, in his missionary work, Peter went to the scattered tribes eastward.

The book was written from Babylon. The date is uncertain, but probably written between A.D. 63-66. It appears to have been written sometime before the destruction of Jerusaleum (A.D. 70). There has been a difference of opinion among expositors as to whether or not Babylon in this passage means "Babylon in Mesopotamia" or "spiritual Babylon" (Rome). The Roman Catholic Church has stressed the idea that Babylon here means Rome; however, such a view completely overthrows all reasonable exegesis. It is true that there is a mystical Babylon in the Book of Revelation, but that book is entirely different from 1 Peter. Revelation is filled with signs and figures of speech which are not to be taken literally, but 1 Peter is written from a much more literal standpoint. If Babylon here means Rome, then we are in grave doubt as to whether Corinth means Corinth, Rome means Rome, etc. There is much argument as to whether Peter ever visited Rome. Romanists hold that he was Bishop of the church there for 25 years. This view appears ridiculous in that the New Testament never once mentions such a fact. Furthermore, Paul wrote one letter to Rome and got letters from Rome (Colossians, Philemon, Ephesians, Philippians, and 2 Timothy), but he never once referred to Peter. However, Paul did refer to Peter when he wrote to the Galatians. It is possible that Peter did visit Rome and did suffer martyrdom there (as many Protestant authorities gladly admit), although even this fact is not absolutely certain.

This letter gives us the fulfillment of the commission of Christ to Peter recorded in Luke 22:31, 32, "When thou art converted, strengthen thy brethren." Peter was comforting churches which were suffering severe persecution, being falsely accused as evil doers (2:12; 3:16; 4:4). The Holy Spirit seems to have been preparing these Jewish Christians for the great destruction of A.D. 70, as he shows how the church fulfills the Old Testament theocracy. Many in the early church (as well as in later times) thought that Peter and Paul did not agree on the fundamentals of the Christian faith; Peter is refuting such an idea; and shows that he has been delivered from the bondage of Judaism and has accepted the same views as those which were held by Paul.

The prominent theme is "Sojourners and Pilgrims." Peter is "The Pilgrim's Progress of the New Testament." Peter traces the Christian's place in this world and in the world to come. The sojourner is a citizen of another country; he must expect trial and suffering, since his Master underwent great suffering in shedding His precious blood for the sojourner. He must subject himself to every ordinance of man for the Lord's sake. He must not suffer because of his own evil doings. He must exercise love toward all men, especially toward fellow-believers. He must ever have his eyes fixed on the great glory to be revealed at the second coming of Christ when he shall receive rewards for faithfulness. The Word of God is his guide in making Jesus precious to his soul.

The key text is 2:11: "Strangers and Pilgrims" and the key word is *suffering*. Another suggested key text is 2:7.

The epistle was taken by Silas or Silvanus. "Silas" is a contracted form of "Silvanus." It is possible that Silas may have helped in writing the epistle. He is always called by the longer name in the epistles. He went with Paul on his second missionary journey, after he had been sent with Paul to give the decision of the Jerusalem Council to the Gentile church at Antioch (Acts 15, 16). He is especially noted for his suffering with Paul in the jail when the Philippian jailer was saved (Acts 16).

No real heresy is evident. However, Peter spends much time in showing that the Church is a fulfillment of the Old Testament theocracy. Thus, he seems to be combating the possibility of any Judaistic heresy which might be taught at any time.

The portrait of Christ is given in the titles of Him. He is called "Jesus Christ . . . Our Lord Jesus Christ . . . a Lamb without blemish and without spot . . . a living stone, rejected of men, but with God elect, precious, chief cornerstone, the stone which the builders rejected, the Shepherd and Bishop of your souls, Christ as Lord, the chief Shepherd." Great emphasis is laid upon the fact that our Lord fulfilled the Old Testament prophecies which were two-fold in meaning: The Messiah was to be first a suffering Messiah; and then the Messiah was to come later in glory. A foretaste of the fact that He will one day come back to this earth is found in His resurrection (1:3, 4). We should never fear suffering, then, since this crucified, risen and coming Lord is our daily portion. Christ is shown to be the center of the New Dispensation, which is the fulfillment of the old. Peter loves to call Christ the "Rock." Not once does he call himself the rock. For a good outline on "Christ Crucified as the Rock" check the footnote in the Scofield Reference Bible.

Let us get a chapter by chapter view of this book to help us in our detailed study. 1. Precious trial and precious blood; 2. Precious rock and precious subjection; 3. Precious subjection and precious hope; 4. Precious suffering (much like the first part of chapter 1); 5. Precious crown and precious trust!

For our study we shall use the following basic outline:

Salutation 1:1, 2
The *Salvation* of the Christian—His Privileges 1:3—2:10
The *Submission* of the Christian—His Practices 2:11—3:12
The *Suffering* of the Christian—His Perils 3:13—5:9
Summation 5:10-14

In *1:1, 2* we have the introduction to the epistle. Several things are noted in these verses. The identification of the author is given (verse 1a), "Peter, an apostle of Jesus Christ." Following the identification of the author, you have a description of the addressees (verse 1), "To the strangers scattered throughout." Now as to their physical situation, they are scattered peoples, exiles of the dispersion, gathered in these many different congregations in the particular geographical areas (verse 1b). But as to their spiritual status, they are chosen, elect; whatever others may think of them, or whatever others may do, they are elect of God (verse 2). They have been chosen by God the Father, converted by God the Son, and cleansed by God the Spirit. This election has its source in the foreknowledge of the Father, its sphere in the sanctification by the Spirit, and its sign in the life of obedience (verse 2). Then we have the benediction of the author on the addressees (verse 2b), "May *grace* . . . as the *fount* of your salvation . . . and *peace* . . . as the *fruit* of your salvation be multiplied."

In 1:3—2:10, we have the first main division of the epistle. This first section deals with the appeals related to the *Privileges of Salvation.*

The *Doctrine of Salvation* is expounded in 1:3-12. The unsaved person is without "hope" (Ephesians 2:12); yet the believer has a *living* hope (verse 3) because he has a living Savior. The believer does not work for his hope; it is a part of his spiritual birthright. We are born again (John 3:5) unto this *living* hope. It is not only a living hope but it is a lasting hope (verses 4, 5). It is reserved in Heaven for the believer, and the believer, too, is kept by the Lord. We are kept by the power of God through faith. Peter stresses that salvation is reserved for the future (verses 3-5), received in the present (verses 6-9), and revealed in a former time (verses 10-12). The believer is saved (justification); he is being saved daily (sanctification); and he will be saved (glorification) (Romans 8:15-25).

So as we live steadfastly in hope, let us praise God for the *prospect* we cherish beyond our troubles (verses 3b, 4), for the *power* we may experience in our troubles (verse 5), and for the *profit* we receive from our troubles (verses 6, 7). Troubles should be expected but they will not last forever. However, until Christ returns, the believer must go through testing. A faith that cannot be tested cannot be trusted. Our suffering is but "for a season" as the Lord sees we need it; but the glory will be forever. The suffering we endure here means more glory when Christ comes; and, knowing this, we love Him the more. Faith, hope, and love are all combined (verses 6-9).

The *duty* of *Saints* is enjoined in 1:13-25. In verses 13-21 Peter exhorts us to live *sensitively*, in *holiness.* First, be sensitive as to your *status* (verses 13-19). "As obedient children, not fashioning yourselves according to the former lusts in your ignorance: But as he which hath called you is holy, so be ye holy in all manner of conversation" (verses 14, 15). The logic of Peter's appeal will appear in full force only after we discover the privileged status that God in His grace has conferred upon His redeemed people. First, we have the status of children (verse 14). Second, we have the status of pilgrims (verse 17). And third, we have the status of freedmen (verse 18). Now the logic of this—conduct yourselves as obedient *children*. You are *pilgrims* in transit, and the homeland that calls you speaks of holiness. Since God has conferred, in His infinite grace, such status upon you, children in the family, pilgrims on the journey, and slaves who were made free by the precious blood of Christ, the blood that cleanseth from all sin, He wants you to bear His likeness (verse 15). Second, be sensitive to the *Savior* (verses 20, 21). Here we see the Lord Jesus and His place in what God designs (verse 20a), His place in what history discloses (verse 20b), and His place in what the Church declares (verse 21).

In verses 22-25, Peter exhorts us to live *sincerely*, in *harmony.* The heart of what Peter has to say here is in the last clause of verse 22, "Love one another with a pure heart." Salvation gives us a living hope, a longing for holiness, and a love for the people of God. The Spirit of God loved us and brought us to Christ; and this same Spirit has planted within us a love for the people of God. Peter uses two words for love in verse 22—brotherly love and Divine love.

The Christian possesses brotherly love; but he needs to exert spiritual energy and love others the way God loves him. This, then, is the obligation to live sincerely in love. Now if we are going to do this, there must be not only the purifying of our souls, the bringing of the new life in Christ through the Word of God which liveth and abideth forever, but there must also be the recognition that we must deal with the things that stand in the way of this harmony between Christians. Christian harmony is a blessing to the Lord, the church, and the believers themselves (Psalm 133). If every believer is obeying the Word and practicing love, there will be harmony.

The *Design* of the *Sovereign* is exhibited in 2:1-10. The sequence of thought, linking chapter 1 with chapter 2, is clear. "Wherefore" of verse 1 connects this section with the theme of 1:23, "being born again." Birth (1:23) and then growth. A believer in Christ is born again. He is to grow in grace (2:2), leading to establishment in grace which is a testimony to the world. One of the features of the passage (verses 1-10) is the reference back to the Old Testament for illustration and comparison (verse 6). There are three thoughts in our passage. Verses 1-3 speak of the truth that we are children in God's family, and we are to express that by taking our *food.* Some preparation is needed. Renunciation of all that hinders must clear the ground for healthy growth. So Peter urges his readers to "put away" the sins of a pagan and of a Christian society. The repetition of the word "all" indicates a new kind of peril to avoid. The life that does not put away these things will be handed over to them. While all this is being done, and as the secret of winning this battle, there is the feeding upon the Word of God. Note the *diet* God provides, "Sincere milk of the word"; the *desire* God presupposes, "As new born babes, desire . . . "; and the *development* God planned, "Grow thereby" (verse 2). Verses 4-8 speak of the truth that we are stones in God's temple and we are to express that by finding our *feet.* Here the metaphor changes from *food* to *foundation*, and the corporate character of the church comes into view: "To whom coming . . . " to Christ, with the continuity and devotion of an adherent. Then Christ is named as a "Living stone," "living" because He is alive and communicating life to those who believe in Him; elect of God; rejected by men; esteemed by believers. "Ye also, as living stones" . . . built upon the foundation and builded together to partake of the foundation character.

Christ is further pictured as a "corner stone," foretold of God in Isaiah 28:16, and here described in terms similar to those already named in verse 4. He is elect and honorable, for those who trust in Him shall not be put to shame. The "corner stone" refers to extremity rather than height. It binds a building together and is visible above the foundation level. "Unto you . . . which believe," those built upon the foundation and bound together by the cornerstone, share the honor (verse 4). So, "Unto you therefore which believe he is precious," not only of Christ, but of our being built into Him. Christ is finally pictured as a "stumbling stone." Christ is not just taken or left. To those who disbelieve, He is the cause of their stumbling (Matthew 12:30). Compare John 6—many came for the bread, but few stayed for the Bread of Life. Let us enter into the life of the foundation being bound together in the fellowship and guarding against any measure of stumbling.

Verses 9, 10 speak of the truth that we are citizens in the new nation, and we express that by exalting the *family*. It is helpful to compare "offer up" (verse 5) and "shew forth" (verse 9); they tell of the priestly and the prophetic ministries of the Christian community. The first is in the temple; the second is in the family. Within this family we see some native characteristics (verse 9) and some high privileges (verses 9, 10). This is the family, entered by calling and evidenced by character.

In 2:11—3:12, we have the second main division of this book. This second section deals with the appeals related to the *Practice* of *Submission.* This section begins with a foreward that is personal (verses 11, 12). These verses speak of our *cardinal* conduct . . . *holiness.* We are to walk holy and to talk holy—"as pilgrims" and "to glorify God"—The aim is the conversion of the Gentile world. It involves inward discipline (verse 11) and outward deportment (verse 12). In verses 13-25, Peter speaks of our *citizenship* conduct . . . *humility.* Verses 13-17 speak of our submission in *civil* relationships . . . (the Christian in the state). Romans 13:1-7 should be read in connection with this passage. Note the command (verse 13a), the compulsion (verses 13b-15a), the characteristics (verse 16), and the categories (verse 17) of submission. In verses 18-25, Peter speaks of our submission in social relationships as servants—(the Christian in his employment). The "servant " here is in the household, a necessary part of the whole. The Christian in this position is to be in subjection to his master, without *discourtesy*, "with all fear," without *distinction*, "good and gentle," and to the froward; without *discouragement*—"take it patiently"; without *disgrace*—"thankworthy" and "acceptable with God" are both "grace" in Greek. So we have the *mandate* (verse 18) and the *motive* (verse 19) for our behavior as servants!

In verses 21-25, Peter gives us our *model* as servants—Christ Jesus. We have been called to suffering because we have been called to Christ. He has left "us an example." Taking Christ as our example is important, not for our justification; we are not saved by following Him, but we are sanctified by following Him. Note His example in relation to sinning, sinners, and sin. We see the sinlessness of Christ (verses 21, 22), the suffering of Christ (verses 23, 24), and the shepherding of Christ (verse 25). So we close with a review of the whole. We were going astray like sheep, and we are now returned unto the Shepherd and Bishop of our soul. He who has the "oversight" must be acknowledged as the "overseer."

In 3:1-7, Peter speaks of our *connubial* conduct—*honoring* (the Christian in his family). Peter speaks first of the submissively obedient wife (verses 1-6). Wives are to be known for their *ministry*, second in command "subjection to your own husbands"; first in commendation "the Word" as a message given, "the walk" as the illustration. They are also to be known for their *manner;* "chaste," holy in heart and habit, coupled with fear (verse 6). Their adorning . . . not; hair and jewelry, dress (c. Isaiah 3:18-24); but a meek and quiet spirit, which bears but does not inflict disturbance. The illustration takes the reader back to the holy women of old time, Sarah called Abraham, Lord (Genesis 18:12). Wives are to be respectful (verse 1), faithful (verse 2), and modest (verse 3). Peter speaks, second, of the sacrificially loving husband (verse 7). "Likewise" indicates a similar attitude of love and respect on the part of the husband. Their submission to the life of the marriage bond is to be governed by "knowledge," due regard paid to the wife. This is based on two things: (1) The wife is the weaker vessel. (2) They are heirs jointly and equally of the grace of life, eternal life. The motive to govern the relationship is that "your prayers be not hindered."

Now verses 8-12 give us the final word which is *relative* in this second section (cf. verses 11, 12). Whether married or not, all Christians are linked together by a common life in the body of Christ. That life is to be lived in mutual submission to each other. The verses gather details under three heads: a. *thoughts* to be entertained (verse 8); b. *tongues* to be disciplined (verses 9-11); c. *truths* to be remembered (verse 12). In the midst of suffering he must be a blessing (verse 9), he must keep clean (verses 10, 11), and he must remember that God is watching (verse 12).

In 3:13—5:11, we have the third division of this epistle. This section deals with our appeals related to the *Perils* in *Suffering.* Chapters 3:13—4:6 relate to our *discipline* in the *world.* Suffering for righteousness' sake has always been the hardest thing to endure. Yet this epistle is about suffering in the experience of Christ, and of those who are on "the Christward road." The *principle* of Christian discipline is given in verses 13-18. Verse 13 asserts that "no virtue is safe that is not active." Pursue the good and so be protected against evil. Yet in the emergency the life of submission wins. Submission should be manifest: a. To the *Lord*—"sanctify Christ as Lord" . . . ever the need of the Christian, but especially so when falsely accused. b. To the *inquirer:* should any ask a "reason," be ready to give it with meekness, and no pride; with fear, as in the sight of God. c. To the *persecutor:* keeping the conscience clear, and the conduct right; you may expect that the conclusion will be the shame of the evildoer!

The Lordship of Christ confers an immunity (verse 13), creates a serenity (verse 14), compels a testimony (verse 15), and carries a sensitivity (verses 16, 17).

The *pattern* for Christian discipline is given in verses 18-22. Peter reminds them of the sufferings of Christ, how He was falsely accused, yet left the matter with His Father. Note several things in this passage— a. the *Christology* of the passage (verse 18), b. the *Communication* in the passage (verse 19a), and c. the *Congregation* of the passage (verse 19b). Following the reference to the days of Noah, Peter makes a statement about Christian baptism; the ark is the true picture of your salvation. The waters carried it safely—so the waters of baptism bring you into salvation (our initiation into Christ by the Spirit of which baptism is the sign). The requirement for baptism—not outward washing—but inward renewal and the pledge of a good conscience. All this through Jesus Christ . . . risen, ascended, and victorious. There is no suggestion here, or anywhere, that those who have had the gospel preached to them on earth will have it preached to them again after death. The "larger hope" is not taught. How wonderful to know that the victory of the Cross has been proclaimed in earth and Hell and Heaven. The ultimate is sure.

The *power* for Christian discipline is given in 4:1-6. Here Peter moves from doctrine to practice once again . . . so set your mind for "the rest of your time." Verse 1 gives us the combat expected. There must be a preparation of mind for this life of suffering. Begin with what Jesus did, consider what Jesus did, and be identified with what Jesus did (verse 1). Verse 2 gives us the contrast examined. There is a contrasted service and a contrasted sphere. Verses 3-6 give us the characteristics expounded . . . the activities of the past life is reviewed and renounced. We renounce the shame of it (verse 3), the pride of it (verse 4), and the judgment of it (verse 5). These things have gone! What wonders the grace of God can do!

Chapters 4:7—5:7 relate to our *discipline* in the *church.* Christian *Fellowship* is in focus in verses 7-11 (avoid complacency). Peter suggests that suffering unifies the church. "Remember this," writes Peter, "the end of all things is at hand" (verse 7). It is clear that the early church idea of the second coming is in view here. To be prepared is the important thing, and the purpose here is to give some characteristics of the prepared life. We are to be *awake* to prayer (verse 7), "sober," all desires under control, "watch" unto prayers. The end is near, then, all to prayer. The tense is imperative, as if they needed to be aroused. We are to be *aglow* with love (verses 8, 9). There is the need to intensify what is there already. We are to be *alert* in ministry (verses 10, 11). The picture is of varied gifts entrusted by grace. In all this . . . the glory of God through Jesus Christ . . . doxology (verse 11).

Christian *Fortitude* is in focus in verses 12-19 (avoid consternation). Peter shares that suffering glorifies the Lord. As the writer draws to a close, he returns to the main burden which has linked together "the sufferings" and "the glory." Verses 12-16 speak of the

Christian's fortitude in the *glory* of the *persecuted* life. "Beloved," love is the characteristic quality of the Christian community. Peter looks around and ahead . . . the sufferings were already "among you," and will remain to "prove you." Therefore, be not bewildered (verse 12) but rather rejoicing (verse 13). Peter follows this with some suggestions about the suffering; how it should come and when it is to be avoided. Let us summarize what he has to tell us here. 1. Let the issue be clear (verse 14). 2. Let the heart rejoice (verse 14). 3. Let the motive be pure (verse 16).

Verses 17-19 speak of the Christian's fortitude in the *purging* of the *redeemed* life. This closing paragraph takes the thought of persecution as a refining influence upon the godly, and sees both in it and beyond it the ultimate judgment of God and the ultimate salvation of the believer. Peter gives us the certainty of judgment (verse 17), the difficulty of salvation (verse 18), and the security found in well doing (verse 19).

Christian *faithfulness* is in focus in 5:1-9. Verses 1-4 speak of faithfulness in *service* to the *flock* (avoid covetousness). What an opportunity we have as pastors! Our appointment to serve is given in verse 1. Our deliverance from the pitfalls in service of personal gain and domineering leadership (wrong motive and manner) is given in verses 2, 3. Our expectation of Christ to reward for service is given in verse 4. So there is a fellowship in service to be affirmed, eagerness in preaching (verses 1, 2a), a flow in service to be anticipated, and expectation from prophecy (verse 4). Verses 5-9 speak of Christian faithfulness in *submission* to the *Father* (avoid conceit and compromise). The opportunity of service and the difficulty in service is rooted in pride (verses 5, 6) and the devil (verses 8, 9). "Humble yourselves" . . . the willingness to humility (verse 7). This is often difficult for the human heart resists humility and yields to the devil. "Resist the devil" . . . the watchfulness for the adversary (verse 8) and walking steadfastly (verse 9). Note "anxiety" (verse 7) may arise from the shattering of pride, or the snarling of the devil. But the thing to do is clear—"Cast it on Him"—for "He careth for you."

The letter has reached its close and is soon to travel by the hand of Silvanus until it reaches the scattered churches of Pontus, Galatia, Cappadocia, Asia, and Bithynia. There was no lithographer in those days; not even a church duplicator. Yet copies would go far and wide, to be read by hard pressed believers in hundreds of tiny churches. Peter must have experienced a great thrill as he uttered the doxology of verses 10, 11 and then tucked in the covering note of verses 12-14.

The benediction (crowning doxology verses 10, 11) suggests grace in *prelude*, grace for *interlude*, and grace to *conclude*. So the doxology has been penned. It sings itself and makes us sing in harmony with it, for we have no need to create it; it is God's work throughout. The bearer is named in verse 12. Also a summation is given. In verses 13, 14 we have the blessed salutations. This seems to be the style of the closing three verses; and they refer to people, and places and greetings! Let us close our study with the final words, "Peace be with you all that are in Christ Jesus."

A SURVEY OF THE EPISTLE OF

Second Peter

by Rev. Milton Worthington

The purpose of our study of this epistle is to discover together, not what we think Peter is saying, but what God is saying through Peter. It is not my purpose to go into a detailed, verse by verse commentary, but to get an overall view of the book as a whole and of each chapter in particular. As we go along, we shall discern the basic *plan* of the book, and we shall discover the Biblical *principles* for our behavior.

Let me make just one simple statement as we commence our study. If we are to discover the truth God has for us, we must remember that there is ONLY ONE indispensable aid to Bible study and that is the ministry of the Holy Spirit (2 Peter 2:21). We must depend upon the illuminating ministry of the Holy Spirit. This will involve heart preparation—a dedication to Christ, and also head preparation—a diligence in Christ. So now let us approach this epistle in full confidence that the Holy Spirit will give us oneness of mind, openness of heart, and obedience of will to God's truth.

This book contains three chapters with sixty one verses. It takes about ten minutes to read.

There can be no reasonable doubt but that Peter, the athletic apostle, was the author, despite the contentions of the destructive critics whose objections can be very satisfactorily and scholarly answered. Internal evidence is not only strong but satisfactory that Peter did write the second epistle. (1) The writer was an apostle (3:2). (2) He was one of the three on the Mount of Transfiguration (1:18). (3) He had written an earlier epistle to this same people (3:1). (4) The style and subject matter is such as would be expected from Peter. (5) The claim is made in the very opening verse (1:1).

Since the authorship of this epistle has been questioned, perhaps more than any other of the New Testament books, it might be good for us to look briefly at the objections raised. First, the critics state that doubts were raised as to Peter's authorship as far back as the third century. We answer that objections concerning other books were also raised in the third century. Moreover, modern discoveries have shown how groundless the objection was. Second, the critics contend that it could not have been written in Peter's lifetime inasmuch as "all" of Paul's epistles had not been written (see 3:16). We answer that the plain sense of 3:16 is "all his epistles" then written. Third, the critics say that the language and style are different from that found in 1 Peter. We answer that 2 Peter was written for a different purpose which is naturally reflected in a change in the language and style which are still emphatically Petrine. Fourth, the critics charge that chapter 2 is a copy of Jude and that Peter would never have been guilty of plagiarism. We answer that neither Peter nor Jude copied from the other, but in chapter 2 Peter prophesies (note the future tense "there are").

Simon Peter was one of the "inner circle" of three of our Lord's disciples. Two of the three in the "inner circle" wrote books of the New Testament. His name was originally "Simon" but Jesus changed his name to "Peter—Cephas" (Greek and Aramaic, respectively) meaning "a rock—stone." He was the son of John and the brother of Andrew, who introduced Peter to Jesus (John 1:42; 21:15, 16). By trade he was a fisherman who lived at Capernaum on the shores of the Sea of Galilee. Peter received three separate calls from his Master: (1) to become His disciple (John 1:40); (2) to become His constant companion (Matthew 4:19; Mark 1:17; Luke 5:10); and (3) to be His apostle (Matthew 10:2; Mark 3:14-16; Luke 6:13, 14). He was the leader of the apostles, and his name is always listed first in the lists of the apostles (Matthew 10:2; Acts 1:13). His name is also first in the list of the "inner circle" of disciples (Matthew 17:1; Luke 8:51; 9:28). As the natural spokesman of the apostles he was the first to confess that Christ was the "Christ" of God (Matthew 16:16; Mark 8:29). Peter's life naturally divides itself into three parts: (1) the period of training and preparation recorded in four gospels; (2) the period of leadership recorded in Acts 1:12; and (3) the period of humble retirement, when Paul took the leadership of the church. This period is represented by 1 and 2 Peter. "He was eager, ardent, impulsive, a man of action, self-confident, true, loving, and faithful." Jesus predicted Peter's martyrdom in John 21:19. Tradition says that he was martyred in Rome, crucified with his head downward, because he would not die with his head upward since his Master had died in that manner, and he was not worthy of his Lord's death.

Simon Peter penned this second epistle either from Rome or enroute about A. D. 63-66. Peter was an elderly man, ready to die (2 Peter 1:14). He wished to leave for Christians his assurance of the verity of the truths of the gospel. He wanted to show the necessity of growth on the part of Christians, to keep them from falling into false teaching. Peter was warning that the Lord's coming might be long delayed. He wanted it known that he and Paul were preaching the same gospel, and that there was no conflict between them.

This letter was written to warn the Christians against false teachers and their teachings. There were many false teachers. "Probably no definite sect is referred to, but corrupters of the Christian church, whose errors subsequently developed into the various forms of reckless immorality and extravagant asceticism known as Antinomian Gnosticism" (Angus Green). In 1 Peter the concern was for enemies without the fold assaulting; in 2 Peter the concern is for enemies within the fold apostatizing. The first dealt with soldiers from outside; the second, with saboteurs from within. The first was to woo to constancy; the second was to warn from inconstancy. Thus, in 2 Peter, Peter exhorts to respond to the sure revelation of God for true surety in salvation and service.

The theology of Peter is certainly expressed in the hymnology:

> Only to be what He wants me to be
> Every moment of every day
> Yielded completely to Jesus alone
> Every step of this pilgrim way
> Just to be clay in the Potter's hands
> Ready to do what His Word commands
> Only to be what He wants me to be
> Every moment of every day.

Second Peter bears very much the same relation to 1 Peter that 2 Thessalonians does to 1 Thessalonians. Second Peter and 2 Thessalonians concentrate very much on the dark side of things to come. Second Peter is to the life of Peter what 2 Timothy is to the Apostle Paul and John 14—17 is to the Lord Jesus Christ. All three sections are the farewell discourses of their respective authors. Second Peter assumes that Christians have already been taught the truths of the gospel on the whole.

The prominent theme of this epistle is TRUE knowledge and FALSE knowledge. The way to escape false knowledge is to follow the knowledge of the true (read 1:16; 2:20; 3:18). Dr. Campbell Morgan gives as the theme, "The Responsibility of Grace." The key text is 3:17, 18. "Ye therefore, beloved, seeing ye know these things before, beware lest ye also, being led away with the error of the wicked, fall from your own stedfastness. But grow in grace, and in the knowledge of our Lord and Saviour Jesus Christ." Chapter 1:19 is another good one. The key word is knowledge.

The *addressees* were the Christians in the northeast part of Asia Minor (Pontus, Galatia, Cappadocia, Asia, and Bithynia). Most of those addressed were Jewish Christians of the Dispersion, but there were also Gentiles as well (2:10). It is thought that these churches had been founded principally by Paul. The opening sentence of the book makes clear, however, that the epistle was not limited to these churches but was written to all believers of all time.

The epistle is characterized by warnings spoken with great solemnity and with a tone that is at times severe. The severity is mingled with real tenderness, since the apostle expects to die very soon.

The Lord Jesus Christ is called by several titles: "Jesus Christ, our God and Saviour Jesus Christ, Jesus our Lord, our Lord and Saviour." The knowledge of Christ is the only thing that will keep a man from falling into the pitfalls of false knowledge. The glory of Christ is also very prominent.

Various analyses of the book have been suggested. I. Exhortation to holiness (chapter 1); False teachers condemned (chapter 2); Judgment may be delayed but will surely come (chapter 3). II. Gracious Provision of God. 1. The evils to come through false teachers. 2. Future of the earth and the conclusion. III. "The Lord is not slack": (1) When days are dark. (2) When times are hard. (3) When men are heady. For our purpose we shall use the following outline: Chapter 1—Foundational Truth; Chapter 2—False Teachers; Chapter 3—Future Things.

As we begin our chapter by chapter study, let me make this suggestion—that you read the Book of Second Peter through once each day for one month to firmly fix the facts in your mind.

Chapter 1: Foundational Truth (where we discover our responsibility to *grow*). In verses 1-4 our ample *provision* is shared.

In verses 1, 2, we are introduced to the author and the readers (addressees). This was the customary greeting, of course, of the day. Paul's greetings are very much like it. Peter tells us who he is; he tells us to whom he writes; and he gives us some clue as to the theme he is going to write about and the desires that were in his heart.

Several things are worth noting in these verses: First, the way in which he refers to himself. He is "a servant and an apostle," a title of absolute authority. He is our brother, and he stands among us as our brother to lead us into the powers of Christ. But he is more than our brother—he is our authoritative teacher. We do not stand on the same level as he does. What he has to say is uniquely Scripture to us and uniquely authoritative; therefore, although he is our brother, he is also our teacher and what he says is indeed the Word of God to us. Then notice how he refers to his Christian readers. They are not his servants, nor are they his inferiors. They are those who have obtained a faith of equal standing with ours in the righteousness of our God and Savior Jesus Christ. These were second generation Christians, but that does not mean that they were second class citizens of the Kingdom of Heaven. Then there is the way he refers to his Lord and Master. At the end of verse 1, he talks about our "God and our Saviour Jesus Christ." Right at the beginning of his letter he shows us the very high position that his Master, Jesus Christ, has in his thinking. Then, fourth, notice the way in which he refers to the Christian life. It is essentially a KNOWLEDGE of God and of Jesus. May "grace and peace be multiplied unto you through the KNOWLEDGE of God, and of Jesus our Lord."

In verse 2 in a delightful way, Peter hints at the real theme of 2 Peter. It is the theme of both 2 Peter and 1 Peter; the theme of spiritual growth, progress, and multiplication in the Christian life. Peter's desire is that a young Christian may grow still more. His desire is that the grace and peace of God may be multiplied in your life and in mine, through the KNOWLEDGE of God and Jesus our Lord.

In verses 3, 4, we are told of the two things that have been granted to us. First, the power of God. God has called us, as verse 3 says, through the knowledge of Himself, to His glory and excellence, to holiness. So, as in the same breath, He tells us that He has called us to His glory and excellence, and also that He has provided the means by which such a life can be lived. He has given us His Divine power. And to put it more exactly, that Divine power has given to us "all things that pertain unto life and godliness, through the knowledge of him that hath called us to glory and virtue" (verse 3).

With the power of God comes the promises of God, by which He has granted to us His exceeding great and precious promises (verse 4). In verse 4 we find a tremendous description of conversion. First, from the negative side. The negative side is that we may escape from the corruption or pollution that is in the world through lust. The new-born Christian is a man who has escaped. Second, from the positive side we have been made a partaker of the Divine nature. A positive note is needed from the Christian church today so that when a person comes into our church he sees there is a feast spread before him; that people there are obviously satisfied with the food of God; that they have escaped from those things that he knows to be wrong; and that they are partakers of the Divine nature; and that alone is their satisfaction and joy. What has God *granted* to us (verses 3, 4)? The *Power* and *Promises* of God! Where the provision is so great, the obligations will be great also, and these are set forth in the next section.

In verses 5-11 our actual *Progress* is suggested. Having revealed what has been granted to us, the apostle turns his attention to what is demanded of us. "And beside this, giving all diligence, add . . . " (verse 5). There is something beyond salvation. It is not enough for a man to be born into God's family; he must also grow up in spiritual things. For this very reason, because of what has been given to us, this is what I demand of you. What does he demand? That we should make every effort, strain every nerve, do our best, to grow in grace. It demands consecrated diligence and clear direction. We are to exert ourselves to be holy, to richly supply, with our faith and through our faith, all these things. Now I prefer to take this, not as a ladder, although it is a lovely ladder, with rungs commencing with faith and climaxing in love, but rather as the parts of a telescope—one leads into the other. We add to faith (saving faith) virtue or praise. We have been saved to show forth God's praises (1 Peter 2:9). The only way to prove our faith is by living a life of virtue. We add to virtue, knowledge or moral discernment. It is tragic how many Christians do not know right from wrong. After knowledge comes temperance or self-control. Self-control leads to patience or endurance. This is the "staying power" of the Christian in times of trial. We add to patience godliness (cf. verse 3). This word means "right worship" or a dependence on God that reveals itself in a devoted life. Brotherly kindness is the next virtue, meaning a love for the brethren. The final virtue Peter names is charity or love. Spiritual growth commences with FAITH and is crowned with LOVE.

What kind of Christian are you (verses 8, 9)? Peter pictures very skillfully two kinds of Christians. First, those who are increasing and growing (verse 8) and then those who are static and do not grow (verse 9). This is the natural thing for a teacher to do; having said what it means to grow, he pictures the man who does grow and the man who does not grow. Those that grow will not be idle or unproductive (verse 8); but those that do not grow or lack these things are marked by three traits. In the present he is *blind*, with regard to the future he is *short-sighted*, and with regard to the past he has *forgotten* (verse 9). What a tragic picture! Blind, short-sighted, and having forgotten the past. That is an exact picture of the back-slidden Christian. It is an exact picture of the Christian who has not grown.

In verses 10, 11 we have this conclusion—"Wherefore . . . brethren, give diligence," make more effort still to secure your security, for if you do this by living a godly life, by growing in grace and knowledge, by a fruitful and productive life; if you do this, blessings will be yours. First, here and now, FREEDOM from FALLING. We shall have stability. Second, hereafter there will be a glorious entrance into the eternal kingdom of our Lord and Savior, Jesus Christ (cf. 5, 11). So we leave this section looking back to the Cross that availed and forward to the crown that awaits.

In verses 12-21, our abiding *pledge* is stressed. This pledge is two-fold, covering the entire Scriptures. First, the *Apostolic* Testimony in verses 12-18. As we go through these verses and allow them to speak for themselves, I would call verses 12-15, Peter's anxiety. The readers already are fairly mature and established; nevertheless, Peter intends to remind them; and the theme of this section is "constant reminder of truth." In verses 13, 14, he says that he will remind them as long as he is alive. In verse 15, he says he will make arrangements to see that when he has departed from this earthly scene, they are still reminded of what he has to say. Quite a persistent teacher! This was probably done by Mark's Gospel.

Verses 16-18 give us the substance of the apostolic testimony. It concerned "the power and coming of our Lord Jesus Christ." These facts were revealed on the Mount of Transfiguration and witnessed by Peter himself. This is the New Testament pledge and leads the apostle back to the Old Testament, to the testimony of Hebrew prophecy (verses 19-21). This is the *Prophetic* testimony. By the happenings on the Mount, together with all the facts of the earthly life and ministry of Jesus, the word of Old Testament prophecy concerning the Messiah, is made more sure (verse 19); and to that word we should take heed in our hearts, knowing that such is not the "invention" of men, but the work of the Holy Spirit through chosen men (verse 21).

We thank God that our Bible is sure. We can trust it because God gave it to us.

Chapter 2—False Teachers (where we discover our responsibility to *Guard*)! The mention of "prophecy" in chapter 1:19 leads Peter to say that there were false teachers among the true prophets. He said that in these days the false would abound, and that these constituted a real danger, threatening the Christian's progress. Thus, chapter 2 treats the subject of false teachers—the peril to progress. Peter begins this chapter by defining the *doctrine* of the false teachers in verses 1-3a. Christians are alerted to the danger here. The connection between 1:21 and 2:1 is suggestive.

The *prediction* of false teachers is given in verse 1. Peter declares that false teachers are bound to come, but that they would ultimately be condemned by God. They deny the atonement and perhaps the deity of the Lord Jesus Christ. They appear among the people as members of the church. They work secretly, under cover of hypocrisy. They replace the truth with their lies. They bring their false teaching in alongside of true doctrine, and then replace the truth with their lies. Their lives deny what their lips teach. In other words, "heresy" is not simply false doctrine; it is false living based upon false doctrine.

The *popularity* of false teachers is given in verse 2. Unfortunately, the false way will be more popular than the true way. People will choose to follow the false teachers because they exalt themselves, rather than Christ; and men love to worship popular and successful people. Also, the false way makes it easier to live in sin while practicing a religious life. Such brings the truth into disrepute.

The *perversity* of false teachers is given in verse 3. Peter is saying that these false teachers depart from the spirit-given words in the Bible (cf. 2:9-16) and manufacture their own words to fit their own theories. Or like the "neo-orthodox" teachers of today, they take the Bible words that we use and manufacture new meanings for them. They use our vocabulary, but not our dictionary. It is not what a man says, but what he means, that counts. Their motive is seen to be covetousness (verse 3a). So we see the church divided—the

Lord denied—many attracted—the way of truth reviled—and Christian people exploited!

Peter continues this chapter by declaring the *doom* of the false teachers in verses 3b-9. Having alerted the readers, now Peter assures them that the false teachers will be punished. He speaks of the nearness of this destruction in verse 3b. He speaks of the nature of this destruction in verses 4-9. Peter cites three Old Testament examples: verse 4, the doom of the angels; verse 5, the flood; and verse 6, the overthrow of Sodom and Gomorrah. This reveals the *perdition* that the godless will experience.

In verses 7-9, we discover the *preservation* the godly can expect. God not only assures that the false teachers will be delivered to judgment, but that the faithful troopers will be delivered from judgment (verse 9).

Peter concludes this chapter by describing the *doings* of the false teachers in verses 10-22.

In verses 10-14, we find the *conduct* of the false teachers described. They are spiritually insensitive. It is quite clear that to Peter the thing to say about these men is that they are lawless; they indulge their passions and break God's law; they despise authority, which means they challenge God's law. These are the two sides of lawlessness: I will not keep His law, and I challenge His right to lay down the law. The actual precepts of God, and the authority of God I hold in small regard. They reject authority.

In verses 15-19, we find the *claims* of the false teachers denoted. They promise their followers satisfaction but do not quench their spiritual thirst. Nothing could be more useless than wells without water! These teachers with their great swelling words give the appearance of being truthful and helpful; but they turn out to be clouds driven by the wind; beautiful but of no help to the thirsty man. Millions today are following false religions that promise help but can give none; they promise liberty, but lead people into bondage. Peter uses a bit of sarcastic logic here. How can people who are slaves of sin themselves ever set anybody free? They are sensually incited and proclaim liberty while being slaves of sin!

In verses 20-22, we find designated the *converts* of the false teachers. They are sadly impoverished and lost. They are entangled in perversity (verses 19, 20). They are estranged from purity (verse 21). They are established in pollution (verse 22).

This chapter makes me tremble as a pastor, a minister in the church of God. It causes me to hold very carefully to the Word of God, and to live very carefully in the presence of God.

We turn now to chapter 3. *Future things* (where we discover our responsibility to *glorify).* This chapter reveals Peter as the loving pastor, caring for his lambs and sheep, for he uses the word "beloved" four times. Each time he gives a solemn admonition (verses 1, 8, 14, 17).

In verses 1-4, the Second Coming is *assailed.* Peter restates his purpose for writing the letter in verses 1, 2. He, like John, has a delightful habit of telling us quite plainly why he is writing. "Remembrance" has been the key to this letter (see 1:12-15). Peter himself had been guilty of forgetting (Luke 22:61), so he wanted to warn his readers against forgetting the Word of God. He wanted them to have "sincere" minds; that is, minds not mixed with the false doctrines named in chapter 2. He points them back to the Old Testament prophets and the New Testament apostles—the entire Word of God (see 1:19-21). He then notes the presence of scoffers who would arise and who would ridicule the idea that Christ was to return to this world. The scoffers would appear to have the uniformity of history on their side; however, the apostle shows this is not the case.

In verses 5-10, the Second Coming is *affirmed.* Peter begins with a refutation of what the scoffers were saying in verses 5-7. He cites the Old Testament examples to prove that God does break into history and judge men. He begins with the created world in Genesis 1:1 (verse 5), made by the Word of God. He then introduces the world of Genesis 1:2 which had been judged by God (verse 6). Verse 7 indicates that the world that now is is "reserved unto fire" and already prepared for judgment. He shows that the former world did perish, and that these scoffers were "willingly ignorant" of that fact. They were not lacking in capacity, neither was there a scarcity of evidence. And as surely as the world was destroyed by water, this world will be destroyed by fire (verse 7).

After the refutation, comes the explanation of the delay of which the scoffers had made so much (verses 8-10). In verse 8 the Lord's relation to time is set forth. He does not reckon time as we do. Man views history in terms of days and years; but to God, time is always eternal present. A thousand years are but a day to Him. In verse 9, the Lord's relation to man is declared. The delay is not an evidence of indifference on the Lord's part, but of His tender longsuffering, not willing that any should perish (verse 9). But God will not be slack. When the right time arrives, He will act. Why is He delaying His judgment, that awful Day of the Lord? Because He wants men to be saved! In verse 10, the Lord's relation to evil is revealed. He will, being what He is, visit all the works of the world with judgment, and as predicted throughout the Scriptures, that "day of the Lord" will come suddenly (verse 10).

The apostle finally brings these truths home to the hearts of his readers. Having declared the manner of Christ's coming and the moment of Christ's coming, he now applies this truth to the mode of conversation (manner of life) of the Christians. Our conduct must take shape in the light of these facts. In a practical way, Peter says this involves *Diligence* (verses 11-14). This is the third time Peter has mentioned diligence. Be diligent to be sure you are saved (1:12); be diligent to grow (1:5); now be diligent to be ready when Jesus comes (3:14). Why live for the world and the things of the world when all is to be burned up? We should have the attitude of watchfulness. We must both "look for" and "hasten" the day of God, and give diligence to be found, when He comes, spotless and blameless; for in the new earth and Heaven beyond the judgment, only righteousness dwells. Not only is diligence involved, but *discipline* as well (verses 17, 18). On the subject of the second coming, there is perfect harmony between the teachings of the apostles (verses 15-17). Therefore, knowing these things, we must "BEWARE" and "GROW"; beware of evil and grow in grace and knowledge.

The theme of 1 Peter is *grace;* the theme of 2 Peter is *knowledge*. So, Peter sums up both books by admonishing us to grow in "GRACE" and "KNOWLEDGE." This is not merely knowledge of the Bible; it is knowledge of Christ through the Bible. We must know Him better (Philippians 3:10). It is possible, unfortunately, to grow in knowledge (have the Bible truth in our heads) and never grow in grace (show the Bible truth in our lives). Peter wants us to have balanced lives. *Learning* the Word and *living* the Word.

So, as the epistle began, so it ends; with the affirmation that in the "full knowledge of God" peace, power, and progress are to be found.

A SURVEY OF THE EPISTLE OF

First John

Rev. Milton Worthington

The Epistle of 1 John is one of five books written by the beloved disciple (see also John; 2, 3 John; and Revelation). This book appears to have been written after John's Gospel as a supplement: It takes up where the Gospel concludes. The Gospel starts "In the Beginning"; the epistle starts "From the Beginning." The Gospel writes particularly about "The Son of God." The epistle was written to those that believe that they might know they are saved and might experience a life of *fellowship* and *victory*. Bishop Westcott well said: "The Gospel shows that 'JESUS IS THE CHRIST'; John's epistle shows that 'THE CHRIST IS JESUS.' " This first epistle is one with 2 and 3 John; the keynote of all three letters is FELLOWSHIP with God. Second and Third John give practical illustrations in everyday life of the truths found in 1 John. Paul is the writer of the law court; he is interested in the legal RELATIONSHIPS and privileges of the believer . . . thus, he views the Christian as a full-grown son before the law. John is preeminently the "writer of the FAMILY." Not once in his writings does he use the term "son" (in the original) of the Christian. He uses the tender word "child-born one," showing his FAMILY RELATIONSHIP. It is a joy to compare the truths of 1 John with our Lord's farewell discourse and prayer in John 14—17. There is a wonderful parallel between the two Scriptures.

External and internal evidence make it quite clear that John, the beloved apostle, wrote 1 John, as well as 2 and 3 John. Dr. B. B. Warfield says that it is very clear that the Gospel of John and the First Epistle of John were written by the same person: "(1) The language and the style of the two are the same; (2) the circle of theological ideas is the same; (3) the personality lying back of the writing is the same in both books; (4) there are numerous passages which are truly parallels between the two writings, the phenomena of which lead to the belief of identity of authorship." The testimony of antiquity has almost entirely agreed that John was the writer, although his name was not attached.

It was probably written at a late date because the epistle combats heresies which were not prevalent earlier. Heresies within the church did not cause great trouble until the persecutions from the Jews ceased. A.D. 90-100 is suggested by Ramsay and is accepted by many scholars. First John was written at a time when John appears to have been the only surviving apostle. The book was almost certainly written after the Gospel of John, since it supplements the Gospel and apparently takes its existence for granted. It was probably written from the city of Ephesus, according to Irenaeus and ancient tradition generally. This epistle was occasioned shortly after the Gospel of John when erroneous views were springing up concerning the Person of Christ. False teachers had gone from Ephesus to the surrounding cities; and they held many different kinds of error. The Gospel of John was written in order that men might BELIEVE that Jesus is the Christ; the first Epistle of John was written that Christians who had believed might know that they have eternal life and might live victoriously in FELLOWSHIP with God.

We must take a clear look at the heresy combated by the important letter. During the lull after the Neronian persecution, there was much heresy in the church. Heresy usually comes when the church is prosperous and when there is little persecution. Persecutions and heresy seldom go toghther. "Incipient Gnosticism" was the error refuted by John. The Gnostics were the "Knowers" (the word comes from the Greek "ginosko" which means to "know"). In coloquial English they were the "know-it-alls." Gnostics differed among themselves on many things, but they agreed that knowledge has a higher place than faith. Gnosticism itself was a composite of four things: Oriental Theosophy, Greek Philosophy, a little Judaism, and a slight tint of Christianity (just enough Christianity to make it dangerous). Many of the Gnostics divided into three main classes: Hylic, Psychic, and Pneumatic. The "Hylic" pertained to matter; they were hopelessly bound by matter and had no hope of salvation. The "Psychic" pertained to the mind; they could attain to "a certain degree of salvation." The "Pneumatic" pertained to the spirit; he was the Gnostic, who was the only one who could attain to fullness of salvation. Since Gnosticism was in its infancy when 1 John was written, it was not fully developed. There were three types of Gnosticism, however, when 1 John was written: 1—denied the Deity of Christ; 2—denied the true humanity of Christ; 3—denied the union of two natures, the human and the Divine, before the baptism of our Lord. First John is unusually helpful to use with Christian Scientists (since Christian Science is a modern revival of ancient Gnosticism), Unitarians, and "know-it-all" university professors and students who deny the authorship of God's Word.

After John died in A.D. 100, Gnosticism began to flourish as never before. It reached its peak between A.D. 135 and 160. At that time there were three main types of Gnosticism: (1) Docetic Gnosticism: believed that Christ's body was not real; it was but a ghost or phantom. (2) Dualistic Gnosticism: believed in the eternal conflict between God and matter. God is good; all that pertains to matter is evil. Many of these Gnostics believed in an inferior God (the God of the Old Testament according to some) called the "Demiurge." He was the one who originated evil matter. (3) Gnosticism which believed in Aeons and Emanations. These Aeons were angelic beings who served as connecting links between God and man. Christ was one of these Aeons (this view is especially refuted by Paul in Colossians). According to traditions, John the Apostle refused to bathe in the same public bath with Cerinthus (one of the foremost Gnostics) because of his non Christian views.

The prominent theme is "Christian Assurance." The key-word is "know." It occurs 32 distinct times in the five short chapters. The following things are eternal certainties to the Christian: "We do know that we KNOW him" (2:3). "We know that we are in him" (2:5). "We know that it is the last time" (2:18). "Ye know all things" (2:20). "Ye know it . . . the truth" (2:21). "Ye know that he is righteous" (2:29). "We know that, when he shall appear, we shall be like him; for we shall see him as he is" (3:2). "Ye know that he was manifested to take away our sins" (3:5). "We know that we have passed from death unto life, because we love the brethren" (3:14). "Ye know that no murderer hath eternal life abiding in him" (3:15). "Hereby we know that we are of the truth, and shall assure our heart before him" (3:19). "Hereby we know that he abideth in us, by the Spirit which he hath given us" (3:24). "Hereby know ye the Spirit of God: Every spirit that confesseth that Jesus Christ is come in the flesh is of God" (4:2). "We know the spirit of truth, and the spirit of error" (4:6). "Hereby know we that we dwell in him, and he in us, because he hath given us of his Spirit" (4:13). "By this we know that we love the children of God, when we love God, and keep his commandments" (5:2). "These things have I written unto you that believe . . . that ye may know that ye have eternal life" (5:13). "If we know that he hear us, whatsoever we ask, we know that we have the petitions that we desired of him" (5:15). "We know that whosoever is born of God sinneth not" (5:18). "We know that we are of God, and the whole world lieth in wickedness" (5:19). "We know that the Son of God is come, and hath given us an understanding, that we may know him that is true, and we are in him that is true, even in his Son Jesus Christ" (5:20).

Another way to express the theme is to call it "FELLOWSHIP WITH GOD THROUGH CHRIST." Dr. James M. Gray says, "The idea is presented to us, not in a progression of thought, but after the manner of the law of recurrence, which we have come to recognize in other instances. Perhaps it might be said, rather, that the apostle gives us three distinct cycles of thought, which form in their combination a beautiful picture of truth, and a cumulative application of the main line of instruction. For example, God is *Light* (1:5); hence, fellowship with God depends on our walking in the light. Again God is *Righteous* (2:29); hence, fellowship with God depends on doing righteousness. And finally, God is *Love* (4:7, 8); hence, fellowship with God depends on our possessing and manifesting love." Concerning fellowship, John is talking about its joy, victory, safety, and certainty.

The key-text is 1 John 5:13. "These things have I written unto you that believe on the name of the Son of God; that ye may know that ye have eternal life, and that ye may believe on the name of the Son of God." If the theme be taken as "FELLOWSHIP WITH GOD" a good key-text is 1:3: "That which we have seen and heard declare we unto you, that ye also may have fellowship with us: and truly our fellowship is with the Father, and with his Son Jesus Christ."

Christ is given these titles in 1 John: "That which was from the beginning. . . that which we have heard . . . that which we have seen with our eyes . . . his Son Jesus Christ . . . . Jesus his Son . . . an Advocate with the Father, Jesus Christ the righteous . . . the propitiation for our sins . . . Jesus is the Christ . . . the Son . . . the Son of God . . . his only begotten Son . . . the Saviour of the world . . . this is the true God and eternal life." The true humanity of our Lord is emphasized, for He was not a phantom or ghost but "very man of very man." He was "very God of very God." First John blends in a beautiful way the humanity and deity of Christ, both of which were questioned by the Gnostics with their subtle speculation. The blood of Christ as our Advocate is emphasized, in order that we may walk in the light with Him, the Holy One. John is talking about how to have fellowship with the Father and with His Son Jesus Christ. Thus, we see complete victory over sin through Christ, "Greater is He that is in you, than he that is in the world." Christ is the indwelling One.

Now just before we give some outlines and proceed with the analysis, let me give you a good chapter by chapter summary. 1—Fellowship, 2—Abiding or knowledge, 3—Holiness or Sonship, 4—Love, 5—Life!

Two good outlines have been suggested: (1) The Logos (introduction) 1:1-4, (2) Light 1:5—2:11, (3) Love 2:12—5:3, (4) Life 5:4-21. Another is: (1) The family with the Father, chapters 1—3, and (2) The family and the foe, chapters 4, 5.

For our purpose we shall use the following general outline . . . . . Introduction 1:1-4; Fellowship Assured Through the Addition of Convicting *Light* 1:5—2:29; Fellowship Assured through the Admonition of Consistent *Love* 3:1—4:21; Fellowship Assured through the Assurance of Continuous *Life* 5:1-20; Conclusion 5:21.

Before we get into our verse by verse study let us look a

moment at the addressees of this book. No particular church is mentioned in the writing of the book. The book was written especially to the Gentiles. Most of those addressed give evidence of having truly been born again. It is possible that John wrote to believers in Asia Minor. Many believe that he addressed this epistle to the same churches which he addressed in the Revelation. (They are Ephesus, Smyrna, Pergamos, Thyatira, Sardis, Philadelphia, and Laodicea.) It would seem that John was intending for 1 John to be circulated.

Be sure to read the book through each day for a month to get the facts firmly fixed in your mind.

The *Introduction* of the epistle is given in 1:1-4. We note here how it began and how it begins . . . this fellowship. If there is going to be fellowship there must first be faith and in these opening verses John reveals how faith came into his own heart and life. In verses 1, 2 John speaks of the *person* of whom he writes, the Christ. He is the eternal one, the beginning whom John had heard (audibly), seen (visually), and handled (tangibly) verse 1. He is described as the "Word of Life" because in Him there is life and those who come to trust in Him and receive Him become partakers of that life, that newness of life which God's intention for men into whose experience the malady of sin has come. In verse 2 John moves quite emphatically on to the historical event of the Incarnation and describes Christ as the "life manifested" . . . . "which was with the Father, and was manifested unto us." Here we see a close parallel between the opening verses of John's Gospel and John's Epistle (John 1:1—2:14). The incarnation (virgin birth) is the very foundation upon which both faith and fellowship rest. Someone has said, "In Jesus we know all of God we shall ever know on earth, and in Jesus we have all of God we can ever need on earth." "The Word was made flesh, and dwelt among us," John records in his Gospel: In his first letter he writes, "For the life was manifested . . . which was with the Father, and was manifested unto us" (verse 2). In verses 3, 4 John speaks of his purpose for writing. Having spoken of his experience of faith (verse 1) and God's eternal FOUNDATION (verse 2), he now speaks of the envisioned (established) FELLOWSHIP which the sharing of our Christian faith will produce—that partnership, that togetherness, that participating with others of like faith which is so vital a part of Christian living. We do well to remind ourselves that the Christian experience is never portrayed in Scripture as being lived in isolation but always in relationship to other Christians as well as to God. It has indeed been well said that God never has an only child. The implication underlying verse 3 is surely that the restoration of fellowship both between man and God and between man and man is indeed the ultimate purpose or goal of God's saving grace in Christ. The final experience into which Christ would bring us is one in which separation has been removed and fellowship has been restored. Note the design (verse 3) and the delights (verse 4) of this Divine fellowship!

First John 1:5—2:29 give us our first main division . . . *Fellowship* assured through the addition of convicting *Light!* The *Conditions* of fellowship are given in 1:5-10. Verses 5-7 speak of the first condition of fellowship; the reception of the *Light*, or the conformity to a standard. The character of God is revealed in verse 5. He is the Light . . . in Him is no darkness at all. It follows that the company of God must be compatible. Even believers sometimes walk in darkness (verse 6). That does not mean that they have clouded or forfeited the Life in Christ, nor strangled the love of Christ, but that they have clouded the Light by Christ. It is falsehood to claim fellowship and "not the truth." Thank God for those in the family who have unbroken fellowship . . . . who live daily in obedience to Him and rejoice in His way and His will (verse 7). Such believers have a happy sense of communion with other believers and also a peculiar sensitiveness to sin and a looking for a continual cleansing (verse 7). The source of light is the omnipotent Sovereign (verse 5), the saints of light are the obedient saints (verses 6, 7a), and the salvation through light is the operation of the Savior (verse 7b).

Chapter 1:8-10 speak of the second condition of Fellowship: the *reliance* upon the Light or the confession of sin. The condition of sin is *declared* (verse 8). God demands the confession of the principle of sin. The confession of sin is *demanded* (verse 9a). God demands the confession of particular sins. The cleansing from sin is described (verses 9b, 10). God demands the confession of personal sins (verse 10). Christians do sin; but this does not mean they must be saved all over again. Sin in the life of the believer breaks fellowship. The word "confess" means "to say the same thing." To confess sin means to say the same thing about it that God does. Keep in mind that Christians do not have to do penance, make sacrifices, or punish themselves when they have sinned. It has been taken care of at the Cross. Does this give a license to sin? The reply to this thought is a definite *NO!* The believer who truly understands God's provision for a life of holiness does not want to deliberately disobey. If communion with God is to be observed, then these conditions must be fulfilled (1:5-10) . . . *Reception* of the Light and *Reliance* upon the Light!

The *Conduct* of Fellowship is given in chapter 2:1-29. John now deals with the conduct of the Christian who walks in the Light. The *character* of our conduct, *LOYALTY* . . . is given in 2:1-11. Verses 1, 2 suggest the *principle* of our loyalty . . . "That ye sin not." One might be tempted to treat sin lightly in the light of the assurance of forgiveness (1:9) and the universal guilt (1:8, 10), so John here shows the standard of conduct and the nature of the remedy for sin in order that his readers might not sin. Verses 3-6 show the *pattern* of our Loyalty . . . "Even as he walked." This will involve obeying the words of Christ . . . and imitating the walk of Christ. As the token of our first loyalty was the law of obedience (verses 3-5), so then the mark here is the law of imitation (verse 6). That is the rule of the fellowship . . . "walk as he walked." That is the outward sign of abiding in Christ. So here we have the commandments to obey (verses 3-6). Chapter 2:7-11 stress the *proof* of our Loyalty . . . Love . . . see John 13:34. When a person is in fellowship with God and walking in the Light, he also walks in Love. It is a basic spiritual principle that when Christians are out of fellowship with God, they cannot get along with God's people. We are all members of God's family; so we ought to love one another (Leviticus 19:18). So here we have the church to be loved (verses 7-11).

The *challenge* for our conduct . . . Separation . . . is given in chapter 2:12-29. Verses 12-14 give us the *progress* God planned we achieve. Like a loving father, John calls the saints "little children"; and all of God's children have been forgiven, but we ought to grow in the Lord, become strong young men in the faith, and ultimately "fathers." Note the characteristics of each of these levels of Christian experience. Dr. Griffith Thomas points out in his commentary that although these may appear to us as successive stages of development, yet, in a sense, they can co-exist simultaneously. There is always something of the infant in us; there is always something of the adolescent in us; but let us pray that there must, and there will surely be a great deal of spiritual maturity about our Christian living.

Verses 15-29 give us the *perils* God previews we are to avoid. The first *peril* is that of the WORLD (verses 15-17). It is the wish of God that we avoid these perils, each and every one of them. This idea of the world being a danger to us is of course concerned with the area of Christian *behavior.* There is a conflict between the love for the Father and the love one would have for the world. The "world" according to this sense means all that belongs to our life that is opposed to Christ. It is Satan's system. If we love the world, we lose the love of the Father and we cease to do His will. Anything in my life that dulls my love for spiritual things, or that makes it easy for me to sin, is worldly and must be put away. John mentions three specific problems: the desire of the flesh, the desire of the eyes, and the pride of life. Is this not what the people in the world live for? By living for the world, like Lot, we lose everything. If we live for God, like Abraham, we will abide forever (verse 17).

The second *peril* is that of error (verses 18-29). This is in the area of Christian *belief.* There needs to be an *apprehending* of the Christless (verses 18-23). John gives how they are described (verse 18) and how they are disowned (verse 19). There needs to be also an *abiding* in Christ (verses 24-29). This means an abiding in the person of God (verse 24), the promises of God (verses 25, 26), and the placements of God (verses 27-29).

Let me just share a summary of the first section . . .

1:5—2:29 . . . Conditions of fellowship with Christ (1:1-10), Commandment to fellowship with Christ (2:1-17), and Continuance in fellowship with Christ (2:18-29). Another way to divide it is: 1:5—2:2 Communion with God observed, 2:3-11 Commandments of God obeyed, and 2:12-29 Commendation of God obtained!

Now we come to the second division of the book . . . 3:1—4:21 . . . *Fellowship* assured through the admonition to consistent LOVE!

The *Characteristics* of the Fellowship are given in chapter 3:1-24. In verses 1-10a John explains our *station* in the love of God. We have received salvation through the love of God. Verse 1 reveals a priceless privilege . . . "called the sons of God." Verse 2 reveals a positive promise . . . "we shall be like him," and verse 3 reveals a purifying power "even as he is pure." Having given us our appointment as sons of God (verse 1) and our appearance as sons of God (verse 3) he now appeals to the sons of God. Purity versus perversity (verses 3-6), pardon versus perversity (verses 7-9), and profession versus perversity (verse 10). The motives, meaning, and marks of love . . . the family characteristics of the child of God are given.

In verses 10b-24 John expounds our *service* in the love of God. We are to render service in the love of God. John contrasts what should be with what happened in the slaying by Cain (verses 11-15). The action of Cain violated the law of love. It reflects the persecution the righteous receive even today from the perverse. He continues with the perception that the righteous are to have . . . evidenced by sacrifice (verses 16-18). He climaxes this section by requiring the spirit of consecration to prevail . . thus, exhorting us to be partakers of the providential dealings of God. The foregoing teaching would no doubt raise misgivings in some minds. So John hastens to add that the fruit of love is confidence, and confidence expresses itself in prayer, and confident prayer is answered in the love of God. John envisions our steadfastness in the love of God, but only through the love of God can this steadfastness be reached. Chapter 4:1-6 speak of the *surveillance* of the spirits. He cautions them concerning the *lying* spirits . . . false prophets. He speaks of the existence of lying spirits (verse 1) and says we are to test the spirits. He speaks also of the examination of the lying spirits as to their creed (verses 2, 3) and their crowd (verses 4-6). He speaks of testing the spirits (verses 1-3), the triumph of the saints (verse 4), and the truth concerning the spirits (verses 5, 6).

In verses 7-21 he speaks of the *salvation* of the saints. He cautions them concerning a *Loving* spirit, false profession. In verses 7-10 John gives us the mystery of Love. Love is of God and of Christ. There is an exhortation to love (verse 7) and the evidence of Love (verses 8, 9). In verses 11-16a we have the motive of love. Men cannot see God, but they can see God's children revealing Him in their love. This love is not something that we work up; it is the work of the Spirit within (Romans 5:5). God's love flows from us as we yield to the Spirit. As Christians we do not love each other because of our good qualities, but in spite of our bad qualities. As we abide in His love, we have no problem loving other Christians. In verses 16b-21 John gives us the marks of love. Love becomes the force working within us (verses 11-16b) that causes us to have boldness in the day of judgment (verse 17), love will cast out all fear (verse 18), love proves the reality of our profession (verses 19-21).

Someone has summarized this section thusly: Divine Love is Love that is *pure* (3:1-9), Love that is *practical* (3:10-24), and Love that is *perfect* (4:1-21).

Now we come to the final division. Chapter 5:1-21—Fellowship assured through the assurance of continuous *LIFE!* Verses 1-12 speak of the place of *FAITH*. Faith is the bond of possession. Faith in Christ is exhibited by the conduct we practice (verses 1-5). As begotten ones we love the brethren (verses 1-3). As believing ones we live victoriously (verses 4, 5). Faith in Christ is also exhibited by the credentials we possess (verses 6-12). These facts are the proof of possession . . . the witness in Heaven (verses 6, 7), the witness in earth (verse 8), and the witness in man (verses 9-12).

Verses 13-17 speak of the promise of the *FUTURE!* The certainty of eternal life is given in the purpose of the writings (verse 13). The confidence in the eternal Lord is exhibited in the prayers of the worshipers (verses 14-16). The cautions to the exemplary life are to be reflected in the prudence of the worshipers (verse 17).

Verses 18-21 speak of the presentation of *FACTS*. There is a word of *assurance* concerning the Christians (verse 18), the *acceptance* of Christians (verses 19, 20), and the *appeal* to Christians (verse 21).

Yes, as we come to a close . . . WE KNOW who a Christian is (5:1-5), Life received by FAITH! WE KNOW who Christ is (5:6-13), Life recorded in FACT! WE KNOW who a Conqueror is (5:14-21), Life revealed as FRUIT! This fruit reflects itself in confidence at the *THRONE* (verses 14-17) and confidence of the TRUTH (verses 18-21).

A SURVEY OF THE EPISTLE OF

Second John

by Rev. Milton Worthington

Second John is one of the three private, personal letters in the New Testament (3 John and Philemon are the other two). It is one of the five shortest books in the Bible (see also Obadiah, Philemon, 3 John, and Jude); all five contain but one chapter. Second and Third John are, in a sense, appendices to First John. Eight of the thirteen verses in 2 John are found, in substance in 1 John. Second and Third John both center in the subject, "Truth." Second and Third John also give a practical application of the command to hate evil and to love God. Second John says to withdraw from those not holding the Truth. Third John says to have fellowship with those who do hold the Truth.

This is the only epistle in the New Testament exclusively addressed to a lady: a woman's epistle . . . woman is always "the elect lady" in the Bible, a great tribute to the dignity of womanhood, wifehood, and motherhood. Second and Third John are all we have left of John's private correspondence just as Philemon is all we have left of Paul's. Great stress is laid on correct doctrine. It is one of the two epistles of the New Testament mentioning the "Antichrist" by name. In spirit and in style it is much like 1 John. It combines gentleness with severity. It is very personal, since it is a private letter.

The author was John the Beloved, who wrote when he was about the age of ninety. He was the last of the twelve apostles, outliving the others by twenty or thirty years. He was the only one of the twelve who did not die a martyr's death, but he lived a martyr's life. He calls himself the "Elder" or the "Presbyter." The idea that "John the Presbyter" was a different man from John the Apostle was invented by Papias about two and a half centuries after the time of Christ. It is accepted widely by critics, but we believe, without true internal or external foundation.

The date of the writing is rather uncertain, but it bears the same tone and appears to have been written at approximately the same time as the first epistle. It was probably written soon after the first epistle and was among the last books of the New Testament to have been written. Tradition says that John labored toward the end of his life in Ephesus and that this letter was written from that city. Some think that John was the guest of nephews of this woman when he wrote (verse 13). John had heard that this godly lady and her children were walking in the truth; and he was expecting to make a visit to them in the near future. He wrote to warn this benevolent lady against entertaining some false teachers who traveled about in an itinerate manner teaching antichristian doctrines.

This epistle was written to the "elect lady and her children." There are three main opinions as to who "the elect lady" was: (1) A church, probably located in the neighborhood of Ephesus. It seems strange that a church should be called "the elect lady." (2) Martha of Bethany. A tradition says that Martha was the "elect lady." Bengel says that the Greek "Kyria" answers to the Hebrew word "Martha." The word "sister" in verse 13 would thus refer to Mary. (3) A wealthy lady in the vicinity of Ephesus. This is the most probable view and is held by a majority of scholars.

Several key texts have been suggested, verse 4 or verse 10. Either is a good one. There is no question that truth is the key word to this epistle. The word "truth" occurs five times in the short chapter. One should really spell it with a capital "T" because this Truth is personal (see John 14:6). John here discusses the nature, test, fruit, character, and defense of truth. The word love occurs four times (1, 3, 5, 6), and the word truth five times (1, 2, 3, 4). Thus, he both woos and warns, teaches tenderly and thunders terribly, in advocating truth. The word "truth" is used in two senses: 1—the body of Christian teaching (verses 1, 4,), and 2—the Christ Himself (verse 3, meaning "truly"). The epistle gives us a homily on the province, products, and preservation of the truth. Supremely it presents HIM as the Truth without us, within us, and with us. The central theme of the book is definitely "The Truth." We are simply to withdraw from those who do not hold the truth.

Several outlines have been helpful to me. I. Salutation verses 1-3, Warning against entertaining false teachers verses 4-11, Concluding Salutation verses 12, 13. II. Walking in Truth verses 1-6, Warning of Traitors verses 7-13. III. Introduction verses 1-3, The Path of the Believer verses 4-6, The Peril of the Believer verses 7-11, Conclusion verses 12, 13.

Now as we begin our detailed study let me remind you to read the book through each day for a month to firmly fix the facts in your mind.

John *Commends* the lady for Perceiving the Truth in verses 1-4. In verse 1 John gives his *Address.* It reveals the deep humility of the author. He, who might have called himself not only an apostle but the last of the apostles and even the apostle whom Jesus loved, is content to describe himself as the "elder" (1a). He also reveals the tender regard for the elect lady (addressee) in Christ to whom he writes; but it is as a sister in Christ that he addresses her, whom he loves in the truth . . . in Christ: a love, spiritual, eternal, holy (1b). In verse 2 John gives his *attestation.* He relates the actual perception of truth by him (2a), and the abiding presence of truth with him (2b). In verse 3 John gives his *ascription.* It refreshes with a benediction and a blessing. The solicitude for the honor and majesty of Jesus Christ . . . the mercy and peace which come to us are not only from God the Father, so to speak, but the second person of the Godhead as well, Jesus, the Christ. And He is the Son of the Father, not a Son, but The Son. How like this is to John's emphasis on the same truth in his first epistle.

In verse 4 John concludes his commendation with a word of rejoicing for the testimony of her children whom he found "walking in the Truth." Note that truth and love go together; Christians cannot have fellowship where there is false doctrine and lies. Note the repetition of the word walk. The truth is not something we study or believe; it is a motivating force for our lives. It is not enough to know truth; we must show it through our actions wherever we are. John rejoiced because certain of this lady's children were walking in truth. This is the same as "walking in the light" which was discussed in 1 John 1. They had received the truth and were doing the truth.

John *Commands* the lady to *Practice* the Truth in verses 5, 6. He reminds the lady of the great commandment which embraces all other commandments, the command to love one another. This burden is the old one of John, the message he reiterates . . . LOVE. But love in the New Testament means not a passion, not an emotion, but a life. An abiding and controlling principle of being influential for righteousness, this is love . . . Christian love. Is not that what John says again and again in his first epistle, and is it not what he says here (verse 6)?

Christian love is not an emotion that we work up. It is simple obedience to the Word of God. When children love their parents, they obey them. "If ye love me, keep my commandments." Christians too often love the Bible but hate the brethren. While saints may differ in their interpretations of certain passages in the Word, they must all agree on loving one another. Where there is a sincere love for the Bible, there will be a love for God's people. Loving the truth and loving the brethren cannot be separated.

John *Cautions* the lady to *Protect* the Truth in verses 7-13. In verse 7 she is to protect the Truth from those that *deceive.* Here John is referring to the false teachers discussed in the first epistle. He reminds us that the test of a false teacher is what he believes about Jesus Christ. If he denies that Jesus Christ came in the flesh, then he is a false teacher and from the Antichrist. While there will be one great Man of Sin (or Antichrist) in the end times, the spirit of the Antichrist is already in the world (see 1 John 4:3). John tells us that the deceivers are in the world (7a) and that they are deniers of the Word (the Christ) 7b. In verse 8 she is told to protect the truth from those that *destroy*. Here John warns the Christian that he is not to destroy the things that have been wrought in Christ. The best way to get detoured on your Christian walk and to lose all spiritual ground you have gained is to get tied up with false doctrine. Satan is a destroyer, and he uses lies to rob saints of their blessings. There needs to be a realization of the danger we face (8a) and the dividend for fidelity (8b).

In *verses 9-11* she is to protect the truth from those that *depart.* What does it mean to transgress as given in verse 9? By the "doctrine of Christ" there is more meant than merely the things He taught with His own lips while here in the flesh, but also the whole doctrine or teachings concerning Him . . . the whole Old Testament and New Testament. To deny the truth concerning Christ is to deny His first and His second coming in the flesh, and he who denies this "hath not God." He may speak much of the Father but he only has the Father who has the Son. To have one you must have the other (verse 9).

The word transgress here means to "go beyond." That is, these false teachers are not content to stay within the limits of the Word of God (Old Testament and New Testament). They are progressive, modern, and prefer to depart from the Bible and go beyond what God has written. This is the wrong kind of progress. While a Christian is to make progress in his walk, he is never to go beyond the bounds of the Bible. We are to "abide" in the doctrine, affirming the basic fundamentals of the Word of God.

In verse 10 John warns us not to entertain these fellows in our homes . . . or even to greet them. Any aid that we give to false teachers is to share in their evil deed. Find out what a man believes before you let him in the house or give him a donation. Check with your pastor if you have any questions.

Just an observation here. I think the command, "receive him not into your house," is not absolute but relative. I do not think it means that we are to deny him meat and shelter, if he be in need of them, but only that we are not to fellowship him as a brother. Even our personal enemies we are commanded to bless and pray for; if they hunger, we are to feed them, and if they thirst, give them drink. But, those who are enemies of God by being enemies of His Truth, we are to have nothing to do with in the capacity of fellow Christians. We must not aid them in their plans or bid them Godspeed (verse 11).

The apostle closes the letter with a word concerning his writings (verse 12) and his wishes (verse 13). He spoke of the brevity of his writing and the expectation of a visit with them shortly to speak with them face to face. He closes with a word of greeting to the "elect sister" (verse 13).

A SURVEY OF THE EPISTLE OF

Third John

by Rev. Milton Worthington

Third John could be called the book of hospitality. It has one chapter with fourteen verses and takes about three minutes to read. It is one of the shortest books in the Bible. Second and Third John are appendices to 1 John, for they give a practical view of working out in every day life the principles laid down in 1 John. Jerome called 2 and 3 John "twin-sisters." The subject of both epistles is truth. Third John is one of the three private letters of the New Testament (see also 2 John and Philemon). Third John especially opposes schisms (cf. 1 Corinthians 1-3). It has a very affectionate tone. "Beloved" keeps recurring (verses 1, 2, 5, and 11). Both 2 and 3 John end with the prospect of a coming, face-to-face meeting. This epistle gives excellent insight into the church life of the first century. The Scofield Bible says: "Historically, this letter marks the beginning of the clerical assumption over the churches in which the primitive church order disappeared." Second and Third John are the only books in the New Testament which do not mention the Second Coming (2 John does speak of the Antichrist in his present manifestation). There is no direct references to the Old Testament.

Internal and external evidence lead us to believe that John, the beloved disciple, was undoubtedly the writer. It was probably written about the same time as 2 John . . . A. D. 90 from Ephesus, where John spent his later years.

John was expecting soon to make a personal visit to the home of Gaius. At that time, there were many itinerate preachers who refused to take any money from the heathen (verse 7). Diotrephes, "who loveth to have the preeminence, " refused to receive these itinerant preachers. One of John's letters seems to have been lost (verse 9). John is writing this time to condemn Diotrephes and to urge Gaius to entertain these itinerant preachers who labor for Christ.

The practical heresy that is combated is domineering church leadership. Diotrephes was "the pope in embryo." This is the first instance we have in the New Testament of such overpowering leadership.

The key word is "fellow-helpers," and the key verse is verse 8. The Lord Jesus is pictured as "The Truth." The only title given to Him in this book is simply "The Name" (verse 7).

There are three prominent characters in this book: (1) The beloved Gaius to whom the epistle was written, Diotrophes, who loved to be preeminent, and Demetrius, the man of good report. There are five men named Gaius in the New Testament. (1) Gaius of Macedonia, Acts 19:29; (2) Gaius of Derbe, Acts 20:4; (3) one whom Paul baptized, 1 Corinthians 1:14; (4) one of Paul's hosts, Romans 16:23; and (5) the one to whom John wrote. It is probable that the last three were the same. If this be true, the Gaius to whom John wrote was converted through John (verse 4), baptized by Paul, and was a wealthy and hospitable member of the church of Corinth. He appears to have been a very generous Christian (verses 5, 6).

Several outlines may help as we begin . . . . . I. Salutation verses 1-4, Encouragement to hospitality verses 5-8, Condemnation of Diotrephes verses 9, 10, Closing Exhortation verses 11-14. II. Gaius, A Confirmed Christian verses 1-8, Diotrephes, A Condemned Christian verses 9, 10, and Demetrius, A Complimented Christian verses 11, 12. III. Commencement verses 1-4, Confirmation of Gaius verses 5-8, Condemnation of Diotrephes verses 9, 10, Commendation of Demetrius verses 11-13, and Conclusion verses 13, 14.

Again as we begin our verse by verse study let me suggest that you read the book once a day for a month to get the facts firmly fixed in your mind.

In verses 1-8 we have the *Confirmation* of a delightful *Gaius.* What a prosperous Christian he was. In verse 1 he was *acknowledged* by John, the beloved, as the beloved Gaius. We are told in 1 Timothy 5:21 that the pastor should show no partiality whatsoever to any member of his congregation. He should consider every member alike. This is true; yet, the pastor cannot help but feel a little more tender to those who love the Lord. Gaius was one of those with whom John was delighted in the Lord. How we thank the church for members like Gaius. John used the word "beloved" four times when referring to him (verses 1, 2, 5, 11). In *verses 2-4* he is *acclaimed* for truth. Verse 2 suggests that he may not have been in good health, or that he was just recovering from an illness. But this we know, he had a healthy spiritual life. Whatever the condition of the outer man, the inner man was prospering. John informs this brother that he has the highest hopes of his success in the things of God. He had heard of the man's conduct and character and was assuring him that he would be rewarded. His prosperity has been declared in verses 1, 2 and demonstrated in verses 3-8 . . . in his character (verse 3), in his children (verse 4), and in his charity (verses 5-8). No doubt Gaius was one of John's converts, as he counts him one of his children. In verses 5-8 he is *accredited* with love. Gaius was the kind of Christian others enjoyed talking about. The brethren (probably traveling evangelists and missionaries) had met Gaius and been entertained in his home. They reported that Gaius was "walking in the truth" and faithfully trying to help the different Christian workers who came his way. Keep in mind there were no hotels or motels in John's day. Traveling evangelists depended on the saints for food and lodging. Gaius was the kind of Christian who loved to entertain the brethren and "bring them forward" as they went from place to place. Why did Gaius help the brethren? Because he loved them, for one thing, and because he wanted to share in their ministries and further the truth. A man might not be a preacher himself, but he can help others preach.

In 5-8 we learn that Gaius was never deceived by false prophets though he ministered to strangers whom he had just met. He had the gift of discernment by which he knew that they were born again. His love was manifested in his hospitality toward these brethren, and as they went all over the known world, they had nothing but praise for this dear man. In verses 7, 8 John teaches us that Christians must take care of the brethren. If the Christians do not take care of Christ's ministers, who will? These Christian brethren whom Gaius aided would take nothing from the unconverted. John calls these unconverted people heathen, and also he terms them as Gentiles. Let every Christian resolve that he will manifest the love of God which is in his heart toward God's ministry by supporting the preachers in their labors.

In verses 9-11 we have the *Condemnation* of a disappointing Diotrephes. One of the greatest disappointments in a young minister's life is when he learns that not all of the brethren are like the beloved Gaius. There is always one Diotrephes in the local assembly. This is the kind of church member easy to do without. In verse 9 his pride is revealed. He wanted to be the "boss" of the church; he loved to have the preeminence (cf. John 3:30). How did this member act? Well, for one thing, he refused to acknowledge the leadership of John (9b). Whenever a church member wants position and prestige he usually attacks the pastor either privately or publicly. Usually he starts a whispering campaign and tries to undermine the pastor's character and ministry. Like Absalom in the Old Testament he hints that the present leadership is not efficient (2 Samuel 15: 1-6), but that he could handle things better. Hebrews 13:7, 17 settle this matter once and for all. In verses 10, 11 his pride is rebuked. Diotrephes told lies about John. "Prating" in verse 10 means to bring false charges and is similar to "tattlers" of 1 Timothy 5:13. If church members would remember that they are to listen to no accusation against their pastor without witnesses present, this would solve the gossip problem (1 Timothy 5:19). He also refused to help the brethren and even went so far as to domineer the church and throw some of them out (verse 10b). The New Testament teaches in some cases of discipline, members are to be dismissed; but Diotrephes dismissed people without giving them opportunity to defend themselves against the accusations and to be heard by the congregation (1 Corinthians 5:3).

It is this kind of member that destroys churches. Eager for power and authority, he tramples on truth, ignores the Bible, grieves the Spirit, and scatters the flock. John rebukes him by reminding him that when he came he would remember his works and words. Verse 11 is the challenge to Gaius and a condemnation of Diotrephes.

In verse 12 we have the *Commendation* of a determined *Demetrius.* It is a joy to turn from Diotrephes to Demetrius. He was the kind of person others could follow ("mimic"). He had a good report both from the brethren and from the Word itself. You could test his life by the Bible, and it passed the test.

Churches today need more men like Gaius and Demetrius, men who love the Bible, the brethren, and the souls of men. We can do without Diotrephes.

Verses 13, 14 give us the conclusion. John speaks of many other things he wishes to say but does not wish to write down (verse 13) and expresses a hope that he will soon be able to visit Gaius (verse 14). He prays that Gaius may have the Christian blessing of peace, sends salutations from the friends of Gaius, and asks him to greet John's friends by name for him (verse 14).

A SURVEY OF THE BOOK OF

Jude

by Dr. Robert Picirilli

Our survey of the New Testament brings us now to the last two books; namely, the brief epistle from Jude and the dramatic book called Revelation. I am going to spend about half of this lesson on Jude, and in the other half I will give you an introduction to Revelation. Then in another complete lesson on Revelation we will survey the contents of that rather strange book.

So now to Jude's little letter. Turn there in your Bible, please. As with all parts of the Bible, we will understand and appreciate this letter better if we first see what can be said about its historical circumstances. Who wrote this letter? To whom? When? Why? The answers to such questions as these, when they can be given, help clarify our grasp of the message of the text itself.

Before going any farther, let me suggest that you review the lesson on Second Peter, or at least reread chapter 2 of Second Peter. If you will read that chapter and then read Jude's one chapter, you will find that the two epistles are very similar in content. Understanding one helps our understanding of the other. Some interpreters suggest that one or the other of the two writers, either Jude or Peter, consciously repeated some of the other writer's material. I do not suppose there is anything wrong with that view, since the Holy Spirit could easily have led one of them to repeat instruction that was still needed. Good things often need to be said over and over again.

The only trouble is that we cannot tell which writer, Jude or Peter, wrote first. Some interpreters feel Jude wrote first and Peter repeated. Others take the opposite opinion. Lenski, for example, feels sure Jude repeated Peter's material. To argue for his view, Lenski points out that Peter usually uses the future tense and says, "There *shall* be false teachers," and so on. Jude speaks of a present reality, as in verse 4, when he says, "There *are* certain men crept in unawares." So Lenski believes that Jude wrote later than Peter, and that Jude wrote when the false teachers that Peter only predicted had really come.

This view is about as good as any other, though we cannot prove the point beyond any doubt. Another question is closely involved, though. Did Jude and Peter write their similar letters to the same general group of people? If you will notice verse 1 of Jude, you will see that no city or region is named. So we cannot prove exactly what original church or churches received this little letter. If Lenski's view is correct, that Jude wrote to expose then present false teachers that Peter had written earlier to predict, then perhaps the two men did write to the same general area. If so, then what area was that? Well, the first verses of Second Peter also contain no specific location. However, in Second Peter, Peter says in 3:1 that he has written his readers two letters, so we can assume Second Peter was sent to the same area as First Peter. And verse 1 of First Peter *does* say that the epistle was to believers scattered throughout Pontus, Galatia, Cappodocia, Asia, and Bithynia. These five Roman provinces covered a large area, almost all of what we now call Asia Minor or Turkey.

So Peter's epistles were sent to a very large group of churches. And if Jude wrote to the same general area, his letter was too. By the way, this lack of specific destination for most of these short letters between Hebrews and Revelation is the reason we call them the *general* epistles. They were more addressed to Christians in general than to specific churches.

Let us assume, then, that Jude wrote this letter sometime after Second Peter and sent it to the same general area, notably Asia Minor. The next question is when? Again, we cannot be dogmatic, but if Jude wrote later than Second Peter, then the year A. D. 65 can be suggested as a likely starting point. We realize full well, however, that the actual date may have been within a few years of this approximate time, perhaps even several years later.

If we cannot be very exact about when Jude wrote or to whom, we can be more sure about the human author. In Jude 1, the writer identifies himself as Jude, a brother of James. Of course the name Jude and the name James were common in New Testament times, as much so as Bob and Bill are to us. But we believe that all New Testament books were written either directly or indirectly under the influence of the apostolic family, and so we look for such brothers in the apostolic family as we know it from the New Testament itself. Were there any such brothers? There were.

You will recall that another of the general epistles was written by one named James. You will also recall that Paul mentions, in Galatians 1:19, an apostle called "James the Lord's brother." And, of course, we know that this James, who was one of Jesus' earthly family, had three other brothers, one named Jude. See Matthew

13:55, where the four brothers of Jesus are named as James, Joses, Simon, and Judas. Consequently, Biblical scholars have usually regarded the author of Jude as this one who was full brother of James and half-brother of Jesus Himself, as we might technically put it. There does not seem to be any reason to question that widely held view. I might add that this view has existed in the church ever since very early church history.

Why, then, did Jude write this little letter to the Christians he felt responsible for? In verse 3 he gives us a hint. He says he had first intended to write about the common salvation but instead felt it needful to exhort his readers to contend for the faith. Let me quote the little commentary on Jude by Charles R. Erdman. He expresses Jude's purpose nicely.

"The occasion of the epistle seems to have been the reception by the writer of news concerning the peril which was threatening the Church. He had been addressing himself to the task of writing a treatise on the subject of the 'salvation' which he shared with his fellow Christians, when he unexpectedly found it necessary to write them this message in which he urges them 'to contend earnestly for the faith which was once for all delivered unto the saints.' He has learned that entrance into the Church has been gained by certain godless men who, in the name of liberty, are living in lawless license, and under the cloak of a Christian profession are hiding their shameless impurity."

And now, with this brief introduction finished, let us look at the text of this one chapter more closely. To outline this letter is not very difficult. Each part is fairly easy to distinguish as the epistle moves logically through its subject matter. We will outline the letter as we survey it, one part at a time.

The first part is the Salutation, in verses 1, 2. Like most all letters written in those times, this salutation contains three elements. First is the writer's identification. He is Jude, brother of James. Some interpreters take this to imply James was now dead and Jude was taking spiritual oversight of James' former territory, but that opinion is based on too flimsy evidence to regard it as anything more than speculation. The second element in the salutation is the address of the letter. As we have already noted, Jude is not specific. He merely addresses those who are sanctified; that is, saints, and who are preserved and called in Christ. Evidently Jude's letter went to a number of churches and believers in a broad area. The third element in the salutation is the blessing. This is pronounced in verse 2: "Mercy unto you, and peace, and love, be multiplied." Such expressions as these were commonly used by the early Christians as greetings.

The second part of Jude is verses 3, 4. These verses give the reason for the writing of this letter. In 3a, Jude says he "gave all diligence to write . . . of the common salvation," which means the salvation we all have in common. This whole sentence means Jude had already begun diligent preparations for writing such an epistle. But, as he indicates in 3b, another more pressing need arose. He felt he must write and exhort them to contend for the faith. "Contend" means struggle. It is an athletic term suggesting a contest, wrestling match, or fight. They needed to get in the "good fight" Paul wrote about in 2 Timothy 4. The Christian faith was under attack, and believers needed to get actively involved in the contest over that faith.

Verse 4 gives the particular circumstances that impelled Jude to write this way. Certain men—false teachers—had sneakily invaded the church and gained a hearing. But their doctrine, warns Jude, will have two effects. The grace of God will be turned into lasciviousness and the Lord Jesus will be denied. This means, at the very least, that the false teachers were using God's grace as an excuse for wicked living, and such a doctrine amounts to a practical denial of the power of Jesus to save and a direct denial of His teachings. So Jude felt impelled to write this little letter and exhort his readers to withstand such false teachers. He notes, by the way, in verse 4, that the sentence of condemnation of these ungodly men has been pronounced long ago. You may remember that 2 Peter 2:3 said the same thing of such false teachers: "whose judgment now of a long time lingereth not, and their damnation slumbereth not." Although false teachers abound now and must be struggled against by the church, their final condemnation is not in doubt.

This brings us to part three of Jude, verses 5-7, in which Jude gives three examples of God's judgment on the wicked. These examples will reinforce the point he has just made, that the false teachers will surely be judged in the end. Jude's first example is in verse 5, and it concerns the Israelites who left Egyptian bondage but did not make it to Canaan. God judged thousands of them at different times in the wilderness.

Jude's second example is given in verse 6 and reminds us of angels who were judged by God. We really do not know much about this, but we assume Jude is referring to those who rebelled with Satan. Jude's third example concerns the ancient cities of Sodom and Gomorrah which were destroyed by fire from Heaven because of fornication and sexual perversion.

Jude's point is very clear: If God judged His own chosen people who believed not, and if God judged angels who rebelled, and if God judged whole cities who practiced immorality, then obviously the false teachers just described in verse 4 cannot hope to escape judgment. You will recall, by the way, that chapter 2 of Second Peter made exactly this same point in exactly the same way. Only Peter's three examples were the sinning angels, the cities of Sodom and Gomorrah, and the world in Noah's day.

Now we come to part four of Jude, verses 8-16; in these verses

Jude describes the character of the false teachers he warns about. The description is quite dramatic and emotional. Without reading the verses now, let us just call attention to the main elements of the description, verse by verse. In verse 8 Jude indicates they are flesh motivated, much like the people of Sodom and Gomorrah in the previous verse. Also in verse 8 Jude shows they do not submit to any authority. Thus they brazenly assert their own independence, more so than even an angel like Michael, in verse 9, who leaves the pronouncement of condemnation to the Lord.

The false teachers' ignorance is stressed in verse 10. They pretend to know much but really do not. In verse 11, they are compared to the self-willed and murderous Cain, and to the self-seeking Balaam, and to Korah, who resisted Moses' authority. In verse 12, Jude observes that these false teachers corrupt the fellowship of the church. Furthermore, like clouds without water they promise much but deliver nothing. They themselves are "twice dead," an expression that certainly means apostasy. Verse 13 compares them to a raging sea that stirs up the dirt.

In verses 14, 15 Jude cites an ancient prophecy of judgment as applying to these false teachers. And in verse 16 he concludes the description of the false teachers by referring again to their seeking after their own advantage. False teachers of any time and place share in most of the characteristics of these whom Jude described in his day.

Part five of Jude is verses 17-23 and is addressed to the faithful believers Jude wrote. Several instructions are included. First, Jude instructs the good Christians to remember and watch for the false teachers.

Second, in verse 20, he instructs them to build themselves up in the faith. Remember that Peter also presented growth in grace as the only sure way to resist false doctrine. Then in verse 21 Jude exhorts them to keep themselves in the love of God, certainly a warning against possible apostasy if they should listen to the false teaching. Fourth, in verses 22, 23, Jude speaks of their attitude toward those who need to be preserved from any sort of error. Compassion is in order. Some will need to have the fear of God put in them.

And now Jude closes out his brief letter in verses 24, 25 with a doxology of praise to God. He it is who has power to preserve and perfect us if we stay in His love. And to Him belongs all glory, majesty, dominion, and power forever.

A SURVEY OF THE BOOK OF

Revelation

PART I

by Dr. Robert Picirilli

Now it is time for us to turn our attention to the last book of the Bible, the Book of the Revelation. Turn there with me in your Bible, please. As I indicated earlier, we will take up the rest of this lecture with Revelation, and devote another entire lecture to it, also. My plan is to use the remainder of this lesson for a general introduction to the book, and then use the other lesson to survey the specific contents of Revelation.

Before we do anything else, let us read Revelation 1:1-3. Follow along in your Bible: "The Revelation of Jesus Christ, which God gave unto him, to shew unto his servants things which must shortly come to pass; and he sent and signified it by his angel unto his servant John: Who bare record of the word of God, and of the testimony of Jesus Christ, and of all things that he saw. Blessed is he that readeth, and they that hear the words of this prophecy, and keep those things which are written therein: for the time is at hand."

I have recorded this especially to call your attention to the blessing that is pronounced in verse 3. We are promised a blessing for reading, listening, and obeying this book. Far too many people are needlessly frightened away from this important part of the Word of God. They have heard that Revelation is too hard to understand. (By the way, the name of the Book is Revelation, not Revelations.) They have heard about the visions and the horses and the strange-looking beasts, and they have been scared away. Well, there may be mysteries in Revelation that are difficult for us, but there is a great deal of clear truth we can grasp and be blessed by. I trust these lessons will help you want to get better acquainted with this book, in spite of what you may have heard.

Certainly there have been some humorous and exaggerated statements made about the deep, dark secrets of Revelation. Jerome—one of the early Christian fathers—is supposed to have said that the book contains as many riddles as words. Martin Luther observed that Revelation 1:3 and 22:18 ask us to observe the teachings of the book. But, he complained, how can we when we cannot understand the book's teachings? Another ancient scholar was reported to have said that Revelation either finds a man mad or leaves him so. But I suggest you discard such inappropriate comments and take Revelation seriously as a significant part of God's Word for us. There is much blessed truth to be learned in the midst of all the strange symbols.

Let us begin with a few words of introduction to the Book of Revelation. Understanding the historical background of any part of the Bible is always helpful. That is especially true with this part. Look a minute at chapter 1 of Revelation again. Notice verse 1: The message was given to John. Notice also verse 4: "John to the seven churches which are in Asia." Notice verse 9: "I John . . . ." Throughout Revelation you will see this first person singular pronoun "I" frequently: I saw, I looked, I beheld, I wept, I said, I heard. All this is John, the one who first received the visions contained in the book and put the contents on paper.

Who was this human instrument given the Revelation for us? This was, without doubt, the Apostle John, the very same as the one who wrote the Gospel of John and the three Epistles of John. You see, then, that John wrote more New Testament books than anyone except Paul. He was the one we often call "The Apostle of Love." We do this partly because John 21:20 refers to John as "the disciple whom Jesus loved." And partly because John's Gospel and epistles contain so much Christian teaching about love—the love of God, love for God, love for each other as believers, and love for the world. Sometimes we forget that John and his brother James—they were Zebedee's sons, you remember—were nicknamed by Jesus "the sons of thunder," as we are told in Mark 3:17. Clearly, as much as John understood love, he also knew how to thunder forth against sin and false doctrine. His writings demonstrate this characteristic, too.

But back to Revelation. Look now at 1:9, which gives us some helpful information about the historical circumstances under which Revelation was written: "I John, who also am your brother, and companion in tribulation, and in the kingdom and patience of Jesus Christ, was in the isle that is called Patmos, for the word of God, and for the testimony of Jesus Christ."

Here, then, was the situation when John wrote Revelation, and part of this we learn from early church history. The year was about A. D. 90 to 95. The Christians were under intense persecution from the Roman Imperial government. You remember that the church was first opposed by the Jews, as when Paul was seized in Jerusalem and spent four years in jail, two in Caesarea and two in Rome. That was in about A. D. 58-61. At that time, the Roman emperors had not yet begun to feel any serious tensions between themselves and the new religion called Christianity.

But before Nero died, in the year A. D. 68, he had gone mad. And in his insanity he began to sponsor official governmental persecution of the church. Under Nero, for example, Paul was arrested again and beheaded in about 66 or 67. Following Nero, some emperors persecuted the Christians; others seemed not to mind Christianity. But the Emperor Domitian, who was in power from 81 to 96, was an especially evil man and was aroused to promote one of the worst persecutions the Christian church has ever experienced. Christians were sought out relentlessly and treated mercilessly. They were given the clear-cut alternative: Either recognize publicly the emperor himself as your god, or suffer the consequences. Those who would not burn incense to the emperor—and what real Christian could?—were jailed, beaten, robbed of all their material possessions, slain, or submitted to some other punishment. Domitian was determined that every person in the empire should give him the worship he thought he was entitled to as the divine being he claimed to be.

This was the problem in the time Revelation was written. According to ancient traditions, all the apostles were now dead but John—martyrs, all of them. John was an old man, 85 or more. During his later years he had been ministering in the Roman province of Asia, especially since A.D. 70 when the Emperor Titus had destroyed Jerusalem and scattered the Jews—Christians or not—all over the empire. Asia, you remember, was a small province on the western end of what we now call Asia Minor or Turkey. Ephesus was the capital city. That Revelation has its background in an Asian context is clear. The seven churches to whom the whole book was sent were in seven cities in Asia. And Patmos, where John wrote, was an island just off the Asian coast, out from Ephesus.

Clearly, John was on Patmos as punishment for his refusal to subscribe to emperor worship. As a Christian, he could recognize but one God. Patmos was a prison island, much like our Alcatraz used to be. John was banished to Patmos, as he puts it in Revelation 1:9, "for the word of God, and for the testimony of Jesus Christ." No doubt the believers in Asia, and elsewhere, were continuing to experience harassment and injury for the name of Christ. On the one hand they were afflicted by the government agents who erected images and altars to Domitian and forced everyone to burn incense to him. On the other hand, they suffered when many of their number submitted to the emperor's demands and pretended it would do no harm.

John was concerned for the flocks of persecuted and cowardly believers. He needed something to reassure and strengthen them. He thought they would listen to him; he was the last of those who had received their commissions from the very lips of the Savior. So God gave John a Revelation of Jesus Christ, a revelation John could pass on to a persecuted church. As Ray Summers aptly says, "The message [of Revelation] is peculiarly relevant today—the call to choose the eternal rather than the temporal; to resist temptation, to refuse to compromise with pagan secularism, to place the claim of conscience above all demands against it; to cherish the confidence of ultimate victory for the kingdom of God, not only in the reign of Domitian, but also in every other chaotic period of world history, including the twentieth century."

In summary, then, this is the picture. Revelation was written in A.D. 90-95, by the elderly Apostle John. He was on Patmos, banished there for his Christian testimony. He wrote to churches in Asia, churches under intense persecution from the Roman Imperial government.

Now let us take a few minutes to observe that there are at least four different methods of interpreting the Book of Revelation as a whole. You will realize that one's basic approach to the book will have everything to do with the interpretation he gets. And through the years, as hundreds of Bible students have grappled with the problems of the Book of Revelation, four different schools of thought have developed, suggesting four different basic approaches to the book. Two of these four are not so popular today. The other two are still widely influential, and I will say more about these last two in the next lecture, when we survey the content and interpretation of the book.

First, one group suggests the book is *allegorical.* They say the details are unimportant, that the book is merely a dramatic portrayal of the eternal conflict between good and evil, teaching us that good will finally triumph. Now there is no doubt Revelation teaches us this, and this is one of the book's primary lessons. But not many Bible students today would say the book teaches nothing more. Many of the allegorical school have been liberals in theology. If you ever want to read a book that takes this approach, try the one by Raymond Calkins entitled *The Social Message of the Book of Revelation.*

A second basic approach is that of the *historicists.* The historical school tells us that Revelation provides us a dramatic picture of the entire course of church history from the days of the early church on through the present age until the final judgment. Historicists usually say that the seven churches in Asia, that were sent the seven letters given in chapters 2, 3, represent seven distinctive periods of church history. Many other interpreters would agree with them. But historicists also say that the visions contained in chapters 4-19 also depict various events of church history from the days of the Roman Empire until now. Martin Luther, for example, was a historicist and believed that some of the visions in Revelation represented the Protestant reformation. If you ever want to read a book from this school of interpretation, try E. B. Elliott's book entitled *Horae Apocalypticae.*

As I have already said, these first two approaches are not too popular these days. Most interpreters now prefer one or the other of the two approaches I am about to mention.

The third school of interpretation for the Book of Revelation is the *futurist* school. The futurists believe that most of the Book of Revelation applies to events that are still future for us. The letters to the seven churches, in the first three chapters, are taken at face value, of course. They dealt with matters that were very real for John and his churches then. But futurists believe that the visions in chapters 4-19 all deal with events to come in the last days, in the day of the Lord. Futurists think Revelation depicts, mostly, the great tribulation that God will bring on the earth before the Lord Jesus stands again on the earth. Most futurists are premillennialists in doctrine, but more will be said about this in the next lecture. Such well-known commentators as Ironside and Newell were futurists. If you want to read the view of a futurist, I would suggest J. A. Seiss's book entitled *The Apocalypse.*

Now, the fourth—and final—approach to the Book of Revelation is called the *preterist* school. (Spelled p-r-e-t-e-r-i-s-t.) The word "preterist" means "past." The preterists believe that the visions in Revelation 4-19 deal mostly with things in the past, things that happened in the days of the Roman Empire, early church history, things going on right when the book was written, and things that were about to happen then, things that would give the churches John wrote information about their own near future. Many amillennialists of our day take this view. Again, more will be said about this in the other lesson on Revelation. If you want to read a book that takes the preterist approach, try the one by Ray Summers, entitled *Worthy Is The Lamb.*

Before leaving this, let me just summarize these four schools once more. The allegorical school thinks Revelation's visions refer to any and all periods alike, with a general truth. The historicists think Revelation depicts all church history specifically, past, present, and future. The futurists think Revelation is mostly future. The preterists think Revelation is mostly past. In the following lesson, I will show you in greater detail how the latter two of these approaches affect the interpretation of Revelation.

And now one more word by way of introduction, in closing. This book as you see clearly in Revelation 1:1, is not a revelation of John, but a revelation of Jesus Christ. "Revelation" means unveiling. The Greek word is *apokalypsis,* and this is the reason the book is often called The Apocalypse. Anyway, this book unveils Jesus Christ. Jesus Christ is revealed. He is revealed in this book in His glorified state. He is the exalted Son of God who has power to walk in the midst of the churches and to sustain His persecuted followers. In that same glory He will return to earth at the end of this age. The exalted, glorified, powerful, returning Lord Jesus Christ is revealed to us in this book. That truth alone makes Revelation worth the reading.

A SURVEY OF THE BOOK OF

Revelation

PART II

by Dr. Robert Picirilli

You should go over Part I of Revelation before this lesson. In that lesson I gave background information that is essential for understanding this unique book we call Revelation or The Apocalypse.

And with that background information in mind, we are ready now to survey the actual contents of Revelation. I have three goals in mind for this lesson. First, I want you to see the contents of Revelation as they are. Second, I want you to understand the contents of Revelation as they are interpreted by two major schools of thought. And third, I want you to appreciate the most impressive lessons that Christians should find in this book regardless of their point of view.

So let us first make an effort to get acquainted with the contents of this book as they are. To start with, I would like for you to turn the pages of the Book of Revelation with me. As we do this, I will suggest the major divisions of the book, and you can jot them down if you are making notes.

First, look at chapters 1, 2, and 3. These three chapters make up Part One of Revelation. I call this part "The Introduction and Letters to the Seven Churches." We will look at this part more closely after a bit, but for now just glance at chapter 1, verse 4: "John to the seven churches which are in Asia." Now look at chapter 2, verse 1: "Unto the angel of the church of Ephesus write." In 2:8, another letter starts, to the church in Smyrna. In 2:12, another one, to Pergamos. In 2:18, the letter to Thyatira begins. In 3:1, the Sardis letter starts. In 3:7, the letter to Philadelphia. In 3:14, the letter to the church in Laodicea begins and continues on through the end of chapter 3. Thus the first three chapters contain the introduction and seven letters.

Part Two of Revelation contains chapters 4—11. Let us call this part "The Vision of the Opening of the Book with Seven Seals." Most people never realize this, but these chapters, 4—11, contain one single vision that runs continuously through from beginning to end. All the action of this vision is built around a sealed book and the breaking of the seals. Again, I will come back to this after a bit, but let us just glance through these chapters for a minute. In chapter 4, verse 2, we are introduced to a throne, and to one who sat on the throne. In chapter 5, verse 1, we are introduced to a book in the right hand of the one seated on the throne, sealed with seven seals. Verse 5 of chapter 5 tells us that Jesus will open the book, and in verse 7 He takes the book from the hand of the One on the throne and prepares to open each seal, one at a time. The rest of the vision, on through chapter 11, tells what happens after each seal is broken.

Turn on now to chapter 12. Part Three begins here and continues on through chapter 20. Let us call Part Three "The Great Cosmic Conflict Between the Forces of God and the Forces of Satan." These chapters contain a series of visions rather than one single vision, as in Part Two. But all the visions in Part Three, chapters 12—20, have a central theme. These visions reveal that there is a great universal warfare between God and Satan, and thus between the followers of God and the followers of Satan. These visions also show us how this conflict will turn out in the end. With what I have just said, both premillennialists and amillennialists can agree. They will differ, however, about the specific timing. More about this in a few minutes, when we will look at chapters 12—20 again.

Now glance at chapters 21, 22. These last two chapters make up Part Four of Revelation. In this part we are given "A Glimpse of the Eternal and Final State of Things." Note 21:1, for example, where the new Heaven and new earth are introduced. Chapter 22 continues the description of this final Heavenly reward, and concludes the book in 22:20 with the promise of the Lord's soon coming.

And now let us go back and look at these four parts of Revelation more closely. Turn back to chapter 1. As I said, the first three chapters make up Part One and contain the "Introduction and Letters to the Seven Churches." Let us subdivide this part into two smaller sections. Chapter 1 is the Introduction. Chapters 2, 3 contain the seven letters.

Verses 1-3 of chapter 1 provide us with a heading for the whole book. This heading speaks of the importance of the book and identifies it as "The Revelation of Jesus Christ." Jesus Christ, glorified and coming again, is revealed in this book.

Verses 4-8 contain the address of the book. John is the human writer, and the book goes to the seven churches. Jesus Christ, in verse 5, is the real author, and verse 7 already speaks of His coming in glory.

Notice verses 9-20 more closely. These verses contain a vision of the real Author of this book, Jesus Christ, in His glory, as the Lord of the church. In verses 9, 10 we see the circumstances: John, in exile on Patmos, was worshiping alone on the Lord's Day and received this vision. First, a voice instructed him to prepare this book for the seven churches, in verse 12. Then John turned and saw Jesus in His glory, in verses 12-16. With eyes like fire (verse 14), and with seven stars in His hand (verse 16), Jesus walks among seven candlesticks (verse 12). The significance of the vision is explained in verse 20. The candlesticks represent the seven churches, and the stars represent the "angels" (which means messengers or pastors) of the churches. The point is clear. Jesus is Lord of the churches. He is not now the humiliated Lamb we saw on the Cross. He is at the Father's right hand with power and glory, and as Head of the Church speaks with authority to the Church. This is also the way He will appear when He returns and calls the Church to judgment. How important, then, the messages He is about to deliver to the seven churches!

These seven messages are presented, one at a time, in chapters 2, 3. As we look through these seven letters briefly, we should pay attention to the structure of each letter. You will see that all seven letters are composed in exactly the same form. Each letter has four main parts. First, each letter has a description of Jesus as the Author of the letter. Some words of description are given, and these words are usually taken from the vision John saw of Christ in chapter 1. Note 2:1, for example, when the letter to Ephesus describes Jesus as the One who holds the seven stars in His hand and walks among the seven candlesticks.

Note also 2:18, where the letter to Thyatira begins by describing Jesus as One who has eyes like fire and feet like fine brass. Exactly these things were said about the glorified Jesus John saw in his first vision. Each of the seven letters begins with some such words about Jesus.

Next, each letter contains what I call an evaluation of the church. In every letter, this evaluation section begins with these words, "I know thy works." Jesus shows He is aware of the spiritual condition of each church. He points out things that are good and things that are bad. We will not take time now to examine the good and bad things about each church. But we will use the letter to Ephesus, in 2:1-7, as an example. In verses 2, 3, good things are evaluated, as also in verse 6. The church at Ephesus has labor and patience and has exposed false doctrine. But a bad thing is evaluated in verse 4: They have lost the keen edge of their first love for Christ.

The third part of every one of the seven letters is exhortation. The exhortation section is based on the evaluation of the church's spiritual condition. Sometimes an evaluation of good things leads to an exhortation to be faithful or hold fast. Look at the letter to Philadelphia, for example, in 3:7-13. In verse 11 the Lord says, "Hold that fast which thou hast." And such positive exhortations as this are usually followed by a promise, as here in 3:11 where Jesus continues: "that no man take thy crown." Many of the exhortations are not positive, however, because they are based on the bad things in the evaluation. Such exhortations as these negative ones usually contain the word "repent," and a warning is almost always attached to such a call for repentance, using the words "or else." Note 2:5, for example: "Remember therefore from whence thou art fallen, and repent, and do the first works; or else I will come unto thee quickly, and will remove thy candlestick out of his place."

Finally, each letter has a conclusion, in two parts. One part of the conclusion is a call for attention: "He that hath an ear, let him hear what the Spirit saith unto the churches." Every letter contains these words. The other part of the conclusion of each letter is a final reward promised to the one that overcomes. Note 2:7: "To him that overcometh will I give to eat of the tree of life." 2:11: "He that overcometh shall not be hurt of the second death." Every letter contains such words as these.

Before we leave these letters I want to point out four main lessons we learn from all seven letters as a whole. First, we learn the importance of enduring in spite of tribulation. Almost every church is complimented for endurance or encouraged to endure persecution. Note 2:3, 2:10, and 2:13, for examples. Remember, the churches John wrote were under intense persecution from the Roman emperor. These letters encouraged them to be faithful in spite of this opposition, even unto death, as 2:10 says.

A second truth stressed in these seven letters is the awfulness of backsliding. Ephesus, in 2:4, 5, is rebuked for having left her first love. Sardis, in 3:1, is rebuked because many who had a name as living were really dead. Laodicea, in 3:15, is neither cold nor hot. And you will recall that many letters urge the churches to "hold fast."

A third important lesson in these seven letters is the need to resist and expose false doctrine. Ephesus, in 2:6, is commended for rejecting the Nicolaitans. Pergamos, in 2:14, 15, is warned against the doctrine of Balaam and the doctrine of the Nicolaitans. Thyatira, in 2:20, is rebuked for tolerating the false prophecies of Jezebel. Time does not permit us to analyze these false teachings, but we are impressed with the need to recognize and resist false doctrine.

The fourth lesson that characterizes all seven letters as a whole is the importance of Second Coming truth. Almost every letter contains some reference to Christ's return. In 2:5, note "I will come unto thee quickly." The same words are contained in 2:16. In 2:25, notice "Hold fast till I come." In 3:3, "I will come on thee as a thief." In 3:11, "Behold, I come quickly." Remember that the vision John saw in chapter 1 was a vision of Jesus in His second coming glory. The blessed hope of Jesus' return is to sustain these churches in their severe persecutions and is to challenge them to be pure in life and doctrine.

But now we must move on to the more difficult portion of the book, starting with chapter 4. I have already told you that chapters 4—11 contain one single vision. In summary, the vision is this. God the Father, seated on His throne, has in His hand a book, sealed with seven seals. The Son—the Lamb of God—takes the book and proceeds to open the seals, one at a time. As each seal is opened, we see dramatic events taking place. The opening of the seventh seal involves a longer chain of events than any of the other six, and these events are presented by the blowing of seven trumpets. Thus, I have called chapters 4—11 "The Vision of the Opening of the Book with Seven Seals."

The question, however, is not so much the content as the meaning of this vision. The interpretation of Revelation is highly debated. So I am going to explain how the two most popular groups interpret the visions in Revelation.

First, a word of introduction to these two groups. We call group one the *preterists.* They believe that the visions in Revelation represent events that transpired in the history of the church in the days of the Roman Empire. They believe that these events were about to take place when John wrote Revelation. Amillennialists are often preterists in their interpretation of Revelation's visions. The amillennialist does not believe there is going to be a future millennium—1,000 years of peace on earth, ruled over by Jesus on a literal throne in an earthly Jerusalem. The amillennialist believes that the Kingdom of God is a spiritual reality in the hearts of believers now. He believes that the return of Christ at the end of this age will be accompanied, simply, by one resurrection and judgment of all men, followed by the eternal state. Thus, amillennialists do not understand the visions of Revelation to represent complicated future events in connection with the day of the Lord. They believe most of Revelation was fulfilled in the past experiences of the early church in the Roman Empire.

The other group, whose interpretation of Revelation I want to explain, takes the opposite approach. These are the *futurists,* and they are usually premillennialists. Premillennialists believe that the Lord Jesus will come back to earth to establish an external Kingdom of God here. They believe that He will reign on earth for 1,000 years—the millennium. They believe that a great tribulation period will precede Christ's coming to earth to set up this kingdom. They believe that the righteous will mostly be raised and judged before the millennium, with the wicked not raised and finally judged until afterward, at the great white throne. So the premillennialists have a much more complicated picture of future events and the day of the Lord. And, as futurists in interpreting Revelation, they believe that most of Revelation represents the events connected with the future day of the Lord.

So I am going to try to give you, briefly, the basic interpretation of each of these two views—the ammillennialists and the premillennialists—about the visions of Revelation. We cannot possibly deal with the small details. Only the broad outlines can be suggested. It is not my purpose to argue these two views, nor to present either one in a good or bad light.

Quickly, then, let us look at "The Vision of the Opening of the Seven Sealed Book" in chapters 4—11. And first, let us look at it as the premillennialist sees it. The premillennialist is a futurist, remember. He believes that this vision is a survey of the great tribulation period that will take place on earth just before Christ returns to earth to establish the millennial kindgom.

In chapter 4, we have the stage set; God is on His throne. The lightnings and thunderings in verse 5 show that He is about to judge the earth. In chapter 5, a book is in His hand. The book is in scroll form, by the way, and seven bands are tied around it. Jesus, as seen in verses 5-7, takes the scroll and prepares to open it. That scroll is the title-deed to the earth and indicates that Jesus is about to come and lay claim to the earth as His rightful possession. As He breaks each seal, judgment will fall on earth during the tribulation period, purging earth in preparation for His coming.

In chapter 6, the first six seals are broken. The first four, in verses 1-8, release four horses: one white, one red, one black, one pale green. Premillennialists agree that these represent war, famine, and death on the earth during the great tribulation. The fifth seal, in 6:9-11, depicts Christian martyrs. The sixth, in 6:12-17, shows natural catastrophes—including great earthquakes—that will be part of God's judgment on earth.

In chapter 7, between the sixth and seventh seal, we see two groups of the Lord's people. The first, in verses 1-8, is 144,000 Jews saved during the great tribulation. The second is a host of Gentile believers who also, as verse 14 puts it, "came out of great tribulation."

In chapter 8, when the seventh seal is broken, seven trumpets prepare to blow—each signaling further judgment on earth during the latter, more intense part of the great tribulation. The first four trumpets sound in chapter 8, and all involve world-wide natural catastrophes on earth that kill millions of people. In chapter 9, the fifth and sixth trumpets blow, releasing strange creatures that inflict misery and death. Interpreters differ as to whether these infernal locusts and infernal horsemen are literal or figurative. But either way, premillennialists see them as indicating more of the misery of evil men during the coming great tribulation.

In chapters 10, 11, between the sixth and seventh trumpets, we see several things, including an angel announcing in 10:6 that "there should be time no longer." In 11:3-14, we see the ministry of the two witnesses on earth during the last half of the great tribulation. In

11:15-19, the seventh trumpet sounds and signals the end of the tribulation and thus a readiness for the Lord Jesus to come and assume authority over the kingdoms of this world, as mentioned in 11:15.

Now let us look again at this same vision of the opening of the book with seven seals, in chapters 4—11. Only this time let us see what the amillennialist says about this vision. Remember, the amillennialist takes the preterist point of view and interprets Revelation as past history rather than future. Those who take this view remind us that the Christians in John's time were under Imperial persecution. The emperor of Rome wanted to force all Christians to worship him instead of Christ. Thus the amillennialist sees this vision of the opening of the seven-sealed book as a picture of the struggle that went on between the Lord and the Roman Empire, showing the means God was about to use to destroy the empire and save His church.

In chapter 4, the vision of God on the throne assures us that He is still in control, even when the church is suffering. The seven-sealed scroll in chapter 5 shows us that God has the unknown destiny of the empire and the church in His hands. When Jesus prevails to open the seals, we see that the Lamb was about to step on the scene of the early church's struggle and become the champion of His people.

Thus, the seven seals are opened to show what means the Lord would use to bring Rome's Imperial power to its knees, as punishment for persecuting the Church. The white horse, seal number one, was enemy invasion of Rome. The red, black, and pale horses represented war, famine, and pestilence that would speed the crumbling of Roman power.

The opening of the fifth seal, in 6:9-11, showed the early church martyrs as the reason for God's judgment on Rome. The sixth seal, in 6:12-17, may either point forward to the final judgment, or may show natural calamities—like earthquakes—also used in destroying old Rome.

The two groups pictured in chapter 7, between the sixth and seventh seals, are both the church, though from two different points of view. As the 144,000 in verses 1-8, the church is on earth, needing protection from Rome. These are not literally Jews. As the innumerable multitude in verses 9-17, the whole church's final destiny in Heaven is glimpsed.

In chapter 8, you recall, the seventh seal leads to seven trumpets. In the preterist's view, these trumpets signal the vengeance God would pour out on Rome. The first four, in verses 7-13 of chapter 8, indicate natural calamities that would destroy partially the Roman population. The strange locusts in 9:1-12, under the fifth trumpet, symbolize internal corruption and decay in the Imperial kingdom. The strange horsemen, under trumpet number six, in 9:13-21, symbolize external invasion from Rome's enemies. The preterist reminds us that Gibbon's history attributes Rome's ultimate fall to three forces: natural calamities, internal corruption, and external invasion. So he sees these three forces in these six trumpets.

Chapters 10, 11 show first an interlude between trumpets six and seven, you recall. The announcement that "time should be no longer," in 10:6, meant no further delay before Rome was to be destroyed. The two witnesses in 11:3-14 symbolized the powerful witness of the early church in spite of her suffering, because the number two was symbolical of great strength. The seventh trumpet, in 11:15-19, reassured the early church of ultimate victory in the conflict with Rome.

You see, then, that the meaning of the long vision in chapters 4—11 is quite crucial. The amillennialists see it as a description of the conflict between the early church and Roman efforts at persecution. The premillennialists see the vision as a description of the conflict that will climax on earth during the future great tribulation.

The same distinction applies to the interpretation of chapters 12—20. I called this part "Visions of the Great Cosmic Conflict Between the Forces of God and the Forces of Satan." Both premillennialists and amillennialists can agree on this title; but again the timing of the conflict described will be entirely different. Amillennialists will still look mostly to the past, the early church's conflict with Rome. Premillennialists will still look mostly to the future, when the conflict climaxes in the great tribulation. Both groups, by the way, believe these visions repeat some of the same history, in greater detail, as was first surveyed in the long vision of chapters 4—11.

Once again, let us look at chapters 12—20 first from the futurist view of the premillennialists. There are seven visions here. The first vision, in chapter 12, introduces the chief characters involved in the conflict of the tribulation period. The woman, in verse 1, represents the people of God of all ages. The red dragon and the stars with him, in verses 3, 4, represent Satan and his followers. The man-child caught up in verse 5 indicates the church already raptured away. The woman left, in verse 13, represents the believers during the tribulation period, a saved Jewish remnant against whom evil forces will make war.

The second vision in this section is that of chapter 13, the two beasts. Premillennialists see the first of these, in verses 1-10, as representing the Antichrist leader of the world in the tribulation period. The second beast, in verses 11-18, represents the false prophet, the leader of a one-world false religion in the tribulation period.

The third vision is chapter 14. This vision anticipates the outcome of the conflict of the tribulation period. God's people will triumph, as seen in verses 1-7, and Satan's crowd will be destroyed, as seen in verses 8-20.

The fourth vision is chapters 15, 16. Here are the seven last plagues of judgment on earth. In 15:7 these are prepared for in the form of seven golden vials of God's wrath to be poured out on earth. In chapter 16, the pouring out of each vial introduces some awful calamity that brings misery and death on men.

Chapters 17, 18 give us the fifth vision, in which the final destruction of Babylon is foretold. Babylon is a symbolical name representing the forces of evil, the people who follow Satan rather than God. This people is presented in 17:3, 4 as a woman clothed in purple and scarlet on a scarlet beast—Satan, of course. This is in direct contrast to the people of God, represented back in chapter 12 as a woman clothed with the sun. Many premillennialists also believe that a literal city, old Babylon restored, or Rome perhaps, will be the center of authority for Satan's crowd during the tribulation. If so, the destruction of "Babylon" referred to in these two chapters will be both of a people and of a city.

In chapter 19 we have the sixth of these seven visions, showing the consummation of our present age, which closes at the end of the great tribulation. That consummation will involve two things. One is the eternal union between Christ and His people, presented in 19:1-10, as the marriage of the Lamb. The other is the destruction of evil forces at Christ's return, as presented in verses 11-21. This is taken by premillennialists to refer to the battle of Armageddon at the close of the great tribulation when Jesus returns to set up the millennial kingdom.

Finally, the seventh vision in this section is given in chapter 20. Premillennialists see in this chapter two things. First is the millennial period itself, described briefly in verses 1-6. Second is the release and final defeat of Satan and final judgment at the end of the millennium, in verses 7-15. This chapter is crucial to the premillennialist's view, of course, since it mentions in verse 3 the 1,000 years while the devil is bound, during which some live and reign with Christ.

But amillennialists, taking the preterist viewpoint, do not agree. So let us look once more at these seven visions in chapters 12—20 to see what they say. Remember, amillennialists look to the past for the meaning, rather than to the future.

In chapter 12, you remember, we saw a vision of a woman, a dragon, a man-child, and the woman's seed. Amillennialists agree that the woman is God's people, and the dragon is Satan. But they interpret the man-child to be Christ and the woman's seed to be the church. To John's readers this would have been the church then existing, against whom Satan raged after Christ's ascension.

In chapter 13, two beasts were introduced. The first beast represented the Roman Emperor Domitian, then living and persecuting the Christians. The second beast was Domitian's emissary who tried to enforce emperor worship on the Christians in the local area of Asia where the seven churches were.

The vision in chapter 14, according to the amillennialists, anticipates the victory of the church, and the announced destruction of Babylon in 14:8 anticipates Rome's fall. In chapter 15, the anticipated rejoicing of the early church is presented.

The seven vials of wrath, in chapter 16, show various ways God would judge Rome. Remember that these, in essence, repeat the picture of judgment by natural calamity already shown in the lengthy vision of chapters 4—11.

Chapters 17, 18, you remember, describe the destruction of Babylon. The amillennialist interprets Babylon, in Revelation, as a reference to the wicked Roman Imperial power then persecuting the church. Thus, these two chapters describe the ultimate fall of the Roman Empire with all her ancient allies.

In chapter 19, we saw a marriage of the Lamb, in verses 7-10 in particular. The amillennialist sees this section as a premature glimpse ahead to the Christian's final destiny, even though the early church was many generations ahead of this as an accomplished fact. In 19:11-21 we saw what the premillennialist describes as the return of Christ and the battle of Armageddon. The amillennialist sees this as Christ's spiritual coming to the rescue of the early, persecuted church, and the overthrow of Rome.

Thus, the amillennialist views chapter 20 quite differently from the premillennialist. He believes Satan was relatively bound (as 20:2 indicates) in the sense that the efforts to enforce emperor worship were defeated in the Roman Empire. The 1,000 years referred to suggest an indefinite period which began when Rome's efforts to persecute the church were crushed. That indefinite period continues today.

Chapter 20, verses 7-10, refer to a release and final defeat of Satan, you remember. The amillennialist sees these verses as futuristic, looking to Satan's increased power as our present age wears on toward the end, but promising His final overthrow at the end of our age. The amillennialist agrees that verses 11-15 describe the last judgment. Only they believe that this is the one and only judgment which will come at the end of this age when Jesus returns and raises all men to stand before Him once and be divided as sheep are divided from goats.

Our time is almost gone, and we cannot carefully examine chapters 21, 22. But these two chapters are not debatable. Both amillennialists and premillennialists agree that these two chapters describe the final and eternal condition of the children of God.

In closing I want to emphasize the important lesson we learn from Revelation, in spite of differences of opinion. We learn that God's people should never give up in their conflict with evil. That conflict always exists, but God's forces will prevail sooner or later, and surely in the end. Satan can operate only so far as God allows him. Still he is relentlessly active and powerful in his war on the saints. But Jesus is always the ultimate Victor and we must never forget it. In the end, His return will bring final and permanent victory, and that blessed hope should sustain us in any period of difficulty, just as it served to sustain the early church. May God help us to live with the confidence we are given when we read the Revelation.

Printed in the USA
CPSIA information can be obtained
at www.ICGtesting.com
JSHW082251280324
60086JS00001B/5

9 780892 650903